LAUDES REGIAE

Plate 1

Carved Wooden Door (*ca.* 430 A.D.) Rome, Santa Sabina
Acclamation to the Pantokrator

LAUDES REGIAE

A Study in Liturgical Acclamations and
Mediaeval Ruler Worship

BY

ERNST H. KANTOROWICZ

WITH

A STUDY OF THE MUSIC OF THE LAUDES AND MUSICAL TRANSCRIPTIONS

BY

MANFRED F. BUKOFZER

UNIVERSITY OF CALIFORNIA PRESS
BERKELEY AND LOS ANGELES
1958

UNIVERSITY OF CALIFORNIA PUBLICATIONS IN HISTORY

VOLUME 33

1946

UNIVERSITY OF CALIFORNIA PRESS
BERKELEY AND LOS ANGELES
CALIFORNIA

———

CAMBRIDGE UNIVERSITY PRESS
LONDON, ENGLAND

SECOND PRINTING, 1958

Price, $6.50

AMICIS OXONIENSIBUS

PREFACE

THE STUDY of mediaeval liturgy, until the beginning of this century, fell almost exclusively to the theologian and the church historian. It is true that some great students of mediaeval art and literature found it profitable or necessary to break into this "reservation." Rarely, however, did it happen that the "professional" mediaevalist, the student of political, institutional, or cultural history of the Middle Ages, swerved so far from his usual studies as to lose himself in the magic thicket of prayers, benedictions, and ecclesiastical rites. We need only skim over the historical writings antedating the First World War or glance at the standard bibliographies to realize that liturgical sources and studies had not then penetrated the sphere of interest of the mediaeval historian. Liturgical problems were rarely, if ever, incorporated in the body of mediaeval history.

In this respect the ancient historian differed profoundly from the mediaevalist. Not even in our age of habitual superspecialization would a scholar in classics venture to study, or pretend to understand, the political and cultural history of antiquity without an intimate knowledge of the cults and the religious customs of Greece, Rome, and the Near East. In the ancient world there was no split between the holy and the profane. The ancient historian, therefore, had the great advantage of being himself the "theologian" and "church historian" of his period.

Far less favorable from the outset was the situation of the mediaeval historian. Religious prejudices, nonexistent with respect to ancient history, have hampered or biased mediaeval studies until almost the twentieth century. History itself seemed to have been split and to have developed that dualism of holy and profane from which eventually the specialized historians of either profession originated. Moreover, the mediaevalist was saddled with an awkward legacy. Academic tradition in almost all countries has it that "Mediaeval and Modern History" are bound together but not "Ancient and Mediaeval." The ideological approach to the Middle Ages, therefore, was much too often determined by problems suggested in view of modern history; and modern problems are far remote from cults of the gods, religious rites, and liturgical functions. Hence, this cultual, or "liturgical," sector—one of the essentials which ancient and mediaeval history have in common—fell deplorably short in the studies of mediaevalists. Eventually it became the task of the ancient historian, church historian, and Byzantinist to account for the period of transition from Hellenistic-Roman cults to Hellenistic-Roman Christianity.

Through the combined efforts of these scholars the ground of the Late Antiquity, a former no man's land, has been tilled so thoroughly that the integration of late antique problems into mediaeval history has become imperative. The admirable and fascinating discoveries of two or three generations of scholars in this field have disclosed the interrelations between the cults of the Mysteries and the early Christian cult, between the worship of emperors and that of Christ. These disclosures, as is natural, have greatly influenced the general appearance of the Middle Ages. The early mediaeval Church, at least until about 1200 A.D. when Gothic mysticism and Renaissance trends of thought began to transform Western religious sentiment, appeared to be linked to the cults of the Late Antiquity—thriving in a near-to-earth climate—much more closely than to any modern ecclesiastical institutions. There arose the necessity of reconsidering early mediaeval problems. A study of the practices and rites of the Early Middle Ages, approached by regarding the Church as still an antique cult integrating within itself the orbits of holy and profane, recommended itself to the mediaevalists.

Recent studies have proved that this approach yielded very considerable results. Mediaeval liturgy, like the rites of the non-Christian cults, turned out to be suitable, not only to theological, but also to politico-historical interpretations. Moreover, an enormous firsthand source matériel was unlocked, and uncounted mediaeval service books, hitherto not utilized by the mediaevalist, were made available for new studies.

The evaluation of these liturgical sources for the purposes of political, cultural, and constitutional history, as well as for the knowledge of mediaeval thought, ideas, and political theories, is as yet in its first phase. Liturgical history in the sense indicated is a new branch of historical science. Edmund Bishop—whose *Liturgica Historica*, published after his death in 1918, discloses a whole program in its title—may be claimed in many respects as the initiator of these studies. On the whole, England and English learned societies have been leading in interpreting and making accessible the liturgical sources. In England, now as in the days of Henry VIII, state and liturgy are still tied together. Only in England has there survived that great mediaeval pageantry, the royal coronation, which evinces the ancient blend of state and liturgy; and perhaps owing to this tradition the ground has proved particularly favorable for liturgico-historical studies. Continental scholarship, however, has contributed its full share. Since 1887 the Roman Catholic Church has published the *Ephemerides Liturgicae*, an official periodical of the Congregation of Rites and at the same time an excellent liturgico-historical review. The great *Dictionnaire d'archéologie chrétienne et de liturgie*, in process since 1907, is the monumental contribution of French scholars whose leading figure for a long time was L. Duchesne. Germany followed with the *Jahrbuch für Liturgiewissenschaft*, published since 1921, which must be considered as one of the most important *historical* periodicals. These publications, along with the works of a great number of individual scholars whose names will be found in the following pages time and time again, are eloquent testimony to the fact that historical and liturgical studies no longer pursue their separate ways; now their courses intersect continuously. It is really no longer possible for the mediaeval historian to ignore these studies and to deal cheerfully with the history of mediaeval thought and culture without ever opening a missal. The liturgy, to say the least, is today one of the most important auxiliaries to the study of mediaeval history.

Presumably four-fifths of the liturgical sources are as yet unpublished or uncatalogued. Of the sources published, a considerable section is almost inaccessible owing either to the purely "local" character of the publications or to their being out of print. Every study in this field, therefore, is bound, despite extensive consultation of manuscripts, to be incomplete and provisional. The *non liquet* as well as the "surprise" upsetting or confirming of a theory will occur more often in this than in other branches of historical research. Moreover, studies on liturgico-political subjects are inevitably technical, hence not easy reading, and the student will notice that many roads are as yet unpaved and that even the highways are not always reliable.

Of these difficulties, which I found stimulating rather than discouraging, indications will be found not rarely in the present volume. I do not pretend to submit a final work on either "Liturgical Acclamations" or on "Mediaeval Ruler Worship." The book offers no more than I have promised in the title, a "Study," or rather a collection of "Studies" braced by a common subject which by chance I became interested in many years ago. It contains the history, if incomplete, of a single liturgical chant, the *Laudes Regiae*. This "Caesarean Litany" received its classical form during the eighth century in the Gallo-Frankish Church under Anglo-Irish and Roman influences, but it represents at the same time the liturgical survival of acclamations tendered to the Roman emperors. The seemingly insignificant changes in the texts of the laudes, traced here from the eighth to the thirteenth century, reflect the various changes in theocratic concepts of secular and spiritual rulership. New light, I believe, is shed on the development of the mediaeval equivalent of the ancient ruler cult. Other items will be likewise new to the reader. The episcopal and papal acclamations have not before been studied in this connection. The laudes of Dalmatia with their strongly legal character hardly have been known to the historian. The liturgical interdependence of Sicily, Normandy, and England is illustrated by some new details. The modern revival of the laudes, here only touched upon, broaches the problem of acclamations, and their function, in modern dictatorial states in which they appear as an indispensable vehicle of political propaganda, pseudo-religious emotionalism, and public reacknowledgment of power. More-over, the collection of a widely scattered and hitherto unsifted matériel, gathered from published and unpublished sources, opens several views into bypaths which often may appear as more important than the subject matter itself. I have tried, not always successfully, to resist the tempta-tion of being sidetracked. Well-known facts have been repeated as little as possible, but the most recent studies on the late antique acclamations, on the rites of coronations and festal crownings of kings and popes, and on political thought in the liturgy have been used amply—and gratefully. Even so I am convinced of having erred more than once, of having neg-lected important points and having overstressed the importance of others. The liturgiologist, to whose indulgence I must appeal, will prob-ably find other faults as well with my conclusions or interpretations.

The studies here offered have been carried through at different times and under various conditions. The first chapter, serving here as a kind of general introduction, started from an investigation on the legend of the Sicilian gold *bullae* of Frederick II. Chapter VI on the laudes in the Nor-man realms originated at Oxford as far back as 1934, when I was for-tunate enough to enjoy the hospitality of New College and its late Warden, the ever-lamented H. A. L. Fisher. In substance the Norman chapter was read as a paper to the Mediaeval Society in Oxford presided over by Professor F. M. Powicke. These chapters, together with parts of IV, V, and VII, were ready for the press by 1936. Conditions made publication impossible, but other students at least could utilize my manuscript; in the first place Professor Percy Ernst Schramm, who pub-lished some extracts and who, in turn, generously placed at my disposal his own collection of matériel on the subject so that some gaps could be filled. Chapters II, III, and parts of IV were added at Berkeley in 1940, when the generosity of Mr. Sidney M. Ehrman, in San Francisco, and of the Emergency Committee in Aid of Displaced Foreign Scholars, in New York, enabled me to revise and translate my manuscript and to complete my studies in leisure.

Some difficulties arose from the war. It was impossible to get any addi-tional information from European libraries about manuscripts which I either had consulted or had failed to consult in former years. For this reason the plan of adding an analytic list of laudes formularies had to be abandoned. My often casual notes, taken years ago, did not always yield a clear answer to questions which arose at a later stage of my studies. Another difficulty derived from the fact that I had no specialized litur-gical library at my disposal. These troubles were at least smoothed down by the untiring readiness of the staff of the University of California Library to provide through the Inter-Library Loan the books which I needed, an assistance which I gratefully acknowledge. However, even the extravagant use which I made of this expedient could not replace the sets of periodicals and books which should have been consulted continuously. Gaps in my bibliography and my knowledge may have resulted from this limitation.

The manuscript of this book was handed over to the University of California Press in January, 1941. By a concatenation of unfortunate circumstances the printing had to be postponed. There is, however, an advantage in the disadvantage. I was fortunate in arousing the interest of Professor Manfréd F. Bukofzer in the musical side of my subject and even more fortunate in persuading him to add an appendix on the music of the laudes which, no doubt, the reader will appreciate and for which I wish to express my profound gratitude. So far as Professor Bukofzer's analysis is based on my manuscript-notes I have to bear the full responsibility for the exactness of my copies. The results of the musical investigation which, needless to say, was carried through quite independently by Professor Bukofzer and without his being acquainted with my analysis of the laudes, fully support the conclusions of my own investigation. Several conclusions which in the text I had to provide, as it were, with a question mark, might subsequently have been rephrased in a more positive form. However, I refrained from making considerable changes and merely referred in the footnotes to the musical excursus.

Finally I wish to express my gratitude to Dr. G. C. Jefferis, Mr. Patrick O'Mara, Professor Max Radin, Mr. Edouard Roditi, Professor Howard M. Smyth, Professor and Mrs. Raymond J. Sontag, Professor John S. P. Tatlock, Mr. Leopold G. Wickham Legg, and Mr. G. H. Williams for various helps, suggestions, and courtesies; to the Committee of Publications for allotting the funds for the printing; and to Miss Lucie E. N. Dobbie of the University of California Press for carefully revising my manuscript. E.H.K.

CONTENTS

PLATES

Senators in togas and citizens in dalmatics acclaim the Kyrios Pantokrator and the Angel of the Covenant. The scene refers to Malachi 3:1.

Cf. E. Kantorowicz, "The King's Advent and the Enigmatic Panels in the Doors of Santa Sabina," *The Art Bulletin*, XXVI (1944), 207 ff.

a, St. Louis (1226–1270), *Écu d'or;* *b*, Philip the Bold (1270–1285), *Reine d'or;* *c*, Philip the Fair (1285–1314), *Masse d'or;* *d*, Philip the Fair, *Chaise d'or.*

Cf. J. A. Blanchet et A. Dieudonné, *Manuel de numismatique française* (Paris, 1916), II, Pl. I, nos. 1–2, pp. 231, 235, nos. 72, 74.

e, Iron shield presented to Don Juan of Austria after the Victory of Lepanto (1571) by Pope Pius V.

Cf. Paul Lacroix, *Vie militaire et religieuse au moyen âge* (Paris, 1873), p. 294, fig. 215.

a, Harbaville Triptych, Paris, Louvre (Tenth century ?).

b, Ivory Triptych, Vatican, Museo Cristiano (Tenth century ?). Both triptychs represent a so-called Déesis, an intercessory supplication. In the upper register are Christ, the Virgin, John the Baptist, the Archangels Michael and Gabriel; in the lower register are the apostles.

Cf. A. Goldschmidt and K. Weitzmann, *Die byzantinischen Elfenbeinskulpturen des X.–XIII. Jahrhunderts* (Berlin, 1934), II, 33 ff., nos. 32–33; cf. no. 31; C. R. Morey, *Gli oggetti di avorio e di osso del Museo Sacra Vaticano* (Vatican, 1936), pp. 21 ff.

Sacring of the king of France: Prostration during the singing of the litany. Paris, Bibl. Nat. Lat. MS 1246, fol. 10: Pontifical of Châlons-sur-Marne (thirteenth century, second half).

Cf. V. Leroquais, *Pontificaux manuscrits ...* (Paris, 1937), Pl. XXXII.

a, *Rex et Sacerdos.* Julius Caesar ordained *Pontifex Maximus* ("Comment Cesar fu euesques ... ce est souuerains sires et maistres des temples et des sacrifices") and crowned emperor. A French manuscript written probably in the surroundings of Charles V of France (1364–1380) and containing the "Histoire ancienne," fol. 199.

Cf. George Millar, *The Library of A. Chester Beatty* (Oxford, 1930), II, 153, Pl. CLXX; see also Sotheby and Co.'s *Catalogue of the Renowned Collection of Western Manuscripts of the Property of A. Chester Beatty, Esq.* (London, 1932), p. 29, Pl. XXVI.

b, Liturgical Reception. Entry of the Emperor Charles IV and his son, King Wenzel at Cambrai, 1377. Paris, Bibl. Nat. Fr. MS 2813, fol. 457ᵛ (late fourteenth century).

Cf. R. Delachenal's edition of *Les Grandes Chroniques de France: Jean II et Charles V* (Paris, 1920), IV, Pl. XXXIII.

ABBREVIATIONS

AA.SS.	Acta Sanctorum. Antwerpen, 1643 ff.
Anal. Boll.	*Analecta Bollandiana.* Paris, 1882 ff.
ArchUF.	*Archiv für Urkundenforschung.* Leipzig, 1907 ff.
Arch. stor. nap.	*Archivio storico per le provincie napoletane.* Naples, 1876 ff.
BÉCh.	*Bibliothèque de l'école des chartes.* Paris, 1839 ff.
Bishop, *Lit. Hist.*	Edmund Bishop, *Liturgica Historica.* Oxford, 1918.
Bouquet, *RHF.*	M. Bouquet, *Recueil des historiens des Gaules et de la France.* Paris, 1899 ff.
Byz. Z.	*Byzantinische Zeitschrift.* Leipzig, 1892 ff.
CSEL.	*Corpus scriptorum ecclesiasticorum latinorum.* Vienna, 1866 ff.
DACL.	*Dictionnaire d'archéologie chrétienne et de liturgie.* Paris, 1907 ff.
De caerim.	*Constantini Porphyrogeniti imperatoris de caerimoniis aulae byzantinae libri duo,* rec. J. J. Reiske. Bonn, 1829.
Eph. Lit.	*Ephemerides liturgicae.* Rome, 1887 ff.
HJb.	*Historisches Jahrbuch der Görres-Gesellschaft.* Munich, 1883 ff.
JLW.	*Jahrbuch für Liturgiewissenschaft.* Münster in Westphalia, 1921 ff.
Jour. Theol. Stud.	*Journal of Theological Studies.* London, 1899 ff.
Liber cens.	Le *Liber censuum* de l'église romaine publié avec une introduction et un commentaire, edited by P. Fabre and L. Duchesne. Paris, 1889 ff. Vols. I, II:1.
Liber pont.	*Liber pontificalis,* edited by L. Duchesne. 2 vols. Paris, 1886–1892.
Migne, *PG.*	J. P. Migne, *Patrologia Graeca.* Paris, 1857 ff.
Migne, *PL.*	J. P. Migne, *Patrologia Latina.* Paris, 1844 ff.
MGH.	*Monumenta Germaniae Historica.* Hanover-Berlin, 1826 ff. The series cited are:

AA. ant.	*Auctores antiquissimi*
Capit.	*Capitularia regum Francorum*
Conc.	*Concilia*
Const.	*Constitutiones et acta publica*
Dipl. Karol.	*Diplomata Karolinorum*
Epist.	*Epistolae Karolini aevi*
Epist. sel.	*Epistolae selectae* (octavo)
LL.	*Leges* (folio)
Poet.	*Poetae latini*
SS.	*Scriptores* (folio)
SS. rer. Germ.	*Scriptores rerum Germanicarum* (octavo)
SS. rer. Lang.	*Scriptores rerum Langobardicarum et Italicarum*

NArch.	*Neues Archiv der Gesellschaft für ältere deutsche Geschichteskunde.* Hanover, 1876 ff.
Num. Z.	*Numismatische Zeitschrift.* Vienna, 1869 ff.
QF.	*Quellen und Forschungen aus italienischen Archiven und Bibliotheken.* Rome, 1898 ff.
RCGr.	*Revue du chant grégorien.* Grenoble, 1892 ff.

RE.	Pauly-Wissowa-Kroll, *Real-Encyclopädie der classischen Altertums-wissenschaft.* Stuttgart, 1894 ff.
Rev. bénéd.	*Revue bénédictine.* Maredsous, 1884 ff.
RHC.	*Recueil des historiens des croisades.* Paris, 1841 ff.
RM.	*Mitteilungen des deutschen archäologischen Instituts.* Römische Abteilung. Rome, 1886 ff.
RQH.	*Revue des questions historiques.* Paris, 1866 ff.
ZfN.	*Zeitschrift für Numismatik.* Berlin, 1874 ff.
ZfRG.	*Zeitschrift der Savigny-Stiftung für Rechtsgeschichte.* Germanistische Abteilung. Weimar, 1880 ff.; Kanonistiche Abteilung Weimar, 1911 ff.
ZKG.	*Zeitschrift für Kirchengeschichte.* Gothe, 1877 ff.

WORKS CITED IN ABBREVIATION

ALFÖLDI, A. "Die Ausgestaltung des monarchischen Zeremoniells am römischen Kaiserhofe," *RM.*, XLIX (1934).

—— "Insignien und Tracht der römischen Kaiser," *RM.*, L (1935).

ANDRIEU, MICHEL. *Les "Ordines Romani" du haut moyen âge.* Spicilegium Sacrum Lovaniense, XI. Louvain, 1931.

BATIFFOL, PIERRE. *Études de liturgie et d'archéologie chrétienne.* Paris, 1919.

BAUMSTARK, ANTON. *Vom geschichtlichen Werden der Liturgie.* Ecclesia Orans, X. Freiburg, 1923.

BIEHL, LUDWIG. *Das liturgische Gebet für Kaiser und Reich.* Görres Gesellschaft. Veröffentlichungen der Sektion für Rechts- und Staatswissenschaft, LXXV. Paderborn, 1937.

BLOCH, MARC. *Les rois thaumaturges.* Publications de la faculté des lettres de l'université de Strasbourg, XIX. Strasbourg, 1919.

BONIZO. *Liber de vita christiana,* ed. Ernst Perels. Texte zur Geschichte des römischen und kanonischen Rechts im Mittelalter, I. Berlin, 1930

BRAUN, JOSEPH. *Die liturgische Gewandung im Okzident und Orient.* Freiburg, 1907.

BRÉHIER, L. and BATIFFOL, P. *Les survivances du culte impérial romain.* Paris, 1920.

BRIGHTMAN, F. E. *Liturgies Eastern and Western.* Vol. I: *Eastern Liturgies.* Oxford, 1896.

CAGIN, DOM P. *L'euchologie latine. Te Deum ou illatio.* Vol. I. Solesmes, 1906.

CASPAR, ERICH. *Geschichte des Papsttums von den Anfängen bis zur Höhe der Weltherrschaft.* 2 vols. Tübingen, 1930–1933.

—— *Roger II. (1101–1154) und die Gründung der normannisch-sizilischen Monarchie.* Innsbruck, 1904.

DELISLE, LÉOPOLD. "Mémoire sur d'anciens sacramentaires," *Mémoires de l'académie des inscriptions et belles-lettres,* XXXII:1. Paris, 1886.

DEUSDEDIT. See Wolf von Glanvell, Victor.

DUCHESNE, L. *Christian Worship: Its Origin and Evolution.* Translated by M. L. McClure. 5th ed., London, 1931.

DÜMMLER, E. *Anselm der Peripatetiker.* Halle, 1872.

EBNER, ADALBERT. *Quellen und Forschungen zur Geschichte und Kunstgeschichte des Missale Romanum im Mittelalter: Iter Italicum.* Freiburg, 1896.

EICHMANN, EDUARD. "Die Ordines der Kaiserkrönung," *ZfRG.*, kan. Abt. II (1911).

—— "Die sog. römische Königskrönungsformel," *HJb.*, XLV (1925).

—— "Königs- und Bischofsweihe," *Sitzungsberichte der Bayerischen Akademie der Wissenschaften,* Phil.-hist. Klasse, 1928, No. 6.

—— "Von der Kaisergewandung im Mittelalter," *HJb.*, LVIII (1938).

—— "Zur Geschichte des lombardischen Krönungsritus," *HJb.*, XLVI (1926).

ELLARD, GERALD. *Ordination Anointings in the Western Church Before 1000 A.D.* Monographs of the Mediaeval Academy of America, VIII. Cambridge, Mass., 1933.

ENGEL, ARTHUR. *Recherches sur la numismatique et la sigillographie des Normands de Sicile et d'Italie.* Paris, 1882.

ENGEL, A., and SERRURE, R. *Traité de numismatique du moyen âge.* 3 vols. Paris, 1891–1895.

ERDMANN, CARL. *Die Entstehung des Kreuzzugsgedankens.* Forschungen zur Kirchen- und Geistesgeschichte, VI. Stuttgart, 1935.

FRANZ, ADOLF. *Die kirchlichen Benediktionen im Mittelalter.* 2 vols. Freiburg, 1909.

GAGÉ, JEAN. "Σταυρὸς νικοποιός. La victoire impériale dans l'empire chrétien," *Revue d'histoire et de philosophie religieuses*, XIII (1933).

——— "La théologie de la victoire impériale," *Revue historique*, CLXXI (1933).

GASTOUÉ, AMÉDÉE. *La musique de l'église*. Lyons, 1911.

——— "Le chant gallican," *RCGr.*, XLIII (1939).

GOLDAST, MELCHIOR. *Rerum Alamannicarum Scriptores*. 3d ed., Frankfort and Leipzig, 1730.

GOODACRE, HUGH. *A Handbook of the Coinage of the Byzantine Empire*. 3 vols. London, 1928–1933.

GRABAR, ANDRÉ. *L'empereur dans l'art byzantin*. Publications de la faculté des lettres de l'université de Strasbourg, LXXV. Paris, 1936.

Graduel de Rouen = *Le graduel de l'église cathédrale de Rouen au XIIIᵉ siècle*, publié par V. H. Loriquet, Dom Pothier et Abbé Colette. 2 vols. Rouen, 1907.

GRANCOLAS, JEAN. *Les anciennes liturgies*. Paris, 1704.

Gregory VII, *Registrum* = *Das Register Gregors VII*, ed. Erich Caspar in *MGH. Epist. sel.*, II. Berlin, 1920.

HASKINS, C. H. *Studies in Norman Institutions*. Cambridge, Mass., 1918.

HEISENBERG, A. "Aus der Geschichte und Literatur der Palaiologenzeit," *Sitzungsberichte der Bayerischen Akademie der Wissenschaften*, Phil.-hist. Klasse, 1920, No. 10.

HELDMANN, KARL. *Das Kaisertum Karls des Grossen*. Quellen und Studien zur Verfassungsgeschichte des Deutschen Reiches, VI:2. Weimar, 1928.

HENZEN, GUILELMUS. *Acta fratrum Arvalium quae supersunt*. Berlin, 1874.

KANTOROWICZ, ERNST. "Ivories and Litanies," *Journal of the Warburg and Courtauld Institutes*, V (1942).

——— *Kaiser Friedrich der Zweite. Ergänzungsband*. Berlin, 1931.

——— "A Norman Finale of the Exultet and the Rite of Sarum," *The Harvard Theological Review*, XXXIV (1941).

KENNEDY, V. L. *The Saints of the Canon of the Mass*. Studi di antichità cristiana, XIV. Rome, 1938.

KERN, FRITZ. *Die Anfänge der französischen Ausdehnungspolitik bis zum Jahr 1308*. Tübingen, 1910.

——— *Gottesgnadentum und Widerstandsrecht im frühen Mittelalter. Zur Entwicklungsgeschichte der Monarchie*. Leipzig, 1915.

KLEWITZ, H.-W. "Die Entstehung des Kardinalkollegs," *ZfRG.*, kan. Abt., XXV (1936).

——— "Die Festkrönungen der deutschen Kaiser," *ZfRG.*, kan. Abt., XXVIII (1939).

——— "Die Krönung des Papstes," *ZfRG.*, kan. Abt., XXX (1941).

KRUSE, HELMUT. *Studien zur offiziellen Geltung des Kaiserbildes im römischen Reich*. Studien zur Geschichte und Kultur des Altertums, XIX:3. Paderborn, 1934.

LAEHR, GERHARD. *Die konstantinische Schenkung in der abendländischen Literatur des Mittelalters bis zur Mitte des 14. Jahrhunderts*. Historische Studien, CLXVI. Berlin, 1926.

LAUER, PH., in *Bulletin de la société nationale des antiquaires de France*, 1910.

LE BRUN DESMORETTES (DE MOLÉON). *Voyages liturgiques de France*. Paris, 1757.

LEHMANN, PAUL. "Corveyer Studien," *Abhandlungen der Bayerischen Akademie der Wissenschaften*, Phil.-hist. Klasse, XXX. Abh. 5. Munich, 1919.

LEROQUAIS, ABBÉ V. *Les sacramentaires et les missels manuscrits des bibliothèques publiques de France*. 4 vols. Paris, 1924.

—— Les pontificaux manuscrits des bibliothèques publiques de France. 3 vols. Paris, 1937.

LUCIUS, JOANNES. De regno Dalmatiae et Croatiae libri sex. Vienna, 1785.

MABILLON, JOHANNES. Vetera analecta. Paris, 1723.

MANSI, J. D. Sacrorum conciliorum nova et amplissima collectio. Florence, 1759 ff.

MARTÈNE, EDMUNDUS. De antiquis ecclesiae ritibus libri tres. Antwerp, 1736.

MASKELL, W. Monumenta ritualia ecclesiae Anglicanae. 2d ed., Oxford, 1882.

MIRBT, CARL. Quellen zur Geschichte des Papsttums und des römischen Katholizismus. 5th ed., Tübingen, 1934.

MURATORI, L. A. Liturgia romana vetus. 2 vols. Venice, 1748.

PETERSON, ERIK. Εἶς θεός. Epigraphische, formgeschichtliche und religionsgeschichtliche Untersuchungen. Forschungen zur Religion und Literatur des Alten und Neuen Testaments, XLI. Göttingen, 1926. Cited as Untersuchungen.

PROST, A. "Caractère et signification de quatre pièces liturgiques composées à Metz en latin et en grec au IXᵉ siècle," Mémoires de la société nationale des antiquaires de France, XXXVII. Paris, 1876. Cited as Quatre pièces.

REISKE, J. J., ed. Constantini Porphyrogenitii imperatoris De caerimoniis aulae byzantinae libri duo. Bonn, 1829. See De caerim.

ROSENSTOCK, EUGEN. "Die Furt der Franken und das Schisma," in E. Rosenstock and J. Wittig, Das Alter der Kirche. Berlin [1927].

RUBEIS, B. M. DE. Monumenta ecclesiae Aquilejensis. Venice, 1740.

SCHRAMM, PERCY ERNST. "Der König von Frankreich," ZfRG., kan. Abt., XXV (1936), and XXVI (1937).

—— Der König von Frankreich: Das Wesen der Monarchie vom 9. zum 16. Jahrhundert. 2 vols. Weimar, 1939.

—— "Die Krönung bei den Westfranken und Angelsachsen von 878 bis zum 1000," ZfRG., kan. Abt., XXIII (1934).

—— "Die Ordines der mittelalterlichen Kaiserkrönung," ArchUF., XI (1930).

—— "Die Krönung in Deutschland bis zum Beginn des Salischen Hauses," ZfRG., kan. Abt., XXIV (1935).

—— A History of the English Coronation. Oxford, 1937.

—— Kaiser, Rom und Renovatio. 2 vols. Leipzig and Berlin, 1929.

STRAUB, A. Vom Herrscherideal in der Spätantike. Forschungen zur Kirchen- und Geistesgeschichte, XVIII. Stuttgart, 1939.

TELLENBACH, GERD. "Römischer und christlicher Reichsgedanke in der Liturgie des frühen Mittelalters," Sitzungsberichte der Heidelberger Akademie der Wissenschaften, Phil.-hist. Klasse, Abh. 1. 1934–1935.

THALHOFER, VALENTIN and EISENHOFER, LUDWIG. Handbuch der katholischen Liturgik. 2d ed., Freiburg, 1912.

TREITINGER, OTTO. Die oströmische Kaiser- und Reichsidee nach ihrer Gestaltung im höfischen Zeremoniell. Jena, 1938.

Wörterbuch der Münzkunde, Hrsg. von Friedrich Freiherr von Schrötter. Berlin, 1930.

WOLF VON GLANVELL, VICTOR. Die Kanonessammlung des Kardinals Deusdedit. Vol. I. Paderborn, 1905. Cited as Deusdedit.

CHAPTER I

A LEGEND ON COINS, AND ITS ORIGIN

THE MOTTO *Christus vincit, Christus regnat, Christus imperat*, is displayed on innumerable mediaeval objects of devotion and art.[1] It is inscribed on the blades of swords that they might gain victory and on church bells that they might announce it. It is engraved on crucifixes in Southern Italy and other Mediterranean regions, and it is carved on the base of the great obelisk which Pope Sixtus V reërected in the center of the great square facing St. Peter's. Apotropaeic forces were said to dwell in these words if they were used as a spell, and rings inscribed with them were believed to protect the bearer from evil. The three clauses were sung as a charm to keep droughts and tempests away. As medical benedictions they are found in ancient dispensatories, and whoever suffered from a disease of the eye needed only to call on St. Nichasius, bishop of Rouen, and repeat the magic words in order to be relieved of his afflictions.[2]

Without forfeiting its magical, exorcist character this motto was placed as a legend on coins. When, in 1474, the Emperor Frederick III permitted

---

[1] See the rich material collected by Erik Peterson, *Untersuchungen*, pp. 162 f.; W. Deonna, "Christos Propylaios ou Christus hic est," *Revue archéologique*, XXII (1925), 73; C. Weyman, "Analecta," *HJb.*, XL (1920), 186; Adolf Franz, *Die kirchlichen Benediktionen im Mittelalter* (Freiburg, 1909), II, 96, 103 f. See also *Recueil de textes relatifs à l'histoire de l'architecture ... en France*, eds. Victor Moret and Paul Deschamps (Paris, 1929), II, No. LIV, 125, n. 2, concerning the foundation-stone of the great altar of the abbey of La Couronne (Charente), which shows the following inscription:

XPC VINCIT XPC REGNAT

Anno ab incarnatione Domini Mᵒ Cᵒ LXXᵒ IIIIᵒ Idus
Mai ego Petrus Engolismensis et ego Petrus Petragoricensis
episcopi et ego Junius indignus abbas de Coro[na]
posuimus hunc lapidem in edificio hujus altaris . . .

AMEN XPC IMPERAT AMEN

[2] Avranches, Bibl. Munic., MS 41 fol. 1, a sacramentary of St.-Benoît-sur-Loire, late twelfth century, has the following entry in a thirteenth-century hand:

In nomine Patris + et Filii + et Spiritus Sancti. Amen.
Sanctus Nichasius habuit maculam in oculo et deprecatus est Deum, ut quicumque nomen suum super se portaret, maculam in oculo non haberet + Christus vincit + Christus regnat + Christus imperat.

Cf. V. Leroquais, *Les sacramentaires et les missels manuscrits des bibliothèques de France* (Paris, 1924), II, 310, no. 157. Fuller details are found in the Oxford, Bodleian Libr. James MS 27, which contains fragments of the partly burnt Brit. Mus. Cotton. MS Otho A. XIII, of the twelfth century, to which Mr. N. Denholm-Young called my attention. On fol. 126 (118) a modern note indicates: "Ex homiliis Saxonicis quas habuit Dominus Cottonus ex dono Episcopi di Kelfanore scriptas manu contemporanea tempore Henrici secundi." There follow Anglo-Saxon fragments, then on fol. 127 (119), a Latin incantation which is doubtless of Norman origin: "In nomine etc. Sanctus Nichasius habuit minutam variculam in oculo et oravit

the city of Cologne to mint municipal money, which was to circulate side by side with the electoral currency,[3] the citizens struck a penny the obverse of which, in accordance with Colognese tradition, bore the names of the three Magi—Gaspar, Melchior, Balthasar—protectors and patrons of the city from the days of Barbarossa. On the reverse, however, the Colognese engraved the words: XPC : VINCIT : XPC : REGNAT : XPC : IMPERAT.[4] There was a good reason for deliberately combining this formula with the names of the Magi. A popular incantation which the Archangel Gabriel was alleged to have brought from Constantinople before handing it over to Charlemagne, and which was well known in the middle of the fifteenth century, was credited with the power to protect its

---

ad Deum, ut quicumque hoc malum habuerit et nomen suum super se scriptum portaret, liberaretur ab hoc morbo.

+ Sanctus Nichasius oret pro isto Rogero.
+ Sanctus Nichasius oret pro isto Rogero.
+ Sanctus Nichasius oret pro isto Rogero.
+ Christus vincit, Christus regnat, Christus imperat.

Christus per intercessionem beati Nichasii liberet hominem Rogerum ab hoc morbo et ab omni alio . . .''
A similar text (Spanish, fifteenth century) has been published by Franz, *op. cit.*, II, 488, n. 1, who assumes, however, that this benediction is found in very late texts only; but it is, at the least, as old as the twelfth century. Only the Norman Nichasius, among many other saints of this name, can be referred to; he was the first bishop of Rouen and his Translation took place in 1122; cf. Migne, *PL.*, LXII, cols. 1165 f.; *Anal. Boll.*, I (1882), 628–632; Martène et Durand, *Thesaurus novus anecdotorum* (1717), III, 1677 ff. On St. Nichasius as a healer of eye diseases, especially of sties, see Franz, *op. cit.*, II, 487 ff.; *ibid.*, p. 497, the *Christus vincit* as a benediction combined with a puff in the eyes, the latter ("sufflatio") being a well-known exorcism, see e.g., V. Thalfhofer and L. Eisenhofer, *Handbuch der katholischen Liturgik* (2d ed.; Freiburg, 1912), II, 309. For another medical application of the triad, see Friedrich Wilhelm, *Denkmäler deutscher Prosa des 11. und 12. Jahrhunderts* (1914), 64, who quotes from a Zurich dispensatory the spell: "Ayos, Ayos, Ayos. Christus vincit, Christus regnat, Christus imperat"; see also Franz, *op. cit.*, II, 484, the spell against cold fits, and Wattenbach, "Aus den Briefen des Guido von Bazoches," *NArch.*, XVI (1891), 113, for a twelfth-century exorcism combined with the three clauses. See also the Psalter of Essen of the tenth century to which a hand of the fourteenth century added the magic formula ("Christus vicit"); H. Dausend, *Das älteste Sakramentar der Münsterkirche zu Essen* (1920), 7. The exorcist character of the triad derives, probably, from the third clause ("Christus imperat"), for the ritual of exorcism in the *Rituale Romanum* has the formulae: "Imperat tibi maiestas Christi. Imperat tibi Deus Pater. Imperat tibi Deus Filius. Imperat tibi Deus Spiritus Sanctus . . .''

[3] J. Chmel, *Regesta chronologico-diplomatica Friderici III Romanorum Imperatoris* (Vienna, 1840), No. 6828.

[4] A. Engel et R. Serrure, *Traité de numismatique du moyen âge* (Paris 1894), III, 1214. The descriptions of the coin always show the abbreviation SPC instead of the correct XPC. The mistake seems to go back to H. P. Cappe, *Beschreibung der Cölnischen Münzen* (Dresden, 1853). Professor Arthur Suhle, Director of the Numismatic Collection in the Kaiser Friedrich Museum, in Berlin, kindly informed me that the two dies of the Colognese *groschen*, which are preserved, display rightly XPC, not SPC. Of the *groschen* not one coined specimen seems to be known at present; on the dies, cf. P. Joseph, "Die Münzstempel und Punzen in dem historischen Museum der Stadt Köln," *Num. Z.*, XX (1888), 114, nos. 146 f.; see also A. Noss, *Die Münzen der Städte Köln und Neuss 1474–1794* (Cologne, 1926), No. 1; A. Suhle, "Zum Münzrecht der Städte Köln, Werl und Marsberg," *ZfN.* XXXIX (1929), 188 f.; cf. below, Appendix II.

bearer from violent death and deadly accident; and this angelic spell
likewise combined the names of the Magi with the motto:[5]

> Gaspar fert mirram + thus Melchior + Balthasar aurum +
> Christus vincit + Christus regnat + Christus imperat +
> Christe libera famulum N. + ab omni malo et periculo.

The formula, as a motto on coins, was almost unknown in central and
eastern Germany; but it appears frequently in the western marches of
the Reich. An interesting variation is found on a *groschen*, minted for
Aachen, which shows the surprising legend:

XC : VINCIT : XC : REGNAT + KAROLUS MAGNUS IMPERAT

St. Charlemagne here has taken the place of Christ the Emperor. Shortly
after 1300, ecclesiastical princes such as those of Trier and Cologne,
Liège and Cambrai, as well as secular princes, for example those of
Luxembourg, Brabant, Jülich, Holland, Hainaut, or Flanders, all used
the motto for their coinages. In doing so, they were imitating and copying, though not counterfeiting, the foreign model of France (see Appendix II). For the Valois kings displayed that device on their *écus* and on
other coins, just as the late Capetians had used it in former days for their
deniers or for those magnificent *floreni ad cathedram*, the so-called *chaises
d'or*, which showed the king enthroned on a high Gothic chair, and which
had been minted in France since the days of Philip the Fair (see Pl. II,
c–d).

In fact, one might say that in the Later Middle Ages only the king of
France was considered legally entitled to the *Christus vincit, Christus
regnat, Christus imperat* device on coins. Like the royal miracle of healing
scrofula by touch, like the Holy Vial containing celestial balm for anointing the king, like the Oriflamme, or the Golden Lilies, the three clauses
had become a symbol of the sacred prerogatives of the crown of France.
The device was usurped, quite logically, by the English monarchs in
their capacity as kings of France;[6] it was transferred to Southern Italy
when Charles VIII began to mint money for his yet unconquered kingdom of Naples;[7] and it was used by French princes of the blood royal

---

[5] X. Barbier de Montault, *Œuvres complets* (1893) VII, 350 f., 408, 513; see also L.
Gougaud, "La prière dite de Charlemagne," *Revue d'histoire ecclésiastique*, XX (1924),
219, 225, 227, 230. See also Lynn Thorndike, *A History of Magic and Experimental
Science* (New York, 1923), II, 483.

[6] See, e.g., Herbert A. Grueber, *Handbook of the Coins of Great Britain and Ireland
in the British Museum* (1899), *s.v.* "Anglo-Gallic coinage"; also A. Blanchet et A.
Dieudonné, *Manuel de numismatique francaise* (1916), II, 285, fig. 135; F. Friedensburg, *Münzkunde und Geldgeschichte der Einzelstaaten des Mittelalters und der neueren
Zeit* (1926), 190, no. 86; and below, Appendix II.

[7] It is found on the silver *Carlini* which were coined in the mints of Naples and Sul-
mona, February–May, 1495; cf. Luigi dell'Erba, "La riforma monetaria Angioina,"
Arch. stor. nap., N. S. XIX (1933), 61.

when they were granted the privilege of coining money.[8] The motto accompanied the French kings like a shadow; it gradually had become a symbol of the *Rex Christianissimus*, perhaps for the very reason that according to tradition, St. Louis was the first to use it for some coins of his country.[9]

This tradition is correct so far as gold currency is concerned. The long series of French coins bearing that device begins with gold deniers which St. Louis had ordered minted in 1266. The adoption of the new legend fits perfectly with all the other achievements of this royal crusader and saint whose reign marks the high tide of the French cult of kings, of the "Religion of Rheims and St.-Denis." It was St. Louis, who in every respect enriched that treasure of grace on which all his successors would thrive. It was he whose kingship was elevated to transcendency by the Spiritualists and Symbolists of his age and who, in turn, bestowed the thin and light air of the angelic kingdoms upon his country and assimilated, for the last time, the French chivalry to the militant celestial hosts.[10] In putting the three clauses as his device on his gold coins, he had, as it were, commended his government to Christ the victorious, the royal, the imperial, whom he himself represented on earth more perfectly, perhaps, than any other king ever did.

With an apparently well-calculated reference to the device of this saintly king and knight, William of Nogaret, when demanding, in May, 1308, the extermination of the Knights Templars, began his address by quoting the words *Christus vincit, Christus regnat, Christus imperat*, thus introducing a comparison between Philip the Fair, St. Louis' grandson, and Christ, "victorious over his foes, ruling over the defeated, and commanding gloriously over the world."[11] And once more, at the very end of the Middle Ages, Calvin, in a most militant letter written after the

[8] See, e.g., Henri Stein, "Charles de France, frère de Louis XI," *Mémoires et documents publ. par la société de l'école des chartes*, X (1921), 487 f., 490 f.

[9] Blanchet et Dieudonné, *Manuel*, II, 48; A. Dieudonné, *Les monnaies capétiennes ou royales françaises* (Paris, 1932), II, No. 1; cf. Nos. 165–167, 222, 233, 237, 306, 308, 333–335. Concerning some later variations of the legend cf. below, p. 24, n. 28. See Pl. II, *a–b*.

[10] The "Christus vincit, Christus regnat, Christus imperat" has hardly been mentioned among the "sacraments" of the cult of French kings; see for the French "royal religion" the fundamental study by Marc Bloch, *Les rois thaumaturges*, Publications de la faculté des lettres de l'université de Strasbourg, 19 (Strasbourg, 1924); more recently Percy Ernst Schramm, *Der König von Frankreich: Das Wesen der Monarchie vom 9. zum 16. Jahrhundert* (Weimar, 1939), a study based upon his two articles in *ZfRG*. kan. Abt. XXV (1936), 222–354; XXVI (1937), 161–284.

[11] William Rishanger, *Chronica Monasterii S. Albani* . . . (ed. Riley, Rolls Series, 28), p. 492:
"Christus vincit, Christus regnat, Christus imperat. Sic fuit de Christo qui primo vicit inimicos suos: ipsis devictis regnavit gloria et etiam imperat in gloria. Sic enim Rex Francie, qui victoriam habuit et invenit de inimicis Christi."
Cf. Robert Holtzmann, *Wilhelm von Nogaret* (1898), 156.

Treaty of Amboise and on the eve of the Huguenot Wars, used that device to justify a military action in the name of Christ.[12]

By the fourteenth century, however, St. Louis' legend for his coins had found a new interpretation in France. The king was said to have chosen this motto in order to prove that the miracle of healing the "king's evil," which often was achieved by the touch of a gold coin, was not really accomplished by the king, but by Christ himself, who merely acted through his royal mediator. And, in addition, the motto showed that St. Louis considered his kingdom dependent not on the sword but on God from whom he held it in fief.[13]

Such a reduction of currency to the relationship with God might be attributed, with no more nor less foundation, to any coin which displayed a frankly Biblical or liturgical legend. To apply Scriptural legends on money was a usage which arose hardly earlier than the age of the Crusades,[14] but which became popular very quickly. These new inscriptions

[12] Calvin, *Opera omnia* (Brunswick, 1879), XX, 1, no. 3942:
"Christus non vult ut arbitremur quod venerit ad mittendam pacem in terram, sed gladium. . . . Sed nunc . . . qui non habet vendat tunicam suam et emat gladium. . . . Insigne regnum Galliae. Christus vincit, Christus regnat, Christus imperat."

[13] See the interpretation of Jean Golein, *Traité du sacre*, written in 1374 (Paris, Bibl. Nat. Fr. MS 437, fol. 44):
"... qu'il (le roi) a à tenir à dieu son hommage, qu'il li a fait de son royaume, qu'il tient de lui et non mie seulement de l'espée, si comme veulent dire aucuns, mais de dieu, si comme il tesmoigne en sa monnoie d'or quant il dit: *Christus vincit, Christus regnat, Christus imperat*. Il ne met mie: l'espée regne et vaint, mais dit: Jhs. vaint, Jhs. regne, Jhs. commande."
This author, one of the leading mystics of the "royal religion" at the court of Charles V of France, has a queer predilection for the "Christus vincit" triad on the royal French coins, for he quotes it time and again. In the manuscript mentioned above (fol. 2ᵛ) he writes, in the preface to his translation of Durandus' *Rationale*, as follows:
"En ceste foy ont ensuyvi les nobles roys de France leur droit patron le dit saint Charles (Charlemagne), et par especial le sage roy Charles regnant en France l'an mil CCCLXXII, lequel, à la forme et manière des ses predecesseurs, donnans l'onneur du royaume à Jhesu Crist, fait mettre ou coïng de sa monnoie d'or *Christus vincit, Christus regnat, Christus imperat*. ..."
And in a similar way he refers to the inscription in the preface to his translation of John Cassian's *Collations* (Paris, Bibl. Nat. Fr. MS 175, written in 1370):
"Mon très redoubté seigneur le très noble prince plain de vertus, le roy Charles, qui tient et gouverne le royaulme et empire de France, l'an M. CCC. LXX, en attribuant tout à Dieu et fait escrire en monnoye *Christus vincit, Christus regnat, Christus imperat*, en desirant que ses vertus particulières soient assemblées avecques les souverains, luy a pleu à moy commander ..."
Cf. L. Delisle, *Recherches sur la librairie de Charles V* (Paris, 1907), I, 98, and 99, n. 1. For Golein's reference to the healing of scrofula, see Bloch, *op. cit.*, p. 489, and *ibid.*, pp. 128 f., for the general tendency to attribute this miracle to Christ; see also Schramm, "Frankreich," *ZfRG.*, kan. Abt. XXV (1936), 321, n. 3.

[14] Cf. W. Froehner, "La liturgie romaine dans la numismatique," *Annuaire de la société française de numismatique et d'archéologie* (1889), 39–55. The first gold coins of St. Louis bearing a Biblical legend originated probably during his first crusade (1249–1254); his gold deniers minted at Acre (1251) show the Scriptural text in Arabic language and Kufic characters; cf. Henri Lavoix, *Monnaies à légendes arabes frappées en Syrie par les croisés* (Paris, 1877), 54 f.; A. Suhle, in *Wörterbuch der Münzkunde* (1930), *s.v.* "Kreuzfahrermünzen"; G. Wegemann, *Die Münzen der Kreuzfahrerstaaten* (Halle, 1934), 7.

frequently evoked, it is true, a satiric rather than a mystic interpretation. When, in later days, a Milanese duke chose to put on his money the verse *Te Deum laudamus*, popular jests almost inevitably made these initial words of the well-known hymn refer not to God but to the coin itself, to Money as God and to the glorification of the deified gold—"We praise thee like God." Or, when a monarch such as Louis XIV issued money bearing the device *Per me reges regnant*, this certainly was all too true and perhaps even meant to be cynical. Also, we cannot assume that the jest-loving Tuscans would not have noticed the ambiguity, though probably involuntary, of the legend on Sienese coins in the thirteenth century: *A et O, principium et finis*. Nor can we suppose that people would have missed the joke, almost forced upon their minds, when Robert II of Artois, in the very same century, provided his deniers with the words from Matthew: *Ego sum Deus*.[15] Minds then were quite open to ambiguous interpretations and very willing indeed to realize the satirical point. We need only recall the widely diffused "Money Gospels" of the wandering scholars, in which the cult of *Sancta Marca* or *Saint Denier* (Denis) and of other similar saints was praised.[16] Even the beautiful legend chosen by St. Louis for his coins did not escape distortion; it had been abused in travesties long before the king had applied it to his deniers.

> Nummus vincit, nummus regnat, nummus cunctis imperat,
> Reos solvit, iustos ligat, impedit et liberat . . .

ran a song of Walter of Châtillon.[17] Alain of Lille had also thought of this travesty: "Quid plura? Nummus vincit, nummus regnat, nummus imperat in universis."[18] Epistolary exercises, likewise, seized upon this saying.[19] Pupils of the cathedral school at Trier, for instance, made

---

[15] See Froehner, *op. cit.*

[16] Dümmler, in *NArch.*, XXIII (1898), 208 ff.; Paul Lehmann, *Die Parodie im Mittelalter* (Munich, 1922), 55 ff.

[17] Karl Strecker, *Moralisch-satirische Gedichte Walters von Châtillon* (Heidelberg, 1929), 110, no. 10, where the two lines are used as a refrain of the song similar to the responses of *Christus vincit* as used in a section of the laudes; cf. below, pp. 15 f. Earlier verses, attributed to Abbo of Fleury, anticipate somewhat this liturgical genre:
> "Publica spes nummus nunc rege potentior omni:
> Extollit presens, deicit aufugiens;
> Nummus nobilitas, nummus sapientia, nummus
> Pretendens superat, pauper ubique iacet."
Cf. A. van der Vyver, "Les œuvres inédites d'Abbon de Fleury," *Rev. bénéd.*, XLVII (1935), 165, n. 1.

[18] K. Strecker, "Walter von Châtillon und seine Schule," *Zeitschrift für deutsches Altertum*, LXIV (1927), 119, who mentions also the line from another rhythm: "nummus regit, nummus regnat, nummus et iustificat."

[19] See the "prayer" in an early Bolognese *ars dictandi*:
> "Per dominum aurum tuum purissimum, qui tecum vivit et regnat et regnavit per omnia scrinia cardinalium tuorum."
The author refers to the finale of prayers "Per dominum nostrum Jhesum filium tuum qui tecum vivit et regnat . . ." Cf. H. Kalbfuss, "Eine Bologneser *Ars dictandi* des zwölften Jahrhunderts," *QF.*, XVI (1914), 5.

Barbarossa expound that Christians seeking justice and impartial law courts should come to Trier, the city of Caesar, where they would find what they were looking for, "non nummo cooperante sicut Rome, ubi nummus et non Petrus regnat et imperat."[20]

Facetious, although in fact very bitter, these early mockeries and derisions of the sacramental formula may elicit the question whether the motto thus ridiculed was perhaps found on French money before the time of St. Louis. Why should the poets and scholars have chosen this formula to honor the Savior Money if the motto had not already appeared on coins? However, these satirists, as is well known, drew preferably from the Scripture or from prayers and litanies. They did not mock the legend of an existing French coin, but they travestied a litany which was popular, above all in France, during the twelfth and thirteenth centuries. This becomes evident from allusions made by an unidentified poet of this period, an imitator of Hildebert of Lavardin. Admittedly, his verse,

> Est dominus terre nummus, quia regnat ubique,
> Imperat et dominis et dominatur eis . . .,

hardly differs from similar productions. But his additional invocation *Exaudi, candide numme!* is, of course, a parody of the liturgical *Exaudi, Christe!* This latter, not too common a liturgical phrase, is repeated time and again—in a very prominent place—in the same litany in which the *Christus vincit* is used like a poetical refrain. Hence, there are two formulae of the same chant which are burlesqued by the poet,[21] and this provides us with the evidence that it was not the coin, but the litany which must be considered the source of these jests.

Who then, we must ask, was the first to put the *Christus vincit, Christus regnat, Christus imperat* on his coins? We should, perhaps, not entirely reject the possibility that the saying appeared on French silver coins of the twelfth century, though no such occurrence seems to be proved and later practice in France restricted the legend to gold coins.[22] It is certain, however, that the triad, as a whole or in parts, can be found on coins issued in the twelfth century in Southern Italy and Sicily, in the realms of Norman princes and kings.

It is particularly interesting to trace the triadic device to Norman Sicily because even this insignificant detail reveals the strange fusion of

[20] Wattenbach, "Iter Austriacum," *Archiv für Kunde österreichischer Geschichtsquellen*, XIV (1855), 88, who refers to a passage in the *Script. Hist. Aug.* (Vopiscus, *Saturn.*, c. 8: "unus illis Deus nummus est"), but fails to recognize the liturgical allusion.

[21] P. Lehmann, "Eine Sammlung mittellateinischer Gedichte aus dem Ende des 12. Jahrhunderts," *Historische Vierteljahrsschrift*, XXX (1935), p. 49, ll. 51 f., 104; the author is one Theodoric (of St.-Troud?) whose model was Hildebert's great *nummus* poem; cf. Migne, *PL.*, CLXXI, cols. 1404 ff.

[22] A. Prost, *Quatre pièces*, p. 196, n. 1; cf. Leclercq, in *DACL.*, VIII, 1908, *s.v.* "Laudes gallicanae."

relations and cultural influences for which the kingdom was famous. Two different streams of tradition must be distinguished from the outset, an Eastern and a Western, or, so far as rites are concerned, a Byzantine and a Gallican tradition. The formula that corresponds to the Latin *Christus vincit*, is the Greek: IC XC NIKA ('Ιησοῦς Χριστὸς νικᾷ). In a way, the Greek form may be called the original, although both sayings derive ultimately from the same source, the ancient Oriental and Roman acclamations.[23] The Greek formula—frequently displayed in such a way that the eight characters were distributed in pairs in the four angles of a cross:

$$\frac{IC|XC}{NI|KA}$$ —became one of the most famous monograms of Christ. It can

be traced back to the fourth century, allegedly to the time of Constantine the Great, and the Greek Church seems to have begun the practice of stamping this symbol on the host in the fifth century.[24] Hosts and coins eventually displayed the same characters, a relationship about which Honorius of Augustodunum, the standard-bearer of Western mystagogues, writes in general terms:[25]

The host receives the form of a denier because Christ, the bread of life, was betrayed at the price of a few deniers, He, the true denier, that shall be given to the laborers in the vineyard. Into the bread is pressed, with characters, the image of the Lord, as in the deniers there are engraved image and name of the emperor.

In the Eastern Empire the relationship was certainly the reverse. For the symbol IC XC NIKA appears on the host before it was applied to Byzantine money by Constantine V, the inconoclast emperor (741–775). During his reign the persecution of image worshipers reached its climax and it was Constantine V who systematically changed the types of Byzantine coinage in order to remove the image of Christ from these "symbols of the State's power par excellence."[26] At any rate, from the time of the

---

[23] On the NIKA acclamations, see Peterson, *Untersuchungen*, pp. 152 ff.; Prost, *Quatre pièces*, p. 199; Leclercq, in *DACL.*, I, 252, *s.v.* "Acclamations"; *JLW.*, X (1930), 373, No. 407.

[24] Joseph Dölger, *Antike und Christentum* (Münster, 1929), I, 21 ff., and pls. 2, 3, 7.

[25] Honorius Augustod., *Gemma animae*, I, c. 35, Migne, *PL.*, CLXXII, col. 555:
   "Panis vero ideo in modum denarii formatur, quia panis vitae Christus pro denariorum numero tradebatur qui verus denarius in vinea laborantibus praemio dabitur. Ideo imago Domini cum litteris in hoc pane exprimitur, quia et in denario imago et nomen imperatoris scribitur . . ."
The similarity of the host with a coin (cf. Leroquais, *Pontificaux*, I, xvii, in connection with the *sacculus*, the lined sack in which the host was carried until the ninth century) applies to the Western form of the host, but not to the Greek which has the form of a bread. However, in the Greek host the image of an emperor, Constantine, is found occasionally, cf. C. M. Kaufmann, "Konstantin und Helena auf einem griechischen Hostienstempel," *Oriens Christianus*, N. S., IV (1915), 85 ff.

[26] Cf. Hugh Goodacre, *A Handbook of the Coinage of the Byzantine Empire* (London 1931), II, 142, No. 19; Gerhart B. Ladner, "Origin and Significance of the Byzantine Iconoclast Controversy," *Mediaeval Studies*, II (1940), 137 ff.

iconoclast rulers, the formula appeared, over and over again, on the coins of the Byzantine Empire.

This usage was observed also in Byzantine southern Italy.The Normans, therefore, when they, too, began to put this sign on their coins and *bullae*, either adopted or simply continued a Byzantine tradition. We can trace the IC XC NIKA on Norman money back at least to the reign of King Roger II who, apparently only after his elevation to the dignity of a king, applied these symbols to his gold *tarì* and thereby replaced the former Arabic coins bearing inscriptions in Kufic characters. Furthermore, a *bulla* of Roger II displays the Greek legend.[27] Hieratic characters have a life and history of their own, which frequently differs from that of the corresponding political development. In the administration of the kingdom of Southern Italy, the Greek language gradually died away, although its official use lasted until the time of Frederick II;[28] but the Greek symbols on coins survived the Norman dynasty. The Hohenstaufen, among them even the last kings, Conrad IV and Manfred, continued to strike money with this Greek inscription,[29] and it was used also by Charles of Anjou.[30]

Ostentatiously indeed, the Norman princes had taken the place of the Byzantine emperors in the former Greek provinces of Italy by either borrowing the imperial legend of coins or continuing an imperial custom. This practice intersected with influences from the motherland of the Normans. The ecclesiastical rite introduced in Southern Italy had a touch of the ancient Gallo-Frankish usage, a fact borne out by that litany, for instance, which began *Christus vincit, Christus regnat, Christus imperat.* Along with the Greek inscription, this triad, too, began to appear on the Norman money during the twelfth century. A coin of Roger II, showing St. Januarius the patron of Naples on the obverse, carries on the reverse the legend, unfortunately badly preserved, XPC VI · XPC . . .; but it is easy to supplement it by . . . RE · XPC IMP. It may be that

[27] In general, see A. Suhle, in *Wörterbuch der Münzkunde, s.v.* "Schrift"; C. A. Garufi, *Monete e conii nella storia del diritto siculo* (Palermo, 1878). For Roger II, see Arthur Engel, *Recherches sur la numismatique et la sigillographie des Normands de Sicile et d'Italie* (Paris, 1882), 37 f., who dates the earliest coin of this type 1141; cf. *ibid.*, p. 43, Nos. 78, 81, 82, 84; for a *bulla* of Roger II with the legend IC XC NIKA, cf. K. A. Kehr, *Die Urkunden der normannisch-sizilischen Könige* (Innsbruck, 1902), 208. Roger Bursa, duke of Calabria and Apulia (1085–1111), however, used a lead *bulla* with this legend even before Roger II; cf. Engel, *op. cit.*, p. 84, No. 9.

[28] E. Kantorowicz, *Kaiser Friedrich der Zweite. Ergänzungsband* (Berlin, 1931), 132 ff.

[29] Cf. Suhle, in *Wörterbuch der Münzkunde, s.v.* "Tarì."

[30] G. S. Sambon, "Monnaies de Charles Ier d'Anjou dans l'Italie méridionale," *Annuaire de la société française de numismatique et d'archéologie* (1891), p. 135, and in *Gazette numismatique française*, III, 138; Luigi dell'Erba, "La riforma monetaria angioina e il suo sviluppo storico nel reame di Napoli," *Arch. stor. Napol.*, N. S., XVIII (1932), 163; Charles' coins as a crusader bear the legend SERVUS XPI, cf. Sambon, "Monete d'oro da Carlo I d'Angiò a Tunisia," *Rivista italiana numismatica*, VI (1893), 341 ff.; dell'Erba, *op. cit.*, p. 165; and, for the title "Servus Christi," Goodacre, *op. cit.*, p. 115; Schramm, *Kaiser, Rom und Renovatio* (1929), I, 141 ff.

this coin was minted at Naples after the last Byzantine Master of the Soldiers had surrendered this place to Roger II (1131), and that the king, in this last stronghold of the Greek government, quite designedly replaced the Greek inscription by the similar Latin version,[31] which by then had become popular. We know, for example, another coin of that age, struck by some local Norman prince in Southern Italy, which likewise permits us to recognize the characters XC · RE · XC · IM, meaning of course *Christus regnat, Christus imperat*.[32] The Latin phrase appears, moreover, not alone on coins. A seal of Roger I clearly bears the Latin version of the Greek inscription: *Jhesus Christus vincit*.[33] There is further a privilege granted to Messina in 1129. It is a later forgery; but it must be noted that the forger, in order to make the document appear worthy of confidence, wrote in the outer ring of the supposedly "royal" *rota* the words *Deum cole. Qui regnat, vincit, imperat*.[34] He thus assumed that this had been the king's device and may have considered the triad "very Norman." It is true, we know of no *bulla* or seal of the early Norman monarchs that bore exactly this legend. Nevertheless, the forger was not quite wrong, for Roger's grandson Frederick II, in his youth and as a king of Apulia and Sicily, used a golden *bulla* which displayed the uncurtailed triad of *Christus vincit, Christus regnat, Christus imperat*,[35] and it is more than likely that the young prince, or rather his advisers, simply continued an older Norman tradition. Frederick II, in any case, changed the inscription once he began to rule independently. His later *bullae* bore the legend *Roma caput mundi*, thus illustrating plainly his great shift from the Norman-Sicilian crusader atmosphere of his earlier days to the intellectual climate of the Hohenstaufen, to the ideal of Roman world-government and of the revival of Rome.

---

[31] Engel, *op. cit.*, p. 40, No. 50.

[32] *Ibid.*, p. 56, No. 166. See also Luigi dell'Erba, "Sui *Follari* longobardi anonimi alla leggenda *Victoria* battuti in Salerno," *Bollettino del circolo numismatico napoletano* (1925), p. 7, according to whom (cf. p. 4) the Lombard princes of Salerno began to use the formula XC · RE · XC · IMPE as early as the tenth century.

[33] For the seal of Count Roger I on a privilege for Catania of 1092, see Roccho Pirri, *Sicilia sacra* (2d ed.; Leyden), I, 464; for the *bulla* of Roger II, cf. above, n. 27.

[34] Kehr, *op. cit.*, p. 166, n. 1; for the literature on this forgery, see Erich Caspar, *Roger II und die Gründung der normannisch-sizilischen Monarchie* (Innsbruck, 1904), 501 ff.

[35] Huillard-Bréholles, *Historia diplomatica Friderici Secundi* (Paris, 1859), Introd., ci, and I, 212; O. Posse, *Die Siegel der deutschen Kaiser und Könige* (Dresden, 1909) I, 27, Nos. 3, 4; the *bulla* was used, once more, for unknown reasons in 1243; cf. Böhmer-Ficker, *Regesta Imperii*, V, No. 3369; *MGH.Const.*, II, 328, No. 239. The formula was reintroduced by the Aragonese kings of Sicily at the end of the thirteenth century, beginning with Peter of Aragon and his Hohenstaufen queen, Costanza (1282–1285), who put it on their gold *reali;* cf. V. Capobianchi, "Immagini simboliche e stemmi di Roma," *Archivio della società romana*, XIX (1896), 369 f.; Mariano Amirante, "Il *reale* di Giacomo d'Aragona," *Circolo numismatico napoletano, Studi e ricerche* (1926), 31 f.; Rodolfo Spahr, "Il *reale* di Federico II d'Aragona," *Bollettino del circolo numismatico napoletano* (1927), 37 f.

To recall the passionate feelings of the crusading age in connection with the *Christus vincit* device on coins and seals of Norman kings or of St. Louis is not unjustifiable. Fulcher of Chartres, in his History of the Kingdom of Jerusalem,[36] narrates how the Franks under King Baldwin marched to the battlefield of Ramleh (1105) and there, advised by the patriarch,[37] shouted the battle cry *Christus vincit, Christus regnat, Christus imperat!* Also, the Armenians in the battle of Adana (1097) answered the *Allah akbar!* of the Muslems with shouting *Christus vincit, regnat, imperat!*[38] The cry *Deus vult!* was on the lips of the first crusaders; it was like the hollow rumbling of Fate. The new invocation of Christ the Victor, King, and Commander revealed distinctly the new idea which had seized upon the crusaders after their first great successes, the clear-cut purpose of reinvesting Christ as king in his kingdom of Jerusalem.[39]

However this may be, the device of the Norman rulers must also be regarded as a reflection of the crusading spirit. Its adoption by the Normans as well as by the warriors in the Holy Land proves not only the popularity and wide diffusion of the liturgical verse, but proves also that this martial saying appealed to the spirit of the crusading age and expressed, like a slogan, the true meaning of the Holy Wars. There may be added an almost posthumous evidence: Pope Pius V presented to Don Juan of Austria after the Victory of Lepanto (1571) an iron shield which showed the legend *Christus vincit, Christus regnat, Christus imperat*, reminiscent of the mood of the early crusaders.[40]

In summing up the inquiry it may be said that Byzantine tradition, Gallican liturgy, and the crusading spirit are jointly reflected in the coins and seals of the South Italian Norman kings. The Latin *Christus vincit* triad, we can see, was not simply a translation or amplification of

---

[36] Fulcher Carnotensis, *Historia Hierosolimitana*, II, c. xxxii, 5, ed. H. Hagenmeyer (Heidelberg, 1913), 497; *RHC: Occid.*, III, 413; see also *Gesta Francorum*, c. 70, in *RHC: Occid.*, III, 540, and the *Historia Hierosolimitana*, II, c. 18, *ibid.*, III, 566; cf. *Notes and Queries*, CLVIII (London, 1930), 65, 118.

[37] "Sicut eis [a patriarcha] iussum fuerat"; the words in brackets are only in the Cambridge manuscript of Fulcher's work.

[38] Radulfus Cadomensis, *Gesta Tancredi*, c. 40, *RHC: Occid.*, III, 636:
   "Ex illo, Allachibar, quod infidelitas orando exclamat, hac in urbe obmutuit, ac pro eo *Christus vincit, regnat, imperat* . . . reboavit."
Professor J. S. P. Tatlock kindly called my attention to Tudebodi Continuatio, *Historia Peregrinorum*, c. 120 (ad a. 1099), *op. cit.*, III, 220: ". . . unde Christo victori laudes referuntur."

[39] An allusion to the triad is perhaps found in the sermon of Pope Urban II at Clermont, at least in the form transmitted by Fulcher, I, c. 3, in *RHC: Occid.*, III, 324: "Presentibus dico, absentibus mando, Christus autem imperat." For the change of the general conception concerning the task of the First Crusade, see Erdmann, *Kreuzzugsgedanken*, pp. 363 ff. For the battle cries of the crusaders, cf. Du Cange, *Glossarium*, X, 38 ff. (Dissertation XI: "Du cry d'armes"); R. Röhricht, *Geschichte des Königreichs Jerusalem* (Innsbruck, 1898), 580, 589; Erdmann, *op. cit.*, pp. 83 ff.

[40] Cf. Paul Lacroix, *Vie militaire et religieuse au moyen âge* (Paris, 1873), 294, fig. 215; see Pl. II, *e*.

the Greek legend IC XC NIKA, since it derived from the Gallo-Frankish liturgy. Yet the fact that the first Latin clause tallies with the Greek motto may have called forth the substitution of the one phrase for the other. Indeed, both the Greek and Latin forms make their appearance almost simultaneously on Sicilian coins in the early twelfth century, long before the Latin version was put on the coinage of France. It therefore seems likely that St. Louis' famous device, which eventually was taken over by many a European lord enjoying the right of coinage (see Appendix II), was applied to coins for the first time by the Norman kings of Southern Italy.

CHAPTER II

THE GALLO-FRANKISH LAUDES REGIAE

ANALYSIS OF A CAROLINGIAN LAUDES TEXT

RÉMY DE GOURMONT's fine and almost poetical definition of litanies as "implorations multipliées de bouches jamais lasses, de coeurs toujours en peur et en pleurs," as orisons which "add love to adoration, to humble petitions tears, and to the surrender to an absolute power the hope for the mansuetude of the suffering Christ" seems to refer to the individual private devotion of the Later Middle Ages and even modern times rather than to the hieratic liturgical forms of the Church at an earlier stage.[1] The litanies of the official liturgies, such as the Litany of the Saints in the Western Church, can hardly be called a matter of private piety. These long sequences of short petitions represent a form of prayer which always encompasses the sum total of Christian society on earth, and often that of the invisible powers and saints in heaven as well. They refer to the peace and welfare of the world, to the Holy Catholic and Apostolic Church, to the bishops and priests, to emperors, kings, and other representatives of the secular government, to the sick, to those traveling, and to those in need and in danger. In the Eastern Churches the suffrages are said by the deacon and responded to by the congregation: "God have mercy," *Kyrie eleison!* In the Western rites, the word *Laetaniae* originally suggested not a prayer proper, but a penitentiary procession which was first introduced in Gaul in the fifth century, a solemnity of three days of fasting and penitence preceding the festival of the Ascension of Christ and inseparably connected with the singing of psalms and deprecatory prayers. How and when the various kinds of prayers and suffrages with their short responses (*ora pro nobis*, *libera nos*, *audi nos*, and others) grew together before the definite form of the liturgical Litany of the Saints of the present *Missale Romanum* was achieved, is a matter for scholarly dispute. The main body of the Litany of the Saints as it is said today, on comparatively rare occasions, is composed generally of invocations to saints whose intercession is demanded; of humble supplications in which the Lord is asked to deliver the faithful from evil and to rescue them through the mysterious forces of his Salvation; and of a number of suffrages which explain the worshiper's desires. Though certainly not a matter of private devotion, the litany is the most genuine expression of the penitential spirit within the Church, of the ideas

[1] Rémy de Gourmont, *Le latin mystique* (Paris, 1922), 143. In the West, the litany first may have been likewise a prayer of "private devotion of individuals" before acquiring official character; cf. Bishop, *Lit. Hist.*, p. 150, 3.

of contrition and humiliation which are emphasized by the fact that on certain occasions the worshipers prostrate themselves when the litany is said.[2]

An exception to this general penitential spirit is formed by the litany which begins with the words *Christus vincit, Christus regnat, Christus imperat.* It is a prayer peculiar to the Gallo-Frankish Church and it is usually called the Laudes.[3] These laudes, which of course must not be confused with the lauds of the canonical hours, are exceptional since neither the suffrages nor the responses are born from "fears and tears." Instead of humble petitions demanding deliverance from evil we find jubilant acclamations; rescue is hoped for not by the mysterious forces of salvation, but by the militant nature of the victorious Christ; and the anxious responses such as *Miserere* or *Libera nos, Domine*, are exchanged for the assured hails of *Christus vincit.* In short, this chant is not directed to the suffering God. The laudes invoke the conquering God—Christ the victor, ruler, and commander—and acclaim in him, with him, or through him his imperial or royal vicars on earth along with all the other powers conquering, ruling, commanding, and safeguarding the order of this present world: the pope and the bishops, the ruler's house, the clergy, the princes, the judges, and the army. The correlations of the two worlds, the present and the transcendental, and the dissolving of the one in the other become manifest on closer inspection of the text of this chant.[4]

---

[2] On litanies in general, see *DACL.*, IX, 1540–1571, *s.v.* "Litanie." The fundamental study is Bishop's "The Litany of Saints in the Stowe Missal," *Lit. Hist.*, pp. 137–164, and *ibid.*, pp. 116–136, on the "Kyrie Eleison." A good analysis of the elements of the Litany of the Saints is offered by Anton Baumstark, "Eine syrisch-melchitische Aller-heiligenlitanei," *Oriens Christianus*, IV (1904), 98–120, and a clear survey of the prayers of intercession by V. L. Kennedy, O.S.B., *The Saints of the Canon of the Mass*, Studi di antichità cristiana, XIV (Rome, Pontificio istituto di archeologia cristiana, 1938), 1–38. For the interrelations between litanies and acclamations, see Peterson, *Untersuchungen*, pp. 166 f. On the prostration, cf. below, p. 90 f.

[3] The most detailed study is still Prost's article published in 1876. Leclercq, *DACL.*, VIII, 1898–1910, *s.v.* "Laudes Gallicanae," is nothing but an extract from Prost's work. See also *DACL.*, I, 242, *s.v.* "Acclamations," now superseded by Erik Peterson, *Untersuchungen*. Ludwig Biehl, *Das liturgische Gebet für Kaiser und Reich*, Görres-Gesellschaft. Veröffentlichungen der Sektion für Rechts- und Staatswissenschaft, Heft 75 (Paderborn, 1937), 102 ff., adds a few observations, but otherwise depends on Prost.

[4] The oldest formulary (cf. below, p. 21, n. 19) displays certain peculiarities. As a model, I therefore reprint the second in age, found in a Psalter from the time of Charlemagne, Paris, Bibl. Nat. Lat. MS 13159, fol. 163 (*ca.* 796–800). Cf. L. Delisle, *Le Cabinet des manuscrits de la Bibliothèque Nationale* (1880), III, 239 f., pl. xxi; *Album paléographique ou recueil de documents importants reproduits par la société de l'école des chartes* (Paris, 1887), Pl. xvii, 3. A very short analysis of the manuscript is offered by A. Gastoué, "Le chant gallican," *RCGr.*, XLIII (1939), 46. The formulary has been printed frequently, cf. Prost, *Quatre pièces*, pp. 173 ff.; *DACL.*, VIII, 1902 f.; *Liber pontificalis*, ed. L. Duchesne (Paris, 1886–1892), II, 37; De Santi, "Le *laudes* nell' incoronazione del sommo pontifice," *Civiltà cattolica*, Ser. XVIII, Vol. XI (1903), 391 f.; H. Dannenbauer, *Die Quellen zur Geschichte der Kaiserkrönung Karls des Grossen*, Lietzmann's Kleine Texte für Vorlesungen und Uebungen, 161 (Berlin, 1931), 57. K. Heldmann, *Das Kaisertum Karls d. Gr.*, Quellen und Studien zur Verfassungsgeschichte des Deutschen Reiches, VI, 2 (Weimar, 1928), 287, maintains that this

I. Christus vincit, Christus regnat, Christus imperat. (ter)

II. Exaudi Christe	R/. Leoni summo pontifici et universali pape vita.
III. Salvator mundi	tu illum adiuva
S. Petre	tu illum adiuva
S. Paule	tu illum adiuva
S. Andrea	tu illum adiuva
S. Clemens	tu illum adiuva
S. Syste	tu illum adiuva
Exaudi Christe	Carolo excellentissimo et a Deo coronato atque magno et pacifico regi Francorum et Longobardorum ac patricio Romanorum vita et victoria.
Redemptor mundi	tu illum adiuva
S. Maria	tu illum adiuva
S. Michahel	tu illum adiuva
S. Gabrihel	tu illum adiuva
S. Raphahel	tu illum adiuva
S. Johannes	tu illum adiuva
S. Stephane	tu illum adiuva
Exaudi Christe	Nobilissime proli regali vita.
S. Virgo Virginum	tu illam adiuva
S. Silvestre	tu illam adiuva
S. Laurenti	tu illam adiuva
S. Pancrati	tu illam adiuva
S. Nazari	tu illam adiuva
S. Anastasia	tu illam adiuva
S. Genovefa	tu illam adiuva
S. Columba	tu illam adiuva
Exaudi Christe	Omnibus iudicibus vel cuncto exercitui Francorum vita et victoria.
S. Hilari	tu illos adiuva
S. Martine	tu illos adiuva
S. Maurici	tu illos adiuva
S. Dionisi	tu illos adiuva
S. Crispine	tu illos adiuva
S. Crispiniane	tu illos adiuva
S. Gereon	tu illos adiuva

formulary was used on November 24, 800, when the Romans offered "venienti laudes" (cf. *Ann. regni Francorum*, ed. Kurze in *MGH. SS. rer. Germ.* [1895] 110). This assumption is not likely to be correct because the laudes offered at the reception of a king were different from the litany of the laudes; cf. below, pp. 73 f. Duchesne in *Liber pont.*, II, 38, suggests that the formulary was used at Paderborn in 799, when Pope Leo III visited Charlemagne. There is no basis for the suggestion and, generally speaking, one should refrain from confining laudes formularies to one occasion only, since they could be used and probably were used repeatedly on various occasions; cf. below, pp. 21, n. 19; 109, n. 146. The Roman figures are added to facilitate the analysis.

IV. Christus vincit, Christus regnat, Christus imperat.

V.		R/.	
Rex regum		R/.	Christus vincit
Rex noster			Christus vincit
Spes nostra			Christus vincit
Gloria nostra			Christus vincit
Misericordia nostra			Christus vincit
Auxilium nostrum			Christus vincit
Fortitudo nostra			Christus vincit
Liberatio et redemptio nostra			Christus vincit
Victoria nostra			Christus vincit
Arma nostra invictissima			Christus vincit
Murus noster inexpugnabilis			Christus vincit
Defensio et exaltatio nostra			Christus vincit
Lux, via et vita nostra			Christus vincit

VI. Ipsi soli imperium, gloria et potestas per immortalia secula
seculorum.   Amen.
Ipsi soli virtus, fortitudo et victoria per omnia secula
seculorum.   Amen.
Ipsi soli honor, laus et jubilatio per infinita secula seculorum.   Amen.

VII. Christe, audi nos!   Christe, audi nos!   Christe, audi nos!
Kyrie eleison!   Christe eleison!   Kyrie eleison!

VIII. Feliciter! Feliciter! Feliciter!
Tempora bona habeas. Tempora bona habeas. Tempora bona habeas.
Multos annos.
Amen.

A few words are needed to analyze and classify the elements of this
litany.

I. The litany begins with the *Christus vincit, Christus regnat, Christus
imperat*. Save for a certain group of texts,[5] the laudes are always opened
by this formula, the origin of which, so far as it can be ascertained, will be
discussed separately.

II. There follows the invocation *Exaudi Christe* with the hailing acclamation proper *N. N. vita (et victoria)*! The acclamations are the pith of
chant and to this nucleus all the other elements are contributive factors.
This acclamatory figure is very old. Within the Church ritual it is known
since the fifth century at the latest; for example:

Exaudi Christe!   Augustino vita![6]

or:

Exaudi Christe!   Theodorico vita!
Exaudi Christe!   Symmacho vita![7]

---

[5] The Franco-Roman and papal forms of laudes; cf. below, pp. 105 and 144.
[6] Augustinus, *Ep.* 213 (Sept. 26, 426), Migne, *PL.*, XXXIII, cols. 867 f.; cf. Peter

However, this combination was not first created by the Church; it is considerably older. The *vita*-acclaim is of indeterminable age,[8] and the *Exaudi*-invocation is likewise pre-Christian. As in so many rites of the Church, Christ has replaced the Roman emperor in the invocation. The imperial form was:[9]

Exaudi Caesar!	Delatores ad leonem!
Exaudi Caesar!	Speratum ad leonem!

III. To invoke a series of saints by name, at least in the form displayed by the model, is a comparatively late usage which on the Continent is not older than the eighth century. In a rudimentary form, however, the invocation of at least one saint in connection with acclamatory hails can be traced back to the fifth century, when Pope Gelasius, in 495, was acclaimed in the following way:[10]

Exaudi Christe!	Gelasio vita!
Domne Petre!	Tu illum serva!

This usage again follows pre-Christian traditions, since the acclamations to the emperor, offered to him by the senate, the people, or religious brotherhoods such as the Arvalians, often contain the formula *Di te ser-*

---

son, *Untersuchungen*, p. 144; Paul Cagin, *L'euchologie latine. Te Deum ou illatio* (Solesmes, 1906), I:1 p. 266; Gastoué, *La musique de l'église* (Lyons, 1911), 183. On episcopal acclamations in general, cf. below, p. 112 ff.

[7] Acclamations of the Roman Council on March 1, 499, cf. *Acta Synhodi, MGH. AA. ant.*, XII, 402–405; Peterson, *Untersuchungen*, p. 151; Heldmann, *op. cit.* 283, n. 1; see also Deusdedit, III, c. xlv, ed. Wolf von Glanvell (1905), I, 288. Cf. below, pp. 68 ff., on conciliar acclamations. In exactly the same way the imperial images were acclaimed; cf., Gregory I, *Reg.* XIII, 1, *MGH. Epist.*, II, 365: "Exaudi Christe! Phocae Augusto et Leontiae Augustae vita!" See also Helmut Kruse, *Studien zur offiziellen Geltung des Kaiserbildes im römischen Reich*, Studien zur Geschichte und Kultur des Altertums, XIX:3 (Paderborn, 1934), 34 ff., and *passim;* Karl Voigt, *Staat und Kirche von Konstantin dem Grossen bis zum Ende der Karolingerzeit* (Stuttgart, 1936), 86 ff.; Treitinger, *op. cit.*, pp. 204 ff.

[8] See, e.g., I Kings, 10:24, I Kings, 1:39, II Kings, 11:12, and in general, Peterson, *op. cit.*, pp. 142 ff., and *passim.*

[9] Lampridius, *Commodus*, c. 18 f., in *Script. Hist. Aug.* Although the testimonies of the *Historia Augusta* are of a doubtful character, they can all the same be here adduced, since they belong to the later Roman or early Christian period. Moreover, the acclamations to Commodus are now considered genuine, cf. W. Ensslin, in *Cambridge Ancient History*, XII (1939), 366. That similar forms of acclamations were used in Rome is proved by the inscriptions of the *fratres Arvales* (cf. below, pp. 66 f.) as well as by others; cf. Dessaù, *Inscriptiones latinae selectae*, Nos. 2608, 5845, 5865a, 8930, 8931. The Christian character of the acclamations in the *Hist. Aug.* is indeed often surprising, but it is only significant of what Alföldi calls the "Litany Style" of the Later Roman Empire; cf. "Insignien und Trachten der römischen Kaiser," *RM.*, 50 (1935), 86 ff.

[10] *Avellana*, ed. Günther (1895), *CSEL.*, XXXV, 478, No. 103, § 13, with reference to the Roman Council in 495. The acclamation then goes on "Cuius sedem et annos! Apostolum Petrum te videmus!" so that this acclamation is also an important document of the early history of the Petrine Doctrine; cf. Erich Caspar, *Geschichte des Papsttums* (Tübingen, 1933), II, 79. Cf. below, p. 125.

vent![11] The group of persons acclaimed meets, in essence, all the requirements concerning the prayer for the magistracies as suggested by St. Paul, the Apostolic Constitutions, Tertullian, and other authorities.[12]

IV. The first part of the litany ends as it begins with the three clauses *Christus vincit, Christus regnat, Christus imperat*, which seem to brace the whole chant and which here, in a very skillful manner, form a transition to the next section.

V. The hails to the military qualities of Christ with the refrain *Christus vincit* have been considered reminiscent of tropes.[13] They are, however, the *laudes Christi* proper, the acclamations to Christ and his specified military virtues, which henceforth will be referred to as the "laudatory section." These hails, too, can be traced to the imperial acclamations of later Rome if we may trust the *Historia Augusta*.[14] Here we find acclaims to the imperial virtues, for example:

> Alexander Auguste!   Di te servent!
> Verecundiae tuae,
> Prudentiae tuae,

[11] *Corpus Inscriptionum Latinarum*, VI, Nos. 2086, 2104, pp. 551, 571; Guilelmus Henzen, *Acta fratrum Arvalium* (1874), 46. See also Lampridius, *Diadumenos*, c. 1: "Juppiter optime maxime, Macrino et Antonino vitam!" Peterson, *Untersuchungen*, p. 143; Heldmann, *op. cit.*, p. 262, n. 8. The pagan "Di te servent" is replaced in the episcopal acclamations (below, pp. 112 ff.) by the Christian "Deus conservet" or also by "Tu illum serva"; cf. above, the acclamation to Gelasius.

[12] I Tim., 2:1–3, is fundamental, as is illustrated by the title page of the Cranmer Bible (Pl. VIII). See also Tertullian, *Apolog.*, c. 30, 4, ed. Hoppe, *CSEL.*, LXIX, 78 f.; *Apostolic Constitutions*, ed. F. E. Brightman, *Liturgies Eastern and Western* (Oxford, 1896), I, 21, ll. 24–28; cf. Kennedy, *op. cit.*, pp. 14 ff., who outlines the development very clearly. A most instructive study on the deprecatory prayers for the ruler in the early Christian period is F. J. Dölger, "Zur antiken und frühchristlichen Auffassung der Herrschergewalt von Gottes Gnaden," *Antike und Christentum*, III (1932), 117–131. See also the interesting description of Apuleius, *Metam.*, XI, 17, adduced by Peterson, *Untersuchungen*, p. 167, and Alföldi (below, n. 18); further, the study of R. H. Connolly, "Liturgical Prayers of Intercession," *Jour. Theol. Stud.*, XXI (1920), 227 f., and *passim*. In general, see Gerd Tellenbach, "Römischer und christlicher Reichsgedanke in der Liturgie des frühen Mittelalters," *Sitzungsber. Heidelb. Akad.*, 1934, Abh. 1, pp. 9 ff., and Biehl, *op. cit.*, pp. 68 ff. For the effects of I Tim., 2:2, see, above all, the rich collection of authorities adduced by Anton Michel, *Humbert und Kerullarios* (Paderborn, 1930), II, 194 ff.

[13] Léon Gautier, *Histoire de la poésie liturgique au moyen âge: les tropes* (Paris, 1886), 82 f., 86 ff., 150. He refers to the laudes formularies of St. Martial in Limoges (Bibl. Nat. Lat. MS 1240, fol. 65, and Bibl. Nat. Lat. MS 1118, fol. 38ᵛ), of St. Gall (below, p. 32, Autun (Paris, Arsenal MS 1169), Nevers (Bibl. Nat. Lat. MS 9449), and to those in the Munich Cod. Lat. 14322 (cf. below, p. 45, n. 114).

[14] Lampridius, *Alex. Sev.*, c. 10; Vulcacius, *Avidius*, c. 13. It was not a difficult task to "christianize" these imperial acclamations which were soteriological anyhow; see, e.g., Lampridius, *Alex. Sev.*, c. 7: "in te salus! in te vita!" not to mention the earlier Eastern *soter* hails to the ruler; cf. Alföldi, above, n. 9. The four natural cardinal virtues are sometimes inserted in this section; see, e.g., the forms of Nevers (early eleventh century) in the Paris, Bibl. Nat. Lat. MS 9449, fols. 36ᵛ–37, and of Rheims in the Assisi, Bibl. Com. MS 695, fols. 42ᵛ–43, of 1257–1259; cf. U. Chevalier, *Sacramentaire et martyrologe ... des églises de Rheims*, Bibliothèque liturgique, VII (Paris, 1900), 363; Migne, *PL.*, CXXXVIII, col. 901. In the laudes of Metz of the ninth century (Prost, *Quatre pièces*, p. 239), the phrase "fortitudo et *vita*" seems to be an error for "fortitudo et *iustitia*."

Innocentiae tuae
Castitati tuae . . .
Alexander Auguste!   Di te servent!

or:

Antonine clemens!   Di te servent!
Philosophiae tuae,
Patientiae tuae,
Doctrinae tuae,
Nobilitati tuae,
Innocentiae tuae;
Vincis inimicos,
Hostes exsuperas!   Di te tuentur!

It is not surprising to find that in the laudes formulary the virtues and qualities acclaimed have been shifted, so to speak, from the objective to the subjective, from the domain of the eye to that of inner man. Thus, *prudentiae tuae* became *prudentia nostra;* but the forces or virtues of Christ dwelling in man, or aroused by him in man, are counterbalanced in turn by the responsive hails to "Christ who conquers," to the conqueror objectively. That is to say, the manifestations of his virtues in man are many and they may change. But the unchangeable and unshakable nature of his victory is emphasized in the *Christus vincit* which is taken up in this laudatory section and repeated over and over again. Like a musical *leitmotif* the cry dominates especially this part of the chant. It was either the first clause only which was sung (as in our model), or the singers responded with the whole tricolon, or else with one of the three clauses in alternation so that the first response was *Christus vincit*, the second *Christus regnat*, and the third *Christus imperat*, while the fourth would begin again with *Christus vincit*. The last form, however, seems to occur exclusively in English formularies and is unusual.[15] At any rate,

---

[15] The responses seem to have developed in a different form within the various countries. *Christus vincit* alone is the response in the Carolingian, the Franco-Roman, and most of the French royal laudes (e.g., Beauvais, Besançon, Limoges, Nevers, Rheims, Rouen, Soissons, Troyes, and Metz). The three clauses are found especially in Germany (e.g., in Bamberg, Minden, Passau, Ratisbon, St. Gall, but also in the forms of Aquileia, Paris, and Narbonne). The three clauses in alternation are found in the twelfth century, in the Cambridge, Trinity Lat. MS 249, fol. 108ᵛ, and in the thirteenth-century laudes of Worcester, cf. *Paléographie musicale*, XII (1922), 74 f., where, however, the transcription is not correct (see the facsimile of the manuscript, *op. cit.*, fol. 202); for the general tendency in England—as well as in Normandy (cf. below, p. 168)—to draft the *Ordines* of the Coronation in a triadic way, see P. E. Schramm, "Ordines-Studien III," *ArchUF.*, XV (1938), 318, and also the observations made by Bukofzer (below, p. 194) relative to the laudes of Worcester. Gautier, *op. cit.*, p. 150, indicates that the laudes of Autun, in the Paris, Arsenal MS 1169, have the response *Christus vincit, Christus regnat;* that is, two clauses only. An explanation is perhaps offered by the music. Bukofzer (below, p. 195) has noticed that the melodic formula of the *Christus imperat* is frequently used as the music of the invocations in the laudatory part. That is to say that melodically, though not so far as the text is concerned, the phrase would be complete and triadic, for the melodic *imperat* formula would be followed by the two beats of *vincit* and *regnat* which, in turn, precede the *imperat* tune of the then following invocation. The principles prevailing, however, cannot be clearly recognized without consulting the manuscripts once more.

many variations were possible, and the effectiveness of the chant was increased by means of those artificial interlacings and resolutions, repetitions and iterations, which in fact vary with each group of laudes formularies.

VI. The ensuing part consists of hymnic praises, or doxologies, which are not remarkable except for the fact that they refer to Christ alone and not to the triune God as the doxologies usually do. It may be worth while to mention the fact that, as a rule, neither God the Father nor the Holy Spirit are invoked in the laudes, but that the whole chant addresses itself solely to the victorious Son.

VII. There follows, thrice repeated, the *Christe, audi nos*, a cry characteristic of the litanies. Also the *Kyrie eleison*, alternating, as prescribed by the Western Church, with the *Christe eleison*, emphasizes the litany-character of the chant.[16]

VIII. *Feliciter*, thrice repeated and combined with the wishes *Tempora bona habeas* and *Multos annos*, marks the end of the song. Felicitations like these are standard phrases of the acclamations offered to the Roman emperors. The performances of the Arvalian brotherhood, therefore, were styled bluntly *felicia dicere*, whereas in Byzantium it was the *Multos annos* wishes which gave the ceremony the name *polychronion*.[17]

This short analysis of the laudes makes it obvious that most of the formulae can be traced back to Later Antiquity. But even the literary genre of an "Emperor-Litany" was created in that period. We are fortunate enough to have a litany of the early fourth century. It was sung by the legionaries and was directed to the *Summus deus*, the henotheistic supreme deity of that age of transition, who could be invoked, ambiguously, by Pagan and Christian soldiers alike. In 313, the Emperor Licinius is said to have recommended the song to his army, and Eusebius, when ascribing the introduction of this litany to his hero Constantine, added to it a petition for the emperor and his sons. The Eusebian petition is added, in parentheses and in the Latin version, to the text transmitted by Lactantius.[18]

---

[16] Gregory I, *Reg.* IX, 26, *MGH.Epist.*, II, 59 (October, 598). See Bishop, *Lit. Hist.*, pp. 116 ff., and "Liturgical Comments and Memoranda," *Jour. Theol. Stud.*, XII (1911), 411; W. Lockton, "Liturgical Notes," *ibid.*, XVI (1915), 548 f.; L. Duchesne, *Christian Worship, Its Origin and Evolution* (5th ed., 1931), 164 f.; Peterson, *Untersuchungen*, pp. 164 ff.; F. J. Dölger, *Sol Salutis* (2d ed.; Münster, 1925), 60 ff., 98 f.

[17] Henzen, *op. cit.*, pp. 45 f.; Peterson, *Untersuchungen*, pp. 144, 224, n. 1; Heldmann, *op. cit.*, p. 267, n. 1. For the *polychronion*, see A. Heisenberg, "Aus der Geschichte und Literatur der Paläologenzeit," *Sitzungsberichte München*, 1920, Abh. 10, p. 56.

[18] Lactantius, *De mortibus persecutorum*, XLVI, 6; Eusebius, *Vita Constant.*, IV, 20; cf. Henri Grégoire, "La 'conversion' de Constantin," *Revue de l'Université de Bruxelles*, XXXVI (1931), 260 f., who has called attention to these prayers; see also Baynes in *Cambridge Ancient History*, XII, 688 f. Litanies for the emperor in the pagan cults are numerous; they deserve a special study with a view to the Christian litanies for the ruler. See, e.g., the *fausta vota* of the Isis procession in Rome with intentions for "principi magno senatuique et equiti totoque Romano populo, nauticis nautisque

Summe deus, te rogamus
Sancte deus, te rogamus
Omnem justitiam tibi commendamus
Salutem nostram tibi commendamus
Imperium nostrum tibi commendamus
Per te vivimus
Per te victores et felices existimus
Summe sancte Deus, preces nostras exaudi
Brachia nostra ad te tendimus:
Exaudi, sancte summe Deus.
(Supplices omnes te rogamus:
    Imperatorem nostrum Constantinum, cum piissimis
    filiis suis, ad multos annos nobis incolumem et
    victorem conserva, te rogamus.)

The Christus vincit Triad

The oldest Carolingian laudes form known falls in the period between 783 and 787.[19] Except for the omission of the laudatory section and some minor variations, it matches the specimen discussed here. The prayer displays its definite form at its first appearance, and the historian, who is left in the dark concerning any preliminary stages of development, finds himself in the awkward position of knowing the derivation of the general pattern as well as practically every single element of the chant and yet of not knowing when and how these elements were fitted together to form the masterful and quite unique composition of the *laudes regiae*.

This is true also with reference to the tricolon *Christus vincit, Christus regnat, Christus imperat*. Doubtless, this is the most striking element of the laudes, penetrating, bracing, and even molding the whole chant. It opens and concludes the first part of the litany; it is incessantly iterated in the second, and it is the cry which bestows upon the litany its peculiar tone and character. Unfortunately, there is very little known about the origin, not of the single clauses, but of the whole triadic phrase.[20] Nothing

navibusque," which survived in the city until almost 400, an observance brilliantly discussed by A. Alföldi, *A Festival of Isis in Rome under the Christian Emperors of the IVth Century*, Dissertationes Pannonicae, Ser. II, Fasc. 7 (Budapest, 1937), 47 f., with n. 115. See also Peterson, *Untersuchungen*, p. 167, and F. J. Dölger, *Antike und Christentum*, II (1930), 247–251.

[19] Montpellier, Bibliothèque de l'École de Médecine, MS 409, fol. 344, a Psalter of the eighth century. On the manuscript, see *Catalogue général des manuscrits des bibliothèques publiques des départements*, I (1849), 448; *Album paléographique* (cf. above, n. 4), Pl. XVII, 2. The laudatory section and the doxologies are omitted. The authoritative edition is that of Mabillon, *Vetera Analecta* (1723), 170 f., which is repeated by Migne, *PL.*, CXXXVIII, cols. 885 ff. The other editions are lacking the framework of the Litany and therefore must be considered as incomplete; cf. Einhard, *Vita Caroli*, ed. Holder-Egger (1905), *MGH. SS. rer. Germ.*, p. 46 f., App. D; Dannenbauer (above, n. 4), p. 55. Gastoué, *op. cit.*, p. 193, claims the form for the coronation of Queen Fastrada in 783; Heldmann, *op. cit.*, p. 287, suggests that it was sung in Rome at the Easter service in 787; see, however, above, n. 4, and below, n. 92, for the date of the form (hitherto 783–792).

[20] Cf. Peterson, *Untersuchungen*, p. 226, n. 1; Gastoué, *op. cit.*, 192; Prost, *Quatre pièces*, pp. 195 ff.; Deonna, *op. cit.*, p. 73.

conclusive has been brought forth relative to this tricolon, and there is little hope of conducting the investigations beyond the level of hypothesis. We cannot even tell approximately when the formula came into existence. It appears in the earliest Carolingian laudes (783–787), and only one earlier evidence for its existence can be detected, which so far has escaped notice. A brass crucifix, presented to the basilica of Ostia by Pope Stephen II (752–757), bears inscriptions reminiscent of the laudatory section.[21] On one side of the crucifix the inscription reads:

$$\text{Crux} \begin{cases} \text{Romanorum fortitudo.} \\ \text{Romanorum salus} \\ \text{Romanorum arma} \\ \text{Romanorum victoria} \end{cases}$$

This praise of the victorious cross[22] is answered by the inscription on the reverse:

$$\text{Christus} \begin{cases} \text{iubar regni Romanorum.} \\ \text{Dei filius vincit} \\ \text{regnat in aeterna} \\ \text{imperat in saecula} \end{cases}$$

This evidence antedates the earliest Carolingian laudes by some thirty years. However, the inscription falls in the Frankish period of the papacy and the very fact that Stephen II, the pope who entered into the portentous alliance with Pepin, was the donor of the crucifix might make us wonder if Frankish influence had not been effective.

At any rate, the problem of the origin of the tricolon is not solved; it may be approached in several ways. First, there is the possibility of a purely rhetorical origin. What arouses our interest is the rhetorical figure of the tripartite phrase with its hard parataxis of three short clauses whose gradually increasing effectiveness is augmented, and at the same time checked, by the anaphora of the subject. Ancient rhetoric, naturally, knew this artistic figure very well; and it has not escaped the attention of scholars that Quintilian, when explaining the rhetorical power of asyndetic clauses, produces, indeed oddly enough, the paradigm *hic regnat, hic imperat, hic sola* [sc., *eloquentia*] *vincit*.[23] This hint is certainly important

---

[21] Angelo Mai, *Scriptorum veterum nova collectio* (Rome, 1831), V, 3; Muratori, *Novus thesaurus veterum inscriptionum* (Milan, 1742), IV, p. mcmxliv, No. 5.

[22] See the important study of Jean Gagé, "Σταυρὸς νικοποιός. La victoire impériale dans l'empire chrétien," *Revue d'histoire et de philosophie religieuses*, XII (1933), 370–400, a continuation of his earlier study "La théologie de la victoire impériale," *Revue historique*, CLXXI (1933), 1–44. Most interesting material is offered by Felix Rütten, *Die Victorverehrung im christlichen Altertum*, Studien zur Geschichte und Kultur des Altertums, XX, 1 (Paderborn, 1936).

[23] Quintilian, *Inst. orat.*, VII, 4, 23; cf. Weyman, "Analecta," *HJb.*, XXXVII (1916), 79; Peterson, *Untersuchungen*, p. 163, n. 1; Weinreich, in *Philologische Wochenschrift*, XLI (1921), 915.

because it reminds us of the close connection between rhetoric and liturgy in general, a fact commonly known.[24] Although these connections should not be minimized, it is nevertheless difficult to believe that an early liturgist should have drawn on Quintilian's work to produce the acclamatory hails. Rather, we may deduce that Quintilian's paradigm indicates that the combination of the three verbs *regnare, imperare, vincere* was not unknown, but was perhaps even quite popular, in his time.[25]

Second, the liturgy itself seems to offer another possible way of solving the problem. It is legitimate for many reasons to adduce the forms of certain doxological phrases which serve as conclusions of prayers and benedictions. Every official prayer must be "sealed" in a definite way; the form of the finale, however, depends upon whether the orison is directed to God the Father, or to the Son, or to both Father and Son, or to the Trinity. The Church, therefore, uses several phrasings for these conclusions; but always there should appear in these formulae the two verbs *vivere* and *regnare* with reference to Christ,[26] for example: "Per dominum nostrum Jhesum Christum qui tecum *vivit* et *regnat* in unitate spiritus sancti Deus per omnia saecula saeculorum." Variations of these doxological conclusions, and also of the verbs therein, are by no means rare. Some finales show the form *qui vivit et imperat*, others *qui vivit et gloriatur*, and there is even a form which contains three verbs, *qui tecum vivit et gloriatur et regnat*.[27] These formulae are doubtless suggestive of the laudes but are not convincing proofs of a dependency of the tricolon. However, there is one exception; for, a relationship between doxology and laudes can hardly be denied in the finale which sometimes, though rarely, concludes the short prayer for the ruler at the end of the so-called *Exultet*,

---

[24] L. Couture, "Le *cursus* ou rythme prosaique dans la liturgie et dans la littérature de l'église latine du III⁰ siècle à la renaissance," *RQH.*, XXVI (1892), 253 ff.; *Paléographie musicale*, III ("De l'influence de l'accent tonique latin et du *cursus* sur la structure mélodique et rythmique de la phrase grégorienne": Solesmes, 1892); Cagin, *op. cit.*, 247 ff.; Vacandard, "Le *cursus*, son origine, son histoire, son emploi dans la liturgie," *RQH.*, XXXIV (1905), 59–102; F. di Capua, "Il ritmo della prosa liturgica e il *Praeconium Paschale*," *Didaskalion*, N. S., V (1927), 1–23. See also A. Baumstark, *Vom geschichtlichen Werden der Liturgie*, Ecclesia Orans, X (Freiburg, 1923), 84, n. 14; and p. 28.

[25] Weyman, "Analecta," *HJb.*, XL (1920), 186; Weinreich, *loc. cit.*

[26] See, e.g., V. Thalhofer und L. Eisenhofer, *Handbuch der katholischen Liturgik* (2d ed., Freiburg, 1912), I, 331 f. For the Gallican origin of the "vivis et regnas" formula, see J. A. Jungmann, *Die Stellung Christi im liturgischen Gebet*, Liturgiegeschichtliche Forschungen, VII–VIII (Münster, 1925), 105, 184, 196 f. Cf. *Missale Gothicum*, in Migne, *P.L.*, LXXII, cols. 227, 244, for the triad "qui ... vivis, dominaris et regnas."

[27] This last form is rare; it is found in the *Ordo* of the West-Frankish coronation of 888; cf. Schramm, "Westfranken," *ZfRG.*, kan. Abt., XXIII (1934), 198. The form of the finale was subject to controversies as late as the eleventh century; cf. Bernold of Constance, *Micrologus*, c. VI, Migne, *PL.*, CLI, col. 981. For a seemingly Gallican conclusion in the Roman rite, see Baumstark, *op. cit.*, p. 82, n. 3.

that is, the Blessing of the Paschal Candle, on the Saturday in Holy Week. The text of this conclusion is:

Precamur ergo te, Domine, ut nos famulos tuos... quiete temporum concessa in hiis paschalibus gaudiis conservare digneris, qui semper *vivis, regnas, imperas* necnon et gloriaris....

In spite of the replacement of *vivis* for *vincis*,[28] the similarity is so striking that it cannot easily be neglected. This unusual *Exultet* finale makes its first appearance in a South Italian liturgical Easter play, written before 1130; it is found also in several South Italian manuscripts of the twelfth century; it can be traced to Normandy, in or about 1200, and finally to England, where it was adopted by the rite of Sarum during the thirteenth century.[29] That is to say, this conclusion is found, so far as is known, only in the Norman realms, in Sicily, Normandy, and England, and not earlier than the twelfth century. Since the laudes are very much older than the Norman finale of the *praeconium*, it is evident that the tricolon cannot be derived from the doxological conclusion, but that the former has influenced the latter. This fact is of great interest and worth being recorded. It is indicative of the great popularity of the triad, especially in Southern Italy during the twelfth century, and it is quite plausible that the prestige of this formula should have influenced, at least temporarily, another prayer for the ruler, namely the suffrage at the end of the *Exultet*. We know already that other symbols of the Norman kingship of Southern Italy—coins, *bullae*, as well as a forged privilege—contained or reflected the three clauses, and additional evidence of their wide diffusion can be easily established[30] (see below, p. 30). But all this does not help us to discover the origin of the tricolon itself.

There is, however, a third element in addition to rhetoric and liturgy which demands closer inspection, that is the rhythm of the triad. There is no need of seeking far-fetched parallels, for the ancient Roman acclamations offer more than one example of the stirring rhythm of the laudes formula. Suetonius, for instance, mentions the acclaim *Salva Roma, salva patria, salvus est Germanicus!* This is likewise an asyndetic triad of clauses with anaphora, with an implicit climax, and with the longest

---

[28] For the exchangeability of "vivis" for "vincis," cf. below, notes 54, 55. See also Bongars, *Gesta Dei per Francos*, quoted by H. Hagenmeyer in his edition of Fulcher of Chartres (Heidelberg, 1913), 497; *Flores Historiarum* (ed. Luard, Rolls Series, 95) I, 209, where two fourteenth-century manuscripts show the wrong reading "Christus vivit"; see also Gougaud, "La prière dite de Charlemagne," *Revue d'histoire ecclésiastique*, XX (1924), 230, who quotes an incantation "Christus vivit . . ." See also E. Kantorowicz, "A Norman Finale of the *Exultet* and the Rite of Sarum," *Harvard Theological Review*, XXXIV (194), 136, n. 28.

[29] For a detailed discussion, cf. Kantorowicz, *op. cit.*; see below, Appendix III.

[30] Cf. above, pp. 8 ff., for the popularity of the formula in Southern Italy and below, p. 30, notes 54 f. The link between the *Exultet* and the laudes is probably the fact that both prayers refer to the ruler and his worship during the Easter services.

as well as weightiest exclamation at the end.[31] Some other hails, such as *Vincas, valeas! multis annis imperes!* or *Vivas, floreas, vincas! multis annis imperes!*[32] show a wording which recalls the laudes. It was mainly the rhythm by means of which the acclamations, repeated ten, twenty, thirty times, or even more often,[33] achieved their great effect; and all acclamations and liturgical invocations have a natural tendency toward rhetorical anaphora and similar parallelism, not to mention triadic structure.[34] Hence, a Roman acclamation, perhaps a military cheer, the emphasis of which was shifted, as usual, from pagan Caesar to imperial Christ, must have been the model of the laudes hails. However, in Rome itself this form cannot be traced either in pagan or in Christian versions. But Rome, deserted by the Caesars, is not the place to observe the further evolution of acclamations; their continuity becomes obvious only when we turn away from the West toward Byzantium where, thanks to the living presence of an emperor, the acclamations could expand in an almost unbelievable abundance.[35]

The Greek Χριστὸς νικᾷ has frequently been indicated as the main source of the laudes formula.[36] This view is correct so far as the first clause is concerned, but it fails to take into account the other clauses of the phrase. However, the Eastern acclamations allow us to go at least one step farther, for there appears also the formula Χριστὸς νικᾷ · Χριστὸς βασιλεύει. It is found, for instance, in Syrian inscriptions of the sixth or

[31] Suetonius, *Caligula*, 6, 1. For the rhythm, see also the acclamation Εἷς θεός · εἷς Χριστός · εἷς ἐπίσκοπος, quoted by Peterson, *Untersuchungen*, p. 181, from Theodoret, *Hist. eccl.*, II, c. 17, and the remarks of Weinreich, *loc. cit.*, concerning the "crescendo," which is found also in the incantation "Signum Christi, sinnum Crucis, sinnum Sancti Salvatoris" in an eighth-century manuscript; cf. P. David, *Rev. bénéd.*, XLIX (1937), 64. See below, p. 185, n. 23.

[32] Lampridius, *Alex. Sev.*, c. 6 and c. 10. This acclamation remained popular; see, e.g., Sedulius Scotus, *Ad Lotharium*, in *MGH. Poet.*, III, 190, No. XXV, 3–4:
> "Omnes cantemur: multis feliciter annis
> Rex vivat, valeat, vincat, honore cluat,
> Hunc iuvenem populo conserva, Christe, precamur ... "

or, *MGH. Poet.*, I, 671, line 9: "Ac valeat, vigeat, vivat per secula felix." Also, the acclamation to Otto I, in 936, recorded by Thietmar, II, c. 1, ed. Holtzmann (1935), *MGH. SS. rer. Germ.*, Nova ser. IX, 38: "Vivat et valeat rex victor in aeternum!"; and see the laudes of Ivrea (1089–1093) in Ivrea, Bibl. Capit. MS 50 (94); Dümmler, *Anselm der Peripatetiker* (Halle, 1872), 90:
> "Multos annos   Deus adaugeat.
> Vivas et valeas   in domino ... "

Of course, "vivas et valeas" was one of the most common forms of salutation in general, cf. Walther, "Quot-tot," *Zeitschrift für deutsches Altertum*, LXV (1928), 258, Nos. 9, 12, and *ibid.*, LXVI (1929), 69, No. 9.

[33] Hirschfeld, "Die römische Staatszeitung und die Acclamationen im Senat," *Sitzungsberichte Berlin* (1905), 936 ff.; Heldmann, *op. cit.*, p. 281, n. 2. Many cries in the laudes were repeated thrice.

[34] E.g., Cagin, *op. cit., passim;* Baumstark, *op. cit.*, p. 84, and above, n. 24.

[35] On the acclamations in Byzantium, see the careful study of Otto Treitinger, *Die oströmische Kaiser- und Reichsidee im höfischen Zeremoniell* (Jena, 1938), 80 ff., 71 ff., and *passim*, who offers also an account of the modern literature on the acclamations.

[36] Cf. above, n. 20.

seventh century,[37] but may be much older, since the two verbs were closely linked together in the acclamations of the Council of Constantinople in 536 when the bishops shouted[38]

νικᾷ ἡ πίστις τοῦ βασιλέως·   Vincit fides imperatoris,
ὀρθόδοξος βασιλεύει ...   Orthodoxus regnat ...

Or, the bishops used the popular Greco-Roman hails[39]

'Ιουστῖνε Αὔγουστε· τοῦ βίγκας ... Justine Auguste, tu vincas ...
'Ιουστῖνος βασιλεύει.   Justinus regnat.

Once more the two verbs are found closely connected with each other in what has been called the "liturgy of the hippodrome" when the *staurophoroi*, the crossbearers, paraded their crosses crowned with flowers before the emperors, and at this the factions shouted:[40]

ἐν τούτῳ ἐστέφθητε · εὐεργέται.   ἅγιε.
ἐν τούτῳ βασιλεύετε καὶ νικᾶτε.   ἅγιε.
ἐν τούτῳ βασιλεύσετε τὰ ἔθνη πάντα.   ἅγιε.

In hac coronati estis, benifici!   R/. Sancte!
In hac imperatis et vincitis!   Sancte!
In hac imperabitis omnibus populis! Sancte!

Scores of other acclamations in various forms, due to the basileus on every possible occasion, are transmitted in Constantine's *Book of Ceremonies*, and amongst them one particular hail begins directly with Χριστὸς νικᾷ · Χριστὸς βασιλεύει, a shout which the Sardinian soldiers were supposed to proffer on the occasion of a triumph or when the emperor presented the rewards of a victory.[41] That this acclamation was peculiar to the Sardinian troops and orderlies which had been levied in the Western parts of the empire, is interesting. It almost suggests that these hails have been introduced from the West just like the queerly transcribed τοῦ βίγκας (βῖκας). In fact, the Greek βασιλεύειν can mean both *regnare* and *imperare*, so that the two Greek clauses seem to represent a fair translation of the three Latin clauses. On the other hand, there is a more recent interpretation which seems to take the Greek origin for granted. The Latin version, it has been suggested, had to account for both meanings

---

[37] Cf. *Syria. Publications of the Princeton University Archeological Expeditions to Syria in 1904–5.* Division III, 2: Greek and Latin Inscriptions. Section A: Southern Syria, by Enno Littmann, David Magie, Jr., and Duane Reed Stuart (Leyden, 1910), 53, No. 40; cf. p. 45, No. 26: ὃς βασιλεύς · Χριστός · νικᾷς Χριστέ (*ca.* 624–625); cf. Peterson, *Untersuchungen*, p. 226, n. 1.

[38] Mansi, *Sacrorum conciliorum* ... VIII, 969–970 and 1063–1064.

[39] For the acclamation *tu vincas* (τοῦ βίγκας, τούμβηκας, τούμβικας etc.) cf. Gagé, Σταυρὸς νικοποιός," p. 375.

[40] *De caerim.*, I, c. 69, ed. Reiske, I, 324, 12 ff.

[41] *Ibid.*, II, c. 43, ed. Reiske, I, 650, 15; cf. Gibbon, *History of the Decline and Fall of the Roman Empire*, ed. Bury (1898), VI, 85. On the Sardinians, cf. Reiske, II, 774; Gagé, *op. cit.*, p. 396; see also the letter of Pope Leo IV (early in 851) in which he asks the "Judex Sardiniae" to send a Sardinian bodyguard to Rome; Ewald, "Die Papstbriefe der Brittischen Sammlung," *NArch*, V (1880), 383, No. 17.

contained in the verb βασιλεύειν and consequently would at times appear as *Christus vincit, Christus regnat*, at times as *Christus vincit, Christus imperat*, at other times as *Christus vincit, Christus regnat-imperat*.[42] The difficulty of these translations is obvious and there is proof of it. By chance, we have a Greek draft of the Gallo-Frankish laudes in a manuscript of the cathedral of Metz.[43] Why Metz should have used Greek laudes, is not clear; but it may serve our purpose to recall the *schola graeca* in Rome, which used to receive popes, emperors, and other dignitaries with Greek laudes.[44] The cathedral of Metz apparently emulated Rome in the display of a *schola graeca*, and hence, in the ninth century, the Gallo-Frankish laudes were translated into Greek.[45] The translator,

[42] This is the conjecture of Gastoué, *op. cit.*, p. 192, who follows Reiske, cf. *De caerim.*, II, 774.

[43] Metz, Bibl. Munic. MS 351; cf. Prost, *Quatre pièces*, pp. 150 ff., who describes this early tenth-century manuscript which was written probably in the abbey of St. Arnold in Metz; cf. p. 241 ff. for the text and the interpretation of the Greek laudes. J. P. Kirch, "Le chant de l'église de Metz au moyen âge," *Revue Sainte-Odile* (Strasbourg, 1932), was not available to me.

[44] See, e.g., *Liber pont.*, II, 88 (844), 253 (1111); *Gesta Berengarii*, IV, 118 ff., *MGH. Poet.*, IV, 398 f.; *Annal. Fuldenses*, ed. Kurze, *MGH. SS. rer. Germ.*, p. 128; *Graphia aureae urbis Romae, Libellus* c. 19, ed. P. E. Schramm, *Kaiser, Rom und Renovatio*, II (1929), 101 f.; see also Fedor Schneider, *Rom und Romgedanke im Mittelalter* (München, 1926), 107, 144, who styles the Greek laudes in Rome a spectacle which was supposed to impress foreign royalty. The underlying idea, of course, was to offer acclamations in the three sacred languages, i.e., Hebrew, Greek, and Latin in accordance with the trilingual acclamation to the Lord (John, 19:20); see also Schramm, *op. cit.*, I, 208, n. 4, and, for a Jewish acclamation ("Henricus per secula principatum teneat"), Bloch, in *NArch.*, XXII (1897), 121, n. 14. On the other hand, Latin acclamations and laudes were sung also in Byzantium to emphasize the Byzantine claim of universalism; see, e.g., *De caerim.*, I, c. 74 f., ed. Reiske, I, 369 f.; *Liber pont.*, I, 354 (681 A.D.): "In ecclesia S. Sophie publicas missas coram principe et patriarchas latine celebraret et omnes unanimiter in laudes et victoriis piissimorum imperatorum idem latine vocibus adclamarunt." That Latin laudes were sung in Byzantium as late as the eleventh century, follows from a letter of Leo IX to Kerullarios; cf. Migne, *PL.* CXLIII, col. 761: "Quod si contradicitis, ad quid vestro imperatori latine laudes et in Ecclesia Grecis recitantur latine lectiones?"

[45] This translation, most likely, should be linked to the intellectual interests prevailing at the court of Charles the Bald ("par Theodosio," cf. *MGH. Poet.*, III, 243) with which I shall deal in another place. In the cathedral of Metz, as well as in many other Frankish churches, Greek chants and prayers were customarily sung on certain occasions; cf. Michel Andrieu, "Règlement d'Angilramne de Metz (768–791)," *Revue des sciences religieuses*, X (1930), 353. On the survival of the Greek language in the liturgy, a thorough study based upon the manuscripts is needed; A. Tougard, *L'hellénisme dans les écrivains du moyen âge* (Rouen, 1886), offers rich material with many errors; Harold Steinacker, "Die römische Kirche und die griechischen Sprachkenntnisse des Mittelalters," *Festschrift für Th. Gomperz* (Vienna, 1902), 324–341, confines himself to the early period; a very complete bibliography (in addition to Paetow, *Guide to the Study of Mediaeval History*, 1931, 446) of the Greek studies in the Middle Ages in general has been collected by B. Altaner, "Die Kenntnis des Griechischen in den Missionsorden während des 13. und 14. Jahrhunderts," *ZKG*, LIII (1934), 443 f. See also below, p. 143, for the "Cornomanic laudes" in Rome. Genuine Greek laudes were sung to Charlemagne in 812 by the Byzantine ambassadors; cf. *Annal. qui dic. Einhardi*, *MGH. SS.*, I, 99; Regino di Prüm, *ibid.*, p. 566; Schramm, *Renovatio*, I, 199. Pope Gregory X received Greek laudes at the Council of Lyons in 1274; cf. Mansi, *op. cit.*, XXIV, 65: "Quo symbolo finito idem patriarcha, archiepiscopi et logotheta cum aliis cantaverunt laudes solemnes in lingua Graeca domino papae." Cf. Dom A. Strittmatter, in *Traditio*, I (1943), 84, n. 11, for Greek studies in the West.

following the popular mediaeval custom of transcribing Greek prayers in Roman characters, used the expedient of changing the text of the Latin tricolon into

Xps nicha, Xps Uasileuge, Xps epenos.

(Χριστὸς νικᾷ· Χριστὸς βασιλεύει· Χριστὸς ἔπαινος)

He thus replaced the *Christus imperat* by the Greek equivalent of *Christus laudabilis* in order to produce the customary three beats in the Greek translation. This expedient suggests that the Latin triad was the equivalent of the Greek dyad and that there never existed a Greek formula of three clauses which exactly corresponded with the Latin *Christus vincit, Christus regnat, Christus imperat.* Nevertheless, it is important to know that a group of Byzantine soldiers of Western descent acclaimed the victorious emperor with the two Greek clauses. Taken altogether, it is more likely that the liturgical tricolon originated in the crowds in the Byzantine theater, circus, or streets,[46] rather than in the studio of a liturgist who checked on Quintilian's *Institutio oratoria.*

None of the arguments adduced, however, are in themselves strong enough to prove clearly the Byzantine origin of the formula. A continuous taking, giving, and returning is significant of the relations between Byzantium and the West so that it is often difficult, if not impossible, to ascertain whether a usage originated in the Eastern or in the Western part of the Empire. The Sardinians, for instance, may just as well have brought the tricolon from the West to Constantinople, where it was transformed into Greek and restricted to two clauses, as have brought the two Greek clauses, which were known in the East ever since the sixth century at the latest, to the West, where the Greek form then changed into the Latin three beats as a result of the difficulty in translation.[47] All that we know is the fact that in the eighth century the tricolon makes its appearance simultaneously in Frankish Rome and in Frankish Gaul. But no matter whether the formula originated in Rome, in Byzantium, or in Gaul, its connection with Byzantine soldier acclamations brings one momentous point to the fore: the general relationship of the Gallo-Frankish laudes with military life.

The whole character of this liturgical acclamation, in the form valid throughout the Frankish Empire and in its successor states, was soldier-

---

[46] For the acclamations in the circus, see G. Millet, "Les noms des auriges dans les acclamations de l'hippodrome," *Recueil d'études dédiées à la mémoire de N. P. Kondakov* (Prague, 1926), 289 ff.; see also Gagé, *op. cit.,* pp. 372 ff., for the "liturgie de l'hippodrome." Cf. Pl. VI, *a.*

[47] The *tu vincas* formula (above, n. 39) has evidently been taken over by Byzantium from the West. The fact that the tricolon is found in the laudes of Dalmatia, which in general are remindful of Byzantine acclamations, might suggest the Eastern origin of the formula. However, it seems more likely that Dalmatia adopted the phrase from the West, together with the Roman ritual; cf. below, Chap. V.

like. As victor and king, commander or general, Christ was extolled. The army itself was acclaimed, while soldier saints such as SS. George, Theodore, Mercurius, Maurice, or Sebastian were invoked; and the first three were Byzantine army saints.[48] In the laudatory section practically all the invocations are borrowed from the vocabulary of government and soldiership, a lingo of predominant importance in early Christianity, since the great change from paganism to the new faith began, as it were, in the army, where military language, conceptions, and insignia were rapidly transformed into religious ones.[49] "King of Kings," "our King," "our glory," "our auxiliary," "our fortitude," "our victory," "our most invincible weapon," "our unassailable wall," "our bulwark"[50]—these were the very old epithets of Christ, and unrelentingly the choir would burst into the acclaim "Christ is conqueror," "Christ is ruler," "Christ is commander." The same tone lingers on in the doxology, the eulogizing conclusion: "To Him alone the kingdom, the glory and the power . . . , to

[48] Erdmann, *Kreuzzugsgedanke*, pp. 255 ff., who is the first to discuss the "army religion" in the West before the Crusades, seems to suggest a rather late date for the reception of these saints. St. Theodore is found in all forms of the Franco-Roman laudes, that is ever since the early ninth century; cf. below, p. 105. Theodore, George, and Mercurius are jointly the intercessors for the army in the laudes of Besançon— Vatican, Borg. Lat. MS 359, fol. 135ᵛ, cf. Migne, *PL.*, LXXX, col. 411—and of Arles (Prost, *Quatre pièces*, pp. 178 f.; Du Cange, *Glossarium*, V, 46); they are found, however, also in the episcopal acclamations of Minden (1024) in the Berlin, Staatsbibl. Theol. Lat. MS 11, fol. 114ᵛ. Theodore is found also in the laudes of Aquileia which are known only in a twelfth-century copy but which may be considerably older; cf. B. M. de Rubeis, *Monumenta Ecclesiae Aquileiensis* (1740), 588 ff. St. George is first found in the laudes of Autun (early tenth century) written on an ivory diptych; cf. Richard Delbrück, *Die Konsulardiptychen*, Studien zur spätantiken Kunstgeschichte, II (Berlin, 1929), pl. N. 27, and Kantorowicz, "Ivories and Litanies," *The Journal of the Warburg and Courtauld Institutes*, IV (1942), 56 ff.; furthermore, in the laudes of Narbonne of the twelfth century (Paris, Bibl. Nat. Lat. MS 778, fol. 217), which likewise may be a later copy of an earlier form, in the laudes of Ivrea (cf. above, n. 32), in the Norman laudes from the times of William the Conqueror (below, p. 166, n. 46), and in the early eleventh-century form of Bamberg; cf. *AA. SS.*, July III, 699, and Leitschuh, *Katalog der Handschriften der kgl. Bibliothek zu Bamberg* (1895), I:3, p. 147, with reference to the Bamberg, MS lit. 6 (Ed. III. 7), fol. 92. The work of R. Janin, "Les églises byzantines des saints militaires," *Échos d'Orient*, XXXVII and XXXVIII (1934–1935), was not available to me. For St. Maurice in the litanies and laudes, see J. A. Herzberg, *Der heilige Mauritius. Ein Beitrag zur Geschichte der deutschen Mauritiusverehrung*, Forschungen zur Volkskunde, XXV–XXVI (Düsseldorf, 1936), 110–115; cf. Albert Brackmann, "Die politische Bedeutung der Mauritius-Verehrung im frühen Mittelalter," *Sitzungsberichte Berlin* (1937), 279–305.

[49] See, in general, A. Harnack, *Militia Christi. Die christliche Religion und der Soldatenstand in den ersten drei Jahrhunderten* (Tübingen, 1905); see also the two articles by Gagé quoted above (n. 22).

[50] Most of these phrases are very old and go back to Roman ruler-worship, e.g., the τεῖχος-acclamation; cf., Erik Peterson, "Die Einholung des Kyrios," *Zeitschrift für systematische Theologie*, VII (1930), 697, n. 4, and *idem, Der Monotheismus als politisches Problem* (Leipzig, 1935), 116, n. 57. The metaphors are remindful also of the *Apostolic Constitutions*, ed. Brightman, in *Liturgies Eastern and Western*, 1, 12, 23, f.: προστάτης ἐπίκουρος, ταμίας φύλαξ, τεῖχος ἐρυμνότατον, φραγμὸς ἀσφαλείας. See, on the other hand, the *Carmina Mutinensia*, in *MGH. Poet.*, III, 704, 25: "Tu murus tuis / sis inexpugnabilis." Cf. D. L. David, "Acclamations *Christus vincit*," *RCGr.*, XXVI (1922), 6 ff., on the music, and Bukofzer, below, p. 193.

Him alone strength, courage, victory . . . , to Him alone the honor, praise, and hail." It is a martial litany, and the tone of unswerving energy and firmness is preserved from beginning to end.

Thus the cheers proffered, on the occasion of a triumph, by Roman soldiers of the West or East, and perhaps even by Frankish warriors in the Empire, may have given birth to the rhythm and the main idea of one of the most virile, cheerful, and powerful prayers of the Catholic Church. It is not strange that this form of a royal litany should claim Gaul and the Frankish Empire as its home. More than in any other Western Church ritual, an extraordinary space is granted, in the Gallic and Frankish sacramentaries, to the liturgical hallowing of weapons, standards, army, and ruler.[51]

The laudes, however, did not remain soldier acclamations in the narrower sense. They were transformed into a litany and incorporated into the divine service, until finally they were given a very general and purely clerical function in the liturgy of the great festivals. And yet their soldierly and chivalrous character was not entirely lost. It should be remembered that in the Holy Land the *Christus vincit, Christus regnat, Christus imperat* became a battle cry. Also, Pope Innocent III called the *vexillum sancti Petri*, which he handed to the tsar of the Bulgarians, the banner carried against the demons by Christ *qui vincit, regnat, imperat.*[52] Furthermore, Christ is praised as the Conquering Sun in the biography of a martyr pope:

> Sol Christus vincit, regnat, rex imperat almus.[53]

Frederick II is hailed by a poet.[54]

> Vivat Augustus   quantum vult vivere,
> Imperet, regnet   in tanto tempore,
> Ut suos hostes   possit confundere . . .

These lines are likewise reminiscent of the laudes. This is true also of the triumphant greetings which a South Italian master of epistolary style, a former clerk of Edward I, dispatched to England after the king's victory over Llewellyn: *Vivat, regnet, vincat et imperet rex noster invictissimus Edwardus.*[55] The litany which in some places is styled *laudes regiae,*[56]

---

[51] This observation is not new; see, e.g., Grancolas, *Les anciennes liturgies* (Paris, 1704), I, 350 ff. See also Tellenbach, *op. cit.,* pp. 21 ff., 67 ff., who publishes the most interesting texts from the Sacramentary of Gellone.

[52] Innocent III, *Reg.* VII, 12, Migne, *PL.,* CCXV, col. 296.

[53] *Vita S. Clementis (ca.* 1005), in *MGH. Poet.,* V, 131, line 581, to which Mr. N. Fickermann kindly directed my attention.

[54] See the poem of Quilichinus (or Terrisius of Atina?) published by Tina Ferri, "Appunti su Quilichino e le sue opere," *Studi Mediaevali,* N. S., IX (1936), 250.

[55] Paris, Bibl. Nat. Lat. MS 8567, fol. 3, a letter of Stephen of St. George, a late follower of the school of Petrus de Vinea; *ibid.,* fol. 17ᵛ, is a Christmas sermon of the

laudes regales,[57] *regale carmen,*[58] or even *laudes imperatoriae,*[59] was actually called *triumphus* in Paris.[60] Moreover, in certain cathedrals of France, even at a very late date, soldiers served as chanters of this martial litany, two knights in Vienne or six knights in Lyons,[61] who thus still represented, as it were, the cheering army. The military origin of the ceremony had obviously not been completely forgotten. And when the *laudes regiae* were sung at a mediaeval coronation or on festival days, both the text and the tune of this chivalrous responsory could remind the audience that it had once been the legions—Roman, Oriental, and Germanic—that raised the elect to the imperial throne.[62]

THE SEQUENCE OF SAINTS AND ITS INFERENCES

Of the laudes pattern hitherto discussed, the date as well as the country of origin are disputed. However, the matter has never been seriously examined. The traditional name of this pattern is *Laudes gallicanae,*[63] a name which seems to imply that the laudes litany belongs to the ancient Gallican rite. On the other hand, the laudes are claimed to be of Roman origin.[64]

No effort has been made to prove the Gallican origin of the laudes and therefore the assertion always remained vague. In fact, evidence is lacking. It is of little help to refer to the acclamations with which the Mero-

---

same clerk which ends almost like the finale of the *Exultet* suffrage for the ruler: ". . . quod ipse prestare dignetur . . . qui cum Deo patre et spiritu paraclito vivit, regnat et imperat in secula seculorum."

[56] This is the name displayed in all forms of Chartres; Chartres, Bibl. Munic. MS 520 (222), fol. 293ᵛ; cf. V. Leroquais, *Les sacramentaires et les missels manuscrits* (Paris, 1924), I, 62, No. 243; see also the three seventeenth-century copies in De Voisin's *Collectio liturgica* in the Bibl. Nat. Lat. MSS 9497, fol. 172ᵛ (twelfth century), 9508, fol. 92ᵛ (twelfth century), and 9499, fol. 92 (after 1313). Cf. Prost, *Quatre pièces*, p. 171, n. 2; *DACL.*, VIII, 1901.

[57] Theganus, *Vita Hludowici imperatoris*, *MGH. SS.*, II, 594: "fecit ei laudes regales."

[58] Munich Cod. Lat. 14322, fol. 1ᵛ.

[59] *Liber pont.*, II, 88: "imperatorias laudes decantantes." These, however, were laudes sung at the reception of the ruler and therefore may have displayed a different form.

[60] Paris, Bibl. Nat. Lat. MS 9505, fol. 82 (after 1173); Prost, *Quatre pièces*, p. 184. Two other formularies from Paris (thirteenth century) are found in Brussels, Bibl. Royale MS 1799 (Cat. No. 643), fol. 62, and MS 4334 (642); cf. V. Leroquais, *Le bréviaire de Philippe le Bon* (Paris, Brussels, and New York, 1929), 232 f. *Triumphus* is also the technical term for the laudes of Sens of the fourteenth century (Sens, Bibl. Munic., MS 12, fols. 90ᵛ–92ᵛ); but this form was borrowed from Paris and adapted for the usage of Sens; A. Molinier, *Catalogue général des manuscrits*, VI, 12; Leroquais, *Pontificaux*, II, 336 f.

[61] E. Martène, *De antiquis ecclesiae ritibus* (1736), I, 614, with reference to Vienne, and I, 363, 366, with reference to Lyons.

[62] Edmund E. Stengel, *Den Kaiser macht das Heer* (Weimar, 1910); Schramm, *Renovatio*, I, 80 f.; Heldmann, *op. cit.*, pp. 260 f.; see also Johannes A. Straub, *Vom Herrscherideal in der Spätantike*, Forschungen zur Kirchen- und Geistesgeschichte, XVIII (Stuttgart, 1939), 7–75. See below, p. 119, n. 24.

[63] Prost, *Quatre pièces*, pp. 163 ff.; *DACL.*, VIII, col. 1899.

[64] Heldmann, *op. cit.*, p. 286.

vingian kings,[65] like the high imperial officials[66] and the Ostrogothic kings, were greeted.[67] This usage is interesting and even important with regard to legal and constitutional history;[68] but the litany of the laudes, with which we are concerned, has almost nothing to do with the acclamations chanted at a ruler's *adventus*, that is his festal entry into a town. We know the *laudes hymnidicae* of Carolingian times and it is easy to show that their form is quite different from that of the laudes litany. These acclamations need not be discussed. Another argument, though of a general and not very specific nature, is perhaps more persuasive. It has often been stressed that the ancient Gallican liturgy, as compared with the terseness, simplicity, or even puritan aridity of the Roman rite, excelled in flowering eloquence and in luxuriating forms, and that it was impressive in the rich abundance of its ceremonial and ritual style.[69] This consideration, when applied to the laudes, would certainly argue in favor of the Gallican origin; but while valuable as additional evidence, this argument does not disclose the date of the introduction of the laudes nor does it offer a suitable starting-point for further investigations.

On the other hand, the arguments adduced to prove the Roman origin of the laudes are not sound.[70] The assumption is that the formulary was composed in Rome and thence transferred, in Carolingian times, to the Frankish court. This surmise is based on the fact that practically all the formulae of the chant are, in the last analysis, of Roman origin; also it has been pointed out that in the oldest Carolingian laudes two Roman saints, Peter and John the Baptist, are invoked.[71] It is a question open to

---

[65] Gregory of Tours, *Hist. Franc.*, VI, c. 11; VIII, c. 1.

[66] Mommsen, *Römisches Staatsrecht*, III, 950 f.; the acclamations to the Roman officials, on January 1, were still customary in the eighth century; see St. Boniface's letter to Pope Zacharias (742), *MGH Epist. Merov.*, I, 301, No. 50.

[67] Cf. above, n. 7, for Theodoric.

[68] The acclamations to the sovereign king and the imperial "deputy" would often intersect; even Charlemagne, in 774, was received in Rome as though he were an imperial exarch and was therefore greeted with acclamations; cf. *Liber pont.*, I, 497.

[69] Mabillon's *De Liturgia Gallicana libri tres*, in Migne, *PL.*, LXXII, cols. 99 ff., is still fundamental. On the Gallican elaborations, see, e.g., Duchesne, "Sur l'origine de la 'Liturgia Gallicana,' " *Revue d'histoire et de littérature religieuses*, V (1900), 37; H. Netzer, *L'introduction de la messe romaine en France sous les Carolingiens* (1910); Bishop, "The Liturgical Reforms of Charlemagne," *Downside Review*, XXXVIII (1919), 1 ff. See also J. Quasten, "Oriental Influence in the Gallican Liturgy," *Traditio*, I (1943), 55–78, whose important study was published too late to be here evaluated.

[70] For the following, see Heldmann, *op. cit.*, p. 286.

[71] For the formulary, cf. above, n. 19. Heldmann holds that the invocation of St. Peter referred to St. Peter's Basilica in Rome and that of St. John to the Lateran Basilica. He also argues that the formulary must belong to Rome because there is no acclamation to the local bishop. This means very little, as, e.g., Chartres never seems to have introduced this intention and there are several extant forms of the ninth century in which the acclamation to the local bishop is likewise missing, for example, in the laudes to Charles the Bald in the Orléans MS 196 (173), fols. 136–140, of *ca.* 858–867 (or 866–867, if the acclamation to Irmintrude as *regina* be connected with the time after her coronation at Soissons), or in those of the St. Gall MS 381 for Louis the

discussion whether John the Baptist should be considered a saint characteristic of Rome. However, among the five saints invoked in that early form there are found, along with Peter and John, the most famous Frankish patrons, St. Martin and St. Remy, while the fifth, St. Maurice, is a Burgundian soldier-saint and Frankish by adoption; he is a stranger in the Roman liturgy.[72] That these three saints should have been invoked because their shrines were situated on the highways of mediaeval traffic, is a queer idea and far less convincing an argument than the Roman origin of practically all the formulae of the chant.

In order to base the investigation about the date and place of origin of the laudes on solid ground we must examine the extant documents as carefully as possible. Our first question refers to the manuscript transmission of the chant. The laudes first appear in two Frankish Psalters of the eighth century, in the Montpellier MS 409, which contains a formulary of 783–787, and in the Paris MS 13159, which contains laudes of the period 796–800.[73] Chronologically there follows the Verona Codex 92 (87) and, probably dependent on this, the Cologne MS 138, the former falling in the early years of Louis the Pious (*ca.* 820), the latter belonging to the first half, or even first quarter, of the ninth century.[74] The Verona manuscript—it has been called the first liturgical book which could be dubbed a "veritable Pontifical"[75]—as well as the Cologne manuscript are representative of a certain group of collections which have one main feature in common: they are "Gallicanized." That is to say, they contain an alloy of Roman and Gallo-Frankish prayers, orders, and benedictions,[76] and among these there is found also the litany of the laudes in a Romanized form. These Franco-Roman laudes will be discussed later, but in anticipation it may be emphasized that the Verona and Cologne laudes refer to an emperor and not to the Frankish king, and that they represent (adjusted after 800 for Roman needs) a later stage of development of the earlier Frankish forms. At any rate, the two oldest

---

German; cf. Prost, *Quatre pièces*, pp. 175 ff.; A. Schubiger, *Die Sängerschule St. Gallens* (1858), 30 ff. Moreover, the local bishop is not commemorated in the acclamatory conclusion of the *laetania italica* or in the framework of the early Litany of the Saints (cf. below, p. 41). Besides, the prayer for the local bishop and archbishop has been ordered by Charlemagne in 801 (cf. Böhmer-Mühlbacher, *Regesta Imperi*, 1, n. 369); this law shows that hitherto the commemoration of the local ecclesiastical authorities was not the general custom.

[72] For St. Maurice, see above, n. 48; see also A. Wilmart, "Saint Ambroise et la Légende Dorée," *Eph. Lit.*, L (1936), 194 f.: "La fête des martyres d'Agaune est complètement étrangère, en effet, à la liturgie romaine traditionelle."

[73] See above, notes 4 and 19.

[74] Michel Andrieu, *Les 'Ordines Romani' du haut moyen age*, Spicilegium Sacrum Lovaniense, XI (Louvain, 1931), I, 367 ff., 101 ff., 473 ff.

[75] *Ibid.*, p. 474.

[76] That is, they offer the well-known compilation of *Gelasianum* and *Gregorianum* characteristic of the ninth century; Andrieu, *Ordines*, 1, 471 ff.; Bishop, *Lit. Hist.*, pp. 39–61.

forms are found in Gallo-Frankish manuscripts of the eighth century and the following forms in Gallicanized collections of the ninth century. Not a single early formulary has been transmitted in an indisputably Roman collection. This, at least, is a fact which cannot be easily contested.

An observation of minor importance may be added immediately. The laudes in the Montpellier MS 409 display certain dialectal peculiarities. Instead of "tu illum (illos) adiuva" we read *tulo (tu lo, tu los) iuva.* The last editor of this formulary makes a note "Composita est Romae procul dubio . . . et sermone magis Italico quam Latino."[77] It will be difficult to prove the Italian origin of this dialect, since every Romanesque dialect might have developed these forms. Other scholars considered the irregularities Frankish,[78] and they are probably correct. The lingo is reminiscent of forms which abound in Gallic manuscripts of the eighth century, and earlier.[79] Also, there is no reason why a formulary freshly imported from Rome between 783 and 787 should display dialectal abnormalities; Pope Hadrian's *Gregorianum*, imported from Rome in this very period, has no Italian dialect forms. Hence, the oldest specimen of laudes seems to direct us to Gaul rather than to Rome and suggests an older Frankish tradition rather than a new importation.

The main question, however, remains not only to be answered, but to be asked: did all the liturgical formulae of the laudes really originate in Rome? The brief analysis offered above (pp. 16 ff.) has made it clear that except for the triad of the *Christus vincit*, the origin of which remains obscure, almost all the elements can be reduced to prayers or acclamations the primitive forms of which are found in imperial pagan and early Christian Rome. But for the purpose of dating and locating the final redaction of the document we should not ask how far back the single elements can be traced, for this would lead us to Hellenistic times. Rather, we should ask for, and try to ascertain, the latest form-element of the final composition. And this question leads us to the problem of the sequence of saints in the laudes.

It is somewhat surprising to realize how little the series of saints and their order in the laudes has attracted the attention of students.[80] Nor

---

[77] Holder-Egger, in Einhard, *Vita Karoli Magni, MGH. SS. rer. Germ.* (1905), App. D, p. 46.

[78] Gastoué, *op. cit.*, p. 193.

[79] Not to mention earlier works, see the fragments of the Sacramentary of Gellone published by Tellenbach, *op. cit.*, pp. 68 f., or the *Gallican Masses* published by F. J. Mone, in Migne, *PL.*, CXXXVIII, cols. 863 ff., especially the Eighth Mass, *ibid.*, cols. 876 ff.

[80] Eugen Rosenstock, "Die Furt der Franken," in E. Rosenstock and J. Wittig, *Das Alter der Kirche* (Berlin, n. d.), II, 542 f., calls attention to an essential point; for Heldmann's interpretation, see above, pp. 32 f.; Biehl, *op. cit.*, pp. 105 ff., mentions, it is true, the Litany of Saints but does not recognize the implications. Nearest comes

has the question been raised in this connection when the usage of invoking *sanctorum nomina seriatim*[81] became so popular that it eventually affected the laudes. Whatever the primary source of the serial invocations of saints may have been, these so-called "Litanies of the Saints" were propagated not from Rome, but from England and Ireland. Litanies of the Saints containing sometimes two hundred and fifty or three hundred names begin to appear in the British Isles during the late seventh century.[82] Their dissemination to Gaul, and thence to the rest of the Continent, hardly antedates the middle of the eighth century. The Litany of the Saints was adventitious to Rome; it was received there shortly before, or about, 800.[83] The earliest Continental manuscript evidence of the Litany of the Saints is comparatively late. It is found in the Sacramentary of Gellone presenting material of the first half of the eighth century, though written between 770 and 780.[84] Consequently, the date of the first Continental manuscript evidence of the Anglo-Irish Litany almost coincides with that of the earliest manuscript evidence of the laudes, 783–787. But this is not all. Chronologically there follow, after the Sacramentary of Gellone, two other Frankish manuscripts which contain the Litany of the Saints: Montpellier MS 409 and Paris MS 13159, the very two manuscripts which offer also the two oldest texts of the laudes. In other words, our two laudes manuscripts, together with the Sacramentary of Gellone and perhaps one or two additional codices, form the very small group of service books of the eighth century which contain the earliest Continental examples of the Litany of the Saints.[85] Hence, laudes and Anglo-Irish Litanies of the Saints make their first appearance on the Continent simultaneously and in the same manu-

---

Célina Osieczkowska, "La mosaïque de la porte royale à Sainte-Sophie de Constantinople et la litanie de tous les saints," *Byzantion*, IX (1934), 41–83, especially 68 ff.; however, the basis of her article, so far as the West is concerned, is not broad enough, and its purposes are different from those of this discussion.

[81] *Vita S. Austrebertae*, c. III, § 19, in *AA. SS.*, II, 423; cf. Maurice Coens, "Anciennes litanies des saints," *Anal. Boll.*, LIV (1936), 9, and L. Gougaud, "Études sur les 'Ordines commendationis animae,' " *Eph. Lit.*, IL (1935), 4, 11, 24. While Gougaud assumes that the date of the saint's death (704) must be considered the date of our first Continental evidence for the Litany of Saints, Coens rightly emphasizes that the biography in its present form may be of a later date. However, the Litany was certainly sung at burial services in the eighth century; cf. Bishop, *Lit. Hist.*, p. 216, n. 1. See also above, n. 2, for the literature on litanies.

[82] Coens, *loc. cit.*; Bishop, *Lit. Hist.*, pp. 148 f.

[83] No text of a Roman Litany of Saints of the eighth century seems to be extant. The *Ordo of St. Amand*, adduced by Duchesne, *Christian Worship*, pp. 165, 473 ff., has proved to belong to the ninth century and to be under Gallican influence; cf. Bishop, *Lit. Hist.*, pp. 151–160; for the date, see also Andrieu, *op. cit.*, pp. 492 f.

[84] In addition to the references to the Sacramentary of Gellone (Paris, Bibl. Nat. Lat., MS 12048), offered by Tellenbach, *op. cit.*, p. 46, see Gerald Ellard, *Ordination Anointings in the Western Church before 1000 A.D.*, Monographs of the Mediaeval Academy of America, VIII (Cambridge, Mass, 1933), 29 ff., and Pierre de Puniet, "Le sacramentaire romain de Gellone," *Eph. Lit.*, LXVIII (1934), 3 ff.

[85] Coens, *op. cit.*, pp. 8 f.

scripts, and these manuscripts are Gallo-Frankish. This is another fact which should not be ignored.

We turn to the transmission of the laudes texts proper within the manuscripts. The current opinion holds that, until the twelfth century, "die *laudes* literarisch eine selbständige Existenz führen."[86] This independent existence of the laudes is true for the period between the early ninth century and the late eleventh (perhaps early twelfth), for in this period indeed they are usually placed separately as a special song in the manuscripts, devoid of any connection with the liturgical action (see below, pp. 89 f.). Originally, however, the laudes still belonged to what is called the framework of the Litany of the Saints. In the Montpellier manuscript they present themselves as a long acclamatory section within the Litany, and modern editors were not wise in isolating these acclamations by printing them separately and taking them out of their primitive background.[87] In the Paris MS 13159 they are likewise closely connected with the Litany[88] and the continuity of this organic union can be traced to the early ninth century.[89]

It is not difficult to find out the original position of the laudes within the litanies. In the *Ordo* of Angilbert of St. Riquier (*ca.* 800) we find a description of the penitentiary processions such as took place in St. Riquier on the Rogation Days. The *scola puerorum* sings psalms, recites the various creeds—that of the Apostles, that of Constantinople, and that of Athanasius—and after that they sing *laetaniam generalem*, the

---

[86] Schramm, "Ordines," p. 355, n. 2.

[87] E.g., Holder-Egger, *op. cit.*, and Dannenbauer, *op. cit.*, cf. above, n. 18. See, however, Gautier, *op. cit.*, p. 150, who rightly says, "Il nous semble cependant qu'il faut, à tout le moins, y voir une addition qui, très anciennement, a été faite aux *Litaniae*."

[88] Although, at present, there is no access to the manuscript, we can gather all the same the place of the laudes from the scanty descriptions by Delisle, *Le cabinet des manuscrits de la Bibliothèque Nationale* (1881), III, 239 f., and Ph. Lauer in *Bulletin de la société nationale des antiquaires de France*, (1910), 322 f. On fol. 161 is the Athanasian Creed; fol. 163 contains the laudes; 164ᵛ, the *laetania gallica* (as indicated by Delisle and rejected by de Mely, in *Revue archéologique*, IVᵉ ser., XVII [1911], 446. The subject must be reinvestigated, for the *Exaudi* acclamations on fol. 166ᵛ are part of the *italica* so that Delisle was probably correct, after all; cf. Gastoué, "Le chant gallican," *RCGr.*, XLIII [1939], 46: "plusieurs litanies que le scribe lui-même nomme 'gallicanes' "); fol. 165 contains suffrages beginning with *Ut* (which belong to a second litany, probably the *laetania romana* to judge from Delisle, "Sacramentaires," pp. 363 ff.), and fol. 166ᵛ, the *Exaudi* acclamations of the *italica*. See Anglibert's description of the various litanies quoted below, n. 90.

[89] Theganus, *Vita Hludowici*, c. 17, in *MGH. SS.*, II, 594. The passage deals with the coronation of Louis the Pious in 816. The pope (the *ordinator*) and the emperor (the *ordinandus*) prayed in prostration, that is in the usual attitude during the singing of the litany at an ordination; thereafter "*erexit* se pontifex et excelsa voce cum clero suo fecit ei laudes regales." That the expression "surgit (erexit) ab oratione" indicates the rising after prostration is stressed by Thalhofer, *Liturgik*, I, 631. See also E. Eichmann, "Die sog. Römische Königskrönungsformel," *HJb.*, XLV (1925), 528, and Schramm, "Krönung in Deutschland," *ZfRG.*, kan. Abt., XXIV (1935), 312 § 7, for the corresponding phrase in the coronation rite ("Finita autem letania, erigant se").

General Litany. "Deinde vero scola puerorum faciat laudes pro salute totius Christianitatis." Following the laudes, the whole procession, monks and boys, begin to sing the special litanies, the Gallic first, then the Italic, and finally the Roman.[90] This arrangement tallies perfectly with the formulary preserved in the Montpellier MS 409. We find first a litany containing almost two hundred names of saints; then comes the invocation of the various groups of celestials and saints without specified names, the *angeli* and *archangeli*, the *throni* and *dominationes* with the other orders of angels, followed by *Omnes patriarchae*, *Omnes prophetae*, *Omnes evangelistae*, and by the remaining categories of saints. This indeed may well be called the "General Litany." It is followed, in our formulary, by the laudes "for the good estate of all Christendom"—for that of the pope, the king, the princes, the queen, and that of the judges and the army—and is concluded by the *laetania gallica*.[91] At the end of this long chant of, in fact, three or more litanies we find the personal suffrage: "Tu mihi, Christe, concede sororem nomine Rotrudem esse beatam, ut tibi semper serviat illa."

Rothrude was the eldest daughter of Charlemagne and was betrothed from 781 to 787 to the young Emperor Constantine VI. No doubt, the political, if passive, role of Rothrude determines the date of the laudes (783–787), and the suggestion may be advanced that one of her brothers ordered on her behalf one of those general intercessory prayers which in the form of processions and litanies were offered up when important political decisions were imminent.[92]

---

[90] See the text published by Bishop, *Lit. Hist.*, p. 325, and also pp. 330 f.; cf. F. Lot in his edition of Hariulf's *Chronicon Centulense*, in *Collection de textes*, XVII (1894), App. VI, 301.

[91] Migne, *PL.*, CXXXVIII, cols. 885–888. That the litany following the laudes really represents the *laetania gallica* is countenanced by the ninth-century formulary (probably from the abbey of Lobbes) in the Brussels, Bibl. Roy. MS 7524–7533 (3558) fols. 83ᵛ–84, published by Coens, *op. cit.*, in *Anal. Boll.*, LV (1937), 58 f., where an identical pattern of litanies is called "Gallic." Another specimen is found, e.g., in the Berlin, Staatsbibl. MS Theol. Lat. Fol. 452, fols. 1ʳˑᵛ, published by P. Lehmann, "Corveyer Studien," *Abh. Bayr. Akad.*, XXX, 5 (Munich, 1919), 69, a ninth-century litany from Corvey. The same pattern is called "Gallic" as late as the tenth century in the litanies of Mainz in the Vienna, Nationalbibl. MS 1888 (theol. 685), fol. 111, printed in Migne, *PL.*, CXXXVIII, col. 1086; cf. Andrieu, *Ordines*, I, 413.

[92] For Rothrude's engagement, cf. A. Gasquet, *L'empire byzantin et la monarchie franque* (Paris, 1888), 249 ff.; Böhmer-Mühlbacher, *op. cit.*, nos. 226b and 273c. She is frequently mentioned in the poems of her brother-in-law Angilbert, by Theodulf of Orléans, Peter of Pisa, and Paul the Deacon; cf. *MGH. Poet.*, I, 359, 361, 371, 485 f. The singing of litanies in connection with important political events was often ordered by the court; see, e.g., *Chron. Moissiac.*, *MGH. SS.*, I, 312, referring to the three days preceding the coronation of the sons of Louis the Pious, in 817, when the emperor ordered fastings and litanies: "tunc tribus diebus ieiunatum est ab omni populo et laetania facta." In this case suffrages for the princes were probably added to the litanies. Rothrude was of political importance from 781 to 787. Since Queen Fastrada, whom Charlemagne married in 783, is mentioned in the laudes, the date of the chant can be affixed to the period 783–787.

However, we must realize that the laudes, when first they appeared in their definite form, belonged to the general framework of a great Frankish litany to be sung during a procession or on similar occasions. Thus it is obvious that the traditional practice of combining the early Carolingian laudes formularies with the one or the other visits of Charlemagne to Rome is pure guesswork and without a basis.[93] Moreover, the similarity of the laudes with the Litany of the Saints finds an explanation. They represented the middle section of the great chant, and therefore they were harmonized with the preceding *laetania generalis* as well as with the ensuing special litanies. By the insertion of certain series of saints, the laudes themselves became a new variation of the Litany of the Saints. This act of harmonization propounds no problem; but on the technical side, the method of carrying out the assimilation deserves our full attention. In order to disclose it, an inspection of the framework of the Litanies becomes necessary.

The framework of the Frankish Litany of the Saints[94] agrees in essence with that of the early Anglo-Irish Litanies from which, in turn, we know the Greek model.[95] However, the short and simple intentions of the Insular Litany grew in length by elaborations and by the addition of new suffrages which were borrowed from other prayers. It would be premature to advance an opinion concerning the circumstances and the date of the introduction of these accretions because the historical development of this framework of the Continental Litany is as yet not elucidated sufficiently. However, in the Frankish Litanies of the eighth century we find every single type of framework-suffrages, though not all in the same formulary. Of the various sections of suffrages,[96] the first two groups grew in length simply by multiplication of their elements. Instead of the simple imploration of the Insular model

Ab omni malo   libera nos, Domine,

we find additional specifications such as

Ab hoste malo   libera nos, Domine.
Ab omni morbo   libera nos, Domine.
A periculo mortis   libera nos, Domine. ...

These cries, which have clearly an exorcizing or apotropaeic character,[97]

---

[93] Cf. above, notes 4, 19.

[94] See, e.g., the one preserved in the Montpellier MS; Mabillon, *Vetera Analecta*, p. 170; Migne, *PL.*, CXXXVIII, col. 885.

[95] Bishop, *Lit. Hist.*, pp. 142 ff. Except for suffrage 13 ("Per crucem tuam") the framework of the Montpellier Litany contains all the Insular items.

[96] They are discussed by Baumstark, "Eine syrisch-melchitische Allerheiligenlitanei," *Oriens Christianus*, IV (1904), 98 ff.

[97] Baumstark, *op. cit.*, pp. 103 ff. Specimens of the *Ab* and *Per* suffrages are found in Delisle, "Sacramentaires," p. 366.

are followed by a second group referring to the forces of salvation. Here, too, the simple cry

> Per crucem tuam   libera nos, Domine,

has been multiplied by a detailed specification of the various stations in the life of the Lord through which salvation was secured:

> Per passionem tuam   libera nos, Domine.
> Per adventum tuum   libera nos, Domine.
> Per baptismum tuum   libera nos, Domine. . . .

We may neglect these rubrics and concentrate on those in which intentions for the ruler are found. In the Insular model of the Litany there follows the suffrage

> Ut pacem dones te rogamus, audi nos.

In the Paris MS 13159 we find the additional suffrages[98]

> Ut fructum terre nobis dones [te rogamus, audi nos].
> Ut *domnum apostolicum Leonem* in sanctitate et religione conservare digneris te rogamus, audi nos.
> Ut ei vitam et sanitatem dones.
> Ut *domnum Carolum regem* conservare digneris . . .
> Ut ei vitam et victoriam dones.
> Ut *proles regales* conservare digneris . . .
> Ut eis vitam et sanitatem dones.
> Ut *populo Christiano* pacem et unitatem largiaris . . .

The form of these suffrages is that of the ancient *Oratio fidelium* (or *Oratio communis*) of the Mass, a prayer "for all sorts and conditions of men" which was in use at Rome probably until the end of the fifth century before it was replaced by the great *Deprecatio* of Pope Gelasius I (492–496).[99] How this *Oratio fidelium*, which was said in the Eastern Churches on innumerable occasions, survived in Gaul (probably as an independent orison before being attached to the Litany), should not be at all too difficult to ascertain for anyone interested in the matter.[100]

---

[98] Ph. Lauer, *op. cit.*, p. 322.

[99] Cf. V. L. Kennedy, *The Saints of the Canon of the Mass*, pp. 30 f., for the suffrages of the ancient Prayer of the Faithful, and pp. 33 ff., for their replacement by the Gelasian *Deprecatio;* for the latter, see B. Capelle, "Le *Kyrie* de la messe et le Pape Gelase," *Rev. bénéd.*, XLVI (1934), 126–144, a study to which Professor Kennedy kindly called my attention.

[100] These *Ut*-supplications are embedded, for instance, in the *Orationes in Vigilia Paschae* of the so-called *Gallicanum vetus* (Migne, *PL.*, LXXII, cols. 366 ff.) as well as in the *Orationes Paschales* of the *Missale Gothicum* (Migne, *PL,*. LXXII, cols. 270 ff.). That their addition to the Litany of Saints was sometimes meant to be an honor intended to the king, is shown by a later Coronation Order: ". . . et inter cetera inserenda sunt ista: 'Ut hunc famulum tuum N. ad regem eligere digneris, te rogamus! Audi nos! . . .'" with two other intentions for the king following; cf. Eichmann, *HJb.*, XLV (1925), 528; Schramm, "Krönung in Deutschland." *ZfRG.*, XXIV (1935), 326.

A fourth group of suffrages begins with *Pro* [*sc. oremus*]. This set of intentions was derived most likely from the *Orationes solemnes* said during the service on Good Friday, a prayer in which the *Deprecatio Gelasii* survived.[101] As an independent litanylike deprecation these suffrages with *Pro* were very common, for example:[102]

> Pro sancta ecclesia catholica quam conservare digneris.   Kyrie.
> Pro domno *ill.* apostolico et universali papa.   Kyrie.
> Pro domno *ill.* imperatore nostro, judicibus et exercitibus eius.   Kyrie.
> Pro domno *ill.* archiepiscopo nostro et sacerdotio eius.   Kyrie. . . .

To the Litany of the Saints these *Pro*-intentions accreted occasionally; for instance, they are found, in a less elaborate form, in the Montpellier MS 409.[103] Although the reception of these suffrages was not generally effected within the Litany of the Saints, they still provide us with additional evidence of the tendency to append to the Litany suffrages for secular and ecclesiastical rulers.

This tendency is most obvious with a third and less well-known group which occasionally forms the conclusion, not of the *laetania generalis*, but of one of the special Litanies of the Saints which followed after the laudes. The Paris MS 13159 seems to offer the earliest evidence for this type, which is rare altogether. Its scheme is as follows:[104]

> . . . .   intercede pro nobis.
> Omnes sancti   intercedite pro nobis.
> Exaudi Deus   Gregorio pape vita.

---

[101] Migne, *PL.*, CI, cols. 560 f., for the *Deprecatio*. See also Bishop, *Jour. Theol. Stud.*, XII (1911), 408 ff.; Capelle, *op. cit.*, pp. 130 ff.; Kennedy, *op. cit.*, pp. 35 ff.

[102] The specimen, published in *DACL.*, IX, 1599, *s.v.* "Litanies," is of a slightly later date; but these rogations beginning with *Pro* are the nucleus of the early litanies prescribed by the Council of Orléans, in 511, and they are found in the early *preces* ("Dicamus omnes: Kyrie eleison. Ex toto corde et ex tota mente oramus te. Pro altissima pace . . .") published in *DACL.*, IX, 1563 f., and discussed by Gastoué, "Chants des anciennes liturgies gallicanes," *RCGr.*, XLI (1937), 168 ff.; cf. p. 173, the interesting rubric to the *Kyrie* in the Paris, Bibl. Nat. Lat. MS 1118, fol. 12, a sacramentary of Limoges of the tenth century, which indicates the survival of the diaconal litany: "Versum ad Kyrie tunc dicat diachonus."

[103] There are but two intentions:
> "Pro sacerdotibus   te precamus.
> Pro omni gradu Ecclesiae   te rogamus, audi nos."
As a special deprecatory prayer and not in connection with the Litany of Saints, the *Pro*-suffrages are not rare; see, e.g., the Sacramentary of Angoulême (Paris, Bibl. Nat. MS 816, fol. 34ᵛ) in Leroquais, *Les sacramentaires*, I, 9, where all the intentions can be traced back to the *Canon dominicus papę gilasi* preserved in the *Stowe Missal*, ed. by Sir George F. Warner, Henry Bradshaw Society, XXXII (London, 1906), 10 f.

[104] At present, there are but three formularies known to me: (1) Paris, Bibl. Nat. MS 13159, fol. 166ᵛ, published by Lauer, *op. cit.*, p. 323; (2) Berlin, Staatsbibl. MS Theol. Lat. Fol., 452, fol. 2 (827–840 A.D.), published by Lehmann, "Corveyer Studien," p. 69, referring to Corvey; (3) Brussels, Bibl. Roy. MS 7524–7533 (3558), fol. 85ᵛ, published by Coens in *Anal. Boll.*, LV (1937), 58 f., probably from Lobbes and still referring to the Carolingian period. A later specimen of Aix has been published by Gastoué, *op. cit.*, pp. 117 ff. The form here adduced is that of Corvey.

Exaudi Christe	Hludouico imperatori vita.
Exaudi Deus	proli regali vita.
Exaudi Christe	exercitui Francorum vita.
Exaudi Deus	peccata nobis indulge.
Exaudi Christe	orationem populi tui.
Kyrie......	

This song, as a finale of the Litany of the Saints, is remarkable for two reasons: first, for the alternation of *Exaudi Deus, Exaudi Christe*, and second, for the replacement of suffrages by acclamations or hails.

The alternate use of the two invocations is rare, if not unknown, in the Roman rite; nor does it seem to be genuine in the Gallican ritual. It occurs, however, time and again in the "Ambrosian Liturgy," the rite of Milan.[105] To adduce the Ambrosian ritual is fully justified. In a formulary which still belongs to the Carolingian period and may have been written in the abbey of Lobbes, the Litany concluded by this finale is headed by a lemma: "Laetania Italica dicenda die tertia in Rogationibus." That *laetania italica* does not mean "Roman Litany," but "Italian" or "Lombard" is countenanced by the *Ordo* of Angilbert who mentions that the procession on Rogation Days sing, after the laudes, "primo Gallicam, secundo Italicam, novissime vero Romanam" [*sc. laetaniam*]. And if anyone, Angilbert would have known the difference between Italic and Roman, because for seven years, he acted as a tutor and adviser to Pepin, king of Italy and Charlemagne's second son, and went thrice or more often as Charlemagne's ambassador to the papal court.[106]

The second question that concerns us is the replacement of suffrages by acclamations. The Ambrosian Litany, it is true, has the imploration thrice repeated

Exaudi Christe	miserere nobis
Exaudi Deus	voces nostras,

with which the "Italic Litany" of the Frankish manuscripts begins; but

---

[105] Cf. M. Magistretti, *Manuale Ambrosianum* (Milan, 1905), I, 96, 149, 156, 159; II, 47, 129, 246 ff. The invocation of saints' names ends as follows:

"Omnes sancti	intercedite pro nobis.
Exaudi Christe	voces nostras.
Exaudi Deus	miserere nobis."

These are the supplications with which, thrice repeated, the invocations of names open in the Carolingian *laetania italica;* cf. Lehmann, *loc. cit.;* Coens, *loc. cit.*

The litany of Aix to be sung on the second day of Rogations—quoted by Gastoué, *loc. cit.,*—has the following text:

"Kyrie eleison,	Christe eleison.
Domine miserere,	Christe miserere.
Miserere nobis, pie Rex	
Christe, audi nos.	
Exaudi Deus	voces nostras.
Conserva Christe	regibus christianorum vitam.
Exaudi Deus	orationem populi tui.
Sancte sanctorum Deus,	miserere nobis."

[106] Bishop, *Lit. Hist.*, p. 325, and his account of Angilbert's life, *ibid.*, pp. 317 ff.

no acclamations follow,[107] not at least so far as we know. However, the tendency mentioned before of adding to the Litany intentions for the magistracies may have prompted the Frankish liturgist to supplement the cry *Exaudi Christe* in the traditional way by adding *Imperatori* [*Regi*] *vita!* If we consider the general penitentiary climate of the Rogation Days—three days of fasting, contrition, and penitence preceding Ascension—we will find that these cheerful hailing shouts of "Long live the Pope!" and "Long live the King!" seem to be carried into this atmosphere of humility from without. And while the prayers for the ruler beginning with *Pro* and *Ut* displayed the appropriate tone of humbleness, the cheers of the finale with which we are here concerned, are, in fact, nothing but the official and very old Roman *vita*-acclamation offered time and again to the emperor when he made his appearance in public, at solemn processions, or on other occasions.[108] The "suffrages in favor of the ruler" were exchanged for ruler-acclamations, and these shouts were combined with the Litany so that eventually cheers were incorporated into the framework of the great chant of penitence.

The important matter is that the acclamatory conclusion of the Litany of Saints actually elucidates the genesis of the laudes. For, the development presents itself clearly if we compare the scheme of the Litany concluded by acclamations with that of the laudes:

LITANY

S. Maria	intercede pro nobis
S. Michael	intercede ...
S. Gabriel	
S. Raphael	
S. Johannes Baptista	
S. Petre	
S. Paule	
S. Andrea	
S. Johannes	
S. Jacobe....	
S. Stephane	
S. Line	
S. Clete	
S. Clemens	
S. Xyste....	

---

[107] In the "Italic Litany" of the Frankish Church the sequence is inverted: "Exaudi Deus—Exaudi Christe." Cf. above, n. 105. The relationship with Milan deserves attention with regard to the Milanese *Benedictio ad ordinandum regem* of the ninth century; cf. Schramm, "Ordines," pp. 358 ff., 369 ff. See also Gastoué, "Le Chant gallican," *RCGr.*,ᶠXLIII (1939), 44 ff., who believes that the laudes as far as the music is concerned, are "en rapport avec tel recitatif ou tel motif ambrosien." Cf. Bukofzer, below, pp. 207, 210.

[108] Peterson, *Untersuchungen*, p. 144, and *passim*; for Byzantium, see Treitinger, *Die oströmische Kaiser- und Reichsidee nach ihrer Gestaltung im höfischen Zeremoniell* (Jena, 1938), 73 ff., and *passim*.

Omnes sancti	intercedite pro nobis.
Exaudi Deus	Gregorio pape vita.
Exaudi Christe	Hludouico imperatori vita.
Exaudi Deus	proli regali vita.
Exaudi Christe	exercitui Francorum vita. . . .[109]

LAUDES

Exaudi Christe	Leoni summo pontifici . . . vita.
Salvator mundi	tu illum adiuva.
S. Petre	tu illum . . .
S. Paule	
S. Andreas	
S. Clemens	
S. Xyste	
Exaudi Christe	Carolo . . . regi Francorum . . .vita et victoria.
Redemptor mundi	tu illum adiuva.
S. Maria	tu illum . . .
S. Michael	
S. Gabriel	
S. Raphael	
S. Johannes Baptista	
S. Stephane	
Exaudi Christe	Nobilissime proli regali vita.
S. Virgo virginum	tu illos adiuva
S. Silvester	tu illos . . .
[there follow six other saints]	
Exaudi Christe	Omnibus iudicibus vel cuncto exercitui Francorum vita.
S. Hilari	tu illos adiuva.
[there follow six other saints]	

The procedure is so obvious that it hardly requires comment. The Litany of the Saints shows an unbroken sequence of names followed by an unbroken series of acclamations. In the laudes, the sequences both of saints and acclamations are broken up and interlaced with each other. The long series of saints is cut by the insertion of but one acclamation at a time taken "from below," and the series of acclamations is expanded by the infiltration of groups of saints taken "from above." The four groups acclaimed, (1) pope, (2) king, (3) princes, (4) army, are the same as those found at the end of the Italic Litany.[110] They take the place, as

---

[109] The pattern of this litany is found, e.g., in Delisle, "Sacramentaires," pp. 360, 361 f., 363 ff.; it is, on the whole, that of the present *Missale Romanum*.

[110] They represent, at the same time, the four standard acclamations of the Franco-Roman formularies; cf. below, p. 105.

it were, of those general intentions such as *Omnes sancti Apostoli, Omnes sancti martyres, Omnes sancti confessores* [*sc. orate pro nobis*] by which the monotonous enumeration of names is subdivided occasionally in the Litany of the Saints.[111] Thus, the technique of harmonizing acclamations with the Litany proposes no difficulties of understanding. The ancient Roman *vita*-acclamation which in France concludes the *laetania italica* has been combined artfully with the new Anglo-Irish fashion of invoking series of saints. In other words, Roman and Insular elements were fused in Gaul.

However, a seemingly insignificant detail is startling: the order of saints in the laudes has been inverted. The pope is acclaimed first, the king second. But in spite of the pope's taking precedence, it is the king who receives the first group of saints, Mary, the Archangels, John the Baptist, and also the first of the martyrs, St. Stephen, whereas the pope is allotted the second section: the apostles. This queer chiasmus implies that the order of saints sanctioned by the Litany is overthrown, an inversion of the celestial protocol which certainly cannot be dismissed as purely accidental. One explanation offers itself immediately: the pope as successor of the Prince of Apostles quite naturally would be supported by the apostles. But this argument is not conclusive. Why then is St. Stephen, the protomartyr, who in the Litany of the Saints usually heads the file of martyrs, attached to the saints invoked for the king, while the pope has to content himself with martyrs following after St. Stephen such as SS. Clement and Sixtus? The most obvious answer is that these martyrs were the pontiff's predecessors and therefore suitable patrons.

All this may be correct, yet it is not the whole story. At our disposal are sufficient laudes formularies[112] to make it obvious that—"legally," so to speak—the king's suite of saints is composed of the highest ranks of celestial society, whereas the pope in spite of his precedence is but second so far as the *qualitas* of his celestial entourage is concerned. This again is a fact which is incontestable, and if hitherto it has not been stressed by students, it may be due to the fact that in the Montpellier MS 409 the acclamations in the laudes are followed by only one saint at a time and by a rubric "vel alios sanctos quales volueris." This indeed seems to indicate that the saints to be invoked could be chosen deliberately. However, even in this oldest laudes form the name of the pope, Hadrian I, is

---

[111] See, e.g., Delisle, "Sacramentaires," pp. 362 ff.

[112] For the pages following, see my more extensive article, "Ivories and Litanies," pp. 60 f., where a list of some twenty formularies is found classifying the saints of the ruler. St. Mary, the Archangels, John the Baptist, and Stephen are found in at least six forms; Mary, Archangels, and John in five; Mary and Archangels in six; Mary and John in two; the Archangels alone in two; and St. John alone in one formulary. If the queen (or empress) is acclaimed in these laudes, St. Mary is often transferred to her file of saints.

followed "correctly" by St. Peter whereas that of the king, Charlemagne, is followed also "correctly" by that of St. John the Baptist;[113] and by the end of the eighth century we may talk of a customary sequence of saints in the higher brackets of king and pope, even though this order was subjected to certain changes.

If the laudes in the Carolingian successor states, in Greater Burgundy and in Septimania, combined the king's name with less prominent saints (cf. below, Appendix V), the reasons may have been nonhierarchic. It is more important to find that Rome was not heedless of the inverted order of saints in the laudes. The formulary of Franco-Roman laudes found in the Gallico-Roman service books of the ninth century or bound with the Roman *Ordines* of a later period shows some significant changes, among which the rearrangement of the order of saints is not the one least worthy of notice. In this group of Romanized laudes, the pope, who is heading the acclamations as usual, has not St. Peter as his intercessor, but the *Salvator mundi* instead. Then the emperor and the Virgin follow in the traditional order. Peter is left to the princes, the third group of *acclamati*, so that he now appears in the correct order, following after the Virgin. The army is protected, as it often was, by the martyr and soldier-saint Theodore. It is obvious that Rome was anxious both to make up for the "quality" of saints and to restore the correct order observed in the Litany and elsewhere. The two problems were conveniently solved by leaving the Virgin to the emperor, dismissing St. Peter, and associating the *Salvator mundi* with the hails to the pope.[114] In England, to sum up some observations which refer to a later period, this problem of liturgical etiquette was handled in a similar way. The Virgin Mary and the Archangels were left to the king, William the Conqueror; his queen is supported by John the Baptist and the Apostles Peter, Paul,

---

[113] Mabillon, *Analecta*, p. 170; Migne, *PL.*, CXXXVIII, col. 888.

[114] Cf. below, pp. 105–108, for the Franco-Roman laudes. Baumstark, *Vom geschichtlichen Werden der Liturgie* (Freiburg, 1923), 82, n. 3, holds that the invocation *Salvator mundi* is altogether not of Roman but of Gallican origin. The same is maintained, with reference to the apostrophe *Rex gloriae*, by Giuseppe Beran in *Eph. Lit.*, L (1936), 146. The acclamation to the pope is often followed also in the Gallo-Frankish laudes by the invocation *Salvator mundi;* in this case the acclaim to the ruler usually would be followed by the cry *Redemptor mundi* (cf. above, p. 15). A unique collection of such paraphrases of the name of Christ is found in the Munich Cod. Lat. 14322, fols. 1ᵛ–4ᵛ, in a form of laudes of either Ratisbon or St. Gall, in which the series of intercessors for the bishop begins with *Reconciliator mundi*, for the queen with *Amor ecclesiae*, for the king's sons with *Nutritor parvulorum*, for the monks and hermits *Rector angelorum* [!], for the virgins and widows *Sanctitatis et pietatis amator*, for the judges and the army *Victor mundi*, and for the universal Catholic people *Ordinator seculorum*. A similar group of paraphrasing names is found in the "Gallican Masses," edited by F. J. Mone, especially Mass IX; cf. Migne, *PL.*, CXXXVIII, col. 880C. See also Rosenstock, *op. cit.*, p. 479, for the Frankish Church dedications to the *Salvator Christus*, and for the problem in general, Heinrich Linssen, Θεὸς Σωτήρ. *Die Entwickelung und Verbreitung einer liturgischen Formelgruppe*, Bonn, diss., (Münster, 1929), 32 ff., 49 f.

and Andrew; but the invocations are opened by those of *Pater de coelis Deus, Filius redemptor mundi Deus,* and *Spiritus Sanctus Deus* in favor of the pope, the first *acclamatus.*[115] Hence, the pope heads the litany in regard also to the quality of intercessors invoked. Another expedient was preferred in some cathedrals of France. In Beauvais and in Troyes it is the pope who receives the traditional royal saints, the Virgin Mary and the Archangels. The apostles act here as patrons of the local bishop, whereas the king, coming third, still has the Protomartyr St. Stephen associated with some local saints.[116] In Chartres the pope has the apostles as protectors, but the king is expected to bask in the cool light of patrons such as SS. Cornelius, Cyprian, and Quentin.[117] In other words, several attempts have been made to restore the correct order of saints in the laudes by either lowering the quality of the royal intercessors or by topping them with the unrivaled names of the *Salvator mundi* or the Holy Trinity in favor of the pope.[118]

Why was it that the pope, the first *acclamatus,* did not receive the first section of saints from the beginning? How did this chiastic order originate? Could it be that in the Frankish Church the king had originally taken precedence of the pope and that only at some later date the se-

---

[115] Cf. W. Maskell, *Monumenta Ritualia Ecclesiae Anglicanae* (2d. ed.; Oxford, 1882) II, 85. The invocation of the Trinity agrees with the text of the Litany in the present *Missale Romanum.* On the Continent it is first found (with the additional invocations "Qui es trinus et unus—miserere nobis; Ipse idemque benignus—miserere nobis") in the *laetania gallica* in the Montpellier manuscript (Mabillon, *Analecta,* p. 170; Migne, *PL.,* CXXXVIII, col. 888) and accordingly in the other litanies following this pattern; cf. above n. 91. Insular origin is not unlikely.

[116] An early form of Beauvais, falling in the period 1003–1009 or 1024–1031, is found in the Paris, Bibl. Nat. MSS 9497 (fol. 182ᵛ) and 9508 (fol. 390); they are published by Baluze, *Miscellanea sacra,* II, 143, 285, and Prost, *Quatre pièces,* pp. 189 f. A later form, containing acclamations to Pope Alexander III, Bishop Henry of Beauvais, King Louis VII, the queen, and the judges, is mentioned by Pierre Louvet, *Histoire et antiquités du diocèse de Beauvais* (Beauvais, 1631–1635), II, 299 ff., which I found quoted by H. C. Greene, "The Song of the Ass," *Speculum,* VI (1931), 538. A thirteenth-century form is found in the Brit. Mus. Egerton MS 2615, fol. 42; cf. Henri Villetard, *Office de Pierre de Corbeil* (Paris, 1907), 231; E. K. Chambers, *The Mediaeval Stage,* I (1903), 284, n. 2; 286; and Greene, *op. cit.,* Pl. I, facing p. 541. The laudes of Troyes are preserved in a *Processionale Ecclesiae Trecensis saec. XV,* in the Bibliothèque du Grand Séminaire of this cathedral; they are published by Ch. Lalore, "Les acclamations à la messe pontificale dans l'ancienne liturgie troyenne," *Mélanges liturgiques relatifs au diocèse des Troyes,* Iʳᵉ sér. (1891), 106–115 (not available to me), and are reprinted with the musical notes by Joseph Delasilve, "Une acclamation liturgique notée," *RCGr.,* XII (1903–04), 197 ff. Cf. Bukofzer, below, pp. 199 f.

[117] For the laudes of Chartres, cf. above, n. 56.

[118] The saints after the acclamation to the king are changed also for national reasons, especially in later centuries; this is true especially in the English laudes of the twelfth century (cf. below, p. 171, n. 64), in which SS. Edmund, Erminhilde, and Oswald are invoked, and in those of Worcester (below, p. 172, n. 65) which show the same saints and add St. Edward the Confessor. Also, the twelfth-century form of Rouen (below, p. 166, n. 47) may be mentioned; we find only one celestial protector of the king of France, St. Denys, the saint of the French dynasty and of the French nation then in the making. Nationalism thus began to supersede, and to take precedence of the transcendental liturgical etiquette.

quence of acclamations was inverted so that the pope was hailed first? Although this suggestion may appear unlikely, it must nevertheless be considered, since there is evidence extant which seems to support this hypothesis. In the acclamatory conclusion of the *laetania italica* recorded in the Paris MS 13159 we find the following order:[119]

Exaudi Christe	Caroli regi vita.
Exaudi Deus	prolibus regalibus vita.
Exaudi Christe	exercitui Francorum vita.
Exaudi Deus	peccata nobis indulge.
Exaudi Christe	orationes populi tui.
Kyrie eleison . . .	
Omnes sancti	intercedite pro nobis.
Exaudi Deus	R. P. Leoni pape vita.

This is, to my knowledge, the oldest formulary of this type which has been preserved, and its order of acclamations may be called extraordinary indeed. The pope is transferred to the very last place.[120] This seems to be a demotion in rank and such a rearrangement is not beyond all the possibilities when we consider the date of the manuscript: 796–800. That is to say, it falls in the liturgically most agitated period of Charlemagne's government. We have to set the matter against the background of the royal Synod of Frankfort where Charlemagne decided, on his own authority and against both Nicaea and Rome, a liturgic issue of greatest import, namely that of the veneration of images; his decision was given also on the issue of Spanish Adoptianism. At this synod the assembled bishops finally acclaimed him *Rex et Sacerdos!* Certainly, in those years, there was a tense and nervous atmosphere with regard to liturgical questions in Charlemagne's realm.[121] It was in this period, too, that by the king's order Alcuin accomplished his "Supplement" to the Gregorian Sacramentary and that Charlemagne's self-confidence as "controller" of the Church rose to the point of culmination, while in Rome the negligible Pope Leo III was overwhelmed by difficulties. Thus, a rearrangement of the order of acclamations with Charlemagne taking precedence of the pope would be likely to match the general situation between the Council of Frankfort and the Roman coronation in 800.

The evidence, however, is hardly reliable. The order "King-Pope" instead of "Pope-King" would remain without parallel in Western and

[119] Lauer, *op. cit.*, p. 323.

[120] The characters *R. P.* preceding the name of the pope, as found in Lauer's edition, prompted me in the article quoted above, n. 112, to supplement *R*[omano] *P*[ontifici]. I now believe that they mean nothing but "respondent" (or "responsam").

[121] Cf. Bishop, "The Liturgical Reforms of Charlemagne," *Downside Review*, XXXVIII (1919), 1–16, and *idem, Lit. Hist.*, pp. 15 ff.; also Rosenstock, *op. cit.*, pp. 512, 516, 536 ff.

Eastern liturgies;[122] and, moreover, the demotion of the pope to the very last place, if intentional, was carried through in a most inefficient way. The invocation *Omnes sancti* (that is, the transition from invoking individual saints to the voicing of the acclamatory hails) makes no sense in its new place; and to put the acclamation to the pope after the *Kyrie*, that is, after the conclusion of the whole litany, is even more bungling. An error of the scribe is probably the correct solution of this enigmatic order.[123]

This is all the more likely, for the inverted order of saints makes sense when we try to "picture" the names instead of reading them. There are several Byzantine ivory triptychs preserved which illustrate in a most perfect way the Litany of the Saints.[124] The central tablets of the ivories are divided in two sections, an upper and lower. In the upper part, Christ is the central figure. As the ruler of the universe, he is seated on an imperial throne which is humbly approached by the Virgin Mary and John the Baptist, both in beseeching attitude, while the Archangels Michael and Gabriel are guarding the throne or floating in mid-air over the head

---

[122] The intentions for the Church and the reigning supreme pontiff precede, not follow, the suffrage for the king, his family, and his army.

[123] A suggestion may at least be advanced. Tellenbach, *op. cit.*, p. 18, publishes from several ninth-century sacramentaries a *Memoria imperatoris et totius populi Christiani*, a commemoration "pro rege nostro et sua venerabile prole et statu regni Francorum," which is formulary and found by the hundreds in Merovingian and Carolingian diplomata and, in the last analysis, goes back to the times of the Roman emperors. Here the pope is not mentioned at all. Is it possible that the acclamatory conclusion with which we are concerned followed originally a similar *Memoria* and that therefore the name of the pope was added subsequently? There is yet another observation which indeed seems to sanction the hypothesis that the intention for the pope should be considered a later addition. Not only is the sequence of saints reversed in the laudes, but also the sequence of invocations in the acclamatory conclusion of the *laetania italica* (see also above, n. 105).

Ambrosian Litany   Italic Litany
"Omnes sancti   interc. p. n.   "Omnes sancti   interc.
  Exaudi Christe   voces n.   Exaudi Deus   pape vita
  Exaudi Deus   miserere n."   *Exaudi Christe*   regi vita."

In the Paris, Bibl. Nat. MS 13159, however, the acclamatory conclusion begins like the Milanese Litany with *Exaudi Christe* and the response *Caroli regi vita*, whereas the pope with a preceding *Exaudi Deus* appears at the very end of these hails.

While reading the proofs I chanced upon the Mozarabic *Pax* litany which in the so-called Antiphonary of King Wamba (León, Library of the Cathedral Chapter), fol. 173ᵛ, concludes the *Benedictio Cerei*. Here, indeed, the intention for the king precedes that for the Church.

Pax in coelo. Amen.
Pax in terra. Amen.
Pax et plenitudo tua, Domine, super nos descendat. Amen.
Pax regibus et potestatibus seculi huius. Amen.
Pax ecclesie tue catholice, que est in hunc locum constituta, et per
    universum orbem terrarum in pace diffusa. Amen.

Gf. Germán Prado, *Textos ineditos de la liturgia Mozarába* (Madrid, 1926), 51 f.

[124] See Kantorowicz, "Ivories and Litanies," pp. 60 ff., and Osieczkowska, *op. cit.* The subject is equally well illustrated by the later imagery of the Litany of the Saints; see Arthur Haseloff, *Eine thüringisch-sächsische Malerschule des 13. Jahrhunderts* (1877), Pl. XXXI; Sir George Warren, *Queen Mary's Psalter* (London, 1912), Pls. 297–312, pp. 31 f., the most exuberant pictorial representation of the Litany.

of the Savior. It is a so-called Déesis, an intercessory supplication offered up before Christ by the only two human beings believed to dwell in the angelic world: the Virgin Mary, praised time and again as "more honorable than the Cherubim and beyond compare more glorious than the Seraphim" and therefore ranking above the angels; and John the Baptist, who "alone on earth appeared as an angel incarnate" and "participates in the ethereal dignity" because, at the baptism of Christ, the Precursor, "greater than all saints," was assisted by angels as celestial acolytes while he performed the service "in an angelic way though still within human life."[125] In the lower part of the ivories are five apostles, with St. Peter dominating the center, Paul and Andrew on his left, and John and James on his right. If we now try to "read" the names in the two sections, we find the well-known order of the Litany of the Saints restored: the Virgin Mary, Michael, Gabriel, John the Baptist, and Peter, Paul, Andrew, John, and James. (See Pl. III, *a–b*, and Pl. XV.)

Thanks to the ivories, the distribution of saints in the Frankish laudes suddenly discloses its meaning. We now can "see" the implications of the chiastic order. It is manifest, above all, that the names of the Virgin, the Archangels, and St. John are by no means accidentally connected with the acclamation to the king. The attendance of these angelic and superangelic beings and intercessors implies that the person supported by them dwells, so to speak, with them in the upper part of the image, whereas the accompaniment of the apostles—saints, yet human beings—implies a dwelling below. It was a prerogative of the Frankish king and an honor intended for him to have an abode in the most prominent place—and how could it be otherwise in the Carolingian Empire! The king's place is in the "royal box" which he shares with his angelic and superangelic patrons, whereas the pope, with the apostles, occupies the "stalls." It is as if the king's intercessors, through their own superhuman quality, were to indicate and emphasize the king's *character angelicus*,[126] nay to make him through their companionship almost *ipso facto* the human counterpart of the world ruler enthroned in celestial majesty. The Pantokrator in Heaven and the Autokrator on Earth face each other; they reflect and

[125] The basis of this cult is, of course, Mark 1:2 (Matt. 11:10; Luke, 7:27): "Ecce mitto angelum meum." To the places adduced in the article mentioned above (n. 112), there should be added Louis Brou, "Un passage de Tertullian conservé dans un répons pour la fête de St. Jean-Baptiste," *Eph. Lit.*, LII (1938), 237–257. The studies of D. E. Flicoteaux, *Le culte du Saint Précurseur* (1924), and *La Noël d'été et le culte de St. Jean-Baptiste* (Lophem-les-Bruges, 1932), were not accessible to me. See also N. L. Okunev, "Arilje, un monument de l'art serbe du XIIIᵉ siècle," *Seminarium Kondakovianum*, VIII (1936), Pl. IX, 2. I shall deal separately with the fact that St. Mary and John the Baptist are the only saints whose birthdays are celebrated by the Church (in addition to that of the Lord). See also G. La Piana, *Le rappresentazioni sacre nella letteratura bizantina* (Grottaferrata, 1912), 49 ff., on the *encomia* for Mary and John.

[126] The subject deserves a special study. See my quite incomplete notes in *Ergänzungsband*, pp. 72 ff. The basis is probably II Sam., 14:7 and 20.

interpenetrate each other; and both become "transparent," as they stand out against, and become visible through, each other. But admittedly, the imaginative and at the same time mysterious symbolism with which the East represented the monarch and his "throne-sharing God,"[127] was only dimly reflected in the West.

However, there is no need to seek an "original" order of acclamations in which the Frankish king would appear first and the pope second. For the inverted order is sure to have been the original, and the wrong sequence of saints is apparently correct. The Frankish king, it is true, left to the pope the precedence, an honorary privilege. But in substance, he, the king, remains the one who comes first, the true master of the Church, within which he represents the genuine *christus Domini*.[128] The ideological background of the Carolingian Empire-Church and the bases on which it was founded were rarely displayed so impressively as they were by this act of leaving a privilege to the Roman Pontiff and of securing the substance for the Frankish king.

Of the many questions that thrust themselves upon us—for instance, whether the West was familiar with the Déesis representation and conscious of its implications[129]—only one can be dealt with here, and only

[127] Christ's relationship with the Byzantine emperor was in fact that of a σύνθρονος θεός. According to *De caerim.*, II, 1, ed. Reiske, I, 521, the emperor was usually seated in the right seat of the throne which was considered that of Christ; only on Sundays and other feast days, the emperor leaves the right seat vacant and sits in the left part of the throne so as to make it "visible" that he shares the throne with Christ. See also Treitinger, *op. cit.*, p. 33, who, however, does not mention the underlying Hellenistic idea of the "throne-sharing Gods"; for the problem see Arthur D. Nock, "Σύνναος θεός," *Harvard Studies in Classical Philology*, XLI (1930), 1–62.

[128] The anointment of the head of the Frankish king seems to have preceded that of the bishops; cf. Ellard, *Ordination Anointings*, pp. 30 f.; cf. *ibid.*, pp. 20 f., for the anointings of the hands of priests; the general introduction of the episcopal anointments does not seem to antedate the middle of the ninth century; Ellard, *op. cit.*, pp. 55 ff.; Leroquais, *Pontificaux*, I, p. lxxxviii (cf. *ibid.*, I, 29), maintains that the episcopal unction is first found in the latter half of the ninth century, in the Angers, Bibl. Munic. MS 80 (72), fol. 89ᵛ (a Pontifical not mentioned by Ellard); but this date is certainly too late.

[129] The subject needs a special study. For the seventh century and the Carolingian period, however, the following items may be mentioned: the representation in Santa Maria Antiqua in Rome; cf. Myrtilla Avery, "The Alexandrian Style at Santa Maria Antiqua, Rome," *Art Bulletin*, VII (1924), 131–150; Osieczkowska, *op. cit.*, pp. 47 ff., and Pl. III; see also Robert Berger, *Die Darstellung des thronenden Christus in der romanischen Kunst* (Reutlingen, 1926), 156 ff., who refers also to early representations. A Déesis is found in the Evangelary of St. Médard at Soissons (Paris, Bibl. Nat. Lat. MS 8850, fol. 124); cf. A. Boinet, *La miniature Carolingienne* (Paris, 1913), Pl. XXIII, A, first quarter of the ninth century. See also Ermoldus Nigellus, *In honorem Hludovici*, II, vv. 421 ff., *MGH. Poet.*, II, 36, who transfers acclamations into poetical form and enumerates the SS. Andrew, Peter and Paul, John and Mary. For dedications of churches and monasteries to the Déesis saints, cf. J. v. Schlosser, *Schriftquellen zur Geschichte der karolingischen Kunst* (1896), e.g., nos. 274, 277, 594, 601, 823; see also *Regesta Imperii*, I, no. 1667. Of great interest is the cult of the Déesis in the former Lombard kingdom. The gold plate in the Bargello shows King Agilulph in the *Maiestas* with two Victories and two warriors, remindful at least of the Déesis; cf. *DACL.*, IX, 2277, fig. 7165. The same king, together with Queen Theodelinda, dedicated the church of Turin, in 602, to Christ, St. Mary, and John the Baptist; cf.

in a somewhat perfunctory way, namely: what are the sources of the sequence of saints in the Carolingian laudes? The Déesis order of saints (Mary-Archangels-John-Peter) in the Litany is not originally Roman, though finally it was accepted by Rome. It is Eastern, but is found also in the Gallican rites.[130] In essence, though with a slight variation (Archangels-*John-Mary*-Peter), the order is preserved also in some Irish and English Litanies.[131] However, none of these sequences seems to have formed the model of the order of saints in the laudes. The formulary in the Paris MS 13159, as well as in half a dozen other specimens, adds to the Déesis group the name of St. Stephen so that there results the sequence Mary-Archangels-John-Stephen-Peter. It would be plausible to adduce some local cult of St. Stephen and thus explain his role as intercessor for the king.[132] But this would not be correct, for the Déesis group

Paullus M. Paciaudius, *De cultu S. Johannis Baptistae antiquitates christianae* (Rome, 1755), 17; see also, for the Lombard veneration of St. John in general, Paulus Diaconus, *Hist. Lang.*, IV, c. 21 and c. 47; V, c. 6, *MGH. SS. rer. Lang.* 123, 136, 146 f. In this connection the famous chalice of Duke Thassilo of Bavaria (eighth century) must be mentioned; cf. A. Riegl and E. H. Zimmermann, *Kunstgewerbe des frühen Mittelalters* (Vienna, 1923), 53–58, Pl. XXV; Marc Rosenberg, *Geschichte der Goldschmiedekunst auf technischer Grundlage* (Frankfort, 1924), II, 79 ff., figs. 76, 77. The dedication of the church of Turin (602), together with the dream of St. Sophronius in which a Déesis is mentioned (*Encomium SS. Cyri et Joannis*, c. 36, Migne, *PG.*, LXXXVII, cols. 3557–8D), is one of the earliest evidences of this group. See, however, Baumstark, "Bild und Lied des christlichen Ostens," *Festschrift Paul Clemen* (Düsseldorf, 1926), 169 f., who seems to assume an even earlier date for the Déesis (early sixth, or even fifth century). Joseph Wilpert, "Die Kapelle des hl. Nikolaus im Lateranpalast, ein Denkmal des Wormser Konkordats," *Festschrift für Georg von Hertling* (Kempten and Munich, 1913), 230 f., holds that the archetype of the Déesis is found in the Constantinian mosaics of the Lateran Basilica. In 881, a chapel was built in Modena "in honore sancti salvatoris et sanctae Mariae et sancti Johannis"; cf. *Decretales Pseudo-Isidorianae*, ed. P. Hinschius (1863), xix, and the first of the *Carmina Mutinensia*, lines 31 f., *MGH. Poet.*, III, 705. See also the anonymous *Carmen ad Regem* of the late ninth century (Raphael is replaced by Elijah) in *MGH. Poet.*, IV, 136; but here and elsewhere (*ibid.*, pp. 321, 326) the Litany of the Saints is followed. Cf. Haseloff, *op. cit.*, pp. 194 f.

[130] For the Déesis order without the archangels, see F. E. Brightman, *Liturgies Eastern and Western* (Oxford, 1896), I, 40:2, 57:2, 66:7, etc.; *ibid.*, p. 357:29 ff., for the order with angels in the Liturgy of John Chrysostom. See also Theodor Schermann, "Die griechischen Kyprianosgebete," *Oriens Christianus*, III (1903), 317; Baumstark, in *Oriens Christianus*, IV (1904), 117; Gregor Peradse, "Ein Dokument aus der mittelalterlichen Liturgiegeschichte Georgiens," *Kyrios*, I (1936), 76. The sequence exercises influence also on the order of Masses in the *Commune Sanctorum;* see, e.g., the Sacramentary of St. Thierry of the ninth century (Delisle, "Sacramentaires," p. 118), where the Masses for the "Sapientia" and the "Spiritus Sanctus" are followed by those for St. John, John the Baptist, Peter, Stephen, and others. Cf. Leroquais, *Sacramentaires*, I, 24, and 58; in the Sacramentary of Amiens, St. John is left out; *ibid.*, I, 42. For Milan, see Magistretti, *loc. cit.* In the Mozarabic Diptychs the name of St. Zacharias appears between those of Mary and John; cf. Migne, *PL.*, LXXII, col. 421; the same is true in an Ethiopic liturgy; cf. Brightman, *op. cit.*, I, 228:27; S. Euringer, "Die äthiopische Anaphora des hl. Epiphanius," *Oriens Christianus*, XXIII (1927), 111. It may be noted that (in addition to Jesus) Mary, Zacharias, and John the Baptist are the only New Testament names found in the Koran.

[131] Bishop, *Lit. Hist.*, pp. 142 f., 161.

[132] See, e.g., Hincmar's address at Charles the Bald's coronation in Metz (869), Migne, *PL.*, CXXXVIII, col. 740: ". . . et in hac domo, ante hoc altare protomartyris Stephani, cuius nomen interpretatum resonat coronatus, per Domini sacerdotes, acclamatione fidelis populi, . . . corona regni est imperioque restitutus."

including St. Stephen is derived from another source. In the diptychs of the Gothic—that is Visigothic-Spanish—Church of Arles, which seem to belong to the sixth century, we find exactly the same order of saints.[133] This does not necessarily imply that the Frankish Church borrowed from the liturgy of Arles, since that sequence of saints did not originate on the banks of the Rhone. Stephen preceding the apostles and following St. John is an order which is purely "Oriental," not Byzantine or Greek, but Syrian and Egyptian or even Alexandrian. Attention has been called to the existence of this order in the Syriac liturgy of St. James and in the Jacobite liturgy of Cyriacus of Nisibis; also, it is found in the Armenian rite.[134] The most striking parallel, however, occurs in the Egyptian rite, in the liturgy of the Coptic Jacobites, where the priest implores[135]

the intercession of the holy glorious ever-virgin Theotokos *St. Mary*, and the prayers and supplications of the holy Archangels *Michael* and *Gabriel*, and of *St. John* the Forerunner and Baptist and Martyr, and *St. Stephen* the Protodeacon and Proto-martyr, and of our holy Fathers the *Apostles*. . . . .

That St. Stephen in the celestial hierarchy of Eastern Churches held this very high rank among the angelic and superangelic beings of the Déesis may be due not to his quality as Protomartyr, but rather to that as Protodeacon. "He was made a deacon of the dread divine mysteries; and in his ministry he depicted a type of the angels. This type the deacons bear in Holy Church, imitating in their ministry the hosts of the height."[136] Thus, St. Stephen, who represented *in officio* a type of angels, was associated with St. John, the "angel incarnate," and St. Mary, the super-angelic Mother of God, to act together with the archangels as intercessors for the king.

How it happened that this "Egyptian" order of saints reappeared in the surroundings of Aachen and entered the litany of the Gallo-Frankish laudes, is a problem that still needs a thorough study. However, such

---

[133] *DACL.*, IV, 1071; Migne, *PL.*, LXXII, col. 136; see also F. Probst, *Die abend-ländische Messe vom fünften bis zum achten Jahrhundert* (1896), 333.

[134] Bishop, *Lit. Hist.*, pp. 161 f., and *Jour. Theol. Stud.*, X (1909), 447 ff.; cf. R. H. Connolly and H. W. Codrington, *Two Commentaries on Jacobite Liturgy* (1913), 100, 109. For the Armenian sequence of saints, see Brightman, *op. cit.*, I, 440; Baumstark, "Denkmäler altarmenischer Messliturgie," *Oriens Christianus*, N. S. VII–VIII (1918), 22, where the angels precede SS. Mary, John, Stephen, and the apostles; A. Rücker, in *Oriens Christianus*, XXIII (1927), 152. St. John and St. Stephen are commemorated together also in the *Nobis quoque* of the Canon of the Roman Mass, a practice which Kennedy, *The Saints of the Canon of the Mass*, p. 144, suspects as a borrowing "directly from Alexandria" probably of Pope Gelasius; cf. *ibid.*, p. 37 f., his list of Eastern commemorations containing St. Stephen. St. John in the *Nobis quoque* was interpreted by mediaeval liturgists as John the Evangelist; cf. Thalhofer, *Liturgik*, II (1912), 189.

[135] Brightman, *op. cit.*, p. 169.

[136] *The Liturgical Homilies of Narsai*, transl. into English by Dom R. H. Connolly (Cambridge, 1909), Introd., p. xxiv; cf. *ibid.*, pp. 3 f., 7 with n. 1; 55 f. See also Connolly and Codrington, *op. cit.*, pp. 18 f., 35 f.; and H. Lietzmann, "Die Liturgie des Theodor von Mopsuestia," *Sitzungsber. Preuss. Akad.* (Berlin, 1933), 916, §§ 2–3.

"Egyptian" symptoms are not rare in Gaul. They may be accounted a survival, a Gallican remnant of earlier days, or, more likely, a later importation carried on the wave of Eastern influence in the sixth and seventh centuries.[137]

DATE AND PLACE OF ORIGIN

It is relatively easy now to fix the approximate date of the redaction of the *laudes regiae*. Whatever the liturgical acclamations to kings and emperors may have been like in earlier days, laudes in the form of a Litany of the Saints, invoking *sanctorum nomina seriatim* or *plures sanctos invocantes*,[138] cannot have existed before the Litany of the Saints was introduced on the Continent. Thus, the redaction of the laudes litany must fall in the eighth century. The formulary of 783–787 in the Montpellier manuscript is not likely to be the very oldest form. It is disclosed by the *Liber Pontificalis* that Pope Hadrian I, in 774, ordered the laudes sung to Charlemagne. It is not asserted that these laudes, offered to "God Almighty and to Charles, the most excellent King of the Franks and Patricius of the Romans," contained names of saints. But in view of the fact that at the coronation in 800 the invocation of saints is mentioned *expressis verbis* we may assume that also the laudes of 774 resembled the traditional Frankish pattern for the following reasons: Pope Hadrian, in spite of his efforts to court the Frankish king in whose honor he had introduced a special "prayer for the king" on the Saturday before Easter, had, surprisingly, omitted singing the laudes to Charles on Easter Sunday, although the king attended the divine service. This omission was obviously due to the fact that the custom of acclaiming the ruler on feast days—and, most likely, the chant itself—was not known in Rome. Hadrian's attention, however, may have been called to this neglect; for on Easter Monday the pope made up for it and sang the royal litany to Charles, presumably in the form which was customary in the Frankish Church.[139]

If this assumption be correct, the year 774 would mark the *terminus ad*

---

[137] For some suggestions concerning these relations, see Kantorowicz, "Ivories and Litanies," pp. 80 f. See also L. B. Ellis, "The Animal Symbols of the Evangelists," *Ancient Egypt* (1930), 109–118, also his "The Introduction of Christianity in the Rhineland," *ibid.* (1928), 12–16, to which Professor Eugen Rosenstock-Huessy kindly called my attention. The interesting study of Johannes Quasten, "Oriental Influence in the Gallican Liturgy," *Traditio*, I (1943), 55–78, was published too late to be used for the present discussion; but the results of his study support very pleasingly the suggestions here advanced.

[138] Cf. above, n. 82, and *Liber pont.*, II, 7, line 26.

[139] *Liber pont.*, 1, 498, seems to indicate this correction by the emphasis laid on the singing of the laudes on Easter Monday; cf. Biehl, *op. cit.*, p. 107, whose suggestions I follow. That most likely the commemoration of the ruler in the *Exultet* was introduced into the Roman rite in 774, is emphasized by G. B. Ladner, "The 'Portraits' of Emperors in Southern Italian *Exultet* Rolls and the Liturgical Commemoration of the Emperor," *Speculum*, XVII (1942), 194 f.

quem; therefore, the laudes must have existed in the Gallo-Frankish Church before this date. On the other hand, the Gallo-Frankish composition cannot be older than the eighth century owing to the late adoption of the Litany of the Saints. Moreover, it is unlikely that this composition belongs to the time of the last Merovingian kings. There was no reason on the part of the Pepinides, the Merovingian mayors of the palace, for exalting the Merovingian dynasty by introducing a new "royal anthem." This consideration would bring the *terminus a quo* down to the middle of the eighth century, roughly to Pepin's elevation to the rank of king, so that it may be maintained that the litany of the laudes originated in France between 751 and 774, that is, in the time either of Pepin or in the early years of Charlemagne.

The Frankish origin can hardly be doubted. There are too many indications which allow us to draw this conclusion. The transmission of laudes texts exclusively in Frankish manuscripts or in Gallicanized collections of *Ordines* is one important indication. Another is the fact that the Litany of the Saints makes its first appearance on the Continent in Gaul. A third point is the "Gallican," and at any rate non-Roman, sequence of saints observed in the laudes (Mary-Archangels-John-Stephen-Peter). And in addition to these indications we may recall some items of a more general nature: the florid character of the Gallican ceremonial and ritual style; the emphasis in the Gallo-Frankish Church on the liturgical hallowing of the ruler, his army, his standards, or weapons, and the fact that so far as the West is concerned there was no prince of any importance equal to the Frankish king. In Rome there was at that time neither king nor emperor, and it is difficult to believe that Rome should have introduced a new chant to celebrate the Byzantine emperors in the age of iconoclasm, not to mention the fact that the Litany of the Saints was received in Rome probably not before the very end of the eighth century. Thus the Gallo-Frankish origin of the laudes in the times of Pepin or in the early years of Charlemagne can hardly be disputed, unless new evidence is adduced to prove the contrary.

Inevitably there must arise the question whether the laudes can be brought into connection with Pepin's anointment,[140] which marks in several ways—legally and liturgically—the critical moment after which European history turns definitely "mediaeval." Pepin was consecrated twice: in 751 by St. Boniface and in 754 by Pope Stephen II. He was the first Western ruler ever to be consecrated by a pope, and it is well known that this hallowing was a *do ut des* transaction, that the Holy See needed

---

[140] For the introduction of royal anointments, see Eva Müller, "Die Anfänge der Königssalbung im Mittelalter," *HJb.*, LVIII (1938), 322 ff. The surmise concerning the Celtic-Insular origin of anointment is by no means done with and superannuated; cf. Klauser, in *JLW.*, XIII (1933), 350 f.

the help of the Frankish king as much as the king needed the liturgical consecration and ecclesiastical recognition to compensate for his lack of royal blood. Pepin's anointment by Pope Stephen took place not in Rome but in St.-Denis. A Frankish, to say nothing of a Roman, *Ordo coronationis* did not exist. The only relevant precedent was Pepin's own anointment which, as we are told, had been performed by St. Boniface.[141] Whether the early ninth-century benedictions for a king and the formula for anointing the hands of a king preserved in a benedictional of Freising refer to the sacring of Pepin[142] and whether St. Boniface was their compiler[143] are open questions. Actually, nothing is known about them. Hence, it would be a mere surmise to link the name of St. Boniface, Anglo-Saxon by birth and champion of Rome by vocation, with the composition or introduction of the litany of the laudes. It would be interesting if this were so; but there is no evidence whatever to support this conjecture. We do not even know whether laudes were sung at Pepin's coronation.[144]

---

[141] For St. Boniface as "consecrator," cf. *Regesta Imperii*, I, No. 62a.

[142] The Munich Cod. Lat. 6430, fol. 30ᵛ, a ninth-century Benedictionary from Freising, contains four *Benedictiones regis* which G. Morin, in *Rev. bénéd.*, XXIX (1912), 168 ff., claimed as a consecration ritual of the Merovingian kings. This suggestion is not likely correct because there was not an unction of Merovingian kings. Eichmann, "Königs- und Bischofsweihe," *Sitzungsber. Münchener Akad.*, 1928, Abh. VI, pp. 29 ff., considers that these benedictions may be referred to the Coronation Order of Pepin; see also his article, "Die sog. römische Königskrönungsformel," *HJb.*, XLV (1925), 545 ff., where he reprints the texts of these benedictions. Eichmann's hypothesis is as good and as bad as any other because nothing certain can be known about the application of these prayers. Not so good, however, is his argument stressing that the formula

"Unguantur manus istae de oleo sanctificato, unde uncti fuerunt reges et prophetae, sicut unxit Samuhel David in regem, ut sis benedictus et constitutus rex in regno isto . . ."

"fitted the occasion," namely the replacement of the last Merovingian (quasi "Saul") through Pepin (quasi "David"). This theory as advanced by Eichmann ("Königs- und Bischofsweihe," p. 32) and adopted by Erich Caspar, "Das Papsttum unter fränkischer Herrschaft," *ZKG.*, LIV (1935), 136, n. 8 ("Der Hinweis auf David, der an Stelle des verworfenen Saul trat, und auf ein durch einen Besitztitel göttlicher Verleihung begründetes Königtum scheint auf Pippin zu *passen*"), proves less than nothing and cannot be acknowledged as an argument or a basis for the attribution to Pepin. Bishop, *Lit. Hist.*, p. 13, warns of "the attempts that have been made to fix the dates of prayers by means of allusions supposed to be contained in them to current events." This warning should be remembered in the present case. The formula quoted above for the anointment of the king's hands (an unction of the head is not provided for) matches with what Ellard, *Ordination Anointings*, pp. 20 f., calls the "Samuel-David formulary," an early form of prayer found, e.g., in the *Ordo Baptismi* of the Bobbio Missal, which subsequently was adapted to sacerdotal ordination. To this, Th. Klauser, in *JLW.*, XIII (1933), 351, adds that between 700 and 900 the formula is applied to every form of sacramental oilings, namely, baptism, anointing of the dying, sacerdotal ordination, and finally royal sacring. It follows that the formula was used at the royal anointment, not because it "fitted" the special occasion and the political situation under Pepin, but because it was the formulary of all "oil rituals." The same is true, by the way, for the Litany of Saints; it is likewise combined with all "oil rituals." The whole complex seems to require a special study.

[143] Schramm, "Ordines," p. 362, n. 2, does not reject such a surmise.

[144] The laudes and hymns sung by Pope Stephen II at the procession (*Liber pont.*, I, 447) may or may not have contained the laudes litany of the Frankish Church.

BACKGROUNDS AND GENERAL ASPECTS

There is nevertheless some foundation for connecting, in a more general way, the anointment of Pepin with the composition of the laudes. For in the change from the profane to the liturgical of both the king's inauguration and the king's acclamation, neither of which was ecclesiastical in Merovingian times, we can trace the same conditions and the same intellectual forces at work elsewhere in that period. In later Rome, so it has been said, the self-presentation of the Caesars was gradually "litanized" and transcendentalized until an almost independent imperial liturgy developed side by side with that of the Church.[145] In Carolingian Gaul the corresponding development led toward the hallowing of the king by the ordinary liturgy, an instrument which the king first used for his purposes, but which was destined to engulf him.

What Pepin created and Charles continued was, as Frankish doctrine had it, the revival of the Biblical kingship of David. The introduction of the purely Biblical rite of royal unctions was not enforced upon Pepin by merely politico-dynastic considerations. This ritual of the Old Testament and its revival were in full agreement with the drift of the age toward "liturgifying" the secular sphere and toward theocratic solutions of political problems. It may be appropriate to recall, in the first place, the political as well as religious self-esteem and self-reliance which noticeably seized upon the Franks in Pepin's times, although to a lesser degree they had been so disposed earlier. The Franks, ever since their victory over the Arabs, had begun to think of themselves as the new people chosen by God, the "new sacred people of promise," as they were styled by the Holy See.[146] The roots of their history, in spite of the legends of the Trojan descent of the Franks, were sought not in the profane evolution of the Greco-Roman world, but in the sacred tradition of the Old Testament. The Franks endeavored, as it were, to wheel into Church history as the continuators of Israel's exploits rather than into Roman history as the heirs of pagan Rome. Their armies were not considered new legions of a new Caesar: they were compared with the columns of Israel leaving Egypt under the guidance of an angel who preceded the army day and night, with the army that witnessed David's victory over Goliath, or with the three hundred that fought under Gideon.[147] Like other nations in revolutionary times, like the English people under Cromwell, the

---

[145] Alföldi, "Insignien," pp. 86 ff.; Louis Bréhier et Pierre Batiffol, *Les survivances du culte impériale romain* (Paris, 1920) 50 ff.; Treitinger, *op. cit.*, pp. 49 ff., and *passim*.

[146] *Cod. Carol.*, No. 11, *MGH. Epist.*, III, 505; Rosenstock, *op. cit.*, pp. 487 f., whose suggestive discussion is followed closely here.

[147] See the *Missa in profectionem hostium contibus in prohelium* in the Sacramentary of Gellone, published by Tellenbach, p. 68 f.

Franks believed themselves to be God's chosen people destined to execute the plans of Divine Providence. Within these trends of thought, it was quite logical and consistent that the king, to whom the nation looked for guidance, appeared to them under the symbols, not of a Roman Caesar, but of a king who had almost directly descended from the Old Testament. This is the meaning of the idea of the Frankish "Regnum Davidicum." The king began to represent a type of ruler modeled upon David. He was the *novus Moyses*, the *novus David*. He was the priestly king, the *rex et sacerdos*. He was, through his consecration with holy oil, like David the Anointed of God, the *christus Domini*.[148] "Jerusalem" wandered to Gaul; the only Biblical pattern of a hallowed tribe, Israel, helped to shape the tribe that was to shape Europe. Pepin's anointment after the pattern of Israel's kings[149] is the keystone of this evolution and at the same time the cornerstone of mediaeval divine right and *Dei gratia* kingship.

But the Franks were not only the new Israel and the warriors of

[148] The *Codex Carolinus* contains countless examples; also, the metaphors chosen by the pope to address Pepin are preferably taken from the Old Testament; see, e.g., *MGH. Epist.*, III, 539, No. 33, where Pepin is styled "Joshua"; *ibid.*, p. 480, No. 3, p. 554, No. 42, p. 649, No. 98, the king is styled the "New Moses," and, p. 540, No. 33, 552, No. 39: "Novus quippe Moyse novusque David." However, the title of David is considered the highest, *ibid.*, p. 540, No. 33: "Sed in omnibus illis (Moses and Joshua) non ita complacuit eius divina maiestas, sicut in David rege et propheta testante eodem misericordissimo Deo nostro in id quod ait: 'Inveni David servum meum secundum cor meum, in oleo sancto unxi eum.' " See *ibid.*, p. 557, No. 43; p. 652, No. 99; and also Amalar of Metz, *De ecclesiasticis officiis*, in the dedication to Louis the Pious (Migne, *PL.*, CV, col. 988), who in the Byzantinizing acclamation replaces the "novus Constantinus" of Eastern hails by "novus David," "novus Salomon"; for Charlemagne, styled "novus Constantinus" by Pope Hadrian I, cf. *MGH. Epist.*, III, 587, No. 60; cf. G. Laehr, *Die Konstantinische Schenkung in der abendländischen Literatur des Mittelalters*, Historische Studien, Heft 166 (Berlin, 1926), 8 f.; cf. below, p. 74, for Charles the Bald. For these titles in Byzantium, cf. Treitinger, *op. cit.*, pp. 130 ff. For the "rex et sacerdos" idea, cf. H. Lilienfein, *Die Anschauungen von Staat und Kirche im Reich der Karolinger*, Heidelberger Abhandlungen zur mittleren und neueren Geschichte, 1 (Heidelberg, 1902), 28 ff.; F. Kern, "Der *rex et sacerdos* in bildlicher Darstellung," *Festschrift für Dietrich Schäfer* (Jena, 1915), 1 ff.; Franz Kampers, "Rex et sacerdos," *HJb.*, XLV (1925), 495 ff.; see also Schramm, *Der König von Frankreich* (Weimar, 1939), *passim*, for the later periods. The idea of priest-kingship is illustrated in a queer way in a miniature of a former Chester Beatty manuscript which was written probably in the surroundings of Charles V of France and in which Caesar's ordination as bishop and coronation as emperor is depicted; see Sotheby and Co.'s *Catalogue of the Renowned Collection of Western Manuscripts the Property of A. Chester Beatty, Esq.* (London, 1932), Pl. 26, facing p. 29 (Pl. V, *a*). The acclamation to Charlemagne at the Council of Frankfort (794), "Sit rex et sacerdos" (*MGH. Conc.*, II, 141 f.), is significant, too. It is remindful of the acclamation of the bishops at Chalcedon, in 451, when the Emperor Marcian was hailed: τῷ ἱερεῖ, τῷ βασιλεῖ, τὰς ἐκκλησίας σὺ ὥρθωσας, νικητὰ πολεμίων, διδάσκαλε πίστεως; cf. Mansi, *op. cit.*, VII, 177; Treitinger, *op. cit.*, pp. 124 f., and for similar features in Byzantine art, André Grabar, *L'Empereur dans l'art byzantin*, Publications de la faculté des lettres de l'université de Strasbourg, 75 (Paris, 1936), chap. III, and *passim.* The term "christus Domini" is applied also to the Anglo-Saxon kings in the eighth century, since they adopted the rite of anointment in 785 at the latest; cf. Schramm, *A History of the English Coronation* (Oxford, 1937), 8, 118, 258.

[149] For an early Frankish Benediction of Kings and the Old-Testament character of all formulae of anointings, cf. above, n. 145.

Jehovah. They began to look upon themselves as the exemplary Christian people without restriction or competition, as the chosen people of the New as well as of the Old Covenant. Their king was not only the "new David"; he was also the *Rex Christianissimus*,[150] for the Franks prided themselves on representing the core of the universal *populus christianus*. This tribe felt itself to be universal owing to its Christian championship—universal not like the Romans, but far above the Romans. Of this spirit there is a famous utterance, recorded in the *Lex Salica*. In the opening of the second and longer prologue written under Pepin,[151] there is found in language of unsurpassable pride:

> Gens Francorum inclita,
> Auctore Deo condita,
> fortis in arma,
> firma in pacis foedere...

The conclusion of the prologue states that the Franks, after having shaken the Roman yoke from their necks, surpassed the Romans by establishing a dominion better than theirs because it was Christian.[152] A compound of thoughts and antinomies, deeply engrained in mediaeval culture and politics, suddenly rises to the surface in this passage: the antinomy of Christian Biblical universalism and of Roman political world government, of "Jerusalem" and "Rome," of *Regnum Davidicum* and *Imperium Romanum*. These elements were contradictory and yet had to arrange themselves together. In the center of that new prologue to the old lawbook, there is the homage paid to "Chlodoveus torreus et pulcher," who by the favor of God first received the sacrament of baptism in the Catholic rite and whose praise in the preface then dissolves into the litanylike acclamation[153] to an almost Frankish Christ.

---

[150] Cf. Rosenstock, in *ZfRG.*, germ. Abt., IL (1929), 511.

[151] Georg Waitz, *Das alte Recht der Salischen Franken* (1846), 37; for the date of the second prologue, see Mario Krammer, "Zur Geschichte der Lex Salica," *Festschrift für H. Brunner* (Weimar, 1910), 455; Krusch, in *NArch.*, XL (1916), 537; Heymann, *ibid.*, XLI (1919), 434. For the liturgical reminiscences and parallels, see A. L. Mayer, in *JLW.*, VII (1927), 319, No. 386.

[152] See the interesting discussion by Elisabeth Pfeil, *Die fränkische und deutsche Romidee des frühen Mittelalters*, Forschungen zur mittelalterlichen und neueren Geschichte, 3 (Munich, 1929), 80 ff. That the Christian exploits surpassed those of the Romans is, of course, an old topic discussed broadly by Leo the Great; see, e.g., his *Sermo LXXXII*, c. 1, Migne, *PL.*, LIV, col. 423, where further places are quoted; see also *NGH. Poet.*, I, 117, stanza 15 ("neque Caesar et pagani, sed divina gratia"), and the Diptych of Rambona showing the she-wolf with Romulus and Remus overwhelmed by the *Crucifixus;* A. Goldschmidt, *Die Elfenbeinskulpturen aus der Zeit der Karolingischen und Sächsischen Kaiser*, I (1914), No. 181a; A. Haseloff, *Pre-Romanesque Sculpture in Italy* (Florence and Paris, 1930), Pl. 78, and Johannes Reil, *Christus am Kreuz in der Bildkunst der Karolingerzeit*, Studien über christliche Denkmäler, 21 (Leipzig, 1930), 72 f.

[153] The blending of acclamation and litany combined with the usage of rhymed prose is unmistakable. For other poetical acclamations of the Carolingian period, cf. below, p. 70, n. 15.

Vivat qui Francos diligit Christus,
eorum regnum custodiat,
rectores eorum lumen suae gratiae repleat,
exercitum protegat,
fidei munimenta tribuat,
pacem gaudia
et felicitatem tempora
dominancium dominus
Jesus Christus
pietate concedat.

It is difficult to believe that the litany acclamation which concerns us, the *Christus vincit, Christus regnat, Christus imperat,* could have received its last touch and definite form in surroundings other than those of the early Carolingian court.[154] The Biblical atmosphere hovering around Pepin and Charlemagne and increased by Anglo-Saxon and Irish-Celtic influences must be considered the hotbed from which the litany of the Gallo-Frankish laudes arose.

It is not unimportant to realize that these solemn acclamations to the ruler depended upon the Anglo-Irish Litany of the Saints and its adoption by the Franks, for it makes these *laudes regiae* stand out, unexpectedly, against a background which differs from that commonly accepted. This background is hardly to be called simply Roman; it is typically Carolingian; that is, a blending of Gallican and Anglo-Irish elements with Roman ingredients. The central element of the laudes, it is true, is the ancient Roman *vita*-acclaim: *Exaudi Christe! N. regi vita!* But we may ask whether the Frankish kings considered it a Caesarean hail, and may answer: not necessarily. For to their ears the *vita*-hails were probably not Roman-Imperial shouts referring to the Caesars, but they were Biblical. Saul, David, Solomon, and the other kings of Israel had been hailed in a similar manner, and the Biblical shout *Vivat Rex!* remained the acclamation valid at the Frankish, that is, non-Roman, coronations at Aachen.[155] Not the Roman, but the Biblical undertone of the hails facilitated the combination of these cheers with the penitential deprecations of the Litany of the Saints. The laudes thus seem to fall in with the tradition peculiar to the Carolingian court, a tradition which was Biblical and Anglo-Irish in the first place and which, although it was about to amalgamate with the Roman ecclesiastical currents, was Roman-Imperial only in a lesser degree.

There remains one more point to be stressed: the function of the Litany with its well-organized files of saints in the Carolingian political theology.

---

[154] The laudes in the Montpellier manuscript, for instance, refer to a member of the court, Rothrude; cf. above, n. 92.

[155] B. Simson, *Jahrbücher des Fränkischen Reiches unter Ludwig dem Frommen* (1874–1876), I, 5, 103.

We need not recall in detail the liturgical activity of Pepin and Charles, the sponsors of those great reforms in the Frankish Church which ended in the merging or equalizing of Gallo-Frankish and Roman usages,[156] in order to make it clear that in the eighth century, and in Gaul, liturgy was subjected not only to the judgment of priest and bishop; it was in the last resort the business of the king. Ecclesiastical rites as well as ecclesiastical organization became political matters above all once the substance of kingship itself became churchified. The adroitness in liturgical matters displayed by the early Carolingians, their never-relaxing interest in a subject so remote from modern statesmanship, their violence in imposing a new manner of ecclesiastical chanting on their realm, and Charlemagne's personal participation in the redaction of the *Libri Carolini* (his marginal glosses have been recently discovered, proving his careful and passionate scrutiny)[157] are all less surprising if we realize that the enforcement of the word *filioque* on the Roman Creed was a matter of royal prestige, and that the compilation of the *Libri Carolini*, dealing with the veneration of images, was an act of circumspect and refined diplomacy, or that Alcuin's "Supplement" to the Roman *Gregorianum* was a piece of statecraft.[158] Liturgy, in the Carolingian age, was like an additional "Law of the Constitution," and the "Department of Religious Affairs and Public Worship" was kept by the ruler in his own hands.[159]

It has sometimes been emphasized that Pepin, in reorganizing the Frankish Church, had cleared away the uncontrollable and suffocating influence of the innumerable Gallic and Frankish saints whose worship had covered with rank growth the Christian faith in Merovingian Gaul and that with his new measures Pepin had cut right through the jungle of sovereign saints.[160] The so-called Roman Purism, it is true, entered

---

[156] Th. Klauser, "Die liturgischen Austauschbeziehungen zwischen der römischen und der fränkisch-deutschen Kirche vom 8. bis zum 11. Jahrhundert," *HJb.*, LIII (1933), 186 ff.

[157] See Wolfram von den Steinen, "Karl der Grosse und die *Libri Carolini*," *NArch.*, IL (1930), 207–280; and "Die Entstehungsgeschichte der Libri Carolini," *QF.*, XXI (1929–1930), 1–93.

[158] An excellent survey of the political side of Charlemagne's ecclesiastical activity is found in Erich Caspar's posthumous study "Das Papsttum unter fränkischer Herrschaft," *ZKG.*, LIV (1935), 132–264; it is a fragment of the third unfinished volume of his *Geschichte des Papsttums*.

[159] Rosenstock, "Die Furt der Franken," p. 537 ("So sehr ist die Liturgie Staatsrecht"), and Bishop, "The Liturgical Reforms of Charlemagne," *Downside Review*, XXXVIII (1919), 2.

[160] See the Capitulary of 794 (§ 42); Böhmer-Mühlbacher, *op. cit.*, No. 316. It was not always observed. For instance, the litany in the Montpellier manuscript has six, instead of three, archangels, namely, Uriel, Raguel, Tobiel, in addition to Michael, Gabriel, and Raphael. These unorthodox angels, as Mabillon, *Vetera Analecta*, p. 171, indicates, had been deposed by the Roman council in 745, where they were declared demons; Hefele, *Conciliengeschichte*, III (1877), 538 f. Pope Hadrian I, in 791, stressed the fact that Uriel was unorthodox; *MGH. Epist.*, V, 26. Ansegisus († 833), in his collection of Capitulars, adduces the decisions of the councils according to which there were but three archangels known by name; *MGH Capit.*, I, 2, p. 399, n. 16.

into the realm, unifying, centralizing, supporting the aims of the new monarchy and reflecting the monarchic ideals. In the same direction, however, there worked from another side and in a different way the Insular influences as reflected in the orders of the Litany of the Saints. The concise organization of the celestial world offered by the Litany retroacted inevitably on this world, and scholars have not been heedless of the peculiar manner in which the series of saints began to make their appearance in royal charters.[161] It is well known that Dionysius the Pseudo-Areopagite paralleled the celestial hierarchies of angels with the orders of the Church, and in a later age this parallelism was extended to the ranks of the State.[162] In the eighth century, however, the influence of Pseudo-Dionysius was negligible in France;[163] and as the tendency made itself felt to arrange the ranks of the State not only with those of the Church[164] but also with those of Heaven, the Litany with its columns of Angels, Prophets, Apostles, Martyrs, Confessors, and other categories of saints proved to be a helpful expedient. Society on earth was arranged in accordance not with the angelic choirs, as was true in later centuries, but with the choirs of saints found in the Litany. The Litany thus sustained the organizing functions which were exercised, in a later age, by the Pseudo-Dionysian conceptions.

The laudes represent an early and most remarkable example of the new hierarchical-theocratic tendency. In this artfully composed chant the orders of dignitaries on earth, both secular and ecclesiastical, and the

---

However, Uriel and Raguel are invoked, together with Heremiel and Azael, in the *Antiphonary of Bangor*, ed. F. E. Warren, Bradshaw Society, X (London, 1895), II, 85, cf. 92; and Uriel was to survive for many centuries, cf. P. Perdrizet, "L'archange Ouriel," *Seminarium Kondakovianum*, II (1928), 241 ff. See also Schermann, "Griechische Litaneien," *Römische Quartalschrift*, XVII (1903), 336, and the scores of names collected by Erik Peterson, "Engel- und Dämonennamen," *Rheinisches Museum*, LXXV (1926), 394. Many a name is found also in St. Jerome's *Nomina Hebraica*, cf. Migne, *PL.*, XXIII, col. 1173. See also *DACL.*, I, 2086 f., 2156 ff. *s.v.* "Anges."

[161] Rosenstock, *op. cit.*, pp. 543 f., has collected most interesting material on this subject.

[162] For the later period, cf. B. Vallentin, "Der Engelstaat," *Grundrisse und Bausteine zur Staats- und Geschichtslehre zusammengetragen zu Ehren Gustav Schmollers* (Berlin, 1908), 40 ff.; see also Wilhelm Berges, *Die Fürstenspiegel des hohen und späten Mittelalters*, Schriften des Reichsinstituts für ältere deutsche Geschichtskunde: Monumenta Germaniae Historica, II (Leipzig, 1938), 52 ff.

[163] The first Pseudo-Dionysian works, sent by Pope Paul I to Pepin, had entered France about 760; *Cod. Carol.*, No. 24, *MGH. Epist.*, III, 529.

[164] The State-Church parallelism of ranks is, after all, one of the main topics of the *Constitutum Constantini;* see especially § 15 in the edition of C. Mirbt, *Quellen zur Geschichte des Papsttums und des römischen Katholizismus* (6th ed.; Tübingen, 1934), 111; it is likewise found in the Legend of Pope Sylvester ("ut in toto orbe romano sacerdotes ita hunc [sc. papam] caput habeant, sicut omnes iudices regem"); cf. Mombritius, *Sanctuarium* (Paris, 1910), II, 513. The first detailed and systematic discussion of this parallelism seems to have been worked out on the Continent by Walafrid Strabo, *De exordiis et incrementis rerum eccl.*, c. 32, *MGH. Capit.*, II, 515, written about 840. In England, this parallelism is found already in the dooms of Aethelberht of Kent (§ 1) of 604 or thereabouts; cf. Liebermann, *Die Gesetze der Angelsachsen* (1903–1916), I, 3.

series of celestial intercessors reflect, and merge into, each other. Intentions for the powers on earth, it is true, were often added to the Litany of the Saints; but these humble suffrages following after the long enumeration of names seemed to emphasize the chasm between the two worlds rather than their symmetry. This chasm is closed by the laudes. They display, as it were, the cosmic harmony of Heaven, Church, and State, an interweaving and twining of the one world with the other and an alliance between the powers on earth and the powers in heaven. Each terrestrial rank is associated with a group of celestial intercessors. The king as the *christus Domini* is linked to the group of angelic and superangelic intercessors, the pope to that of the apostles, the army to the martyrs, the queen—if she is acclaimed—to the choirs of virgins, and the bishop to the confessors. Human society thus reflects, and is organized after, the model of the hierarchy above. In short, the laudes are among the earliest Western political documents in which the attempt was made to establish in the secular-political, as well as in the ecclesiastical, sphere a likeness of the City of God.

The mediaeval equivalent of ancient ruler worship is the liturgical homage to the ruler. We may safely call it the "Mediaeval Ruler Cult." While full-blown in Byzantium by the fifth century, it began to take shape in the West after the anointment of Pepin, and to develop there its peculiar liturgical form. The achievements of the Carolingian Renaissance and the predilection of Charles the Bald for Byzantine thought and etiquette should not deceive us. The most significant features of early Carolingian ruler worship were hardly borrowed from the Hellenistic-Roman model. The model which was consciously followed, in the eighth century, at least, was the image of the kings of the Old Testament, anointed chieftains of a tribe like the early Carolingians. The antinomy between *Regnum Davidicum* and *Imperium Romanum* was deep-rooted. It can be traced, over and over again, in the writings of that age. Alcuin, in a famous letter, contrasted the dignity of the emperors in New-Rome with the priest-kingship of the Franks in favor, of course, of his royal master;[165] and in the *Libri Carolini*, published in 792, Charlemagne himself approved of the verdict upon the Byzantine rulers and consented to those frequently quoted passages which pour forth invectives against "the gentile and superstitious rites of the Roman Emperors" who permitted their persons as well as their images to be "adored."[166] But in spite of this antagonism, the Franks were destined to become not

---

[165] *MGH. Epist.*, IV, 288, No. 174; cf. Pfeil, *op. cit.*, pp. 97 ff., for the idea of the Franco-Christian Empire and the unwillingness of the Franks to conceive of themselves as Rome's successors; see also Heldmann, *op. cit.*, pp. 289 ff., 305. See below, n. 170.
[166] *Libri Carol.*, II, 19, *MGH. Conc.* II, Suppl., p. 77.

Israel's but Roma's successors. Only a few years after the violent sentence had been launched against the adoration of emperors and their images it happened that Charles himself, in Rome, on that memorable Christmas morning in 800, *post laudes ab apostolico more antiquorum principum adoratus est.*[167]

"Rome," in her combat with "Jerusalem," had conquered once more. By the force of circumstances, Charles was compelled to change from the Gallo-Frankish role of Biblical king to the Franco-Roman role of emperor. Even so he retained the likeness of the Savior. But ever since 800, the older and more powerful image of *Christus imperator* interfered with the Frankish conception of a Davidic priest-kingship. It seems as though Charles aimed at being "Emperor of Aachen," at making his *sedes davidica*[168] the virtual Rome of the Western world, where a "Lateran" was built and the authentic mass book for all the churches of the *orbis Francorum* was kept. It was to Aachen that the enunciation referred: "where the head of the world will be, that place shall be called Rome."[169] Aachen was to outshine Rome on the Tiber and Rome on the Bosphorus. But the idea and image of the Imperator was too thoroughly Roman and one with the Imperial City.[170] *Qui Francos diligit Christus*, though remaining a French symbol until the days of St. Louis and Joan of Arc, became one with *Christus iubar regni Romanorum.* (Cf. above, p. 22).

This change was sponsored, promoted, and effected by the Holy See. Rome, not France, was in need of an emperor; Rome created him. But Rome, and the Church in general, were also recipients. The spiritual climate of the Frankish ideal of rulership affected, in the first place, the Frankish clergy. The rite of anointing the bishop's head, though perhaps first indicated in the Sacramentary of Gellone, belongs to the age of the Pseudo-Isidorian Decretals and of Hincmar of Rheims.[171] This rite thus followed rather than preceded the ritual of the royal anointment. It implied that the bishops, by their unction, became the king's peers; that

---

[167] *Annales Regni Francorum a. 801, MGH. SS. rer. Germ.*, ed. Kurze (1895), 112.

[168] Cf. Modoinus' *Ecloga*, I, 14 f., in *MGH. Poet.*, I, 385; Pfeil, *op. cit.*, p. 146, n. 97. That the palace of Aachen was to represent the Temple of Solomon is a perhaps pleasing, but unproved surmise. "The pre-eminence of the Christian element" concerning this building has been emphasized recently, but also the fact that "the architectural prototype of the Palace has not been established"; cf. Richard Krautheimer, "The Carolingian Revival of Early Christian Architecture," *The Art Bulletin*, XXIV (1942), 34 f.

[169] Modoinus, *Ecloga*, vv. 40 f., in *MGH. Poet.*, 386. I hope to discuss the problem of "Aachen, Jerusalem, and the two Romes" in another connection. See, however, Pfeil, *op. cit.*, pp. 142 ff., and Krautheimer, *op. cit.*, pp. 30 ff., 35 ff.

[170] Unfortunately my attention was called too late to the study of E. E. Stengel, "Kaisertitel und Souveränitätsidee," *Deutsches Archiv*, III (1939), 3 ff., who brings the Anglo-Saxon antecedents of the Carolingian *Imperator* title (Bede, Alcuin, Coenwulf of Mercia) into relief.

[171] Ellard, *op. cit.*, 31, 51 ff.; cf. pp. 30 f., the highly suggestive though not fully convincing interpretation of the *Gellonense*.

they, too, and in their way, became representative of the idea of *rex et sacerdos;* and that perforce certain royal prerogatives such as the acclaim with the *Christus vincit* were passed on gradually to the bishops.

In Rome, however, another image began to rise. At the time of Pepin's anointment the most fateful and influential document of the Middle Ages was invented: the Donation of Constantine. This great forgery prepared the way toward a new stage of the mediaeval ruler cult. For more than two centuries, beginning in the eleventh, the papal mirage of *sacerdos et imperator* was to sway the world and to fascinate the Roman pontiffs.

This development of mediaeval ruler worship can here be traced only in its "vocal accompaniment," in the liturgical acclaim of the *laudes regiae*. This homage to the David-kings wandered from the Frankish palace chapel to St. Peter's. In a slightly Romanized form, this litany would greet the Franco-Roman and Germano-Roman emperor at his coronation in Rome. And it was remodeled once more to fit the Roman emperor-pontiffs when they decided really to wear the crown which allegedly had been bestowed upon Pope Sylvester by Constantine. Thus, the history of the laudes presents itself as a segment of the history of the mediaeval ruler cult.

CHAPTER III

THE FRANCO-ROMAN FORM OF LAUDES

LITURGIFIED ACCLAMATIONS TO THE RULER

THE PHRASE "Roman Simplicity and Frankish Elaborations" indicates the essence of the liturgical antagonism prevailing in Carolingian times.[1] Exuberant forms did not agree with the Roman style. It was in the surroundings of the Frankish court that the simple Roman *vita*-acclamation had been fitted together with the Litany of the Saints and with the militant cry *Christus vincit, Christus regnat, Christus imperat*. But it was in Rome that people were always conscious of the legal and constitutive character inherent in every acclamation, ecclesiastical or secular. And it was in Rome that the Frankish laudes disclosed their import as a legal act. Acclamations composed after the Frankish manner were probably new to Rome, but liturgical acclamations to the ruler in general were not.

The imperial ceremonial of pagan Rome had been gradually transformed into a divine service.[2] To this ceremonial there belonged acclamations, originally spontaneous cheers offered in assemblies and barracks, in the streets or in the circus, cheers whose incessant iterations may have put the crowd into a frenzy and which first had been organized by Nero and his troupe of hired applauders.[3] What had been proffered voluntarily in earlier days, was continued as a duty. To the extent that the public appearance and the forms of representation of the Caesars became stylized the acclamations crystallized. Certain forms of expressing approval or disagreement, joy and thanks, demands and complaints became customary and traditional until, in the later Roman and Byzantine ceremonial, the manner of uttering sentiments in the emperor's presence was subjected to rigid prescriptions. Improvised shouts were not lacking, but they were grouped around a skeleton of standard phrases and formulae which were heard time and again. The formalizing of the acclaims was

---

[1] Ellard, *op. cit.*, p. 14; E. Bishop, "The Liturgical Reforms of Charlemagne," *Downside Review*, XXXVIII (1919), 1–16.

[2] The fundamental studies are Alföldi, "Die Ausgestaltung des monarchischen Zeremoniells am römischen Kaiserhof," and "Insignien und Trachten der römischen Kaiser," *Mitteilungen des Deutschen Archäologischen Instituts, Römische Abteilung,* IL (1934), 1–118 (see, especially for the acclamations, pp. 79–89), and *ibid.*, L (1935) 1–171. See also Richard Delbrück, "Der spätantike Kaiserornat," *Die Antike,* VIII (1932), 1–21, and the important study of Johannes A. Straub, *Vom Herrscherideal in der Spätantike,* Forschungen zur Kirchen- und Geistesgeschichte, XVIII (Stuttgart, 1939), who deals abundantly with acclamations as a constitutive factor; Peterson, *Untersuchungen,* pp. 141 f.

[3] Suetonius, *Nero,* 20. 3; Dio Cassius, LXI, 20, 4–5, and the other places adduced by Alföldi, "Zeremoniell," pp. 79 ff.; Gagé, "Σταυρὸς νικοποιός," *Revue d'histoire et de philosophie religieuses,* XIII (1933), 378.

promoted when the specifically Christian terminology began to bear upon and to remold the imperial style. No matter how much the liturgical language had originally borrowed from that of the court, the language of the court ceremonial stiffened as the terms became filled with ecclesiastical spirit and echoed the language of the liturgy. The formula of dismissing the court dignitaries, *Ite missa est*, became all the more solemn as it now matched the words of the dismissal in church, and a change such as that of the invocation *Exaudi Caesar!* to *Exaudi Christe!* is likewise indicative of the shift from a "Here and Now" to a transcendency beyond time and motion. The introduction of a timeless element and of the ideal of the motionless could not fail to retroact on the emperor's appearance and personal attitude. "Being saluted as Augustus with favoring hails, while hills and shores thundered out the roar, he [Constantius II, in 357] showed himself as motionless [in Rome] as he was commonly seen in the provinces . . . As if his neck were in a vise, he kept the gaze of his eyes straight ahead, and turned his face neither to right nor to left, and like a human statue he did not even nod when jolted by the wheels of his chariot."[4]

Such was the ideal; and we gather that the cries of *Exaudi!* reached the emperor as little or as much as the godhead beyond. It is the remoteness and timelessness which the imperial ceremonial had in common with the liturgy of the Church and which made the imperial acclamations almost *ipso facto* "liturgical."

To hail the emperor was, on the other hand, a priestly function also in pre-Christian Rome. The Arvalian Brotherhood, in imperial times, was always connected closely with the worship of the emperor and the imperial family. The emperor's birthday, his day of accession, his triumphal return from a victorious campaign, the victory fought by one of his generals, and also the more intimate events within the imperial house, all these were occasions on which the *fratres Arvales* would meet and commemorate the name of the emperor by singing their archaic songs, acclamations, and felicitations.[5] These acclaiming songs had their set place after a liturgical banquet granted to the brothers at least once a year by the emperor, and for their acclamatory performance the *Arvales* received a gratuity, the *sportula*, which it has been said corresponded to the small

---

[4] For Byzantium, see Treitinger, *op. cit.*, pp. 71 ff., and *passim;* for the formula of dismissal, see Bréhier-Batiffol, *Les survivances du culte impérial romain* (1920), 51; for the "Exaudi Caesar" invocation, cf. above, p. 17; Constantius' entry: Ammianus Marc., XVI. 10, 9–10; Straub, *op. cit.*, p. 182; R. Laqueur, "Das Kaisertum und die Gesellschaft des Reiches," in R. Laqueur, H. Koch, W. Weber, *Probleme der Spätantike* (Stuttgart, 1930), 33 ff. See Pl. VI, *c*.

[5] Guilelmus Henzen, *Acta fratrum Arvalium quae supersunt* (Berlin, 1874); Wissowa, "*Arvales fratres,*" *RE.*, I, 1, pp. 1484 ff.; Peterson, *Untersuchungen*, pp. 143, 167; Alföldi, "Zeremoniell," p. 86; for the acclamations, see also Gaetano Marini, *Atti e monumenti degli Arvali* (Rome, 1795), II, 581 f.

amount of money, the *presbyterium*, obtained by the singers of the Christian *laudes regiae* in later days.[6]

It is always difficult to tell whether the ceremonies and feasts of the Church are survivals of the pagan past or analogies produced by other formative elements. There is no doubt that the rituals of the Arvalian Brothers were well known to Christians: for instance, Tertullian's polemics against the Roman celebrations of the emperor's birthday and similar festivals condemn and ridicule the performances of the *fratres Arvales*.[7] The Arvalian College was dissolved as late as 382 by the Emperor Gratian, and other pagan sacerdotal organizations, at least in the provinces, even survived the fourth century.[8] A continuity of certain rites should therefore not be ruled out completely. But even though the tradition may have been broken, it was resuscitated in a new form. That the Arvalian Brotherhood should always consist of twelve priests was an observance remindful of the important role which the apostolic figure played not only in liturgical usages and in monastic life, but also in the cult of the Christian emperors ever since Constantine had been buried as the "Thirteenth" among the twelve apostles.[9] Again, in late Carolingian times, Charles the Simple founded a college of twelve canons in Attigny (918) whose function was to commemorate the anniversary of his anointment and some other important events in his life.[10] This custom, it seems, was newly inaugurated by Charles the Bald, and at least the hypothesis may be advanced that later Roman anniversary lists such as that of the *Natales Caesarum* in the *Calendar of 354*, which was copied in Carolingian times, influenced this emperor and truest representative of what is called the Carolingian Renaissance.[11] However this may be, Charles the Bald,

---

[6] Henzen, *op. cit.*, pp. 16, 45 f.; Metzmacher, "De sacris fratrum Arvalium cum ecclesiae christianae caeremoniis comparandis," *JLW.*, IV (1924), 36.

[7] Tertullian, *Apolog.*, 35, 7, *CSEL.*, LXIX, 85. Tertullian even quotes the text of an Arvalian hexameter acclamation: "De nostris annis addat tibi Iupiter annos!" Cf. Henzen, *op. cit.*, p. 46 ("augeat" for "addat"); Peterson, *Untersuchungen*, p. 182.

[8] Henzen, *op. cit.*, p. xxv; Batiffol, *Les Survivances*, p. 15; E. Kornemann, "Zur Geschichte der antiken Herrscherkulte," *Klio*, I (1902), 140 ff.

[9] Henzen, *op. cit.*, p. iii 3. Cf. Otto Weinreich, *Triskaidekadische Studien*, Religionsgeschichtliche Versuche und Vorarbeiten, XVI, 1 (Giessen, 1916), 3 ff., and "Lykische Zwölfgötterreliefs," *Sitzungsberichte Heidelberg*, 1913, Abh. 5, pp. 26 ff., for Constantine and the Twelve Gods; see also R. Delbrück, *Antike Porphyrwerke* (Berlin and Leipzig, 1932), xxi, 26, 118, and the golden diadem from Laodicea published recently by Franz Altheim, *Die Soldatenkaiser* (Frankfort, 1939), fig. 67, and pp. 281 ff. For the Maundy celebrations in Byzantium, cf. Treitinger, *op. cit.*, pp. 126 f.; see also Thietmar, *Chronicon*, VIII, c. 1, ed. Kurze, p. 193, for the coronation of Henry II and his suite of twelve Roman senators who "mistice incedebant cum baculis"; cf. Schramm, "Krönung in Deutschland," pp. 236 f. It would be easy to add many more items.

[10] Bouquet, *RHF.*, IX, 537 f., No. 71; see also the diploma of Charles the Fat (July 30, 883), *MGH. Dipl. Karol.*, II, 142 f., No. 88.

[11] See my forthcoming study on "Charles the Bald and the *Natales Caesarum*."

Charles the Fat, Louis the Stammerer, Charles the Simple, all ordered the monks of various monasteries to celebrate the ruler's birthday, the day of his sacring, his wedding day and the empress' or queen's birthday; and in return for their commemorative songs and prayers the monks, like the Arvalians, were granted an annual banquet.[12] Thus there reappeared, in a modified manner, the usages of the *fratres Arvales* in whose ritual the liturgical acclamation was the outstanding feature.

Moreover, the acclamations became at least semiliturgical when the ancient custom of the Roman Senate of acclaiming the emperor was passed on to the synods which represented, as it were, the Senate of the Christian Church.[13] Whenever the bishops present at a council had come to a final decision, especially at the end of the whole meeting, which frequently was presided over by the emperor himself, the moment arrived for voicing the cheers to the monarch. The text of the Byzantine conciliar acclamations, of which scores have been preserved,[14] was not so definite as that of the Western laudes nor had these acclamations the form of a Litany of Saints. They centered in the customary *multos annos* wishes and retained, on the whole, the form of the ancient senatorial acclaims,

[12] Henzen, *op. cit.*, pp. 51 ff., 63 ff., 71 ff., 77 ff., and Bouquet, *RHF.*, VIII, 577 ff., No. 176, the charter of Charles the Bald for St.-Denis: ". . . ob refectiones annuales fratribus praeparandas . . . videlicet ut (1) in idibus Junii, quando Deus nos nasci in mundo voluit, et (2) octavo idus Junias, quando Sanctus Sanctorum nos ungi in regem sua dignitate disposuit, sed et (3) octavo decimo kal. Febr., quando me Rex Regum, fugatis atque contritis ante faciem divinae potentiae nobiscum agentibus, in regnum restituit, quae commemoratio post obitum nostrum in depositionis diem . . . convertatur, necnon et (4) in idibus Decembris, quando Deus me dilectam conjugem Hirmentrudem uxoreo vinculo copulavit, verum et (5) quinto kal. Octobris, quando ipsa dilectissima nobis conjux nata fuit . . ., ipsae refectiones fratribus in nostram memoriam . . . praeparantur." For the connections with usages of the Graeco-Roman antique, see Wilhelm Schmidt, *Geburtstag im Altertum*, Religionsgeschichtliche Versuche und Vorarbeiten, VII (1909); Bernhard Laum, *Stiftungen in der griechischen und römischen Antike* (Berlin, 1914), I, 75 ff.; and above, n. 11.

[13] The relationship between senatorial and conciliar acclamations has been stressed already by Casaubonus in his edition of the *Historia Augusta*, Avid. Cass., c. 13; cf. Marini, *op. cit.*, II, 581 f.; furthermore H. Gelzer, "Die Konzilien als Reichsparlamente," in his *Ausgewählte kleine Schriften* (1907), 142 ff., and Pierre Batiffol, "Origines de règlement des conciles," in his *Études de liturgie et d'archéologie chrétienne* (1919) 84–153. For the conciliar acclamations in general, see Peterson, *Untersuchungen*, pp. 146 ff.; Heldmann, *op. cit.*, p. 281; Biehl, *op. cit.*, p. 130; *DACL.*, I, 244, *s.v.* "Acclamations"; Treitinger, *op. cit.*, p. 220, n. 50. Their function is well illustrated by P. Batiffol, "Une épisode du Concile d'Éphèse," *Mélanges G. Schlumberger* (Paris, 1924), 28–39, and their importance is emphasized by Leo the Great (*Ep.* LIX, Migne, *PL.*, LIV, col. 867A), for he writes ". . . de vestrae tamen devotionis pietate gaudemus, et in sanctae plebis acclamationibus, *quarum ad nos exempla delata sunt*, omnium vestrum probavimus affectum."

[14] See, e.g., Mansi, *op. cit.*, VI, 935, 975 (Chalcedon, 451); VII, 94 f. (Chalcedon, 451); VIII, 969 f., 1063 f. (Constantinople, 536); XI, 346 (Constantinople, 680); XI 935 (Trullian Synod, 692); XII, 1153 (Nicaea, 787); XVI, 417 (Constantinople, 867); XVII, 393 (Constantinople, 879); and also *Avellana*, No. 103, §§ 13 and 30, ed. Günther (1895), *CSEL.*, XXXV, 478, 487 (Rome, 495); *Acta Synhodi, MGH. AA. ant.*, XII, 402 ff. (Rome, 499). See also Grabar, *L'empereur dans l'art byzantin* (Paris, 1936), 90 ff., for artistic representations of the emperor presiding over the councils.

Multos annos imperatoribus!
Basilio, Leoni et Alexandro, magnis
    regibus et imperatoribus,   multos annos!
Eudocie, piissime Auguste,   multos annos!
Stephano Porphyrogenito et a Deo
    donato syncello,   multos annos!
Johanni et Photio, sanctissimis
    patriarchis,   multos annos![15]

The observance of proffering conciliar laudes was also introduced to the
Frankish Empire once its rulers had become masters of the Frankish

---

[15] Mansi, *op. cit.*, XVII, 393, 511. The acclaims to the "Orthodox emperors" or to
the "New Constantine" in connection with the *multos annos* wishes are found time
and again. The tradition of putting *multos annos* as a legend on coins survived in
Byzantium; cf. Goodacre, *op. cit.*, pp. 16, 115 f., 134 ff., 140 ff., 200. For "Novus
Constantinus" as a title, see Treitinger, *op. cit.*, p. 131, n. 4. It could be applied also
to two emperors at the same time; see, e.g., Henri Grégoire, *Recueil des inscriptions
grecques chrétiennes d'Asie Mineure*, Fasc. I (Paris, 1922), 21 f., Nos. 79 and 80, for the
inscription Κωνσταντίνων τῶν νέων Ἡρακλήου καὶ Ἡρακλήου . . . πολλὰ τὰ [ἔτη], and Grégoire's discussion of this title (*ibid.*, p. 22).

The Byzantine type of acclamations is altogether rare in the West; see, however,
Liber pont., II, 177, the acclamation to Hadrian II in 868. Remindful of the Byzantine
form, even of the rhythm of the responses πολλὰ τὰ ἔτη, though western in the litanizing
tone, is, e.g., the deprecatory prayer in the dedication of Amalar's *De ecclesiasticis
officiis*, in Migne, *PL.* CV, col. 988:

"Divo Hludovico   vita.
Novo David   perennitas.
Da principi,   Domine, vitam.
Ipsi novo Salomoni   felicitas.
Pax mundi   vos estis.
Pio principi   prosperitas.
Domine, vitam   ei concede.
Vestra fides   vos servet.
Christus, quem vos honoratis,   ipse vos servet.
Potestatem vestram   Deus conservet.
Deus pacificet   regnum vestrum.
Judith, orthodoxe, nobilissime atque
    prudentissime Auguste, salus   per multos annos.
Lumina pacis,   Domine, serva.
Lumina mundi,   Domine, serva.
Vita vestra,   tutela omnium est.
Vestra fides   Ecclesiarum est gloria.
Piissimos dominos nostros imperiales natos,
    Hlotarium gloriosissimum coronatum et
    fratres eius   Christus conservet.
Ex proavis orthodoxos,   Domine, serva.
Custodes fidei,   Domine, serva."

The mixture of acclamations and deprecatory invocations as well as the general litany
character of this dedication is evident. But there is also some similarity with Byzantine acclamations which Amalar may have heard often enough when studying the
Byzantine ritual in Santa Sophia (cf. Migne, *PL.*, CV, cols. 1275 f.). Hails such as
"novo Constantino, novae Helenae" are replaced, in agreement with Frankish style
by "novo David, novo Salomoni," although the latter acclamations are found also in
Byzantium (Treitinger, *op. cit.*, p. 130, n. 2) and the former in the West (Prost,
Quatre pièces, p. 209; Laehr, *op. cit.*, p. 7). The acclamation, even in letters and other
writings, has always a confirmative and corroborative character; see, e.g., the emperor's acclamation to the pope at the end of the *Constitutum Constantini* (Mirbt,
Quellen, p. 112): "Divinitas vos conservet per multos annos, sanctissimi et beatissimi
patres"; or the acclamatory address in the writing of the Synod of Pavia (876) to

synods and, by implication, of those of the Western Church.[16] Possibly from the days of Pepin and St. Boniface, certainly from those of Charlemagne onward, the Frankish sacramentaries contained a *Missa in tempore synodi pro rege dicenda*.[17] The laudes, of course, are not mentioned in connection with this conciliar Mass. But the thanksgiving prayers of the bishops offered to Charlemagne after the Council of Frankfort (794) have the character of acclamations:[18]

> Sit dominus et pater,
> sit rex et sacerdos,
> sit omnium Christianorum moderantissimus gubernator . . .

Further, we have at our disposal the reliable description of the ceremonies observed at the Council of Ponthion in 876. The Emperor Charles the Bald, so we are told, arrived "graecisco more paratus et coronatus"; thereafter, the Empress Richildis was escorted to the assembly, and while she stood at the Emperor's side, all those present arose from their seats. At this moment, two papal legates began to sing the imperial litany and "post laudes peractas in domnum apostolicum et domnum imperatorem ac imperatricem ac ceteros iuxta morem" the synod dissolved.[19] As in Byzantium, the acclamations were sung at the end of the meeting, an ecclesiastico-legal act which implied the recognition of the emperor on the part of the Frankish Church.[20] The text of these hails was evidently that of the customary Gallo-Frankish laudes. This is suggested by the enumeration of the *acclamati*, pope, emperor, empress, "and the others

---

Charles the Bald: "Gloriosissimo et a Deo coronato magno et pacifico imperatori, domni nostro Karolo perpetuam augusto prosperitatem et pacem"; *MGH. Capit.*, II, 99, No. 220; and also Hincmar's acclaim to Louis the Stammerer in his *Mirror of Princes* (Migne, *PL.*, CXXV, col. 983): "Domino Ludovico/regi glorioso sit semper salus et vita!" Cf. Schramm, *Der König von Frankreich*, I, 38; II, 25, n. 5. Acclamations are found very often in Carolingian poetry; for a specimen see, e.g., Alcuin's poem to Charlemagne, *MGH. Poet.*, 1, 257, No. 45:
> "Ut vivat, regnet multis feliciter annis
> Ad laudem populi David in orbe pius."

[16] Charles summoned the councils "more priscorum imperatorum" even when he was a king, *MGH. Conc.*, II, 254. For the "universalism" of the Council of Frankfort, see Rosenstock, *op. cit.*, pp. 491 ff., 526 ff.; and Hans Barion, "Der kirchenrechtliche Charakter des Konzils von Frankfurt 794," *ZfRG*, kan. Abt. XIX (1930), 139 ff., as well as his study *Das fränkisch-deutsche Synodalrecht des Frühmittelalters*, Kanonistische Studien und Texte, V–VI (1931), 216 ff., and *passim*.

[17] It is first found in Alcuin's *Supplementum* to the *Gregorianum*; cf. Muratori, *Liturg.*, II, 189; cf. Biehl, *op. cit.*, pp. 129 f., *The Gregorian Sacramentary under Charles the Great*, ed. H. A. Wilson, Bradshaw Society, XLIX (1915), 315; cf. Leroquais, *Sacramentaires*, I, 26, 88; see also Rosenstock, *op. cit.*, p. 537, n. 2.

[18] *MGH. Conc.*, II, 141 f. The parallel with Byzantine conciliar acclamations is striking, see, e.g., the acclamation at Chalcedon in 451 (Mansi, *op. cit.*, VII, 177), and above, p. 57, n. 148; cf. Treitinger, *op. cit.*, p. 124, n. 2. The styling of Charlemagne as Master of all Christians is a standard phrase; see, e.g., Alcuin's famous letter of 799, in *MGH. Epist.*, IV, 288, No. 174.

[19] *Annales Bertiniani*, in *MGH. SS. rer. Germ.*, ed. Waitz (1883), 131.

[20] Schramm, *op. cit.*, I, 41.

according to custom." Also we know that Arnulf of Carinthia was acclaimed by the Synod of Tribur (895) after the well-known fashion of the laudes: "Exaudi Christe! Arnulpho regi vita!"[21]

The conciliar acclamations rendered to the emperor were certainly ecclesiastical in nature, and gradually almost every official appearance of the monarch, in the East as well as in the West, became "liturgicized" in one way or other. It was an Oriental and Hellenistic-Roman custom to receive the ruler in a most solemn way, whenever he visited a city or entered his capital. This ceremonial entrance, which turned into an *entrée joyeuse* in the Later Middle Ages (in many details it has survived until modern times) and which was called the emperor's *adventus* in earlier centuries, had a definitely religious character.[22] In Later Rome the punctilio of these receptions had developed along the usual lines. On the one hand, the emperor's *felix adventus* was transcendentalized by means of the pagan cults; on the other, the Church adopted the imperial ceremonial and accommodated it to its own needs, until finally the ecclesiastical ceremonial reacted upon that of the Christian emperors.

This mutual borrowing began in an early age. St. Paul already applies the technical term of the imperial reception, ἀπάντησις, to the eschatological return of Christ.[23] In later times, a most elaborate image of a transcendental reception is found in the *Ordo commendationis animae*, which belongs to the Office of the Dying.[24] The resplendent host of angels, the senate of the apostles, the army of martyrs and confessors, the choirs of virgins and the patriarchs, all join, it is hoped, to meet the soul which is guided by St. Michael, the Christian Psychopompos and commander of the *militia coelestis*. The officiating priest prayed for the soul that it might enjoy the angelic reception at the gates of the celestial city: "Obvient tibi sancti angeli Dei, et perducant te in civitatem sanctam Jerusalem." Death, in this prayer and not only in it, means the arrival at man's destination, the *entrée joyeuse* of the soul into the celestial Jerusalem. And vice versa, every city on earth preparing itself for the liturgical reception of one anointed, becomes a "Jerusalem" and the comer a likeness of Christ. Indeed, every liturgical celebration of the *adventus* of a

---

[21] *MGH. Capit.*, II, 213, No. 252. A formulary of laudes for Arnulph as well as a Litany of Saints with acclamatory conclusion containing his name have been published by Lehmann, "Corveyer Studien," pp. 71 f. See below, n. 45.

[22] The fundamental study on the *adventus* in Christian times is Erik Peterson, "Die Einholung des Kyrios," *Zeitschrift für systematische Theologie*, VII (1930), 682 ff. See also Alföldi, "Zeremoniell," pp. 88 ff., 92 f.; Straub, *op. cit.*, pp. 182 ff.; Kruse, *op. cit.*, p. 39; Grabar, *op. cit.*, pp. 46, 130, 234 ff.; C. Erdmann, "Kaiserliche und päpstliche Fahnen im hohen Mittelalter," *QF.*, XXV (1933–1934), 11 ff.; Treitinger, *op. cit.*, p. 232.

[23] Peterson, "Die Einholung des Kyrios," pp. 682 ff.

[24] Migne, *PL.*, CLI, cols. 925 f.; Gougaud, "Étude sur les Ordines commendationis animae," *Eph. Lit.*, XLIX (1935), 12; see also A. D. Nock, in *Harvard Theological Review*, XXXIV (1941), 103 ff.

monarch reflects, or even stages, the Christian archetype of the performance: that is, the Lord's entry into Jerusalem, which was depicted
time and again after the model of an imperial *adventus*. Thus, while
imagery displayed the Lord's entrance into the Holy City as an imperial
reception, the emperor on his arrival was received like the Redeemer
whom he represented. Besides, the singing of antiphones to the ruler such
as "Blessed is he that cometh in the name of the Lord" and the waving of
olive branches and palm leaves on the part of the people, customary long
before Christian times, would always suggest the image of the Lord's
triumphal entry into Jerusalem on Palm Sunday.[25]

All this remained traditional with the Byzantine emperors and was
adopted by the Germanic kings.[26] Eventually, the ruler's *adventus* was
ritualized by the Church, for obvious reasons. The cities visited by a king
would usually be episcopal sees. The clergy naturally attended the ruler's
reception so that the ceremony was brought, almost automatically, into
line with the Church. Moreover, the character of the reception was
inevitably ecclesiastical whenever the king arrived to stay at a monastery. The need, therefore, arose to organize and codify officially the details of the solemn receptions. Since the eleventh century, at the latest,
the Church rituals contain veritable *Ordines ad regem ducendum*, and the
liturgical reception became finally a prerogative of those anointed, bishop
and king.[27]

---

[25] The Palm Sunday procession is first recorded in Jerusalem in the *Peregrinatio
Etheriae*, cf. Duchesne, *Christian Worship*, 505; it was introduced into the Roman
rite probably via Gaul. The famous hymn of Theodulf of Orléans ("Gloria, laus
et honor tibi sit, Rex Christe redemptor," *MGH. Poet.*, I, 558, No. 69) is in fact an
acclamation to Christ on his royal entry into Jerusalem on Palm Sunday; cf. Michels,
"Die Akklamation in der Taufliturgie," *JLW.*, VII (1928), 79, n. 7. Most interesting
in this connection are Charlemagne's alleged entry into Jerusalem on a white mule
(cf. Erdmann, *Kreuzzugsgedanke*, p 277, n. 114) and the Palm Sunday customs observed by the Russian emperors; cf. G. Ostrogorsky, "Zum Stratordienst des Herrschers in der byzantinisch-slavischen Welt," *Seminarium Kondakovianum*, VII (1935),
193 ff. The *adventus* had a Messianic ring, even in pre-Christian times; cf. Nock,
"Σύνναος θεός," pp. 19 f.; Alföldi, "Zeremoniell," pp. 88 ff.; Peterson, "Die Einholung
des Kyrios," pp. 682 ff.; Maskell, *Monum. Rit.*, II, pp. cliv ff. The most impressive
literary documents of the messianic *adventus* are produced by the chancery of Frederick II, cf. Kantorowicz, *Kaiser Friedrich der Zweite*, I, 467; II, 202. A solemn reception was customarily offered to the imperial images; cf. Gregory I, *Reg.*, XIII, *Ep.* 1,
MGH. Epist., II, 365; Kruse, *op. cit.*, pp. 34 ff.; Heldmann, *op. cit.*, pp. 274, n. 1, 191
n. 1; and the *Libri Carolini*, in *MGH. Conc.*, II, Suppl., 133: ". . . imperiales effigies et
imagines emissas in civitates et provincias obviabunt populi cereis et thymiatibus,
non cera perfusam tabulam honorantes, sed imperatorem."
[26] For Byzantium, see Treitinger, *op. cit.*, p. 232, and for Merovingian France,
Gregory of Tours, *Hist. Franc.*, VI, c. 11; VIII, c. 1.
[27] Cf. Bruno Albers, *Consuetudines monasticae*, Vol. I: *Consuetudines Farfenses*
(1900), 170; Maskell, *Mon. Rit.*, II, 322 ff.; Biehl, *op. cit.*, pp. 166 ff., who publishes
several formularies; an additional one, in the Roman Angelica MS B.3.18, fol. 181,
of the eleventh century, is mentioned by D. B. Capelle, *Rev. bénéd.*, XLVI (1939), 135;
for the Pontifical of Durandus, cf. Peterson, "Die Einholung des Kyrios," p. 693,
n. 2, and in general, Leroquais, *Pontificaux, passim*. None of these *Ordines* seems to
antedate the eleventh century. That the liturgical reception was reserved for those

On these occasions the singing of *laudes hymnidicae* was rarely omitted. Hymns are, in many respects, transcendentalized acclamations. They here take the place of the former spontaneous hails of the crowds or of the children who always played, and still play, an important role at all solemn receptions. These chants, however, must not be confused with the laudes litany. They were metrical sequences, usually composed for a single occasion only, so that the monks of St. Gall could boast of having received King Conrad I "novis laudibus dictatis."[28] Of these poetical or metrical reception laudes quite a few are preserved,[29] and we may inspect one of them more closely to make it clear in what way they differ from and agree with the laudes of the Mass.

An interesting specimen is found in a manuscript of Metz which may belong to the ninth century. The song refers to an Emperor Charles, probably to Charles the Bald.[30] It begins with an acclamation:

Ave sacer et alme,	Imperator Carole
[Ave sacer et alme,	Imperator] excelse.
Deus rex coeli	Te conservet.

anointed is inferred by a decree of Honorius III, in 1221: ". . . ne cui principi, nisi sacro oleo inunctus esset, religioso instructo agmine honoris gratia obviam iretur." Cf. Potthast, *Regesta Pontificum*, No. 6584, a decree to which Biehl, *op. cit.*, p. 146, calls attention. The relationship between oil anointings and ἀπάντησις deserves a special study; cf. above, n. 24.

[28] *Casus Sangall., MGH. SS.*, II, 84 (911 A.D.); see *ibid.*, pp. 74, 146, for the receptions of Charles II and Otto I. A great number of these metrical laudes are preserved in the St. Gall. MS 381, cf. *MGH. Poet.*, IV, 323, No. XVIII ("Versus ad regem suscipiendum"), 324, Nos. X–XI; 327 ff., Nos. XVI–XVIII; see also Dümmler, "St. Gallische Denkmale aus der karolingischen Zeit," *Mitteilungen der antiquarischen Gesellschaft in Zurich*, XII (1858–1860), 216 ff., 254 ff. Theodulf wrote an *adventus* poem in Sapphic stanzas for the reception of Louis the Pious in Orléans, cf. *MGH. Poet.*, I, 529, No. 37; the eighth stanza shows that it was supposed to be sung:

"Hoc chorus cleri populique turba
safficum carmen recinens precetur,
det Hludovico ut deus imperandi
tempora longa."

Others, for Louis the German and Charles the Bald as well as for Lothar, were written by Sedulius Scottus, cf. *MGH. Poet.*, III, 183, No. XV, and 217, No. 60; the fifth stanza of the latter clearly displays the messianic background:

"Rex tuus mitis, sapiens, honorus,
Pacifer ductor Salemonis instar
Nunc venit Caesar, tuus, alma, princeps,
Filia Sion."

[29] There are also *adventus* songs for bishops; cf. *MGH. Poet.*, III, 185, n. XVIII, and 220, no. 66, both by Sedulius for Bishop Franco of Liège; see also Prost, *Quatre pièces*, pp. 212 f., for the bishop of Metz, a song which shows a faint similarity to the *laudes pueriles* of the Roman *schola cantorum;* cf. *Liber cens.*, Introd., pp. 112 f., and II, 173; *DACL.*, VIII, 1914 f.

[30] It is published by Prost, *Quatre pièces*, pp. 209 f., from the Metz MS 351. Prost, *ibid.*, pp. 214 ff., believes that the chant refers to Charlemagne. But the formulary of Greek laudes, which follows immediately after the *adventus* songs, has acclamations to Pope John VIII and to Charles the Bald's son Louis the Stammerer. Furthermore, the intellectual atmosphere of the Byzantinizing song and of the Greek laudes is reminiscent of the second Charles rather than of the circle of Charlemagne. Also, the expression *progenies sancta* is used with reference to Charles the Bald by Hincmar

There follow good wishes for the emperor's progeny; then come those for his happy and successful government of the world:

Colla gentium	Tibi sternantur,
Regna mundi	Tibi subdantur,
Ut in perpetuum	Regnes per aevum.
Exulta Polus,	Laetare Tellus,
Constantinus novus	Effulsit in mundum,
Carolus praeclarus	Progenie sancta,
Quem Deus elegit	Regere gentes.

We easily recognize the image of the Kosmokrator: the kingdoms of the world shall obey him; Heaven and Earth shall rejoice; a new Constantine shall radiate in the universe, a most brilliant Charles of saintly birth, whom God elected to rule the nations.[31] In harmony and unison with the celestial vault, the individual city of Metz now jubilates at the *adventus* of the ruler of Messianic promises, of the *Rex Pacificus:*

Gaude civitas,	Laetare Polus
Exulta Mettis	De adventu regis.
Rex pacificus	Advenit tibi,
Laetitia ferens	Gaudiumque per aevum.

Then comes the joy of those who went to meet and escort him:

Laetantur omnes	Occurrentes ei.
Ingredere,	Benedice, benedice, benedice.

Before the chant proper concludes with a prayer to St. Stephen, patron of the Cathedral of Metz, that he may intercede for Charles, we find the

of Rheims (see below, n. 31) as well as by Walafrid Strabo (*MGH. Poet.*, II, 406) in an *adventus* chant for Charles; cf. A. M. Friend, "Two Manuscripts of the School of St. Denis," *Speculum*, I (1926), 67 f. The itinerary of Charles the Bald is not decisive; besides, in October of 876 the emperor was at the gates of Metz, where he wanted to meet the bishops of Lotharingia; cf. Dümmler, *Ostfränkisches Reich*, III, 33. The imperial title of Charles the Bald finds an explanation through the *Annales Fuldenses ad a. 869*, *MGH. SS. rer. Germ.* (ed. Kurze), p. 70: "Se imperatorem et augustum . . . appellare precepit." See also E. E. Stengel, "Kaisertitel und Souveränitätsidee," *Deutsches Archiv*, III (1939), 6 f., 11, 14 f., and below, n. 31.

[31] For the titles of honor, such as "novus Constantinus, novus Salomon," cf. above, n. 15; Charles the Bald is occasionally compared also with Theodosius, cf. the inscription of the Psalter-image (Paris, Bibl. Nat. Lat. MS 1152), published in *MGH. Poet.*, III, 243. "Tellus" and "Polus" are continuously referred to in the Carolingian poetry in connection with either the ruler or Christ; for the latter, see, e.g., John the Scot, *MGH. Poet.*, III, 544, line 77; in miniatures of that period, "Tellus" at least is represented over and over again; cf. Schramm, "Herrscherbild," p. 195, n. 172. The acclamations "Deus conservet" and "quem Deus elegit" are in fact episcopal acclamations; cf. below, p. 117. The *progenies sancta* mentioned in the poem refers to St. Arnulph, the patron of the Arnulfingians (Carolingians), who was closely related to Metz through the famous abbey of St.-Arnould, a coincidence alluded to by Hincmar in his address to Charles the Bald at the latter's coronation in Metz, in 869; cf. Migne, *PL.*, CXXXVIII, col. 740, where also the plurality of Charles' kingdoms ("singularum regnorum diademata") is stressed; cf. Stengel, *op. cit.*, p. 11, for the implications with regard to the "hegemonial" *imperator* title.

usual interlacing of eternal and present rulership which was indispensable to the acclamations of the times:

Ave digne	Imperator benigne,
Sanctae crucis	Triumphator
Te exaltet,	Imperator...
Regnum coeli	Post hoc regnum
Ut capesces	In aeternum.

This is the end of the chant; but there follow, as a conclusion, those shouts which are found similarly in the Gallo-Frankish laudes and elsewhere:

Feliciter, Feliciter, Feliciter!

Tempora bona habeas,	Tempora bona habeas,
Tempora bona habeas,	Tempora bona habeas.
In aeternum.	Amen.

Such were the *laudes hymnidicae* chanted at liturgical receptions, when the emperor was aspersed with holy water, when the thurifers brandished their censers and the crossbearers drew up at the head of the procession to conduct the emperor into the city.[32]

A most impressive liturgical ceremonial was of course staged in Rome at the reception of the Frankish or German king who came to receive the imperial diadem, or for other reasons. The earliest report about a Roman reception of a mediaeval ruler falls in the year 774 when Charlemagne first visited Rome. He was received with the honors due to the exarch, the viceroy of the Byzantine emperor. The various Roman corporations, the *scholae*, went to meet him before the city, carrying palm leaves and olive branches in their hands and singing laudes to him.[33] His entrance into the city had a decidedly messianic note, and the antiphon which was customary on this occasion, at least in later times, the *Ecce mitto angelum meum*, may have greeted Charlemagne also. This verse of Malachi, which

---

[32] See, for instance, the arrangements prescribed in the *Ordo Farfensis*, above, n. 27.

[33] *Liber pont.*, I, 496 f., II, 88 f., 300 f., 340 f., and *passim*. Charlemagne was not received *in lieu* of the Byzantine emperor but of the Byzantine exarch; for at the reception of an emperor the pope himself proceeded to the sixth milestone to meet the ruler, whereas Charlemagne was expected by the pope in front of St. Peter's; cf. *Liber pont.*, I, 343, for the reception of Constans II (663 A.D.), "cui sexto ab urbe miliario Vitalianus papa cum sacerdotibus et Romano populo occurrit." Thus, Charlemagne's reception was modeled after that of the exarch; it remained authoritative for all imperial receptions in Rome. A very detailed description is found in the Coronation Order of Cencius, the so-called *Cencius II*, in *Liber cens.*, I, 1*, and republished by Schramm, "Ordines," *ArchUF.*, XI (1929), 375; cf. Eichmann, "Studien zur Geschichte der abendländischen Kaiserkrönung," *HJb.*, XLV (1925), 24 ff., who analyzes the route observed at the imperial entries into Rome. The crucifix carried before the monarch is conceived of as a "royal standard" (βασιλικὸν σημεῖον) to be displayed also at the *adventus* of the Lord on his return; cf. Peterson, "Die Einholung des Kyrios," p. 701. To have crossbearers heading the procession was a royal and imperial privilege; cf. *Liber pont.*, II, 88, the reception prepared by Sergius II for Emperor Louis II: "Obviam illi eius sanctitas dirigens venerandas cruces, *id est signa*, sicut mos est imperatorem aut regem suscipere." For the *privilegium crucis* within the hierarchy, see Thalhofer-Eisenhofer, *Liturgik*, 1, 577 f.; its imperial origin is indicated by Kruse, *op. cit.*, pp. 76 ff.

in the Gospels refers to the harbinger of the Lord, might give the impression that the ruler himself was looked upon as the *angelus*, the messenger of God. But the underlying idea is more likely another one: as the Lord at his Coming is preceded by the "messenger," so shall the emperor at his Advent be preceded by an angel.[34] This is, at the same time, the ecclesiastical version of a pre-Christian image such as is found on countless imperial coins symbolizing the emperor's *adventus*. The angel leading the emperor is simply the transmogrified winged *Victoria* who guided the triumphant emperor into his city.[35]

Liturgical acclamations to the ruler were not restricted to the occasions mentioned here. The ancient imperial acclamations, though turned into a new form and referring to God or Christ and applied to bishop and priest, are found in practically every range of the divine service. However, the examples adduced suffice to indicate the general development: the transmutation of pagan sacrals to ecclesiastical rites. These changes also affected necessarily the acclaiming *vox populi* by which a new ruler was instituted in the throne.

CORONATION LAUDES

The acclamations so far discussed may be regarded as marks of a customary and traditional devotion to the ruler. Even in their ecclesiastical form, these cheers seemed to express simply the affection owed to the ruler on the part of the people or the respectful loyalty of a clergy and Church which depended on him. However, it is almost self-evident that the liturgicized hails were more than merely joyful cheers in an ecclesiastical language. Like the mention of the ruler's name in the Mass,[36] these hails had a crypto-constitutive meaning. In the acclaims voiced by bishops and patriarchs at a synod, the legal and constitutive character of these hails is quite obvious: the assembled bishops recognized the ruler acclaimed as the legal lord of their territorial, or of the universal, Church. And the most momentous act in connection with which acclamations were not only appropriate but even indispensable, was that of a prince's accession to the throne. To "acclaim" meant: to "create" a new ruler and

---

[34] For the *Ecce mitto angelum meum*, see the Order of Farfa, above, n. 27, and *MGH SS.*, XI, 547; cf. Eichmann, "Zur Datierung des sogenannten *Cencius II*," *HJb.*, LII (1932), 309, n. 147, who rightly corrects me. For the *Benedictus qui venit*, cf. *Liber pont.*, II, 88. See also *ibid.*, I, 451, a reception hymn for Pope Stephen II: "Venit pastor noster et post Deo salus nostra."

[35] See Graber, *op. cit.*, Pl. XXVIII, 1–2, and p. 46, n. 2, and E. Kantorowicz, "The 'King's Advent' and the Enigmatic Panels in the Doors of Santa Sabina," *The Art Bulletin*, XXVI (1944), 207–231.

[36] Biehl, *op. cit.*, pp. 59, 81, mentions a few interesting examples of special permissions for including a ruler's name in the Canon of the Mass; see also Treitinger, *op. cit.*, p. 84, n. 186, and, for a modern example (referring to King Leopold III of Belgium) *Eph. Lit.*, XLIX (1935), 106: "Hodierno tempore singularis est casus in suo genere."

to recognize him publicly in his new dignity. The mere fact of being acclaimed by senate and army, at times by the army alone,[37] had legalized the accession of Roman emperors. It has been rightly emphasized that there was no legal emperor without acclamation[38] and that the acclaiming *vox populi*, represented by one group or another, had a distinctly constitutional effect. It was through the medium of acclamatory election that the *vox populi*, audible through the politically strongest group at the time, elevated the new monarch or assented to the fact of his elevation. Whatever the background might have been in any single case—whether the throne had been achieved by election or bloodright, adoption, or violence—and whatever the customary ceremonies of inauguration, a formal acclamation could not be lacking.

The inauguration of a ruler had originally nothing whatever to do with the Church. It was a constitutive and purely "civil" or "military" act in both Rome and Byzantium, as well as in the Teutonic realms where people and soldiers, or in later times the magnates, assented to the prince's accession by hailing him thrice and raising their hands. His installation then took place in various forms among which the elevation on the buckler[39] or the famous Merovingian drive in the ox-wagon are most familiar to the historian.

[37] In the fourth century, according to Symmachus, the army established itself as *castrensis senatus*; cf. Straub, *op. cit.*, p. 34; see his first chapter for the general development. See below, Chap. IV, n. 24.

[38] The subject has been greatly clarified, as far as mediaeval conditions are concerned, by Heldmann, *op. cit.*, pp. 258–289. The decisive factor at the election was that the candidate was styled *Augustus* and received the acclamations or laudes; cf. Ammian. Marc., XXVI, 2, 3: "Augustusque nuncupatur cum laudibus amplis" (Valentinian, 364 A.D.); *ibid.*, XXVI, 6, 8: "Gratianum declararunt Augustum, clamorum amplissimo sonu"; *ibid.*, XXX, 10, 5: "Augustus nuncupatur more solemni"; cf. Straub, *op. cit.*, pp. 16, 18, 19 f., and p. 20: *"Nuncupare* ist der Begriff für den wichtigsten Einzelakt des gesamten Zeremoniells, die feierliche und offizielle Übertragung des Herrschernamens Augustus oder Caesar, die durch den Zuruf der Truppen erfolgt." We find the terminology unchanged in the Middle Ages; cf. *Annal. regni Franc.*, A.D. 812, *MGH, SS. rer. Germ.*, ed. Kurze (1895), 136, the acclamations of the Byzantine ambassadors before Charlemagne: "more suo, id est greca lingua, laudes ei dixerunt, Imperatorem eum et Basileum appellantes"; Benedict of St. Andrew (ed. Zucchetti), 175, referring to Otto I: "et laudibus ab scolis honorifice laudatus et Augustus est appellatus"; Thietmar, IV, c. 2, *MGH. SS. rer. Germ.*, ed. Holtzmann (1935), 133, referring to Henry II of Bavaria, who was hailed king against Otto III during the Easter celebration at Quedlinburg in 984: "hac in festivitate idem a suis publice Rex appellatur laudibusque divinis attolitur." It is evident that the ancient tradition was unbroken. In all these examples the acclamation is certainly constitutive. Of a more courteous and flattering character, although politically very important because implying the recognition of the Western imperial dignity by Byzantium, were the acclamations proffered in honor of the Emperor Louis II and Empress Angilberga by the Council of Constantinople, in 867; Mansi, *op. cit.*, XVI, 417; Ch. J. Hefele, *Histoire des conciles*, trans. Dom. H. Leclercq (Paris, 1911), IV, 448, n. 2; Dümmler, *Ostfränkisches Reich*, II, 199.

[39] Brightman, "Byzantine Imperial Coronations," *Jour. Theol. Stud.*, II (1901), 367; the usage was probably of Teutonic origin, but was closely connected with Central Asiatic observances; see the most interesting material offered by Peter A. Boodberg, "Marginalia to the Histories of the Northern Dynasties, Chap. 4: The Coronation of T'o-pa Hsiu," *Harvard Journal of Asiatic Studies*, IV (1939), 242 ff.

The establishment and final consolidation of the Christian divine right of rulers, however, implied the recognition through yet another king-maker. The monarch, declares the Emperor Marcian in the fifth century, "is elected to the throne not only by the senate and the army but by God also."[40] A participation by the clergy in a prince's enthronement there-fore became inevitable because only the Church could make the coöpera-tion of the divine kingmaker visible. The first coronation which was actively conducted or assisted by the clergy (whatsoever the political reason of this ecclesiastical participation then may have been) took place in Byzantium at the coronation of Marcian in 450.[41] In the West, how-ever, the coöperation with the Church did not become imperative before the rite of royal anointment was introduced. Byzantium, although the cradle of innumerable rites and among them the ceremony of ecclesias-tical crownings, introduced the imperial unction not earlier than the late twelfth century.[42] Visigothic Spain, where the royal sacring with oil had been exercised in the latter half of the seventh century, collapsed in 711;[43] and the Celtic or Anglo-Saxon anointings, if really they can claim priority before those performed on the Continent,[44] remained without universal effectiveness. Europe, generally, did not observe the rite of anointing kings prior to the time that Pepin required the ecclesiastical legitimation and renewed the Biblical tradition. With Pepin's anointment the royal inauguration was shifted, once and for all, to the sacramental or at least liturgical sphere. Henceforth this action was dominated by sacerdotal functions and the model of Samuel, the prophet and high priest anointing David, enchanted the minds of layman and priest.

Thus the inauguration of a king had been passed on, with certain re-strictions, to the hands of the clergy. By degrees the ruler's first and most important public appearance became ecclesiastical. He even began to depend, with regard to his installation, on the assent of the Church. The clergy, in theory as well as in practice, could refuse to consecrate a candidate considered unsuitable. Recognition by the Church, therefore, gradually gained so much in importance and esteem that the assent of the other king-creating powers, above all that of the acclaiming people,

---

[40] Cf. Peter Charanis, "Coronation and Its Constitutional Significance in the Later Roman Empire," *Byzantion*, XV (Boston, Mass., 1941), 53.

[41] W. Sickel, "Das byzantinische Krönungsrecht bis zum 10. Jahrhundert," *Byz.Z.*, VII (1898), 517 ff.; Brightman, *op. cit.*, p. 377, claims Nov. 23, 602, as the date of the first coronation; see, however, A. E. R. Boak, "Imperial Coronation Ceremonies of the Fifth and Sixth Centuries," *Harvard Studies in Classical Philology*, XXX (1919), 37 ff., and the discussion of Charanis, *op. cit.*, pp. 49 ff.

[42] Eva Müller, "Die Anfänge der Königssalbung im Mittelalter," *HJb.*, LVIII (1938), 333, rightly follows Marc Bloch, *Les rois thaumaturges* (1924), 475 ff., 774 f.

[43] Müller, *op. cit.*, pp. 333–340.

[44] The priority of Anglo-Celtic anointings is generally refused by modern scholars; see, for instance, Schramm, *English Coronation*, p. 6, n. 3; Ellard, *op. cit.*, pp. 11 ff.; Müller, *op. cit.*, pp. 322–330; cf., however, Klauser, in *JLW.*, XIII (1933), 350 f., in his review of Ellard's book.

was more or less overshadowed by sacerdotal functions. This does not imply that the acknowledgment of the new ruler through the people was doomed to vanish entirely. In fact it survived, though in a somewhat stunted form, even at the solemnity of the ecclesiastical inauguration, namely in the so-called *collaudatio* of the people. The insertion into the coronation rite of the *collaudatio*, a shout of agreement, was not regulated uniformly; its place varies in the *Ordines* and so does its form. It could take place at the beginning of the solemn action when the ordaining archbishop inquired whether the people were willing to consent to the consecration of the prince; and the answer would be either the cry *Fiat! Fiat!* or the chanting of the *Te Deum*. Or the acclaims of the assembly—of clergy and people—would be shouted at the end of the consecration proper and would consist of the Biblical *Vivat rex in sempiternum!*, an act of homage rather than a consent. And even this homage was occasionally transformed into an antiphon sung by clerics: "Tunc moduletur antiphona: 'Vivat rex! Vivat rex! Vivat rex in eternum!' "[45] The tendency on the part of the Church was clearly to "clericalize" the whole action and to move the coöperation of the people to the remotest background. Both ecclesiastical ideology and principles of divine right worked together to reduce or even eliminate the participation of the people whose rights, however, emerged once more from insignificance, at least in theory, when the ideas of popular sovereignty as based on the vast complex of the *lex regia* claims became effective again.[46] At any rate, the royal inauguration, once it was removed to the loftiness of a liturgical act, became independent of the acclaim of the people. The Church, in her own and peculiar way, began to promote the ruler by granting him or refusing to him the solemnity of consecration; and sooner or later the priestly functions extended far beyond the Samuel-like act of pouring the balm on the head of the new David. The coronation proper that is—the act of placing the crown on the king's head—was likewise included in the liturgical performance; and the handing over of the royal insignia, ring and sword, scepter and orb, was also liturgicized until the donning of almost every coronation garment became subject to the rites of the Church.[47]

[45] Schramm, "Westfranken und Angelsachsen," p. 228; see also his studies, "Die Krönung in Deutschland," pp. 244 ff., 250, and 191, n. 1, and *English Coronation*, p. 143, n. 1, on the *collaudatio* in general. For the connection of *Te Deum* and laudes, see the interesting procedure at the Council of Tribur (895): "Exurgentes igitur de sedibus suis reverendissimi patres, cum astanti clero, ter quaterque proclamantes . . . *Exaudi Christe, Arnulpho magno regi vita!* et sonantibus campanis *Te Deum laudamus* concinentibus cunctis, glorificantes et Jesum Christum conlaudantes. . . ." Cf. Migne, *PL.*, CXXXVIII, 807D.

[46] For these interrelations see Schramm, *English Coronation*, p. 169, and *idem.*, "Frankreich," *ZfRG.*, kan. Abt. XXVI (1937), 169.

[47] A *Benedictio coronae regiae* and a *Benedictio cuiuscunque regalis ornamenti*, appended to the English Coronation Order of the twelfth century, seem to be the first records of the blessing of royal insignia; cf. P. L. Ward, "The Coronation Ceremony in

Against the background of this evolution, it appears consistent that the formerly profane electoral acclamations of army and people, senate or magnates, should likewise have been liturgicized or should have found an antitype in the divine service. The acclamation as a constitutive and legal act on the part of the people was supplemented by an ecclesiastico-legal act, namely by an acclamation on the part of the Church. This was precisely the function of the laudes at the coronation: they represent the sanction and assent of the acclaiming Church. In other words, the *collaudatio* of the people and the laudes of the Church are two different species of what had originally been one single act: the acclamatory legitimation of a new ruler. This agrees with the intellectual development in general. The two spheres, secular and ecclesiastical, had broken apart; king-making, too, had been divided into two actions, one secular and one ecclesiastical, and, accordingly, the acclamations also had been split in two.

The functions of the two acclamations were not the same. The *collaudatio* took place before unction and coronation were consummated; it therefore represented the will of the people, including the clergy, to see a particular prince crowned king and must be considered a public manifestation of agreement with the action in prospect. The laudes, however, were chanted *after* the consecration, within the ensuing Mass. They symbolized the ecclesiastical recognition of the king consecrated, and signified a manifestation of agreement on the part of the Church with what had been done. Hence, if we may say so, the *collaudatio* referred to the prince publicly elected, whereas the laudes referred to the king anointed and thus visibly chosen. The acclamations of the people conferred on a prince the kingly power, whereas the chant of the laudes presented the new king as the Anointed of God, the χριστὸς ἐπιφανής.

Occasionally these two acts would be condensed and appear almost as one act. In the so-called *Coronation Order of King Edgar* (973) the acclamatory homage of the people had been transformed into an antiphon chanted by clerics. On the other hand, in the *English Order of the Twelfth Century* the homage is again a simple shout, whereas the antiphon is replaced by the laudes which the Normans had introduced.[48] It is one of the rare cases in which the laudes are sung not within the Mass, but at the end of the consecration. Yet in spite of these and other peculiarities,[49] the laudes in general belonged to the Mass, whereas the acclamations of

Mediaeval England," *Speculum*, XIV (1939), 175, n. 1. The handing over of the insignia of course, was always (at least ever since the ninth century) performed in a ritual way and with appropriate prayers, although the raiments as such do not seem to have received a special blessing.

[48] In the Cambridge, Trinity MS 249, fol. 108ᵛ, the laudes follow after the "Sta et retine" and before the coronation of the queen. For the introduction of the laudes to England by the Normans, cf. below, pp. 177 f.

[49] See, e.g., Schramm, "Krönung in Deutschland," pp. 320, n. 7; 312, n. 6.

people and clergy usually preceded the sacring proper so that the two performances were separated from each other by the king's "transfigura-
tion"—his anointment and ordination.

The laudes thus appear as the ecclesiastical antitype of the secular
acclamations. However, the laudes are the acclamation not only of the
visible Church, but also of the invisible one. They contained hails to the
king, it is true, but to the king along with all the other powers on earth.[50]
By means of the laudes, therefore, the newly ordained ruler was fitted
into the social structure of this world and received, at the same time, his
very high place as an executor of the planning of Providence. The new
government was thus linked with the divine government and with that of
Christ, the true governor of the world. During the ceremony of the consecration which preceded the laudes, the images of King and Christ had been
brought together as nearly as possible. The prayers had emphasized that
the king was to be "glorified without end together with the redeemer and
saviour Christ whose name (*christus*) and place he is believed to display."
The "mediator between God and men" had been besought by the priest
that "he may confirm the king as mediator between clergy and people in
the throne of this present kingdom and grant him to rule together with
Him in the eternal kingdom."[51] In addition to this idea, stressed time
and again, of the *condominium* of the Anointed with his God with whom
in after life he was to share the throne,[52] the Orders continually emphasize
the parallelism between Christ and King. Even formulae so insignificant
as the finales concluding the prayers occasionally would display a singular
elaboration by placing Christ, the anointed and ever victorious, in parallel with his royal vicar on earth.[53] When finally the laudes, inserted as a

[50] Schramm, *Der König von Frankreich*, I, 38, seems to forget that the laudes contained an intention for the pope as well. It is true, the acclamation of the "people,"
i.e., of those present, and the laudes sung by the clergy coincided at Charlemagne's
coronation in 800; cf. below, p. 84. As a rule, however, and ever since the early ninth
century, the laudes were voiced exclusively by the clergy or other special chanters; cf.
Bukofzer, below, pp. 197 f. Therefore, it cannot be maintained "dass in den Laudes,
die bei der Kaiserkrönung ertönten, die Zustimmung des Volkes [*sic!*] zum Ausdruck
kam." Also there is no need to raise the question whether those accompanying the
Frankish or German king to Rome were entitled to participate in the singing of the
laudes or whether this was a privilege of the "Romans." The laudes were a purely
clerical performance; the congregation or the "electors" had nothing else to do with
this chant but listen to it in silence. The song was not even a Diaconal Litany with
responses of the congregation, as suggested by R. H. Connolly, "Liturgical Prayers of
Intercession," *Jour. Theol. Stud.*, XXI (1920), 227 f.
[51] See the tenth-century Order of Mainz, Schramm, "Krönung in Deutschland,"
p. 317, § 14, and *ibid.*, p. 319, § 17: ". . . cum redemptore ac salvatore Iesu Christo
cuius nomen vicemque gestare crederis, sine fine glorieris."
[52] *Ibid.*, p. 316, n. 4; cf. above, p. 50, n. 127.
[53] The Order of *ca.* 900 (Schramm, "Westfranken und Angelsachsen," pp. 201 ff.)
has elaborated on the finales in particular; see, e.g., the finale concluding the anointment (*ibid.*, pp. 203 f., § 5):
    "Per dominum nostrum Iesum Christum, filium tuum, qui *unctus est oleo
    letitiae* prae consortibus suis et virtute crucis potestates aerias debellavit,

special festal song in the High Mass which followed the consecration, were voiced, the chant inevitably elicited the vision that not only the visible Church acclaimed, confirmed, and recognized the new ruler, but also that through the Church the Heavens consented to the new *a Deo coronatus*. The chant implied that the new king was acclaimed also by the choirs of angels and saints, as well as by Christ himself, who, in his quality as Victor, King, and Commander, recognized the new *christus* of the Church as his fellow ruler and, at the same time, reacknowledged, along with the new king, all the other powers ruling on earth.

All this is anything but allegorical. It must be accepted with as much of that mediaeval "Realism" as is apparent in every line of the Coronation Orders. In a Munich manuscript, in which the laudes are styled the "Royal Chant," *Regale Carmen*, there is a miniature illustrating this litany.[54] It shows a king with crown, scepter, and orb enthroned in the center of the large "X" with which the *Xristus vincit* begins, as though the artist intended to indicate the king's rule through, with, and in Christ. Much of the passionate emotion of the "Royal Chant" results from this interplay of widest contrasts and from the haziness of the horizontal line where the two spheres, divine and human, still could dissolve into one, just as they did in the pre-Christian past.

"People" and "Church" are not the same thing. The laudes, representing the recognition of the ruler on the part of the visible and invisible Church, therefore cannot be regarded as an "acclamation on the part of the people" and even less so as "the people's consent." They are not simply a form of electoral acclamation, and the fact that the king was not hailed alone, but the king along with the pope and other powers, should prevent us from mistaking the chant for a secular constitutional act of election.[55] Besides, the laudes were sung by the clergy, not by the people.

But was the laudes chant a constitutional act at all? It is interesting to account for the customs observed in Byzantium. Here, there were known, from an early date, the constitutive acclaims of senate, army, and people, the so-called *Euphemia*, as well as the liturgical acclamation during the service, the *Mnemosynon*.[56] It is generally held that the latter did not

---

tartara destruxit regnumque diaboli superavit et ad caelos victor ascendit; in cuius manu victoria omnis, gloria et potestas consistunt, et tecum vivit et regnat Deus in unitate eiusdem Spiritus sancti per omnia saecula saeculorum. Amen."
Or the finale after the tradition of the sword:
"Per auxilium *invictissimi triumphatoris* domini nostri Iesu Christi qui cum Patre..."
It is clearly the intention to present Christ as victor and conqueror and thus to assimilate with him the newly anointed king. See also *ibid.*, pp. 235 ff., 269 ff.

[54] Munich, Cod. Lat. 14322, fol. 1ᵛ.
[55] Cf. above, n. 50.
[56] Heisenberg, *op. cit.*, pp. 55 ff.; cf. below, p. 84, for the coronation of Charlemagne; and *Gesta Innocentii Tertii*, c. 3. Migne, *PL.*, CCXIV, xxi, for the two acclamations to the pope.

own a constitutive character in a legal sense.[57] This may be true so far as our terminology is applicable. The acclamation of the people, the army, and the senate was legally constitutive; probably the act of crowning was also.[58] The acclamations of the Church were certainly not directly "king-making." Still, they were a decisive factor for the establishment of the imperial authority; they were among the many elements disclosing their constitutive power when denied rather than when granted.

Similar conditions prevailed in the West. The laudes acclamation, representing the recognition of the king's legitimacy, was an accessory manifestation, impressive by its festal and solemn character, but not indispensable; for legally the liturgical acclaim added no new element of material power which the king had not already received earlier by his election and consecration. In fact, the French and German Coronation Orders do not contain the laudes, although, for certain reasons, they were probably sung at the sacrings in these countries. Nevertheless, the laudes were a decisive element because the royal authority, and consequently the royal power, were strengthened through this solemn assent of the Church. By means of this chant, the Church professed and publicly espoused the king in a solemn form. However, the weight of this profession or espousal cannot be measured by legal standards.

It has recently been emphasized that the procedure observed at the coronations had much in common with the usages adhered to in Church synods.[59] Especially during the ninth century, and in a rudimentary form in later centuries as well, the routine preceding the consecration (for instance, the proposals of the "chairman," the allocutions of the bishops, and several formulae applied) was remindful of the routine observed in a synod. And just as a synod would end in a solemn acclamation to the ruler to show that a decision was taken, so the coronation would end in a solemn acclaim to the ruler to show that the sacring was consummated. It was, so to speak, the seal placed on the enactment of the Church. A charter, admittedly, does not become legally "more valid" if furnished with a gold *bulla* in place of a seal of wax; but the importance of the issue becomes more obvious. This is true also of the laudes. They do not imply an increase of the legal force of the decision made, but they stress the weight of the decision. This weight is imponderable. But in the imponderables, then and now, the legal power is sometimes more effective than in legally constitutive enactments.

Although the mediaeval laudes must be considered an act of recognition rather than of constitution, there is nevertheless an exception to this

---

[57] Heisenberg, *loc. cit.*; see, however, Treitinger, *op. cit.*, p. 84, n. 186.

[58] Cf. Charanis, in *Byzantion*, XV (1942), 49–66.

[59] Cf. Schramm, *Der König von Frankreich*, I, 27 f., who refers to H. Barion, *Das fränkisch-deutsche Synodalrecht des Frühmittelalters* (1931), 97 ff.

rule, namely the coronation of Charlemagne in Rome. This event was extraordinary in every respect, and it was extraordinary also with reference to the ceremonial. The sources do not allow us to distinguish all the ritual acts with the clarity desired. However, even through the dimness of the extant accounts there seem to be discernible the two acclamations, those of the people and those of the Church. It is a question of interpreting the two main sources[60] whether or not we are to make a distinction, on the one hand, between the hails of the "faithful Romans" who, after the pope had placed the crown on Charlemagne's head, shouted their "Karolo, piissimo Augusto a Deo coronato, magno et pacifico imperatori, vita et victoria," and, on the other hand, the chant of the laudes proper, in which this hail was repeated by the Roman *clergy*, "ante sacram confessionem beati Petri apostoli." However this may be—and it is not very satisfactory to press sources which have been turned over and over again—the shouts of the Romans and the laudes, as they then followed one after the other without a break, seem to have formed one single tumultuous outburst of voices in which it is idle to seek the particular cry which was "constitutive" and legally effective. In this case, the acclamation of the Church, as it intermingled with that of the people, or of "those present," for once had also a legally binding character.

Charlemagne's crowning forms the one great exception. When coronations became a routine, the laudes were voiced by one or two chanters, and the *schola* or choir responded. The performance took place within the Mass, and the laudes received their set place after the first Collect and before the Epistle. They were heard at every Roman coronation of an emperor until the end of the Middle Ages. Yet, we have to proceed to the twelfth century before finding this chant incorporated into a Roman Order proper; nor do any Orders of the Royal Coronations contain the laudes earlier than the twelfth century. However, the scores of laudes forms which have survived from almost every century during the Middle Ages, make it clear that the custom of singing the liturgical acclamations was widespread for a long time. What remains doubtful, however, is whether or not this observance should always be linked in a direct way with the royal coronations. It may be that the laudes, when chanted at the German, French, and early Anglo-Norman crownings, were voiced, not on account of the coronations, but because in general the coronation would take place on one of the feast days of the Church.

[60] The fundamental accounts, in this respect, are the *Annal. regni Francorum, ad a. 800*, and the *Vita Leonis III* in *Liber pont.*, II, 7. See the careful account of Caspar, "Das Papsttum unter fränkischer Herrschaft," *ZKG.*, LV (1935), 257 f.

FESTIVAL CROWN-WEARINGS, CROWNINGS, AND LAUDES

The Western coronation rite may have borrowed single features from Byzantium, but on the whole it must be maintained that the Western Church developed her most impressive and spectacular pageantry out of her own liturgical resources. Possibly, however, the Byzantine model was effective with reference to the liturgical acclamations which were voiced for the ruler on the great feast days of the Church: Christmas, Easter, and Pentecost. That the Byzantine emperor received acclamations at the Church festivals in Constantinople does not mean very much, for every festal appearance of the emperor was accompanied by these hails. It is of greater importance to realize that apparently in the provincial cathedrals, too, the imperial acclamations were chanted on these and similar occasions.[61] When and in what connection this usage was started is not sufficiently clarified, and merely as a hypothetical thesis the question may be raised whether the custom of acclaiming the absent ruler on feast days may not perhaps be connected with the veneration of the imperial images which, in the provinces, were exposed and vicariously acclaimed on festal occasions.[62]

In the Carolingian orbit the usage can be traced back to the eighth century. The form of these festival acclamations was apparently that of the laudes litany; at least, we assumed (p. 53) that the laudes which Charlemagne received on Easter Monday in 774 followed the Frankish pattern. The following time, at Christmas 800, the laudes in the Frankish form are described quite clearly. Here, however, the festival laudes were combined with the emperor's coronation. It seems useless to try to find out whether the chant represented festival or elective laudes, for probably they were both. The festival laudes, on this occasion, broke up and turned back again to what they had been originally—a constitutive acclamation. After 800 the matter becomes clearer. Early in the ninth

---

[61] See Johannes Diaconus, in *MGH. SS.*, VII, 32, where the bishops of certain Dalmatian cathedrals promise the doge of Venice, "quod feriatis diebus, quibus laudis pompam in aecclesia depromere solebant, istius principis nomen post imperatorum laudis preconiis glorificarent." The chanting of laudes to Constantine IV on the Easter Octave in 681 (*Liber pont.*, I, 354) was due to special circumstances. The whole question is in need of a special study, probably in connection with the "Imperial Hours" followed by a *polychronion* in the present orthodox service on Christmas and Epiphany.

[62] *Cod. Theod.*, xv, 4, 1: "Quando nostrae statuae vel imagines eriguntur, sive diebus (ut adsolet) festis, sive communibus, adsit iudex . . ." Already Joannes Lucius, *De regno Dalmatiae et Croatiae* (Vienna, 1758), lib. II, c. vi, p. 72, has called attention to this law in connection with the laudes and refers to Guido Pancirolli's Commentary on the *Notitia Dignitatum*, cf. J. G. Graevius, *Thesaurus antiquitatum Romanarum* (Utrecht, 1698), VII, 1399F. Kruse, *Studien zur offiziellen Geltung des Kaiserbildes im römischen Reich* (1934), who mentions the law several times, thinks of a display of the images in the circus (p. 40), but does not discuss the feast days; see, however, p. 61, for the *natalis imperatoris*, and below, note 107.

century, we learn from the lemmata of certain laudes formularies[63] that this chant was sung on feast days:

Incipiunt laudes festis diebus. Quando laudes canendae sunt, expleta oratione a Pontifice, antequam lector ascendat ambonem, pronuntiant duo Diaconi sive Cantores respondente illis schola ho modo . . .

This rubric appears in all the Franco-Roman, or Romanized Gallo-Frankish, formularies; the phrasing survives as long as these forms were copied, that is, until the fourteenth century. A similar arrangement is found in a non-Romanized Gallo-Frankish formulary. It refers to the Emperor Louis II and Empress Angilberga, to Pope Nicholas I and apparently to the bishop of Chieti, and seems to fall in the year 865–66, when the imperial couple sojourned at Chieti. It has the following heading:[64]

In Christe nomine hec sunt laudes de nativitas Domini sive in nativitate [MS: "et in" for "nativitate"] sanctorum cuilibet.

Thus, this formulary represents Christmas laudes which, however, could be sung on other saints' days as well. We have a formulary of Orléans of the same period (858–867), referring to Pope Nicholas I, King Charles the Bald, and Queen Irmintrude, which cannot be connected with Charles' coronation at Orléans in 848, or that of his son Charles, when the latter became king of Aquitania in 855. It is a general formulary for festal days, transmitted in a casual way on the last four pages of a collection of homilies and introduced by the heading: "Finita oratione post *Gloria in excelsis Deo* dicat sacerdos *Christus vincit, Christus regnat, Christus imperat.*"[65] After the ninth century, rubrics such as "Incipiunt laudes in Pascha sive in Pentecosten,"[66] or simply "Laudes Paschales,"[67] or similar lemmata are not rare.

---

[63] In the Cologne MS 138, and in the Munich Cod. Lat. 14510; cf. Andrieu, *Ordines*, I, 107, 233; *MGH. LL*, II, 78 f.; Fabre, in *Mélanges d'archéologie et d'histoire*, X (1890), 387.

[64] Vatican, Reg. MS 1997, fol. 160ᵛ; cf. F. Maassen, *Geschichte der Quellen und der Literatur des canonischen Rechts*, I (Graz, 1870), 527; Gaudenzi, in *Bulletino dell'Istituto Storico Italiano*, XXXVII (1916), 376, n. 1.

[65] Orléans, MS 196 (173), fols. 136–140; cf. *Catalogue général des manuscrits des bibliothèques publiques*, XII, 102. The manuscript contains nothing but homilies except for the last four folios which contain the laudes. In addition to the three intentions mentioned, we find one for the "noblissima proles regalis" (i.e., the Gallo-Frankish form of this hail) and the likewise Gallo-Frankish acclamation "omnibus iudicibus et cuncto exercitui Franciae." The form "Franciae" is extraordinary but seems to be correct if we take the usage of the language at the court of Charles the Bald into consideration; cf. G. Kurth, "Francia et Francus," in *Études franques*, I (1919). Although the Orléans formulary preserved cannot refer to events in 848, the "acclamation" mentioned in Charles' *Libellus proclamationis* might nevertheless imply the singing of laudes at the coronation; *MGH. Capit.*, II, 451; Schramm, *König von Frankreich*, I, 16, n. 4, and II, 14.

[66] Early tenth-century troper of St. Martial in Limoges, Bibl. Nat. Lat. MS 1240, fol. 65; cf. Delisle, *Cabinet des manuscrits*, III (1881), 271 ff., and Pl. XXXI, n. 3; G. M. Dreves, *Prosarium Lemovicense*, in *Analecta Hymnica*, VII (1889), 4 ff.

[67] Thus, in the laudes of Freising, in Munich Cod. Lat. 27305, fol. 241; cf. G. T. von Rudhart, in *Quellen und Erörterungen zur bayrischen Geschichte*, VII (1858), 473 f.

The fact that the earliest rubric referring to feast days is found in Franco-Roman formularies might suggest that the voicing of the laudes chant on festivals of the Church was a Roman usage. It might be conjectured that the rendering of laudes continued simply an ancient pre-Frankish, city-Roman tradition and that, let us assume, Pope Hadrian I revived merely acclaims to the Byzantine emperor on feast days, which now he applied to the Frankish king after that custom had been dormant in the times of the Iconoclast emperors. This may be so, but it is not likely. The laudes of Chieti, as well as those of Orléans, have not the Franco-Roman but the Gallo-Frankish form, and yet they are "festival" laudes. Moreover, materially, the lemmata of the Franco-Roman forms do not seem to agree with the urban Roman customs, for in Rome, so far as we know, the laudes litany was not sung unless the emperor in person was present in the city; but we know that in France and in Germany the laudes actually were chanted in the cathedrals on Church festivals even though the king or emperor was not present. The lemmata of the Franco-Roman formularies, therefore, seem to reproduce the Frankish rather than the Roman custom.

The place of the laudes within the Mass is mentioned quite frequently in the ninth century and thereafter. They were always inserted in the introductory sections of the service,[68] but here their place would vary. The ordinary place for the acclamations intended for the ruler was between the first Collect and the Epistle.[69] It may be by mistake that once they are mentioned after the Epistle.[70] More often they preceded the first Collect and followed after the *Gloria*[71] or even after the *Kyrie;*[72] but there is reason to believe that the laudes in these last two cases were "episcopal" acclamations rather than *laudes regiae*. Such acclamations after the *Kyrie* are mentioned, for instance, by Bonizo, bishop of Sutri, the partisan of Gregory VII. On the festal day, writes Bonizo, the bishop is to be seated in his chair, where he is seen by clergy and people, and thus enthroned he remains during the solemn singing of the *Kyrie eleison* and during the chanting of the laudes for the Roman pontiff and all bishops,

---

[68] The only exception so far is apparently the English Coronation Order of the twelfth century; cf. above, n. 48.

[69] This is true of all the Franco-Roman laudes, those of Normandy (below, chap. VI, n. 48), of England, allowing for the one exception mentioned in note 68 (cf. below, chap. VI, notes 68, 69, 80), and of those of several French cathedrals, e.g., Troyes, Narbonne, Laon; it is true also for St. Gall, cf. Goldast, *op. cit.*, II, 147.

[70] In the Sicilian Coronation Order of the twelfth century; cf. below, chap. VI, n. 44.

[71] For instance, at Orléans, Nevers, and Soissons. This is, according to Eichmann, "Die Ordines der Kaiserkrönung," *ZfRG.*, kan. Abt. II (1912), 10, the place of the laudes in the Byzantine Mass. But this is not correct. In *De caerim.*, I., c. 38, p. 193, it is said that the *people* acclaimed the emperor with the Trishagion and with the Δόξα, that is, with the angelic acclamations (cf. Peterson, *Untersuchungen*, pp. 226, n. 2, and 234); but this is not the *Gloria* of the Mass.

[72] In the Durandus forms mentioned below, Chap. IV, notes 2–4.

the emperor and empress, and for the judges and the whole Christian army.[73] This description agrees, on the whole, with the rubric of a later form of "imperialized" episcopal acclamations,[74] so that we must assume that they belonged to a different category even though the text may have tallied with the *laudes regiae*. The laudes were one of those chants of the Church which were subjected to certain restrictions. Like the *Gloria*, the singing of the laudes was reserved to episcopal masses; they could not be voiced unless the archbishop or bishop himself was present or his place taken by another person of episcopal rank.[75] That is to say, the bishop in person had to receive—and to pay the *sportulae* for—the acclamations to the ecclesiastical and temporal powers whose representative he was. Of course, it would be difficult to tell whether the bishop received the festal ruler acclamations as a royal or as a hierarchical representative. The stress may have varied according to time and occasion. If the ruler himself was present, the intention for the ruler was certainly in the foreground; and if a cardinal or the pope was present, the laudes would accentuate the hierarchical side. In the earlier times, the bishop receiving the laudes may have represented both powers; but there can be no doubt that after the eleventh century and especially in the Later Middle Ages the laudes were completely hierarchized and directed so exclusively to the bishop as representative of the hierarchy that the intentions for the ruler and the other secular powers were sometimes omitted.[76]

The place of the laudes in the divine service calls our attention to a

---

[73] Bonizo, *De vita christiana*, II, c. 51, ed. Ernst Perels, in *Texte zur Geschichte des römischen und kanonischen Rechts im Mittelalter*, 1 (Berlin, 1930), 59:

"(Episcopus) ascendat sedem, in qua spectante clero et populo resedeat, donec Kyrieleyson a clero sollempniter decantetur et quamdiu laudes Romano pontifici et omnibus episcopis, imperatori quoque et imperatrici, iudicibus et cuncto exercitui christiano sollempni cum reverentia fuerint decantate."

Cf. Biehl, *op. cit.*, p. 108, n. 1.

[74] See the forms indicated above, n. 72. The rubric reads as follows:

"Laudes sive rogationes sequentes dicuntur in precipuis solemnitatibus videlicet in diebus illis in quibus pontifex sedet post altare, quod fit hoc modo: Precentor cum quattuor bonis cantoribus et cum totidem pueris bene cantantibus immediate post Kyrie eleison incipit post altare alta voce: 'Christus vincit...'"

There follows the form adduced below, p. 113, which contains intentions for pope, bishop, and king, though not for the judges and army; see, for the rubric, Martène, *De antiquis ecclesiae ritibus*, I, 584. Cf. Pl. IX. An impressive description of the performance, referring to Rheims, is found below, chap. IV, n. 31.

[75] "Sequitur triumphus qui nunquam nisi celebrante episcopo cantatur," says a form of Paris (Paris, Bibl. Nat. Lat. MS 9505, fol. 82), cf. Prost, *Quatre pièces*, p. 171; see also the form of Rouen in the Bibl. Nat. Lat. MS 904, fol. 108ᵛ: "Si archiepiscopus presens fuerit, cantetur ante epistolam *Christus vincit*"; or the prescriptions at Rheims mentioned in Ulysse Chevalier, *Sacramentaire et martyrologe ... des églises de Rheims*, pp. 104, 132, 205, and, above all, p. 200. Concerning the singing of the *Gloria*, cf. Duchesne, *Christian Worship*, p. 166; *DACL.*, IV, 1525 ff., *s.v.* "Doxologies."

[76] See, e.g., the later laudes of Orléans; Le Brun Desmorettes, *Voyages liturgiques*, p. 189.

change which it is easier to indicate than to explain. The chant, when making its first appearance in the eighth century, belonged to the framework of the great Litany of the Saints of which it was but one section. This fact, as we have seen, is recorded in the first two laudes formularies transmitted; it is sanctioned by the *Ordo* of Angilbert, and it is intimated by the ceremonial observed at the sacring of Louis the Pious, in 816.[77] It may be that the place of the laudes mentioned by Bonizo and in some formularies (after the *Kyrie* of the Mass) is still indicative of the ancient connection with the Litany of the Saints.[78] From this association, however, we find the laudes removed by the early ninth century. They have become an independent liturgical chant to be sung usually between the first Collect and the Epistle. We know nothing about the practice observed in this respect during the eighth century. Our sole evidence is the visit of Charlemagne to Rome in 774; but whether the acclamation was sung after the *Kyrie* or was inserted in another place we do not know. In 800, the laudes were probably not sung in connection with the Litany of the Saints or the *Kyrie*, but were chanted after the pope had placed the crown on Charlemagne's head and after the Romans had given their acclamatory shouts. At the consecration of Louis the Pious, in 816, the laudes immediately followed the prostration of both the emperor and pope; an association which seems to imply their connection with 'the Litany. However, this connection is henceforth given up. By the first quarter of the ninth century, they are definitively separated from the Litany; and ever since that time they have been transmitted separately and as a special song. We find them on flyleaves in Collections of *Canones* or of homilies or, once, among the writings of Boethius;[79] or we find them at the beginning or at the end of liturgical manuscripts.[80] They always

---

[77] See above, pp. 36 f. For the coronation of Louis the Pious, cf. Theganus, *Vita Hludowici Imperatoris*, c. 17, *MGH. SS.*, II, 594; the form of the laudes chanted by the pope is actually preserved in the poem of Ermoldus Nigellus, *In honorem Hludovici*, II, v. 420 ff., *MGH. Poet.*, II, 36:
"*Exaudi*, precibusque meis, pete, flecte benignam,
   Christe, aurem; votis, rex pie, quaeso, fave.
   Adiuvet Andreas, Petrus, Paulusque, Johannes
      Atque Maria Dei mater opima pii . . ."
Cf. Eichmann, *op. cit.*, p. 6.
[78] Above, notes 72, 73. Cf. Bukofzer, below, pp. 208 f.
[79] Ivrea, MS 50 (94), has the laudes on a flyleaf between Books 19 and 20 of the *Collectio canonum* of Burchard of Worms; cf. Bethmann, in *Pertz' Archiv*, IX (1847) 626, and Dümmler, *Anselm der Peripatetiker*, pp. 89 f. The Vatican, Reg. Lat. MS 1997 has the laudes on the last leaves of a *Collectio canonum* which is followed by a Roman Order, cf. Maassen, *Geschichte der Quellen und der Literatur des canonischen Rechts* (Graz, 1870), I, 527. In the Orléans MS 196 (173), they are found at the end of a collection of homilies; cf. above, n. 64. For laudes in a Boethius manuscript (Rouen, MS 489 [A 254]), cf. *Graduel de Rouen*, I, 69; and for those written on an ivory, see E. Kantorowicz, "Ivories and Litanies," 56 ff.
[80] See Andrieu, *Ordines*, I, 107, 371 f. For laudes in a Troper (Bamberg, Cod. Lit. 5), see below, n. 120, and Bukofzer, below, pp. 190, 198.

appear in the form of an *additamentum* along with other liturgical odds and ends and without a proper place, thus roaming about in the service books just as many another Franco-Gallic prayer.[81] It is true, a rubric would often indicate where and on what occasions the chant should be sung. But the festival laudes, like the coronation laudes, do not seem to have been inserted in the service books proper—as a part of the Christmas, Easter, or Pentecost liturgy—before the twelfth century, even though Bonizo mentions them and even though once they are added, loosely and without organic connection, to an Ottonian Order of the Coronation.[82]

It is always a delicate task to try to explain such changes which usually have a definite reason. But at least a suggestion may be offered. To begin with, *laudes in festis diebus* could not be connected with the Litany of the Saints because the Litany, as a rule, was not offered on these days. Hence, if the laudes were to be sung, they had to be cut out of the framework of the Litany of the Saints to which, in the eighth century, the acclamations had adhered and been assimilated. Moreover, the endlessly long processional Litany of the Saints was shortened when introduced into the divine service, for instance, at ordinations and coronations.[83] Finally, the general change within the rite of sacerdotal ordinations must be considered. Together with the new observance of oil anointings at episcopal and other ordinations—an observance spreading slowly in the eighth century and rapidly in the ninth—the Litany of the Saints was introduced into the ordination ritual because this prayer was, or gradually became, inseparable from and one with all oil anointings. Further, the singing of the Litany of the Saints implied the prostration of ordainer and ordinands, including the clergy participating, a custom which, in connection with ordinations, was considerably older than the introduction of the Litany of the Saints.[84] However, this observance (the Litany of

---

[81] This agrees somewhat with the remarks of E. Bishop, "The Liturgical Reforms of Charlemagne," *Downside Review*, XXXVIII (1919), 15 f., about benedictions and other prayers derived from the Gallicanized "Gelasianum of the Eighth Century": they "were added to the official mass-books on fly-leaves, or were brought together as a sort of unauthorized appendix."

[82] Andrieu, *Ordines*, I, 397; Migne, *PL.*, CXXXVIII, col. 1119.

[83] The Coronation Orders of Mainz (tenth century) prescribe that the Litany was to be sung "breviter" with twelve apostles, twelve martyrs, twelve confessors, and twelve virgins invoked; cf. Schramm, "Krönung in Deutschland," pp. 311, § 6, and 326, § 6; his interpretation of this place (p. 236) is not correct, cf. Funk, in *HJb.*, LVI (1936), 590. For an illustrated specimen of this dodecadic arrangement, see Haseloff, *Eine thüringisch-sächsische Malerschule*, Pl. XXXI.

[84] To investigate the relations between oil anointings in general, the Litany of the Saints, and prostration is far beyond the scope of this study. The statement of M. Buchner, "Grundlagen der Beziehungen zwischen Landeskirche und Thronfolge im Mittelalter," *Festschrift Georg von Hertling* (Kempten and Munich, 1913), 236 f. (cf. Schramm, "Das Herrscherbild in der Kunst des früheren Mittelalters," *Vorträge der*

the Saints with prostration at the anointment) was transferred to the rite of royal sacrings. Our first evidence refers to the crowning of Louis the Pious in 816, for here the prostration of the emperor and the consecrating pope is indicated quite clearly. Moreover, the king's prostration is described circumstantially in the Coronation Order of Mainz (*ca.* 961).[85] The king, so we are told, is led by his ordainer and other bishops to the steps of the altar. Here, on the pavement covered with tapestries and cloth, the elect prostrates himself with both his arms extended so as to form a cross. The same position is taken by the bishops and priests while the other clergy in the choir chant the Litany of the Saints in an abbreviated form with the invocation of twelve apostles and the same number of martyrs, confessors, and virgins respectively.[86] It is a gesture of deepest humiliation and contrition. That the laudes, a festal and joyful acclamation, could not be received in this attitude is obvious. Even the rapid change from one extreme to the other was not suitable, although the proceedings in 816 suggest such a change without transition. Hence, when the Litany with prostration became the custom at the sacring of the ruler, the separation of the acclamatory laudes from the Litany recommended itself. But the close connection of some festival laudes with the *Kyrie* of

---

Bibliothek Warburg, II, 1, 1924, 220), holding that the penance of Louis the Pious in Attigny (822 A.D.) combined with a prostration before the altar remained authoritative for the coronation ritual, is sure to be wrong. The prostration of priests and bishops at their ordination along with the chanting of the Litany is found in the *Ordo Romanus VIII*, and Duchesne (*Christian Worship*, p. 356, n. 1) stresses that "the prayer, which was usually offered up in silence by the congregation (cf. *ibid.*, p. 107), was here replaced by the Litany." On the other hand, the Litany with prostration at an oil anointment is found, in the latter half of the eighth century, in the burial rite of Monte Cassino; cf. Bishop, *Lit. Hist.*, p. 216, n. 1. A full description, and perhaps the earliest one, of an episcopal ordination with anointment of the head, chanting of the Litany, and prostration is offered by Hincmar of Rheims, who refers to his own ordination in 845; cf. Migne, *PL.*, CXXVI, col. 186; Eichmann, "Königs- und Bischofsweihe," *Sitzungsberichte München*, 1928, Abh. 6, p. 40; Ellard, *op. cit.*, pp. 55 f. There can be little doubt that the *tertium comparationis* between royal and episcopal consecration was the anointment. After the anointment had been added to the episcopal ordination, the ceremony of inaugurating the king became likewise an "ordination" which was accompanied by the Litany and the Prostration of *coronator* and *coronandus*. The ordination anointings of bishops, however, do not antedate the later eighth, or even the early ninth century. The prostration of the ruler in imagery should be taken into account; cf. Grabar, *L'Empereur dans l'art byzantin* (1936), 100 ff. An interesting letter concerning the prostration (though not in connection with the ordination) has been published by Andrieu, *Ordines*, I, 320, 350. It is directed to either Hadrian II (867–872) or Hadrian III (884–885).

[85] Cf. above, n. 83.

[86] Schramm, "Die Krönung in Deutschland," p. 311, § 6. ". . . inter manus episcoporum perductus in chorum usque ad altaris gradus incedat; cunctoque pavimento tapetibus et palliolis contecto, ibi (rex) humiliter totus in cruce prostratus iaceat una cum episcopis et presbyteris hinc inde prostratis, ceteris autem in choro letaniam breviter psallentibus . . ." See also the letter of Berno von Reichenau to Henry III, published by A. Duch, "Berno von Reichenau," *ZKG.*, LIII (1934), 424; the writer reminds the emperor of his mourning at the death of the Empress Gisela (1043) and mentions: "expansis in modum crucis manibus coram omni populo in terram corruistis." See Plate IV.

the Mass is still reminiscent perhaps of the former practice.[87] (See Pl. IV.) At first glance, the singing of laudes on Church festivals seems to be far remote from coronations or ecclesiastico-political manifestations in general. However, this is not so. Church festivals and coronations were correlated so far as a certain predilection prevailed for deferrring the consecration of a king to one of the great feast days of the Church; or, if this was not feasible, considering the long delay of the ruler's final installation, at least a Sunday would have been chosen, an observance, by the way, which had a parallel in the ordaining of bishops whose consecration took place traditionally on Sundays though rarely on the great festival days.[88] The intention combined with this usage is obvious. The king's day of exaltation was to coincide with the days of the exaltation of the Lord in order to make, by this coincidence, the terrestrial kingship appear all the more transparent against the background of the kingship of Christ. This tendency, however, had also a retroactive effect. The commemoration of the Lord's days of exaltation was to recall the most solemn celebration in a king's life, his coronation. Hence there originated one of the queerest customs of the Middle Ages, the *coronamenta* or festival coronations of emperors and kings.[89]

We should distinguish, as far as this is possible, betwéen festival "crown-wearings" and festival "coronations"; but admittedly the line between these two institutions fluctuates. It is natural that the great feasts of the Church called for a full-dress pageantry on the part of the clergy as well as of the secular power, especially when the latter became

---

[87] In the later Order of Mainz *ca.* 980 (cf. Schramm, "Krönung in Deutschland," p. 326, § 6) certain intentions for the king were added to the Litany:
"... et inter cetera inferenda sunt:
Ut hunc famulum tuum N. ad regem eligere digneris,
te rogamus, audi nos.
Ut eum benedicere et sublimare digneris,
te rogamus ...
Ut eum ad imperii fastigium producere digneris,
te rogamus ... "
They agree, *mutatis mutandis*, with the intentions added to the Litany in the Gallican *Ordo de sacris ordinibus*, Migne, *PL.*, CXXXVIII, col. 1011D; for the manuscripts see Andrieu, *Ordines*, I, 576, *s.v.* "Psalmista id est cantor ... "
[88] Thomas Michels, *Beiträge zur Geschichte des Bischofsweihetages im christlichen Altertum und im Mittelalter*, Liturgiegeschichtliche Forschungen, Heft 10 (Münster in Westphalia, 1927).
[89] On the *coronamenta*, cf. Schramm, *English Coronation*, pp. 31 f., 56 f., and *passim*, and the same author's "Der König von Frankreich," *ZfRG.*, kan. Abt., XXV (1936), 273 ff., as well as his "Ordines-Studien III," *ArchUF.*, XV (1938), 324 ff., where further evidence may be added from *Vita Lanfranci*, c. VI, 52, *AA. SS.*, May VI, 835. The crown-wearings in Germany have been carefully studied by Hans-Walter Klewitz, "Die Festkrönungen der deutschen Kaiser," *ZfRG.*, kan. Abt. XXVIII (1939), 48–96, beginning with a *coronamentum* of Otto I in 970. For Byzantine crown-wearings on the festivals, see the material gathered by Heldmann, *op. cit.*, pp. 297 f., 295, n. 4; on Easter in 526, Pope John I performed the festival crowning of Justin I, cf. Mansi, *op. cit.*, VIII, 457; *Liber pont.*, I, 175. See also the discussion of Du Cange, *Descriptio ecclesiae S. Sophiae*, chap. 43, in the edition of Paulus Silentarius by Immanuel Becker (Bonn, 1837), pp. 100 f.

more and more "clericalized." On these days the archbishops would wear their palls which they were entitled to don only on very few occasions.[90] And correspondingly, the king would wear his crown on Christmas, Easter, and Pentecost. Exactly when this custom arose, we do not know. Such "crown-wearings" were certainly an old tradition in Byzantium.[91] In the West, they were customary ever since Carolingian times at the latest. Charlemagne, on that Christmas morning in 800, apparently strode to St. Peter's with the crown on his head and probably removed it, according to Byzantine usage, on his entrance into the church.[92] We know that Charles the Bald wore a diadem with a silk veil, an *epirriptarion*, on his head when on festivals or Sundays he went to church. It is this Byzantine headgear, not the custom of going to the High Mass under his crown, which makes the slightly irritated Annalist exclaim: "He contemned the customs of the Frankish kings and considered the Greek glories highest."[93]

With this usage we have to connect the singing of *laudes in festis diebus*. It is as though the exposition of the crown—and correspondingly of the pall of the metropolitans—required an acclamation. And this practice became all the more imperative, when gradually these "crown-wearings" became much more than merely a full-dress pageantry to recall to the people, by the display of the royal insignia, the power and splendor of regality. By the tenth century, perhaps even earlier, the crown was no longer a headgear which the king was entitled to put on and off at his pleasure, as obviously Charles the Bald still had done. The golden circle

[90] For the pall, see Joseph Braun, *Die liturgische Gewandung im Okzident und Orient* (Freiburg, 1907), 620 ff.; *DACL.*, XIII, 931 ff.

[91] Cf. above, n. 89; Treitinger, *op. cit.*, p. 152, emphasizes that the imperial crown-processions do not seem to antedate the eighth century.

[92] Heldmann, *op. cit.*, pp. 295, n. 4, 297 ff., 300, does not style this coronation a festival "crown-wearing," but the evidence adduced by him makes it clear that the celebration started as a festival *coronamentum* in accordance with Byzantine customs. Not the crowning, but the interpretation of the crowning as an enhancement to the imperial rank by the means of the *Augustus*-acclamation was the deciding act. So far as all this is concerned, Heldmann has greatly clarified the problem of Charlemagne's coronation in 800.

[93] *Annales Fuldenses (ad a. 876)*, *MGH. SS. rer. Germ.*, ed. Kurze (1891), 86: "capite involuto serico velamine ac diademate desuper inposito dominicis festisque diebus ad aecclesiam procedere solebat. Omnem enim consuetudinem Francorum contemnens Graecas glorias optimas arbitrabatur." On the raiments alluded to, see Eichmann, "Von der Kaisergewandung im Mittelalter," *HJb.*, LVIII (1938), 278, who indicates the connections with the contemporary miniatures and the nonliturgical character of these raiments at that time. See also Nithart, II, c. 8, *MGH. SS. rer. Germ.*, ed. Pertz (1839), 21 f., who relates the arrival of envoys on the Saturday before Easter, in 841, "qui coronam et omnem ornatum, tam regium quam et quicquid ad cultum divinum pertinebat, ferebant." Cf. Schramm, *Der König von Frankreich*, I, 13. Also, the second imperial coronation of Louis II in Rome, in 872, refers obviously to a particularly solemn crown-wearing, an interpretation which would render unnecessary the all-too-complicated theories of A. Henggeler, *Die Salbungen und Krönungen des Königs und Kaisers Ludwig II. (844–850–872)*, Fribourg, diss., 1934; cf. Levillain, in *Le Moyen âge*, XLV (1935), 276–284. The question arises whether the Old Testament was not the model of repeated coronations; cf. 1 Chron. 29:22: "Et unxerunt secundo Salomonem filium David."

in itself had become "sacramental" and had the character of a quasi-liturgical raiment. The theory arose that it was not the king's office to put on in his chamber this insignia of the anointed, but that it was the privilege of the competent metropolitan to place the crown on the king's head, in a ritual way and with appropriate prayers, whenever he was to wear it.[94] This act of "crowning" the king anew on feast days became a punctilio of liturgical ceremonies. In fact, the "crowning" was but a simplified repetition of the inaugural coronation, lacking, of course, the anointment which could not be repeated. If one adds to these recurrent coronations the practice observed by some rulers of confessing or even of fasting before every crown-wearing, just as he might have done before his inaugural coronation, or as the bishop did before the feast days,[95] it becomes obvious that every wearing of the crown, rare altogether, was removed from the profane to the sacramental level. Moreover, it is striking how far the assimilation of royal and episcopal rites had proceeded. The king, in fact, adopted episcopal customs just as the bishops adopted royal customs and prerogatives, and often it is difficult to tell whether priority should be sought in the royal or in the episcopal orbit. By and large, however, pall-wearings and crown-wearings coincided. The crown-wearing days were multiplied in later times,[96] apparently with the pall-wearings, whereas on the other hand, the *laudes regiae* finally were called *Acclamatio pallii*.[97] In short, the celebration of Church festivals

---

[94] The right of crowning the king on festivals was claimed in England by the archbishop of Canterbury, cf. Schramm, *English Coronation*, pp. 42 f. In France it finally became a prerogative of the archbishop of Rheims, on whom this right was conferred by Pope Urban II; cf. Migne, *PL.*, CLI, col. 310, and Schramm, "Der König von Frankreich," *ZfRG.*, kan. Abt. XXV (1936), 281. See also above, n. 47.

[95] Schramm, "Der König von Frankreich," p. 273, notes 2 and 3, and the same author's *English Coronation*, p. 31.

[96] Schramm, Der König von Frankreich," p. 275, n. 1, quotes Pseudo-Turpin's fabulous relation that Charlemagne celebrated four annual *dies coronae*. The "classical" crown-wearings were limited to the three great festivals. See, e.g., *Anglo-Saxon Chronicle* (ed. Thorpe, Rolls Series, 23), 189. See also Barbarossa's privilege for Bohemia, *MGH. Const.*, I, 236, No. 170, where the days of the Bohemian saints, Vencislaus and Adalbert are added; Bonizo *op. cit.* (cf. above, n. 72), on the other hand, enumerates a list of feast days (in addition to the three festivals we find Epiphany, Ascension, All Saints, the Days of St. Mary and the Apostles Peter and Paul, the dedication of the respective cathedral and the bishop's anniversary) as laudes days which indicates the close relation with the days of wearing the pall as far as metropolitans are concerned. In Rome, after the eleventh century, there were eighteen *dies coronae*; cf. *Liber cens.*, II, 90; for the English usages under Henry III, cf. below, pp. 100 ff. The rise of the cult of St. Mary added several new laudes days, and for Mary's Coronation there has been composed, in 1922, an acclamatory song from parts of the *Te Deum* and of the *laudes regiae*, cf. *RCGr.*, XXVI, 227.

[97] Klewitz, "Festkrönungen," p. 68 f., very discreetly indicates the possibility of a parallelism between days of crown-wearing and of pall-wearing. He is apparently quite correct; cf. Fred R. Gale, in *Notes and Queries*, CLVIII (1930), 118, who describes a little pamphlet distributed at Rouen which has the title *Christus vincit, Acclamations pour le Pallium* (Imprimatur of the Archbishop Albert of Tours, December 8, 1916). The hierarchic aspects, as far as the laudes are concerned, clearly prevail in Bonizo's *De vita christiana*, II, c. 51.

and of the most prominent festival of kingship began to grow together and became inextricably interlaced during a period of nearly three centuries.

The change from festival crown-wearings to festival crownings was not a rapid one. Repeated crownings occurred above all when the king married or remarried, because on this occasion the inaugural crowning of the queen would usually be preceded by a festival re-crowning of the king. The earliest example belongs either to the year 865 when Lothar II recognized Thietberga as his legitimate queen, or to 866, when Charles the Bald had his Queen Irmintrude crowned at Soissons.[98] By the tenth century, the growth of festival crownings had increased; it is traceable in most of the European kingdoms, in France under Hugh Capet and in Germany under Otto I, but also in England after the Conquest at the latest.[99] The eleventh and twelfth centuries seem to mark the high tide of this practice which rapidly faded away during the thirteenth.

These *coronamenta* or repeated crownings were not only an increase of solemnity owing to the Church festival. They were, it has been said, "an ecclesiastico-legal act which bestowed no new status on the king but did exhibit him anew, in the language of symbolism then understood, as the manifest ruler of his people."[100] It was essential that the king, in that capacity, should be seen by as many of his subjects as possible. The act of re-crowning within the church certainly was important. But the spectacular pageantry for the crowd that could not enter the cathedral, was the king's great procession with the crown on his head, a performance which often has been considered the ecclesiastical equivalent of the ancient triumphal procession of the Imperator.[101] And indeed, the elaborate processions of the Byzantine emperor on the Church festivals, as well as on other occasions, make the uninterrupted survival of the Roman tradition quite obvious.[102] The imperial procession in Byzantium, unless it circulated within the palace, took its way from the emperor's chambers to Santa Sophia or another church. A festival coronation proper did not take place, since the emperor placed the crown on his own head and

---

[98] Schramm, *Der König von Frankreich*, I, 23, n. 1.

[99] Richer, *Historiae*, IV, c. 13, *MGH. SS. rer. Germ.*, ed. Waitz (1877), 134, referring to Christmas in 987; cf. Schramm, "Der König von Frankreich," p. 275, n. 2. For Otto I's crown-wearing on Easter in 970, cf. Klewitz, *op. cit.*, p. 51. For England, cf. the *Anglo-Saxon Chronicle* quoted above, n. 96.

[100] Schramm, *English Coronation*, p. 31.

[101] See the *Constitutum Constantini*, c. 14, ed. C. Mirbt, *Quellen*, 111, for the imperial and papal processions respectively. For the connection between *triumphus* and *processio*, see the *Graphia aureae urbis Romae: Libellus*, c. 10 and 19, ed. Schramm, *Kaiser, Rom und Renovatio*, 11, 97, 101. The "procession" is sometimes closely related with the *adventus* of a ruler; see Peterson, "Die Einholung des Kyrios," p. 693, n. 3, on the relation between reception and triumph.

[102] Above, n. 91.

consequently left the palace crowned.[103] The Western ritual was more complicated owing to the act of crowning. In fact, two churches were needed for the accomplishment of the full program.[104] In the one church, the king was crowned by the competent archbishop or bishop, so that he could wear the crown on the street. Then followed the second part of the great public show: the king paraded in solemn procession together with the bishop, or occasionally even with the pope,[105] from the first church to the cathedral. Here he attended the service at the beginning of which, after the introductory prayers, selected cantors chanted the *laudes regiae.* After Mass the king returned, again in procession, to the palace, where a banquet, presided over by the king, who still wore his crown, concluded the day. The acme of the pageantry, and in every respect its central part, was the High Mass in the cathedral at which the king presented himself as the vicar of Christ. And the symbolism of this display was increased on the part of the Church by repeating the acclamations of the inaugural crowning and thus recognizing, once more and publicly, the king as the Son crowned by the Lord and adopted by His Church.[106] The laudes chant, therefore, was not merely an additional festival song, but a legal, or crypto-legal, act as well, and must be considered an integral part of the royal presentation within the framework of the Church. Here, too, it is clarifying to recall the practices in ancient Rome, where the Caesar, at intervals, was publicly acclaimed as *Imperator*—when a victory of one of the generals was announced, or at an imperial triumph, or when important administrative changes or laws were proclaimed. These acclamations likewise added nothing new to the status of the Caesar, but they represented a recognition and new acknowledgment of the Caesar as *Imperator* and were considered important enough to be recorded on the imperial coins.[107] The form of these acclamations and the occasions on which they were offered changed in Christian times; the underlying idea, however, was merely modified and accommodated to new conditions.

These customs must be taken into account in order to understand why so many provincial cathedrals possessed service books containing "Orders for the Coronation of Kings" and texts of laudes, although a real corona-

---

[103] Cf. Treitinger, *op. cit.,* p. 150, n. 31; see, however, also *ibid.,* p. 63, n. 78.

[104] See the paragraph in Benzo of Alba's *Ad Heinricum,* in *MGH. SS.,* XI, 656 f., and Klewitz' (*op. cit.,* pp. 71, 73 f.) clear interpretation of this passage.

[105] Pope and emperor together paraded, on *Laetare* in 1131, in Liège, and, in 1133, on Witsun, in Rome; Klewitz, *op. cit.,* p. 56, notes 3, 4.

[106] See, for this very complex problem, the study of Eichmann, "Die Adoption des deutschen Königs durch den Papst," *ZfRG.,* germ. Abt., XXXVII (1916), 291 ff.

[107] They are recorded with a figure so that, e. g., *IMP. XVI* on a Roman coin would refer not to the sixteenth year of the reign but to the sixteenth acclamation as *Imperator;* cf. Mommsen, *Römisches Staatsrecht,* II, 2 (3d ed., 1887), 782 ff.; Rosenberg, *RE.,* IX, 1139, *s.v.* "Imperator" as well as under the names of the individual emperors.

tion had never taken place nor was ever likely to take place in that cathedral. The manuscript transmission of laudes, we cannot doubt, is often connected in one way or another with the *coronamenta*. Yet, there are merely inner relations between festival crownings and laudes, and one should refrain from trying to establish general rules where there are none.

However, one of these inner relations can be recognized in the fact that the number of laudes formularies increases with the increasing diffusion of the *coronamenta* and that, in turn, the laudes disappear or undergo essential changes at the time the festival coronations become obsolete.[108] A further link between the transmission of laudes formularies and *coronamenta* must be sought in the "festival itinerary" of the various kings. Where did the king spend Christmas, Easter, or Whitsun? This is important to know. For frequently, though not always, the recording of laudes in liturgical manuscripts may have depended upon whether or not the king customarily spent one of the great feast days in that cathedral town. General convenience, as well as economic considerations, would be decisive in the choice of place, all the more so as the custom arose to defer the royal diets to one of the great festivals, usually Easter or Whitsuntide. This combination of diets, crown-wearings, and Church festivals, when it became effective, influenced the itinerary of the kings not inconsiderably. The German kings, for instance, who in former days celebrated the festivals in their rural palaces, began to favor, from the early eleventh century, the episcopal towns for staging their elaborate ceremonial;[109] and this custom depended upon, and at the same time promoted, the general development toward a reurbanization of mediaeval life. Hence, economic-social development and court ceremonial moved in the same direction.

In some of the European countries the kings, therefore, would move for these celebrations in somewhat regular turns to one of the favored cathedral towns. In England, this festival itinerary of the king was worked out meticulously by William the Conqueror. His program prescribed the celebration of Christmas at Gloucester, of Easter at Winchester, and of Pentecost at Westminster.[110] Consequently, we should expect to have laudes texts preserved from these three cathedrals. How-

---

[108] The increasing number of manuscripts containing laudes in twelfth-century France (Schramm, in *ZfRG.*, kan. Abt., XXV, 1936, p. 340, n. 4) proves very little because the number of manuscripts then increased in general. Their disappearance is more striking. The crown-wearings, e. g., continue in the Empire during the Hohenstaufen period and thereafter, but the laudes disappear about 1100 A.D.

[109] Klewitz, *op. cit.*, pp. 77 ff., 85 f.; see also Bruno Heusinger, *"Servitium regis* in der deutschen Kaiserzeit," *ArchUF.*, VIII (1923), 65 ff., who points out that the German kings and emperors, shortly after 1000 A.D., began to spend the festivals preferably in episcopal towns.

[110] *Anglo-Saxon Chronicle*, ed. Thorpe, p. 189. The Anglo-Saxon itineraries here may be disregarded, since there were no pre-Norman laudes.

ever, we possess only the laudes formulary of Winchester. It is usually brought into relation with William I's festival crowning and the inaugural crowning of Queen Matilda in 1068, since the names of William and Matilda are mentioned; but of course it could just as well refer to any other crown-wearing at Winchester.[111] Furthermore, there are two thirteenth-century texts transmitted from Worcester Cathedral.[112] In this case it is easy to prove the coincidence, because the singing of laudes to Henry III on Christmas, 1232, at Worcester is recorded.[113] For two reasons, however, a perfect correspondence between festival coronations and laudes cannot be expected. In the first place, not all the laudes texts preserved have as yet been brought to light; and secondly, the custom prevailed in England that royal chaplains of the king's suite would chant this litany, hence there was no need to record the texts in the liturgical books of local cathedrals.[114]

It may be that similar conditions prevailed also in Germany; namely, that sometimes royal chaplains sang the laudes. Moreover, it is almost certain that not all the texts extant have been discovered. Finally, our knowledge of the royal itineraries is most fragmentary.[115] All this makes the task of coördinating laudes and festival coronations even more difficult. Nevertheless, in some cases a coincidence can be demonstrated. We know that Conrad II celebrated Christmas in 1024 at Minden; a laudes formulary in a manuscript of Minden mentions the name of Conrad, emperor since 1026, as *rex*, that of Gisela as *regina*.[116] The same monarch spent Christmas in 1033 at Minden, and another manuscript of Minden mentions him as *imperator*.[117] Conrad celebrated Easter of 1029 and 1034 at Ratisbon, where his predecessor, Henry II, also spent

---

[111] Cf. below, Chap. VI, notes 62–63.

[112] Below, Chap. VI, notes 65–66.

[113] *Calendar of Liberate Rolls*, I, 197.

[114] The cantors under Henry III were the royal chaplains Walter of Lench and Peter of Bedinton; cf. *Liberate Rolls*, I, 14, 441, and *passim*. Once in a while, the precentor of Westminster, Stephen of London, was ordered by the king to sing the laudes together with the monks of Westminster; *ibid.*, I, 234, 496. The cantors of King John, Eustace and Ambrose, were likewise royal chaplains; cf. *Rotuli de Liberate ac de misis et praestitis regnante Johanne*, ed. T. Duffus Hardy (London, 1844), p. 1; cf. E. Jamison, "The Sicilian Norman Kingdom in the Mind of Anglo-Norman Contemporaries," *Proceedings of the British Academy* (1938), 261, who suggests that Ambrose may be the author of the original *Estoire de la Guerre Sainte*.

[115] Klewitz, *op. cit.*, pp. 88–96, 85 f., has reconstructed the festival itineraries as far as it was possible; the evidences for the dates quoted here refer to his lists.

[116] Berlin, Staatsbibl., MS Theol. Lat. 11, fol. 114ᵛ. Conrad is "rex," Gisela "regina"; their names are preceded by those of an Emperor N. and Empress Chuonigunda, dowager of Henry II.

[117] Wolfenbüttel, Helmst. MS 1110 (1008), fol. 257; Conrad is emperor, Gisela still "regina" (which means very little as the consorts, e.g., in Carolingian times, were often styled "Queen" although they might be consorts of emperors). The date is not certain, since the names of Archbishop Piligrim of Cologne (1021–1036) and Sigebert of Minden (1022–1037) leave a scope of fourteen years (1022–1036) for dating the formulary.

this feast in 1007 and 1010; an eleventh-century formulary from Ratisbon would fit both monarchs for the king's initial "C" is written over an erasure.[118] Henry II was too often in Bamberg to allow any convincing suggestions with reference to the date of the laudes of this cathedral; however, a formulary mentioning Henry as emperor might well refer to the Easter celebrations in 1016 and 1020.[119] The coincidences are not always so striking as in these few cases. We know, for instance, that Freising was a "crown-wearing" place under Henry III, in 1048, and under Henry IV, in 1059, 1062, and 1069; but the Freising formulary at our disposal refers to a "King Otto." This might indicate that Freising had been the scene of a crown-wearing as early as the second half of the tenth century.[120] On the other hand, there is a formulary extant from Passau which can be dated accurately because the acclamations refer to Pope Sylvester II and "King" Henry II; hence, the form falls in the year 1002–03.[121] This, however, does not agree with the king's festival itinerary so far as it is known. It may be that these laudes were offered to him at his inaugural circuit after his coronation at Aachen. Yet, there

[118] Munich, Cod. Lat. 14322, fols. 98ᵛ–99ᵛ. The name of the bishop of Ratisbon, Gebhard, means very little, as three bishops of this name followed one another; the name of the abbot of St. Emmeram is lacking; Georg Swarzenski, *Die Regensburger Buchmalerei des 10. und 11. Jahrhunderts* (Leipzig, 1901), 191, suggests the time of Gebhard II (1023–1036) and Abbot Ridolfus. The form may have referred originally to Henry II, king from 1002 to 1014, who was twice at Ratisbon during this period; the laudes in the Cassel, Landesbibl. MS 4° theol. 15, seem to fall in this period, too. A second text of laudes in the Munich manuscript (fols. 1ᵛ–4) displays archaic forms and refers probably to St. Gall.

[119] Bamberg, Cod. Lit. 6 (Ed. III. 7), fol. 92; cf. F. Leitschuh, *Katalog der Handschriften der kgl. Bibliothek zu Bamberg*, I, 1 (Bamberg, 1898), 147; Migne, *PL.*, CXL, cols. 54 f.; *AA. SS.*, July III, 699. The text refers to the "Emperor" Henry II, but to "Queen" Cunigunda (cf. above, n. 116). That a *nobilissima proles* is acclaimed, although it was the Joseph-like marriage of Henry II which made him a saint, shows that this acclamation was formulatory. The conclusions drawn from this formula are therefore bound to be wrong. P. Kehr, in his Introduction to *MGH. Dipl. Karoli Tertii*, p. xl, is quite correct when stating with reference to the various *proles*-prayers: "Als historische Zeugnisse sind diese formelhaften Bestimmungen . . . ohne Bedeutung."

[120] For manuscript and editions, cf. below, Chap. IV, n. 12, p. 114. The bishop acclaimed is Abraham of Freising (957–994). Otto is styled "king"; the queen's name is Oda, i.e., the name of King Arnulph's queen, which, however, does not occur in the Saxon dynasty.

Another form of laudes referring to an Emperor Otto, his Empress, and the *proles regalis*, is found in the Bamberg Cod. Lit. 5 (Ed. V. 9), fol. 46; cf. Leitschuh, *op. cit.*, p. 143. The manuscript is a Troper, written perhaps in the monastery of Reichenau; cf. P. von Winterfeld, in *Zeitschrift für deutsches Altertum*, XLVII (1904), 328; Clemens Blume, in *Analecta Hymnica*, XXXIV (1900), 6. The date suggested by Winterfeld is 1008 A.D. which would make the acclamation to "Otto" a commemorative acclaim such as is found in laudes of Pope Hadrian II (868 A.D.) in which Pope Nicholas I is acclaimed "sempiterna memoria"; *Liber pont.*, II, 177. But this practice does not occur in the *laudes regiae* during the Middle Ages (cf. Chap. VII, n. 4, p. 181, for the sixteenth century). The name Otto as that of the king had itself become a formula after three kings of this name had ruled.

[121] Vienna, Nationalbibl., Cod. Lat. 1817 (theol. 277), fols. 183ᵛ–184; cf. Andrieu, *Ordines Romani*, I, 388, 397; the form has been published by M. Gerbert, *Monumenta veteris liturgiae Alemannicae* (St. Blasien, 1779), 110. The reference to Passau is found in the acclamation to the clergy: "Omni clero Pataviensis aecclesiae vita et victoria."

always remains the possibility of a much simpler solution: the laudes were sung in the king's absence.

Thus, in spite of a few agreements between texts and itineraries, it seems difficult to establish any plausible general rule. It is surprising, for instance, that no formulary seems to be extant from Merseburg where the kings and emperors celebrated the festivals so frequently. Was it in this cathedral that the king's chaplains voiced the laudes? Or were these acclamations unknown in the non-Frankish eastern German cathedrals? Also, it is remarkable that not one German formulary seems to be preserved from a date later than the reign of Henry IV. Was it because of the Investiture Strife and its implications that changes in the liturgy had taken place? Was the ecclesiastical worship of the ruler then cut down to a minimum?[122]

A course different from both England and Germany was apparently taken in France. Correlations between laudes and crown-wearings can hardly be detected. The distinction between laudes referring to a special crown-wearing and laudes referring to Church festivals in general is most problematic in Germany; in France such a distinction is almost impossible. It seems that the chanting of laudes in France was more closely attached to the various Church festivals than to the inaugural or festival crownings of the king. That is to say, the laudes were sung because it was Christmas, Easter, or Pentecost, and not because the king was crowned or re-crowned. If the laudes were really sung at an inaugural coronation, the reason was probably that the celebration took place on a feast day. But the decisive factor for voicing this litany was obviously the feast day as such, not the king's coronation or *couronnement au petit pied*. This connection with the ecclesiastical calendar implied, on the other hand, a much greater popularity of the laudes in France than in any other country. They were sung, on the Church festivals, in a great many French cathedrals.[123] And the primary connection with the calen-

---

[122] The laudes for Henry IV (Dümmler, *Anselm der Peripatetiker*, 89 f.) are not even of German origin; they are "Burgundian." The bishop acclaimed was Henry IV's chancellor, Ogerius of Ivrea. The only twelfth-century form of non-Roman imperial laudes is from Aquileia; cf. Bernardo Maria de Rubeis, *Monumenta Ecclesiae Aquileiensis* (1740), 588 ff. The date of these laudes, 1145–1153, is determined by the acclamations to Pope Eugene III (1145–1153) and to Patriarch Pelegrinus (1130–1161); the other intentions refer to an Emperor N., his Empress, to a King N. and his Queen, to the clergy, and to the judges and Christian army. For certain changes in the liturgy within the Empire during the eleventh century, see also Ladner, in *Speculum* XVII (1942), 197, and Klauser, "Die liturgischen Austauschbeziehungen," *HJb.*, LIII (1933), 188 f.

[123] I have noted within modern France, laudes in the following cathedrals: Aix, Arles, Autun, Beauvais, Besançon, Châlons, Chartres, Elne, Laon, Limoges, Lyons, Narbonne, Nevers, Orléans, Paris, Rheims, Rouen, Senlis, Sens, Soissons, Tours, Troyes, and Vienne. This list of twenty-two cathedrals is far from complete. Many of these cathedrals served, at some time or other, as stages for royal crown-wearings. To synchronize these crown-wearings with the respective laudes, if it were possible, would require a special study on each individual cathedral, which is beyond the scope of this study. For Tours, see Martene, I, 363, 568 f.

dar of the Church resulted not only in a wider diffusion, but also in a longer survival of the laudes in France than in any other country. For when the observance of solemn crown-wearings died away in the thirteenth century, and with it the singing of the *laudes regiae* proper, the old tradition was not discarded in France. The song became attached exclusively to the bishop or archbishop; it changed into *Acclamations pour le pallium*, chanted on the days when the archbishop wore the pall.[124] It finally referred to the hierarchy alone and not to the ruler as well, although frequently parts of the original laudes or even the whole form were adapted for the exaltation of the princes of the Church.

FRANKISH PSALTERS AND ROMAN ORDINES

By a most unfortunate combination of circumstances the terms "Gallican" and "Roman" were applied, seventy years ago, to two different types of laudes.[125] Whatever the meaning of these terms may then have been, today these distinctions are both too narrow and too wide; their semicorrectness obscures rather than clarifies the problem, and with regard to the historical development these designations miss the essential point because they do not elucidate the mutual borrowing. The terms "Roman" and "Gallican" have forfeited much of their former simple meaning. The various relations, interpenetrations, and mutual exchanges, in short the whole crisscross of give and take between the two rituals, proves to be too complicated to be covered by two simple catchwords.

As far as the laudes are concerned, these terms are greatly misleading. It is not even convenient to style the form that begins with the *Christus vincit, Christus regnat, Christus imperat* "Gallican" and a type different from this "Roman." In the first place, the "Gallican" laudes are Frankish. Second, most of the elements, though not the textual composition, of the so-called Gallican laudes can be traced to Rome. Third, every so-called Roman form is influenced by the Frankish composition which retroacted on Rome. Furthermore, the truly essential feature of the so-called Roman laudes is not their being "Roman" but their being "episcopal" or "papal," as will be shown in the next chapter. Finally, the terms are obstructive to a more careful analysis. For there is indeed a Frankish formulary which might be called Roman because eventually it was adapted to Roman usage. Its significance has hitherto never been recognized, since it has not even been clearly distinguished from the Gallo-Frankish form.

For all these reasons it is advisable to apply distinctions of greater precision to the various forms and to choose designations which really

---

[124] Cf. above, n. 97.
[125] The terms were introduced by Prost, *Quatre pièces*, pp. 163 ff., and have since been generally adopted; cf. *DACL.*, VIII, cols. 1898–1910, *s.v.* "Laudes Gallicanae."

explain what they indicate and at the same time expose the historical unfolding of the laudes. Hence, the form mainly dealt with until now has been called "Gallo-Frankish," a name which indicates the genuine Frankish and Transalpine, though not ancient "Gallican," character of the composition. The laudes customarily called Roman will here figure always as that which they are, namely "Papal" laudes. And the Frankish form adapted to Roman practice and bound up with the *Ordines Romani*, though not incorporated into them, will be styled "Franco-Roman." And with this last pattern we now concern ourselves.

The formulary first appears about a score of years after the coronation of Charlemagne in 800. Rome, by that time, had accommodated herself to the liturgical worship of the Frankish ruler. Pope Hadrian I had introduced the name of the Frankish king as Roman Patricius into the prayers of the urban Roman ritual. It was Hadrian I who ordered everyone to bend his knee for Charles on Saturday during Lent. It was he who introduced a special prayer to be said for the king on Wednesday in Holy Week. It was probably Pope Hadrian who introduced the commemoration of the Frankish king into the Roman *Praeconium Paschale*, whereas this *Memoria* previously seems to have figured only in the prayers of the Frankish rite.[126] And it was Pope Hadrian who first had the laudes sung to Charles in a Roman service. There is every reason to believe that the liturgical acclamations in the form of the Gallo-Frankish litany were not heard in Rome before Easter Monday of 774.[127] This date, therefore, may mark for our purpose the terminus of the first entrance of the *Christus vincit, Christus regnat, Christus imperat* with the ensuing saints into a service held in a Roman basilica. It is doubtful whether, before that date, even the classical *vita*-acclamation, though by itself Roman of the Romans, was voiced in Rome during the Mass. The only precedent is in 602 when Gregory the Great ordered the clergy and senate of Rome to acclaim the imperial icons in the *basilica Julii* of the Lateran; and in this case nothing indicates that the cry *Exaudi Christe! Focae Augusto et*

---

[126] For Hadrian I and Charlemagne, see Hans Hirsch, "Der mittelalterliche Kaisergedanke in den liturgischen Gebeten," *Mitteilungen des Oesterreichischen Instituts für Geschichtsforschung*, XLIV (1930), 1 ff.; Ladner, *op. cit.*, pp. 194 f.

The commemoration of the ruler at the end of the *Exultet* is older than the Sacramentary of Rheinau (end of the eighth century). It is already in the Antiphonary of León (so-called Antiphonary of King Wamba); it refers, like many old texts, to a plurality of rulers, and is couched very archaically as follows:

"Tribue etiam, Domine sancte, pater omnipotens Deus, Ut diei huius sollemnia sacre paschalis, in quo redemptoris nostri gloria predicatur et gratia, cum antistite nostro Illo aepo., cum *gloriosis principibus* Illis, cum presbiteres, diaconibus, clero adque omni populo sub multorum curriculo celebrare mereamur annorum."

There follows the *Pax* litany quoted above, p. 48, n. 123. Cf. G. Prado, *Textos ineditos de la liturgia Mozarába* (Madrid, 1926), 51 f.

[127] Cf. above, Chap. II, n. 139.

Leontiae Augustae vita! was inserted into a Mass. However this may be, it seems that the Roman legal acclamation became really "presentable" at Mass only after it had been passed on to the Frankish Church and there brought, as a special chant, into the solemn framework of a Litany of the Saints. That is to say, only after the ancient constitutive acclaim of the Romans had been established in France as a festival psalmody was it acknowledged in Rome as a liturgical chant which found its orderly place within the Roman service. At any rate, in its Frankish accouterments the legal acclaim of the Romans became admissible at the divine service within the city, and it may be taken for granted that on Charlemagne's later visits to Rome, especially on Easter in 781, when his sons Pepin and Louis were baptized and consecrated, the chant was offered to him in the traditional Frankish form.

There followed Christmas 800, and therewith the chant of the Frankish Psalters became decisive in the making of world history. Instead of the customary hail sung in the Christmas laudes to "Charles, the Frankish and Lombard king and Patricius of the Romans," the indignant monarch heard acclaims to Charles, the *Augustus* and *Imperator*. The litanized laudes of the Frankish Church, which had been incorporated along with the Litany of the Saints into the Frankish Psalters, suddenly demonstrated, on Roman soil, their original legal power. The Frankish chant had not changed, but the significance of the chant and, metaphorically, its place also. For it had wandered, so to speak, from the Frankish Psalters to the Roman *Ordines*, from a book of hymns, jubilant or penitential, to a book of legal orders and ecclesiastical organization. Rome lent no ear to the beautiful phrases of the *Christus vincit*. There was audible to Roman ears merely the electoral shout *Exaudi Christe! Imperatori vita et victoria!* The Frankish litany, on this occasion, reverted to the constitutive acclaim of the emperors which it had been originally; and the token of Frankish David-kingship came back to Rome as an instrument of statecraft by means of which, according to papal conception, the *Imperium Romanum* was legally turned over to a new Emperor of the Romans. Whatever Charlemagne may have had in mind or have felt, eventually Pope Sergius II, two generations later, was right when coining the formula: Charlemagne "united as one body the Empires of Romans and Franks" ("Romanorum Francorumque concòrporavit imperium"),[128] a statement which felicitously expresses the main point of papal policy ever since the days of Pepin or even Charles Martel.

Of this *concorporatio* of *Regnum Davidicum* and *Imperium Romanum*, of Frankish Psalters and Roman Orders, the new Franco-Roman formulary of laudes, a by-product of Charlemagne's Roman coronation, is

---

[128] *MGH. Epist.*, V, 583 (844 A.D.).

merely another symbol. It is transmitted, in Carolingian times, exclusively in such collections of *Ordines* which are themselves characteristic of the blending of Frankish and Roman liturgies. Moreover, though the new chant still shows unmistakably the pattern of the Gallo-Frankish litany, its new redaction betrays the work of a hand that tried to fit the formulary into the Roman program and Roman style. In fact, it represents a form not of *laudes regiae* but of *laudes imperiales*, for it always refers to an emperor.

The changes were made, quite obviously, in Rome and presumably in the early years of Louis the Pious. A laudes form referring to Charlemagne as emperor has not survived. In Rome, there was no need of drafting a formulary of imperial laudes for Charles. He never again set foot on Roman ground as though he shunned the city to which he owed his enhancement. Rome did not need a formulary of imperial laudes before Louis the Pious was crowned at Rheims, in 816. We learn that Pope Stephen IV when coming to Rheims brought with him the "Crown of Constantine" to place on the emperor's head. He thus was prepared to perform a coronation in France. Also, we know that the pope chanted the laudes to Louis the Pious on this occasion. Therefore, we are probably not too far from the truth if we surmise that the laudes chanted at Rheims, in 816, was a redaction made in Rome before Pope Stephen's departure. At any rate, from the time of Louis the Pious two redactions of laudes coexisted side by side: the old Gallo-Frankish and the new Franco-Roman forms. From the Gallo-Frankish form there eventually branched off the French, German, Anglo-Norman, and Siculo-Norman laudes, whereas the Franco-Roman pattern survived only in the Roman ambit, although on one occasion, in the time of Louis the German, it pressed on into Bavaria.

This juxtaposition of the two forms is illustrated by the Verona Codex 92 (87), our earliest evidence for the Franco-Roman laudes and at the same time the earliest manuscript of the Franco-Roman *Ordines* Collections.[129] At the very end of the book (fols. 67^r–71^v), we find three formularies of laudes, all of them mutilated and fragmentary. The first form is arranged for "general" usage; that is, the proper names are replaced by an anonymous *ille;* it is the earliest "general" form known. It contains intentions for the bishop of Verona, an emperor, and an empress. It seems to represent a form similar to that of Chieti for Pope Nicholas I and Emperor Louis II—"festival" acclamations of the Gallo-Frankish type.[130]

---

[129] Andrieu, *Ordines*, I, 367 ff., 371 f. I can refer only to the reliable, though fragmentary, notes offered by Andrieu, since, unfortunately, I missed inspecting the manuscript and was too late in securing photostats before the war.

[130] This is intimated by the fact that (1) there is an acclamation to the local bishop, that (2) the acclaim to the bishop precedes those to the emperor and the empress, and

There follows another form of which the beginning is destroyed. The acclamations refer to the two Emperors Louis the Pious and Lothar ("augustis a Deo coronatis et pacificis imperatoribus") and to the Empresses Judith, married to Louis in 819, and Irmingarde, Lothar's empress since 821. The form, probably, falls in the early 'twenties of the ninth century: that is, in the time of Lothar's activity in Northern Italy; it seems to represent our first evidence of Franco-Roman laudes.[131] We are sure of this in respect to the equally mutilated third formulary, for it contains, preceding the acclamation to the Empresses Judith and Irmingarde, the intention for the imperial princes in the Franco-Roman manner: "Eius precellentissimis filiis regibus vita." The Verona Codex is so far the only manuscript to offer at the same time the Gallo-Frankish and Franco-Roman types of laudes referring to the same persons.

The Cologne MS 138 belongs also to the first quarter of the ninth century. It contains almost the same "Gallicanized" collection of *Ordines* and other liturgical forms as the Verona Codex, and the laudes again are found on the very last folio (44^r-v). Their text, which here may serve as a model, is as follows:[132]

Exaudi Christe	R/ Domino nostro a Deo decreto summo pontifici et universali pape vita.
Salvator mundi	Tu illum adiuva.
Exaudi Christe	Domino nostro N. augusto et a Deo coronato magno et pacifico imperatori vita et victoria.
Sancta Maria	Tu illum adiuva.
Exaudi Christe	Eius precellentissimis filiis regibus vita.
Sancte Petre	Tu illos adiuva.
Exaudi Christe	Exercitui Romanorum et Francorum vita et victoria.
Sancte Theodore	Tu illos adiuva.

Christus vincit, Christus regnat, Christus imperat.

	R/ Christus vincit, Christus regnat, Christus imperat.
Rex regum	R/ Christus vincit.
Rex noster	Christus vincit.
Spes nostra	Christus vincit.
Gloria nostra	Christus vincit.

that (3) more than one saint at a time is invoked. All this disagrees with the Franco-Roman forms and matches the form of Chieti found in the Vatican, Reg. MS 1997, fol. 160^v; cf. Maassen, *op. cit.*, I, 527; Gaudenzi, in *Bullettino dell'Istituto Storico Italiano*, XXXVII (1916), 376.

[131] This is intimated by the invocations of St. Martin and St. Benedict which conclude the laudes in the Munich Cod. Lat. 14510 (see below) apparently in a similar way. In the third form of the Verona manuscript, the acclamation to the princes is followed, as usual in the Franco-Roman forms, by the invocation of St. Peter; the empresses follow, consequently, with that of St. Paul, who in the Munich manuscript is the protector of King Louis the German, acclaimed after the princes.

[132] Andrieu, *op. cit.*, I, 107; cf. *ibid.*, I, 472. The laudes are printed in J. Hartzheim, *Catalogus historicus criticus codicum mss. bibliothecae ecclesiae metropolitanae Coloniensis* (1752), 103 f.

Misericordia nostra	Christus vincit.
Auxilium nostrum	Christus vincit.
Fortitudo nostra	Christus vincit.
Liberatio nostra	Christus vincit.
Arma nostra invictissima	Christus vincit.
Murus noster inexpugnabilis	Christus vincit.
Defensio et exaltatio nostra	Christus vincit.
Lux, via et vita nostra	Christus vincit.

Ipsi soli imperium, gloria et potestas per immortalia secula seculorum.   Amen.

Ipsi soli virtus, fortitudo et victoria per omnia secula seculorum.   Amen.

Ipsi soli honor, laus et jubilatio per infinita secula seculorum.   Amen.

This model is found also in the Munich Cod. Lat. 14510 the central and older part of which, including the laudes, agrees on the whole with the contents of the two manuscripts mentioned above.[133] The date of the laudes is ascertained by the acclamation to Pope Eugenius II (824–827); there follow the acclamations to Louis the Pious as Emperor, to the "precellentissimi filii reges," and to King Louis the German. Moreover, intentions are added for Bishop Baturic of Ratisbon (817–847), for the clergy ("pastores et rectores"), and for the monks of St. Emmeram. These last three hails are preceded by the acclamation to the army which is styled, uniquely in this group of formularies, "exercitus Francorum" instead of "Romanorum et Francorum." The reason is obvious. The Franco-Roman model is adapted here to the use of the king of Eastern Franconia or Bavaria, and therefore it was *his* army, a Frankish army, that was to be hailed and not that of the emperor. Hence the imperial designation "Romanorum" is omitted. It is thus far the only formulary of this type which might be called a form of "Royal" laudes, whereas all the other formularies are exclusively "Imperial." The three additional intentions for the bishop, clergy, and monks are likewise unusual;[134] but since the whole formulary is followed by episcopal laudes, which normally have no place in a Roman formulary, it is quite clear that here the Franco-Roman form was accommodated to "provincial" needs.[135]

---

[133] Andrieu, *op. cit.*, I, 232 ff. Cf. Ellard, *op. cit.*, pp. 47 f., who is surely correct when emphasizing the singular character of the manuscript. The laudes are printed in C. Höfler's *Die deutschen Päpste*, I (Regensburg, 1839), 285.

[134] These intentions, apparently, are found also in the Verona MS 92; cf. above, n. 130.

[135] This "provincialization" of the Roman form probably implies more than has been realized hitherto. The manuscript contains (fol. 72ᵛ) a *Benedictio super principem* and (fol. 73) a *Benedictio regalis*. Eichmann, "Die sog. römische Königskrönungsformel," *HJb.*, XLV (1925), 544 f., suggested a consecration of Louis the German; his main argument, stressing that in the laudes of St. Gall King Louis is styled *coronatus*, is, however, so unfortunate that his hypothesis has unjustly been rejected; cf. Schramm, "Krönung in Deutschland," p. 189, n. 1; C. Erdmann, "Der ungesalbte König," *Deutsches Archiv*, II (1938), 311–340, ignores Eichmann's suggestions completely. I am inclined to believe that indeed a "consecration" of Louis the German took place in Regensburg in April or May, 826.

A fourth Carolingian form of this type is transmitted in an eleventh-century manuscript in Rome, the Biblioteca Vittorio Emanuele, Lat. MS 2096 (Sessorianus 52), in which the laudes (fol. 126^r) are placed between Gelasian formulae and the *Ordo Romanus IX*.[136] They refer to Pope Nicholas I and Emperor Louis II and follow closely the model of the Cologne manuscript.[137]

These are the Carolingian formularies of the Franco-Roman type. We find no traces of them during the decline of the papacy in the tenth century, a fact which is not surprising. Their survival, however, is indicated by the Sessorianus 52, of the eleventh century, and they reappear in the twelfth century when they are found in close connection with the Roman *Ordines* of Benedict of St. Peter's[138] and Albinus.[139] Although this Franco-Roman form fell into desuetude at the end of the twelfth century, it still was copied in later manuscripts, for instance in the late thirteenth-century Vatican Lat. MS 7114,[140] which is closely related, at least in respect to the laudes, to the mysterious Codex Gemundensis,[141] the date of which is unknown, but can hardly precede that of the Vatican codex.

[136] Andrieu, *op. cit.*, I, 289; cf. p. 287 for the manuscript. The text has been published by G. Morin, "Notice sur un manuscrit important pour l'histoire du Symbole, cod. Sessorianus 52," *Rev. bénéd.*, XIV (1897), 484; H. Grisar, *Analecta Romana*, 1 (Rome, 1899), 229; cf. *Civilià Cattolica*, XI (1903), 396.

[137] The deviations are trifling. That the emperor is styled "magno *pontifico* imperatori" is not a joke but an error ("pacifico"). The army shows four saint invocations: Paul, Andrew, John, and Theodore. Theodore is found in Morin's edition only.

[138] Cambrai, Bibl. Munic., MS 544 (twelfth century) and Rome, Bibl. Vallicell., MS F. 73, fol. 46 (fifteenth century); cf. Fabre, in *Mélanges d'archéologie et d'histoire*, X (1890), 387 f.; *Liber cens.*, II, 171.

[139] Rome, Bibl. Vat. Ottob. MS 3057 (twelfth century); for the variants from Benedict's form, see *Liber cens.*, II, 171, n. 2. In Benedict's form the acclamation to the princes has been omitted, but the invocation of St. Peter with the response "tu illos adiuva" shows that this rubric has been omitted by a mistake which found its way also into the Vallicelliana manuscript of Benedict.

[140] H. Ehrensberger, *Libri liturgici Bibliothecae Apostolicae Vaticanae* (Freiburg, 1897), 516; the form has been published by Eichmann, *Quellensammlung zur kirchlichen Rechtsgeschichte* (Paderborn, 1912), I, 60; cf. the same author's "Die Ordines der Kaiserkrönung," *ZfRG.*, kan. Abt. II (1912), 10 f., who claims that the form refers to the coronation of Arnulph, in 896, which is certainly wrong. The assertion of Eichmann's pupil Biehl, *op. cit.*, p. 110, that Arnulph came without his queen to Rome because the form contains no acclamation to the empress is pure fiction, since the Franco-Roman laudes are standardized, as a rule, to four acclamations; likewise wrong is his statement that the opening *Christus vincit* is lacking in some eighth-century formularies; and, in addition to many other distortions, his assertion is incorrect that the singing of the laudes between Collect and Epistle implies that the coronation took place between Collect and Epistle (p. 111). See also below, Appendix IV, n. 5.

[141] The Codex Gemundensis has not been rediscovered after Martène's publication; the laudes are published in *MGH. LL.*, II, 78 f. The date of this codex is controversial; Eichmann thinks it is ninth century; Erdmann, *Kreuzzugsgedanke*, p. 257, n. 32, suggests "a much later date"; Schramm, "Die Ordines der Kaiserkrönung," *ArchUF.*, XI (1929), 355, n. 2, emphasizes that the Coronation Order of this manuscript represents an abbreviation of the so-called *Cencius I* (ca. 900); the laudes suggest a remodeling at any time after the *Cencius II*. Cf. below, Appendix IV.

The most striking feature of the Franco-Roman formularies is their fixed form. Whereas the Gallo-Frankish forms gradually were adapted to the needs of various nations and therefore would reveal some diversity, the Franco-Roman form appears fixed in all details from the beginning. Without an exception, these laudes refer to an emperor.[142] They contain, as a rule, only the four acclamations for the pope, the emperor, the princes, and the army.[143] The invocations of celestial beings remain likewise unchanged: the *Salvator mundi* for the pope, St. Mary for the emperor, St. Peter for the princes, and St. Theodore for the army.[144] There is always only one invocation of saints after each acclamation, and the sequence of saints makes it more than likely that additional invocations were not provided for.[145] Furthermore, there is never an acclamation found to the *judices*, who appear in most of the Gallo-Frankish forms along with the army. The army, too, would always (except in the Munich MS 14510) display the designation "Romanorum," which never appears in the Gallo-Frankish chant. On the other hand, the designation "Christianorum," which is the rule in the Gallo-Frankish hails to the army, never occurs in the Franco-Roman forms (cf. Appendix IV). In the Gallo-Frankish forms, the princes are traditionally styled "nobilissima proles regalis"; in the Franco-Roman forms they are the "precellentissimi filii reges," an immutable part of this formulary, which makes it futile to try to use this stereotyped phrase as a basis for attributing the anonymous form to an individual emperor who has sons and whose sons

---

[142] This is true also with reference to the Munich Cod. Lat. 14510.

[143] The Munich Cod. Lat. 14510 makes an exception; cf. above, notes 130, 131.

[144] See, however, the Munich Cod. Lat. 14510 and below, n. 145.

[145] Evidence is offered by the Munich manuscript, in which we find the following sequence of saints:

Salvator mundi	(pope)
S. Maria	(emperor)
S. Petre	(princes)
S. Paule	(King Louis the German)
S. Andrea	(army)

And similarly in the Verona MS 92 (Andrieu, *op. cit.*, I, 372):

S. Petre	(princes)
S. Paule	(empresses),

as well as in the Sessorianus 52 (above, notes 136–137), where we find the following sequence:

Salvator mundi	(pope)
S. Maria	(emperor)
S. Petre	(princes)
S. Paule ⎫	
S. Andrea ⎬	(army)
S. Johannes ⎪	
S. Theodore ⎭	

That is to say, it is the sequence of the early form of the Roman (?) Litany of the Saints, without John the Baptist (cf. Duchesne, *Christian Worship*, p. 475, in the Order of St. Amand), and an insertion of other groups of saints (after the invocation of the single saints as indicated above) would not make sense and would be without parallel.

are kings.[146] Finally, there is the title of the pope which may arouse our attention. In all Gallo-Frankish forms, except the laudes of Rheims,[147] the pope is acclaimed: "N. summo pontifici et universali pape vita!" In the Franco-Roman formularies, his title is invariably: "Domino nostro N. a Deo decreto summo pontifici et universali pape vita!" The additional "a Deo decreto," by itself hardly remarkable, is however, the typically curial form of the papal title so that this change, too, indicates a close connection with Rome. Moreover, the papal "a Deo decreto" counterbalances the imperial "a Deo coronato" far better than the Gallo-Frankish hail to the pope; it therefore must be evaluated as a Roman "improvement" of the Gallo-Frankish form. And in this connection it may be stressed once more that the Gallo-Frankish sequence of saints has here been modified.[148] The pope, in the Gallo-Frankish forms, has the apostles as intercessors who rank lower than the Frankish royal patrons Mary, Archangels, and John the Baptist; in the Franco-Roman forms he heads the order of acclamations with the *Salvator mundi*, an invocation of probably Gallican origin.

If we now sum up the items discussed—the transmission of the formulary in the Romano-Frankish *Ordines* collections, the general unchanging character of the composition, the unvaried acclamation to an emperor, the consistency in adding the word "Roman" to the army acclamation, the curial title of the pope, and finally, the sequence of saints invoked— there remains but one possible conclusion: namely, that this formulary is related to Rome, is revised by Rome, and is intended to be the Roman form of laudes arranged for imperial visits and coronations. It represents the Frankish laudes in Roman attire and therefore deserves its name of Franco-Roman laudes.

If anyone is inclined to suggest the priority of the Franco-Roman laudes and could prove that the Gallo-Frankish forms derived from the Franco-Roman, he would be certain to secure fullest attention. For in this case items such as the change of the papal title, of the army designation, and, above all, of the sequence of saints, would betray an intentional revision made at the Frankish court, which would give these matters an unexpected importance. The priority of the Gallo-Frankish form, however, becomes highly probable if we take another detail into consideration.

---

[146] E.g., Eichmann, in *ZfRG.*, kan. Abt. II (1912), 10 (". . . was gerade auf Ludwig den Frommen passt"); see also the vain efforts of Wattenbach, in *Neues Archiv,* II (1877), 439, to solve the question whether the "proles regalis" in the laudes of Minden might imply that Conrad II's son Henry was already crowned king; cf. above, notes 119, 140, and Chap. II, n. 142.

[147] Migne, *PL.*, CXXXVIII, Col. 901; Chevalier, *Rheims*, p. 363; the acclamation reads: "Domno N. a Deo decreto apostolico et reverentissimo (or: sanctissimo) pape vita!" There is no indication how to explain this exception.

[148] Above, Chap. II, p. 45. Also, the sequence itself (omitting the archangels and John the Baptist) is probably Roman; above, n. 145.

A striking, and somewhat irritating, difference between the two forms is the omission in the Franco-Roman laudes of the opening *Christus vincit, Christus regnat, Christus imperat* which is found regularly in the Gallo-Frankish chant. The Romanized forms, without exception, begin with the *Exaudi Christe* and the acclamation proper. The tension, if it may be so expressed, between Frankish Psalters and Roman Ordines becomes visible once more. To the laudes as a martial Frankish litany belongs the triumphant opening, belongs the shout of *Christus vincit* which rolls forth in this song with ever-increasing vehemence. It catches the attention of the listener from the outset. Also, from an artistic point of view the triad is indispensable as an opening: it produces the unity of the whole song. It is, in fact, this triad which braces and fits tightly together the two main divisions of the song, the hails with saint-invocations and the laudatory section with the ensuing doxology. That this well-balanced unity should represent the original composition can hardly be doubted. If we now look at the Roman form, we find that the two parts—the hails and the laudatory section—follow one after the other without any inner urge. The two divisions break asunder, since there is nothing to knit them together organically. In fact, the Romanized form gives the impression that the second part (which, by the way, matches completely with the Gallo-Frankish texts) has simply been patched on something to which it does not belong. Rome, as it often happens, has enfeebled the force of the "Gallican" prayer.[149] But was the omission of the Gallo-Frankish opening merely a bungle or does it make sense?

Any number of Roman acclamations, from the earliest times, can be adduced which would consist mainly of, or begin with, the *Exaudi Christe* formula and the acclaim:[150]

Exaudi Christe!	Theoderico vitam!...
Exaudi Christe!	Symmacho vitam!...
Exaudi Christe!	Gelasio vita!...
Exaudi Christe!	Focae Augusto et Leontiae Augustae vita!

This is the constitutive Roman acclamation. We found it, four times repeated, at the end of the *laetania italica* the rubrics of which agree in essence with the four intentions of the Franco-Roman laudes. It may be surprising to find that the invocatory shout *Exaudi Christe!* is by no means a very common liturgical formula. *Exaudi Domine* or *Exaudi nos Domine*, it is true, is found by the hundreds as the initial invocation of prayers; but *Exaudi Christe* occurs only rarely, except in combination

---

[149] For a good example, see Thomas Michels, "La date du couronnement de Charles-le-Chauve (Sept. 9, 869) et le culte liturgique de S. Gorgon à Metz," *Rev. bénéd.*, XLVI (1939), 2, n. 1; see also, Kantorowicz, in *Harvard Theological Review*, XXXIV (1941), 132.

[150] Cf. above, Chap. II, notes 6, 7, 9, 10.

with an acclaim, especially with the old Roman *vita*-acclamation. Hence in the Roman ritual the *Exaudi Christe!* was almost a call suggesting "Attention! Now comes the imperial or papal salute!" That is to say: *Exaudi Christe!* as an opening had a meaning to Roman ears, and the *Christus vincit* triad obviously did not. The *Christus vincit* in the Frankish Church announced a martial chant which contained acclamations also; the *Exaudi Christe!* in Rome announced a constitutive or legal acclamation embellished, almost reluctantly, by laudatory hails and other accessories. As usual in Rome, legal thinking came before aesthetic feeling. It complied with Roman acclamatory custom to begin acclamations with *Exaudi Christe!*, and thus the redactor of the Franco-Roman formulary has omitted the opening triad of the Gallo-Frankish chant. This omission, therefore, does not seem to be due to negligence. It agreed with the *genius loci*, with Roman tradition. The four *Exaudi* cries are the core of the original Roman acclamation. Everything else—beginning with the *Salvator mundi*—is Frankish accretion adjusted to Roman needs.

The Franco-Roman form, to our knowledge, remained authoritative in Rome at the coronations of emperors. It was used until the twelfth century. Thereafter, probably in 1209, a new form of laudes to the emperor was introduced which remained in force for all the later mediaeval coronations of emperors, including the very last one performed by a pope, the coronation of Charles V at Bologna in 1530.[151] The transition from the Franco-Roman type to that of the Later Middle Ages is clearly marked out by the Coronation Order of Cencius Savelli (later Pope Honorius III), the so-called *Cencius II*. The laudes of this *Ordo* indubitably fall in the last decade of the twelfth century;[152] their text is still based on the Franco-Roman forms, but displays a significant change: the laudes to the emperor are transformed under the influence of the *laudes papales* which had come into prominence in Rome during the twelfth century.

---

[151] Below, Chap. VII, n. 2.
[152] At any rate, they are later than the laudes transmitted by Benedict; cf. below, Appendix IV. The article of Klewitz, "Papsttum und Kaiserkrönung. Ein Beitrag zur Frage nach dem Alter des *C. II*," *Deutsches Archiv*, IV (1941), which the same author announced in *ZfRG.*, kan. Abt., XXX (1941), 130, n. 101, was not available to me.

CHAPTER IV

THE LAUDES OF THE HIERARCHY

Laudes to the Bishop

MEDIAEVAL STATECRAFT and political theory vacillated between two extreme solutions of the *imitatio Christi:* priest-kingship and royal priesthood. Neither was a true solution, and the problem by its very nature could not be solved in the political sphere at all. The history of the mediaeval state is, to a great extent, the history of the interchanges between royal and sacerdotal offices, of the mutual exchange of symbols and claims. To the extent that the idea of kingship became sacerdotal, priesthood became regal. That the rite of anointing kings was revived in Gaul in the same decade that Constantine's "Donation" was drafted in Rome, is perhaps a coincidence, and yet the two events belong together.[1] The divine right of kings and the imperial right of pontiffs are diverse manifestations of the same idea, for they derive from the model of Christ the *Rex et Sacerdos* which both king and bishop emulated. In the times of the rising tide of theocratic and hierocratic thought, the ruler in his claims, functions, and forms of representation appeared more and more bishoplike. The bishop, in turn, took over royal claims, functions, and prerogatives. Among the many royal rights of honor which were gradually passed on to the bishop, there was also that of being offered the laudes in a form similar to, and sometimes identical with, that of the Gallo-Frankish royal chant.

There is a formulary of liturgical acclamations which has confused scholars for a long time. It begins with *Christus vincit, Christus regnat, Christus imperat,* like the Gallo-Frankish forms, and yet it differs widely from all the specimens hitherto discussed. It belongs to a comparatively late period, as no evidence placing it earlier than the end of the thirteenth century has so far been detected.[2] It is first found in the Pontifical of

---

[1] There are reasons of great weight suggesting that the "Donation" had been drafted in 753 with a view to Pope Stephen II's journey to France; cf. Robert Holtzmann, *Der Kaiser als Marschall des Papstes,* Schriften der Strassburger Wissenschaftlichen Gesellschaft in Heidelberg, N. F., VIII (Berlin and Leipzig, 1928), 21 f., n. 3, cf. n. 2. The opinion advanced by Eichmann, "Kaisergewandung," *HJb.,* LVIII (1938), 275, who follows Buchner, *HJb.,* LIII (1933), 137 ff., and maintains that the document falls in the period between 813 and 816, is not convincing.

[2] Martène, *De antiquis ecclesiae ritibus,* I, 584, has published a formulary from Châlons based upon the Pontifical of Durandus; two additional formularies are found in the Durandus Pontificals (1) of Aix-en-Provence (Aix, Bibl. Méjanes, MS 13, fol. 209; 1329–1348 A.D.) and (2) of Peter of Saint Martial, bishop of Rieux and Carcassonne and archbishop of Toulouse (Paris, Bibl. Sainte-Geneviève, MS 143, fol. 247ᵛ; 1359–1401 A.D.), mentioned by Leroquais, *Pontificaux,* I, 6, II, 241, and showing the rubric:

"Quando, ubi et qualiter laudes sive rogationes sequentes dicuntur ... "

William Durandus († 1296)[3] whence it was introduced into the *Pontificale Romanum*.[4] The form has been published several times.[5] Its text is as follows:

Christus vincit, Christus regnat, Christus imperat.

	R/ Christus vincit, Christus regnat, Christus imperat.
Gloria nostra	Christus vincit.
Hunc diem	leti ducamus.
Summo pontifici N. integri- tatem fidei	Deus conservet.
[Episcopum nostrum N.	Deus conservet.]
[Regem nostrum	Deus conservet.]
Istam sedem	Deus conservet.
Populum Christianum	Feliciter. (ter)
Tempora bona habeant	Feliciter. (ter)
Multos annos	Christus in eis regnet.
In Christo semper vivant.	Amen.

The laudes of Châlons and those adduced below, n. 5 (cf. n. 24, and Pl. IX), have the following rubric:

"Laudes sive rogationes sequentes dicuntur in precipuis solemnitatibus, videlicet in diebus illis in quibus pontifex sedet post altare, quod fit hoc modo: Precentor cum quattuor bonis cantoribus et cum totidem pueris bene cantantibus immediate post *Kyrie eleison* incipit post altare alta voce *Christus vincit* ... "

This arrangement must have been also that of the Pontifical of Peter of Saint-Martial, since a miniature illustrating the performance of the laudes displays the four chanters; cf. Leroquais, *op. cit.*, II, 245; A. Boinet, *Les manuscrits à peintures de la Bibliothèque Sainte-Geneviève de Paris* (1911), 107 ff., No. 143. The note referring to the bishop ("pontifex sedet post altare") is remarkable. It suggests an architecture as yet unfamiliar with the High Altar backed by a retable which became the general fashion in the thirteenth century though it was not rare before. It implies that the episcopal throne had its place in the apse of the cathedral and not yet on the Gospel side of the altar. This might suggest a date earlier than the thirteenth century; but for this there is no evidence, moreover, episcopal churches seem to have observed the old custom (the bishop behind the altar and facing the nave when celebrating the Mass) longer than other churches. Cf. Joseph Braun, *Der christliche Altar*, I (Munich, 1924), 411 ff.

[3] Above, n. 2, and below, n. 4.

[4] It is first found in the Paris, Bibl. Nat. Lat. MS 968, fols. 197ᵛ–198, cf. Leroquais, *op. cit.*, II, 93, a *Pontificale Romanum* of the end of the fourteenth century. At the end of the fifteenth century the form was introduced into the official Roman Pontifical which was prepared under Innocent VIII (1484–1492) and first printed in 1485. From a *Pontificale Romanum*, printed at Venice, in 1520, Biehl, *op. cit.*, pp. 159 f., publishes the formulary, and from another edition (Venice, Heredes Luccantonii Junte Florentini) the text together with the neumes has been edited in *RÇGr.*, XXVI (1922), 84 f.

[5] In addition to the form of Châlons (above, n. 2), a form of Elne is found in Du Cange, *op. cit.*, V, 47, *s.v.* "Laus." The laudes in the Vatican Lat. MS 4743, fols. 19ᵛ–20ᵛ, of which Professor G. B. Ladner kindly provided me with a photostat, are mentioned by Ebner, *op. cit.*, p. 215, and Ehrensberger, *Libri liturgici Bibliothecae Apostolicae Vaticanae* (Freiburg, 1897), 458. The part of the manuscript to which the formulary belongs suggests a fragment of a Durandus Pontifical; see the rubrics enumerated by Ebner, *loc. cit.*, and compare them with Leroquais, *Pontificaux*, I, 6; Pierre Batiffol, *Études de liturgie et d'archéologie chrétienne* (Paris, 1919), 23. Ehrensberger styles the manuscript a Missal of Franciscan friars; Ebner suggests origin from Gubbio. The two additional acclamations (bishop and king) found in the Vatican Lat. MS 4743 and in the printed Roman Pontificals are here placed in square brackets.

This chant has merely the opening and concluding cries, the *Christus vincit* and the *Feliciter—Tempora bona*, in common with the Frankish laudes. Of the other invocations and responses none occur in the Gallo-Frankish or the Franco-Roman forms. In the rubric preceding the chant it is mentioned that the litany was sung between *Kyrie* and *Gloria*, that is not between the first Collect and the Epistle, which was the customary place of the *laudes regiae*. (Cf. above, pp. 86 f.) Students, however, have been misled by the *Christus vincit*. They styled the chant either "pseudo-laudes," for they considered it an imperfectly developed and apparently incorrect form of royal acclamations, or a simplified and late form of "Roman" laudes, whatever this term is supposed to indicate in this connection.[6] Yet, the true meaning of the chant and its genealogy have never been investigated and remained obscure.

Nothing could be more erroneous than to dub these acclamations "simplified Roman" or "degenerate Frankish" laudes, for they represent, in fact, an enriched and inflated and thoroughly un-Roman form of what were originally very simple acclamations. The formulary may appear less strange if the introductory *Christus vincit* and the first phrase ("Gloria nostra—Christus vincit") are disregarded so that the original nucleus is severed from the trimmings.[7]

Thus purified, the acclamations begin with *Hunc diem* and display a text which tallies on the whole with forms transmitted from Autun,[8] Beauvais,[9] and Chartres,[10] and which are very similar to others from St. Gall,[11] Freising,[12] Minden,[13] and Aquileia.[14] These forms, it is true,

---

[6] *RCGr.*, XXVI (1922), 84; Prost, *Quatre pièces*, pp. 187 f., 191; Biehl, *op. cit.*, p. 159, who dubs these laudes "Roman, late form."

[7] A specimen lacking these accretions is found at Vienne:

Hunc diem	multos annos.
Istam sedem	Deus conservet.
Summum pontificem Apostolicae sedis	Deus conservet.
Episcopum nostrum	Deus conservet.
Populum Christianum	Deus conservet.
Feliciter (ter)	
Tempora bona habeant (ter)	
Multos annos	Christus in eis regnet.
In ipso semper vivant.	

Cf. Le Brun Desmorettes, *Voyages liturgiques de France* (Paris, 1757), 18. A form of Vienne is mentioned also by Martène, *op. cit.*, I, 363, 614 (*Ordo XXVI*), in which, however, royal laudes (to be sung after the first Collect) seem to precede the episcopal acclamations.

[8] Below, n. 21.   [9] Cf. above, Chap. II, n. 116.

[10] Above, Chap. II, n. 56. The episcopal laudes are printed also by Du Cange, *op. cit.*, V, 49, and Prost, *Quatre pièces*, p. 185.

[11] St. Gall MS 381; M. Goldast, *Rerum Alamannicarum Scriptores* (3d ed., Frankfort and Leipzig, 1730), II, p. 2, pp. 147 f.; Migne, *PL.*, LXXXVII, col. 34 f.; Prost, *Quatre pièces*, p. 188; cf. below, n. 37.

[12] Munich, Cod. Lat. 27305, fols. 241–245. Extracts have been published by G. T. von Rudhart, "Auszüge aus einer lateinischen Pergamenthandschrift der Freisinger Domkirche vom Ende des 10. Jahrhunderts," *Quellen und Erörterungen zur bayrischen Geschichte*, VII (1858), 473 ff.; cf Maurice Coens, "Anciennes litanies des saints,"

all differ from one another in details as the chant proceeds, but most of them would show the phrases:

Hunc diem	multos annos [or: leti ducamus]
Istam sedem	Deus conservet.

These acclamations had their place sometimes at the end of the Mass before the Dismissal—"Post missam dicat Pontifex," says the rubric to the form of St. Gall. That is to say that these short acclaims were chanted at exactly the same place in the divine service where in the liturgical books of other Frankish and Burgundian cathedrals, for example, Rheims,[15] Nevers,[16] Besançon,[17] Metz,[18] Arles,[19] or Ivrea,[20] a very simple acclamation would be found which has the following text:

Te pastorem	Deus elegit.
In ista sede	Deus conservet.
Annos vite	Deus multiplicet.

The meaning of these acclamations is disclosed by a rubric in the formularies of Minden, "Ista laus die qua Episcopus sublimatur in sede cantanda est," or in more general terms in the form of Ivrea "Ad salutandum

---

Anal. Boll., LIV (1936), 24 ff., who discusses the *laetania antiqua* of this manuscript. The text of the episcopal laudes, as yet unpublished, is as follows:

Hunc diem	multos annos.
Domnum Abraham episcopum	Deus conservet.
Salvator mundi	tu illum adiuva
S. Maria	tu illum adiuva ...
S. Paule	
S. Corbiniane	
S. Prime	
S. Stephane	
S. Vite	
S. Cypriane	
S. Tertuline	
S. Castule	
S. Innocenti	
S. Pare	
S. Andrea	
S. Urbane	
S. Feliciane	
S. Alexander	
S. Corneli	
S. Candide	
S. Quirine	
S. Cassiane	

Feliciter (ter)	
Tempora bona habeat (ter)	
Multos annos.	Amen.

[13] Below, n. 36.
[14] De Rubeis, *Mon. Eccles. Aquil.*, 588 ff. The form consists of two deprecations: "Hunc diem—multos annos, Istam sedem—Deus conservet."
[15] Cf. above, Chap. II, n. 14; Migne, *PL.*, CXXXVIII, cols. 901 f. Rémy de Gourmont, *Le latin mystique* (1922), 150, publishes a fragment from Rheims which seems to be only an extract from the last part of normal *laudes regiae*. It is remarkable that the northern bishoprics of the province of Rheims do not seem to have observed the singing of laudes, whereas they are found in the southern cathedrals, at Châlons

pontificem." Hence, the *Hunc diem* and *Te pastorem* hails prove to be episcopal acclamations, and the same is true with reference to the pseudolaudes: they, too, are nothing but so far correct though amplified and even "regalized" episcopal acclamations the "kingliness" of which fits well with the general tendencies of William Durandus. I shall refer to this form as the "Durandus laudes"; its antecedents are now in need of being clarified.

A form of Autun, written shortly after 900 on the inner side of an ivory plate—one of the Consular Diptychs preserved from the time of Justinian[21]—is instructive and therefore may serve here as a model. The

(above, n. 2), Beauvais (above, n. 9), Soissons, Senlis, and Laon. See, for Soissons, the *Rituale* of Bishop Nivelon, Paris, Bibl. Nat. Lat. MS 8898, fols. 30–32, published completely for the Société d'archéologie de Soissons by Abbé Poquet, *Rituale seu mandatum insignis ecclesiae Suessionis tempore episcopi Nivelonis exaratum* (Soissons, 1856); cf. Martène, *op. cit.*, I, 369 ff.; Prost, *Quatre pièces*, p. 183; G. L. David, "Acclamations *Christus vincit,*" *RCGr.*, XXVI (1922), 6 f. The laudes of Senlis are found in the fourteenth-century Antiphonary of St. Fraimbaud, Paris, Bibl. Sainte-Geneviève, Lat. MS 1297, fol. 98; Martène, *op. cit.*, I, 363. For Laon, see the Ordinale of the Deacon Lisiardus (1155–1173), Laon, Bibl. Munic., MS 215 (457); U. Chevalier, *Ordinaires de l'église cathédrale de Laon*, Bibliothèque liturgique, VII (Paris, 1897), 51, 120, 152.

[16] Paris, Bibl. Nat. Lat. MS 9449, fol. 36ᵛ. This seems to be the formulary mentioned by Delisle, who in the *Revue des sociétés savantes des départements*, 11ᵉ sér., Vol. III (1860), 561, refers to Bibl. Nat. Lat. suppl. MS 1704. The laudes are eleventh century, ca. 1060, and unpublished. The form is Gallo-Frankish. There are acclamations to an unnamed pope ("Summo pontifici et universali pape vita") with invocations of the *Salvator mundi*, Peter, Paul, and Andrew; to Bishop Hugh de Champ-Aleman of Nevers (SS. Efricus, Nazarius, Genesius, Symphorianus); to the Kings Henry I and Philip I (*Redemptor mundi*, Maria, Michael, Gabriel, Raphael); and to the judges and the Christian army (Denis, Martin, Rémy). The laudations contain the four cardinal virtues (cf. above, Chap. II, n. 14) and begin with "Lux, via et vita nostra" like those of Rheims (above, n. 15), Soissons (*ibid.*), and of Troyes (cf. J. Delasilve, *RCGr.*, XII, 1903–1904, 197 ff.); but the second phrase shows the queer form "Rex regum et *deus deorum,*" remindful of a hymn in the *Breviarium Gothicum* (Migne, *PL.*, LXXXVI, col. 204) which begins "Domine, Domine, *Rex Deorum*"; cf. A. W. S. Porter, "Cantica Mozarabici Officii," *Eph. Lit.*, XLIX (1935), 141.

[17] Vatican, Borg. Lat. MS 359, fols. 135–136; Ebner, *Iter Italicum*, p. 153; Migne, *PL.*, LXXX, col. 411, and the footnote p. 421; De Santi, "Le *laudes* nell'incoronazione del sommo pontifice," *Civiltà cattolica*, Ser. XVIII, Vol. XI (1903), 393. Their date is eleventh century. A rubric heading the acclamations to the bishop indicates "Antequam dicatur *Ite missa est.*"

[18] Prost, *Quatre pièces*, pp. 238 f.

[19] Du Cange, *op. cit.*, V, 46, from an unknown manuscript "ecclesiae Arelatensis." Cf. Migne, *PL.*, CXXXVIII, cols. 889 f.

[20] Dümmler, *Anselm der Peripatetiker*, p. 90. The text is somewhat archaic and differs slightly from all the others; it is as follows:

Te pastorem	Deus elegit.
In hac sede	Dominus conservet.
Annos vite	Deus multiplicet.
Tempora bona habeas	Summo Patri placeat.
Vitam tuam	Dominus disponat.
Multos annos	Deus adaugeat.
Vivas et valeas	in Domino.
Per infinita secula seculorum.	Amen.

[21] Richard Delbrück, *Die Konsulardiptychen*, Studien zur spätantiken Kunstgeschichte, II (Berlin, 1929), plate N 27; cf. E. Kantorowicz, "Ivories and Litanies," pp. 57 f.

ivory plate first shows a formulary of Gallo-Frankish, or rather Franco-Burgundian *laudes regiae*. There follow the episcopal laudes which have the following text (Pl. XII):

(I) [Te pastorem]	R/	Deus elegit.
[In ista sede]		Deus conservet.
[Annos vite]		Deus multiplicet.
		Amen.
(II) [Hunc diem]	R/	Multos annos.[22]
[Domnum Apos]tolicum		Deus conservet.
[S. . . . . . .]		tu illum adiuva.
[S. . . . . . .]igi		tu illum adiuva.
S. Silvester		tu illum adiuva.
[Domnum N. (?)] Regem nostrum		Deus conservet.
S. Dionisi		tu illum adiuva.
S. Euratine		tu illum adiuva.
S. Medarde		tu illum adiuva.
[Domnum N. (?)] pontificem nostrum		Deus conservet.
S. [. . . . .]		tu illum adiuva.
S. Simplici		tu illum adiuva.
S. Heufroni		tu illum adiuva.

Feliciter. Feliciter. Feliciter.

Tempora bona habeas. Tempora bona habeas. Tempora bona habeas.

The two types of the original episcopal acclamations are found here in one formulary, but the *Amen* indicates an incision. Nowhere are we told what difference there is between the *Te pastorem* and the *Hunc diem* hails. It is obvious, however, that the first section refers to the bishop and his see, whereas the second section refers to the day or occasion on which the chant is sung. We are, therefore, probably not amiss when assuming that the first section originally represented the acclaims offered to the bishop at his ordination and perhaps at his *natalicium*, the anniversary of his ordination, as well. The second section suggests a pattern of "festival" laudes sung to the bishop on Church festivals. The intentions for the pope and king as well as the invocations of saints are accessory; they are by no means the rule. As contrasted with the ordinary *laudes regiae* which precede the *Te pastorem* group, the second section might seem to be a *laudes regiae* form *au petit pied;* but the responses *Deus conservet* indicate episcopal laudes. Thus, it would be more correct to style this form episcopal acclamations *au grand pied*. However this may be, doubtless the two sections of *Te pastorem* and *Hunc diem* hails were considered interchangeable and frequently they merged with one another.

The specimen of Autun elucidates the origin and the composition of the Durandus laudes. The latter begin with the *Hunc diem* scheme of Autun, though without invocations of saints; then there comes the com-

---

[22] "Leti ducamus" for "Multos annos" in the Beauvais forms.

memoration of the episcopal see which is found in the first section of Autun; finally, the *Feliciter* wishes conclude the song. The opening *Christus vincit* followed by one of the laudatory hails is an elaboration borrowed from the *laudes regiae*. Thus, the Durandus laudes do not turn out to be an imperfectly developed form of royal acclamations. On the contrary, they are an amplified form of episcopal acclamations. Moreover, text and structure of this form are anything but Roman. The Durandus formulary is French, probably southern French. It began to penetrate the *Pontificale Romanum* during the Avignon period of the papal court, when the second great wave of French influence affected the Roman liturgy. Along with other elements of the Durandus Pontifical, the chant was incorporated as a curiosity of some foreign cathedrals into the *Pontificale Romanum* published under Innocent VIII in 1485. It disappeared from this service book apparently in 1596.[23]

To discuss in any detailed manner the functions of the episcopal acclamations is beyond the scope of this study. Their function was "inaugural"

---

[23] The propagation of the Durandus laudes compares with that of the Durandus Pontifical. The laudes formulary is found in a fourteenth-century *Pontificale Romanum* (Bibl. Nat. MS 968; quoted above, n. 4). In the fifteenth century it was officially incorporated into the Roman Pontifical prepared by Augustinus Patrizi (Piccolomini) and John Burchard under Innocent VIII (1484–1492) on the basis of the Durandus Pontifical (first printed in 1485); but the editors were conscious of having added to the service book a prayer which did not belong to the Roman ritual, since they changed the rubric (cf. above, n. 2) and said:

"*In quibusdam ecclesiis* fiunt laudes sequentes et rogationes in praecipuis solemnitatibus . . ."

The formulary seems to have been carried through all the editions of this Roman Pontifical, but it was omitted when under Clement VIII a new *P. R.* was published (in 1596). Cf. Batiffol, *op. cit.*, pp. 5–13, and Leroquais, *Pontificaux*, I, pp. xxvii f., who emphasizes that the Durandus Pontifical was popular especially in southern France. The French origin of the Durandus laudes becomes obvious as soon as we organize the episcopal laudes in groups.

    I. Beginning *Te pastorem*: I found this form exclusively in the Western (French, Burgundian, Lotharingian) forms of Rheims, Nevers, Besançon, Autun, Arles, Ivrea, and Metz.

    II. Beginning *Hunc diem*:

        a. *German Form:* It first occurs in the Franco-Roman laudes of Ratisbon which contain intentions for the rulers and others, but no invocations of saints. St. Gall, Freising, and Minden follow the same pattern, but they add an unbroken sequence of many saints (St. Gall with an intention only for the king; Freising and Minden with intentions only for the bishop; and Aquileia with neither intentions nor saints). For the relationship between certain German forms with the acclamations to the pope and to cardinals, cf. below.

        b. *French Form:* Though related to the German forms the French pattern differs from the German in that the various intentions and the invocations of the saints are interlaced with each other just as in the Gallo-Frankish *laudes regiae*. This pattern is very old; it first occurs in Autun (after 900), thereafter in Beauvais and similarly in Chartres. This form is the basis of the Durandus laudes in which, however, the invocations of saints are omitted; the parallelism with the *laudes regiae* is established by the *Christus vincit* (Châlons, Elne, Aix, Peter of Saint-Martial, and Vatican Lat. MS 4743). A stage of development between Autun and Durandus is shown by the form of Vienne, which contains neither saints nor *Christus vincit*; cf. above, n. 7.

before it became "festival" as well. In their quality as electoral or inaugural laudes, voiced at the election or the enthronement of the bishop, they served a purpose equal to that of the royal or imperial acclamations or those performed at the inauguration of the Roman high officials.[24] An interesting specimen of early episcopal acclamations is preserved from the time of St. Augustine; it refers to the election of Augustine's successor in 426.[25] But the episcopal acclamations are older than that. The bishop was elected through the medium of clergy and people by divine inspiration, and the inspiration became manifest through the unanimous acclaim of those present. The election of St. Ambrose, for instance, which was proposed by a 'child, is a famous and early evidence for an "acclamatory election by inspiration."[26] Hence, the acclamation to a bishop, like that to emperors or high-ranking officers, had definitely constitutive power. It was at once a legal and a canonical means of recognizing the bishop at his election and often also at his installation. In this capacity the episcopal laudes were important even at a time when the papal

---

[24] For the parallelism between the elections of emperor and bishop, see, e.g., Hieronymus, *Ep.* CXLVI, 1: "... episcopos presbyteri semper unum de se electum et in excelsiori gradu conlocatum *episcopum nominabant, quomodo si exercitus imperatorem faciat.*" See below, n. 25, for the *dignus*-acclamation, and also the most instructive discussion by Peterson, *Untersuchungen*, pp. 176, ff. See above, p. 31, n. 62.

[25] Migne, *PL.*, XXXIII, cols. 967 f., *Ep.* 213 (Sept. 26, 426):

Augustinus:
"Presbyterum Eraclium mihi successorem volo."
A populo acclamatum est:

"Deo gratias,	Christo laudes.
Exaudi Christe,	Augustino vita.
Te patrem,	te episcopum.
Deo gratias,	Christo laudes.
Exaudi Christe,	Augustino vita.
Te patrem,	te episcopum.
Dignus et	justus est.
Bene meritus,	bene dignus.
Dignus et	justus est
Deo gratias,	Christo laudes.
Judicio tuo	gratias agimus.
Fiat,	fiat.
Dignum est,	justum est.
Fiat,	fiat.
Olim dignus,	olim meritus.
Judicio tuo	gratias agimus.
Exaudi Christe,	Eraclium conserva."

The customary acclamation was simpler than this one; see, e.g., the acclamation to Bishop Solemnis of Chartres, which refers to 507 A.D. (written probably in the eighth century) and has the following text: "Ecce Solemnis! Dignus est, episcopus ordinetur!" *Vita Solemnis episcopi*, in *MGH. SS. rer. Merov.*, VII, 315. See also Peterson, *Untersuchungen*, p. 178, n. 4, for the hails "Dignus et justus est"—the essential cry at all episcopal elections and ordinations; cf. Duchesne, *Christian Worship*, p. 373, n. 6, and, on acclaims to the bishop in general, Peterson, *Untersuchungen*, p. 144; Heldmann, *op. cit.*, p. 275, n. 2. This cry (ἄξιος) was heard also at the coronation of the Byzantine emperor (*De caerim.*, I, c. 38, p. 194), at the promotion of a prefect, and on other occasions (*ibid.*, I, c. 53, p. 268).

[26] Socrates, *Hist. eccl.*, IV, c. 30, Migne, *PG.*, LXVII, cols. 543–544; Paulinus, *Vita S. Ambrosii*, c. 6, Migne, *PL.*, XIV, 31.

monarchy was fully developed and the votes of clergy and people had become *de facto* negligible. The young Frederick II, for example, in the course of his negotiations with the Holy See over episcopal elections in Sicily, could write to Pope Innocent III that no bishop elect, before having acquired the royal assent, was entitled to be enthroned or to have the laudes chanted to him.[27] Thus the Sicilian king recognized this solemnity as an important legal act as late as the thirteenth century.

The custom of voicing episcopal laudes on the festivals of the Church does not seem to antedate the Carolingian period. The oldest forms known to us belong to the early ninth century. They are usually transmitted as an appendix to the Gallo-Frankish *laudes regiae*, though in one exceptional case they are found also at the end of a Franco-Roman form.[28] The transmission of the texts makes it even more likely than it would otherwise have been that the chanting of episcopal laudes on feast days developed in analogy and along with the custom of the royal crown-wearings and the rendering of festival acclamations to the king. The priority of the one observance over the other cannot be ascertained; we must account for mutual influences just as with royal and episcopal unctions. Whether or not the increased prestige and the new significance of the pall, and the restrictions concerning the wearing of this insignia on certain feast days only, should be bound up with the origin of the festival laudes to the episcopate, remains quite uncertain.[29] The earliest forms preserved do not refer to metropolitans. However this may be, the parallelism of rendering royal and episcopal acclamations on Church festivals produced a fusion of the two rites. Yet it would be wrong to treat episcopal laudes and *laudes regiae* alike, although they are usually transmitted together.

Royal and episcopal laudes, it is true, coincided on certain festivals, on Christmas, Easter, and Pentecost. But they did not necessarily coincide on other occasions such as the anniversaries of the bishop, of the cathedral, or of the local patron saint. We have therefore to distinguish between the feast days of Christ and the king on the one hand, and those of the bishop and his cathedral on the other. It seems as though in early times the practice was observed either to omit the episcopal laudes on

---

[27] *MGH. Const.*, II, 544, No. 413: "Antequam assensus regius requiratur, non inthronizetur electus nec decantetur laudis solempnitas, que inthronizationi videtur annexa." See also Thietmar, V, c. 41, *MGH. SS. rer. Germ.*, ed. Holtzmann (1935), 268, for the laudes at an episcopal investiture at Halberstadt in 1004. A thorough study of the history of the episcopal acclamations would be very useful.

[28] In the form of Ratisbon (Munich Cod. Lat. 14510); cf. above, p. 106.

[29] This may have been different in later centuries; in modern times the episcopal acclamations in Rouen were even called "Acclamations for the Pall"; cf. above, p. 94, n. 97. For the significance of the pall in the ninth century, see Nicholas I's *Responsa ad consulta Bulgarorum*, c. 73, *MGH. Epist.*, *VI*, 593, and, in general, Braun, *Die liturgische Gewandung*, pp. 620 ff.

the feast days of the Lord, when the *laudes regiae* were due, since an intention for the bishop was inserted into the general scheme anyhow, or to let the episcopal laudes, in the short form of the *Te pastorem* hails, follow immediately after the *laudes regiae*. On the other hand, whenever royal and episcopal laudes days did not coincide (namely, on the anniversaries of the bishop, the cathedral, and the local saint), the episcopal acclamations were apparently sung *per se*; and on these occasions, when probably the amplified and "regalized" form of episcopal laudes (for example, the second section of the Autun formulary) was due, they either followed after the *Kyrie* or were removed to the end of the Mass and preceded the Dismissal. This, approximately, may have been the underlying idea of the two sets of acclamations which sometimes are found side by side in the service books of the same cathedral.[30] However, the observations advanced here should not be taken as an effort to establish a general rule, for the customs varied in every cathedral. The two performances were very often combined with each other so that the *laudes regiae* were sung on "episcopal days" or might even have passed as episcopal acclamations, while the episcopal laudes proper, trimmed sometimes with scraps of royal glitter, were chanted also on the feast days of the Lord; and often they simply replaced the royal litany.

Despite the fusion of the two sets of acclamations, royal and episcopal, they were nevertheless distinguished within the divine service. A description of the laudes ceremony as performed in the Cathedral of Rheims during the thirteenth century clarifies this point. The performance was started after the *Gloria*. Two chanters took their places on the Epistle side of the altar, where they sang the Gallo-Frankish *laudes regiae*, probably in the form which has been handed down to us from the Cathedral of Rheims. Then, "toward the end of the laudes, when the chanters were about to say *Te pastorem Deus elegit*," they advanced toward the archbishop, ascended the steps to his throne, kissed his hand, and received together with the benediction a gratuity of two sous. That is to say, the chanters sing the laudes proper on the Epistle side near the pulpit, exactly as it is illustrated by a miniature; then, when they switch to the episcopal acclaims and start addressing the archbishop personally (*Te pastorem*), they stride slowly, while still singing, toward the Gospel side

---

[30] This is the case, e.g., in Aix-en-Provence; Paris, Bibl. Nat. Lat. MS 949, fol. 65ᵛ (early fourteenth century), contains *laudes regiae*, whereas Aix, Bibl. Méjanes MS 13, fol. 209 (1329–1348), contains the Durandus laudes; cf. Leroquais, *Pontificaux*, II, 31, and I, 6. In Chartres, the bishop is not acclaimed in the *laudes regiae*, but episcopal laudes follow instead. Also, we must take into account that regional practice may have omitted intentions according to the judgment of the bishop (the prayer for the emperor on Good Friday, e.g., is not said at present, although even the latest edition of the *Missale Romanum* contains it). It is impossible, at any rate, to establish general rules concerning the practice, though we may advance suggestions concerning the origin of the various forms of laudes to the bishop.

where the archbishop has his throne and, while ascending the steps of the dais, offer their felicitations (*Feliciter!* or *Annos vite Deus multiplicet!*)[31].

Exactly when this highly dramatic punctilio, which was certainly the general custom in the Later Middle Ages, may have developed is difficult to tell. It agrees on the whole with a ceremonial observed at the present day when the bishop at his ordination acclaims his consecrator in order to thank him. In three stages the bishop advances toward his consecrator, usually the archbishop, performs three genuflections and sings three times, giving his voice each time a higher pitch, the acclamation *Ad multos annos!* This rite cannot be traced farther back than the twelfth century, when it is first found in the Pontifical of Apamea.[32] It is, therefore, not very much older than the laudes ritual of Rheims, and the possibility of influences of the one ceremony on the other cannot be ruled out. However this may be, it is obvious that the *Te pastorem* section was not simply combined with, or engulfed by, the *laudes regiae*, but that it introduced a shifting of scenes within the performance. The laudes in poetical form which sometimes follow the *laudes regiae* may have served a similar purpose.[33] Moreover, this episcopal ovation was probably omitted whenever the king was present on one of the great festivals, for then—at least according to English usage—the king gave the *presbyterium* to the singers and therefore must have been the recipient of the felicitations.

As a consequence of these general conditions, the tendency to furnish the episcopal acclaims with luster borrowed from the *laudes regiae* becomes comprehensible. An assimilation of the episcopal with the royal laudes occurred. The elements of this assimilation—that is, the adorn-

---

[31] Cf. Chevalier, *Sacramentaire et martyrologe ... de Reims*, p. 132, with reference to the celebration of Easter:
> ". . . procedunt duo presbiteri canonici de choro et incipiunt in sinistra parte altaris. In fine laudum, quando dicturi sunt *Te pastorem Deus elegit*, ascendunt gradus usque ante ipsum archiepiscopum; ibique finitis laudibus accedunt et osculantur manum eius; ipse autem benedicit eis et de benedictione sua dat utrisque ii solidos, et continuo legitur epistola."

Cf. *ibid.*, pp. 288, and also 104, 200, 205.

[32] Cf. Leroquais, *Pontificaux*, I, p. xciii, and *ibid.*, I, 189 ff., for the Pontifical of Apamea (Lyons, Bibl. Mun. MS 570, fol. 298ᵛ), and Michel Andrieu, *Le pontifical Romain au moyen-âge*, Studi e Testi, 86 (1938), I: Le Pontifical Romain du XIIᵉ siècle, pp. 34 ff., who (pp. 151 f.) has published the text of that Order. A similar ceremony took place in the later Byzantine rite of the coronation. The deacons, and following them the priests, approached first the emperor to sing to him with "loud voices" their felicitations, and then walked to the throne of the patriarch to repeat their performance; cf. Codinus, c. XVII, ed. Becker, p. 95.

[33] See, e.g., the English laudes of 1068, published by Maskell, *Monumenta Ritualia*, II, 85 ff. (below, chap. VI). This is the only English formulary to contain episcopal acclamations proper. They differ widely from the Continental patterns:
Benedicat vos divina majestas Domini. . . .
Benedicat Dominus sacerdotium vestrum et introitum vestrum.
For remnants of episcopal acclamations in England, see the forms of Worcester (*Deus conservet* in the acclamation to the archbishop and bishop; cf. Appendix I, n. 20) and below, pp. 171 f., notes 63, 67.

ments and accretions by which the episcopal acclaims were amplified—
were not always the same, and we can clearly distinguish between French
and German customs. In France we notice a trend to add intentions for
the pope and the king to those for the bishop and to interlace them with
invocations of saints. The intentions always follow the episcopal pattern
(that is, they have the response *Deus conservet* and do not display the
vita-acclamation of the royal laudes), whereas the invocations of saints
with the response *Tu illum adiuva* are those of the royal forms. Also, the
Christus vincit, added to the episcopal acclamations, is found only in
France and not earlier than in the Durandus laudes of the thirteenth
century. After this time the triad characteristic of the *laudes regiae* appears more often in the episcopal acclamations. It is predominant, for
instance, in the late mediaeval form of Orléans:[34]

> Christus vincit, Christus regnat, Christus imperat.
>> Episcopo Aureliensi et omni clero sibi commisso pax, vita et salus aeterna.
>> Sancte Evurti   tu illum adiuva.
> Christus vincit, Christus regnat, Christus imperat.
>> Sancte Aniane   tu illum adiuva.
> Christus vincit, Christus regnat, Christus imperat. . . .

The borrowings from the royal laudes are most obvious in this formulary,
which may well be styled "baroque." And quite frequently the royal
laudes in their original form were used as episcopal acclamations.

In Germany, the accretions are restricted to invocations of saints with
the response *Tu illum adiuva*. The result is almost a Litany of the
Saints. A specimen of this kind is found in the tenth-century episcopal
laudes of Freising.[35] There is available an even more elaborate form—an
early eleventh-century text from Minden.[36]

Kyrie eleyson (ter)	
Christe eleyson (ter)	
Kyrie eleyson (ter)	
Christe eleyson (ter)	
Dominum N. episcopum a Deo electum	Deus conservet. Amen (ter)
Hunc diem	bonum habeat. Amen (ter)
Multos annos	Amen (ter)
In hac sede.	Amen (ter)
Tempora bona habeat.	Amen (ter)
S. Petre	tu illum adiuva.
S. Paule	tu illum adiuva.
S. Johannes	tu illum adiuva.

---

[34] Le Brun Desmorettes, *Voyages liturgiques*, p. 189; cf. Pascal, *Dictionnaire de
liturgie catholique* (1844), 743. For a Carolingian form of Orléans, cf. above, p. 86,
n. 65.

[35] Cf. above, n. 12.

[36] The text published is that of the Berlin Theol. Lat. MS 11, fol. 114ᵛ, which agrees
on the whole with Wolfenbüttel, Helmst. MS 1110 (1008), fol. 257.

S. Gorgoni	tu illum adiuva.
S. Dorothee	tu illum adiuva.
S. Theodore	tu illum adiuva.
S. Martine	tu illum adiuva.
S. Columbane	tu illum adiuva.
S. Galle	tu illum adiuva.
S. Magne	tu illum adiuva.
S. Udalrice	tu illum adiuva.
S. Cecilia	tu illum adiuva.
S. Margaretha	tu illum adiuva.
S. Lucia	tu illum adiuva.

Feliciter. Feliciter. Feliciter.
Amen. Amen. Amen.

It should be stressed here that this German form is reminiscent of late eleventh- or early twelfth-century laudes to cardinals and also of certain laudes to the pope.

The current of influence did not always flow from the royal to the episcopal acclamations. A very strange specimen of episcopal laudes applied to the king is found in St. Gall.[37] The song opens with a long deprecatory litany containing intentions for the Church, King Louis the German, and the monks of St. Gall. Then follow laudes in which the king takes the place of the bishop:

Hunc diem	multos annos.
Domnum Hludovvicum regem	Deus conservet.
Salvator mundi	tu illum adiuva.
S. Petre	tu illum adiuva.
S. Paule	tu illum adiuva.
S. Andrea	tu illum adiuva.
S. Gereon	tu illum adiuva.

Feliciter. Feliciter. Feliciter.
Tempora bona habeat. (ter)
Multos annos.   Amen.

This queer inversion of king-bishop is significant of the intellectual atmosphere of the early ninth century when the ideal of *Rex et Sacerdos* was at its height, and similar inversions may have occurred more frequently than the records indicate. However, the form of St. Gall, which already displays the pattern of the "German" episcopal laudes, seems to be

---

[37] Another form of St. Gall (for the one quoted, see above, n. 11) has the normal episcopal laudes, but the intention for the bishop is replaced by one for the congregation:

Hunc diem	multos annos.
Istam congregationem	Deus conservet.
Annos vite	Deus multiplicet.
Feliciter.	

Cf. Migne, *PL.*, LXXXVII, col. 34, where the preceding "litany" is nothing but the last part of normal Gallo-Frankish laudes.

unique. There is known, thus far, but one parallel which is almost a caricature, namely, the papal acclamatory cry which was shouted to (or rather: at) Henry V at his Roman coronation in 1111:

Henricum regem   sanctus Petrus elegit![38]

Episcopal Laudes to the Pope

Of the ceremonial observed at the election and inauguration of the bishop of Rome we know very little so far as the early centuries are concerned. It is not likely, however, that it differed in any considerable manner from that of other bishops. The pope, too, was elected by clergy and people and was acclaimed on this occasion, since every election was acclamatory. The earliest known evidence of a papal election refers to Pope Fabian (236–250). The report, though legendary, is nevertheless remarkable because for the first time we find an acclamatory election of a pope "by inspiration." The shout then heard was a simple *Dignus.*[39] Examples of more impressive acclamations to the pope are not rare in the following centuries, but they are usually connected with the observances of synods and therefore the hails to the pope appear within the general framework of Eastern conciliar acclamations without showing any peculiar features.[40] Yet there is one formulary of laudes which presents itself as genuinely "papal" and was voiced by the Roman Synod in 495 for Pope Gelasius.[41] This is the text:

Exaudi Christe	Gelasio vita!
Domne Petre	tu illum serva!
Cuius sedem et annos!	
Apostolum Petrum te videmus!	

---

[38] *Liber pont.*, II, 300.

[39] Eusebius, *Hist. eccl.*, VI, c. 29, Migne, *PG.*, XX, cols. 587–588. On the *dignus*-acclamation, see above, n. 25. In the acclamation to Fabian's successor, Pope Cornelius, we find the phrase characteristic of the *Te pastorem* and later papal laudes, *electum a Deo* (below, n. 44); cf. Cornelius' description of these events in his letter to Cyprian, in Cyprian, *Epistulae*, No. 48, § 2, *CSEL.*, III, 1, p. 611. On the acclamatory election by inspiration, cf. Heldmann, *op. cit.*, pp. 281 f.; Erich Caspar, *Geschichte des Papsttums*, I, 49.

[40] An exception is formed by the acclamation of the Roman Synod in 499, cf. *MGH. AA. ant.*, XII, 402 ff.; above, Chap. II, n. 7. For an interesting specimen of papal acclamations, see those offered to Hadrian II at Rome, in 868, by an assembly of Oriental clerics from Jerusalem, Antiochia, Alexandria, and Constantinople. They have the following text:

> "Domno nostro Hadriano a Deo decreto summo pontifici et universali pape vita!
> Reverentissimo et orthodoxo domno Nicolao a Deo decreto summo pontifici et universali pape sempiterna memoria!
> Novo Heliae vita perennis et inmarcescibilis gloria!
> Novo Finees aeterni sacerdotii infulas!
> Sequacibus eius pax et gratia!

Liber pont., II, 177.

[41] *Avellana*, No. CIII, §§ 13, 30, *CSEL.*, XXXV, 478, 487; cf. Caspar, *op. cit.*, II, 79.

This acclamation has often attracted the attention of scholars as a testimony of the Petrine Doctrine in its early stages. Indeed, the fourth acclamation intimates that the Holy Council considered the successor of St. Peter a reincarnation of the *heros eponymos* of the Roman See. There are other points to arouse our interest. The third root (*Cuius sedem*) betrays the true character of these laudes, namely that of an episcopal acclamation. The first hail is the well-known imperial and generally Roman *vita*-acclamation, while the second is an invocation of the papal patron saint. Normally in the episcopal acclamations we would find the pagan formula *Di te servent* replaced by the Christian *Deus conservet*. In Rome, however, the bishop is always recommended to and elected by St. Peter, a peculiarity never to be discarded. As usual in Rome, history with its metaphysical inferences proves stronger than transcendency.

This is borne out by the *Ordo Romanus IX*, the first authentic ceremonial in which papal electoral acclamations are mentioned. The order is transmitted in manuscripts of the ninth century but may be somewhat older, since the ritual of inaugurations seems to refer to Pope Leo III (795–816).[42] Laudes to the new pope are mentioned following the *Gloria in excelsis*. They were offered by the *schola cantorum* and repeated by the patrons of the seven Roman regions. Unfortunately, the Order does not record the text of these laudes, and not before the twelfth century is there again evidence for laudes sung to the pope during Mass. But the Order has preserved another formula of acclamations. When the pope, after the divine service, had the pontifical headgear, the so-called *regnum*, placed on his head by the equerry and prepared to mount his horse for the triumphal circuit through the city, the seven *patroni regionum* would approach him to voice the very simple *laudes:*

Domnus Leo papa,   quem sanctus Petrus elegit.
In sua sede   multis annis sedere.

Here again the character of episcopal laudes cannot be mistaken, because the chant contains a reference to the episcopal see. Yet there is a difference between the papal and episcopal acclamation. The latter begins *Te pastorem—Deus elegit*, whereas the former praises the active part taken by St. Peter as elector of the pope. This hail to the Prince of Apostles, in his quality as elector of the pope, has survived until modern times; and although the Roman pontiff would adopt imperial insignia and the im-

---

[42] Migne, *PL.*, LXXVIII, col. 1006, §§ 5–6; for other editions see Andrieu, *Ordines*, I, 19 f., No. XXXVI. The oldest manuscript of this Order is the St. Gall MS 614; cf. Andrieu, *op. cit.*, I, 343. For the manuscript problem, see Klewitz, "Die Krönung des Papstes," *ZfRG.*, kan. Abt., XXX (1941), 111, 50. My efforts to get photostats from St. Gall were as unsuccessful as those of Professor Klewitz because the manuscripts of the abbey have been stored for the duration of the war.

perial titles of *Vicarius Christi* and *Vicarius Dei*,[43] hardly ever would the newly elected pope be saluted by a cheer other than *Domnus N. papa quem sanctus Petrus elegit.*[44]

The election by St. Peter and the reference to it in the acclamation was, of course, a Roman privilege; not one of the provincial episcopal acclamations would display this formula. But what was barred to the "Line" was yet open to the "Household Guards." The acclamations to the cardinals, sung to them on their inauguration, likewise referred to their master's master:

J. cardinalem	sanctus Petrus elegit.
Domnum J. cardinalem	Deus conservet.
S. Maria	tu illum adiuva.
S. Michael	tu illum adiuva....[45]

If we compare these cardinal laudes with the episcopal formulae (*Te pastorem—Deus elegit, In ista sede—Deus conservet*), agreements and disagreements seem to make sense. The cardinals, at least the cardinal-priests and cardinal-deacons, had no flock proper nor had they really a see. They had a *titulus* and not a *sedes*. Hence the formula *In ista sede* is omitted and replaced by a repeated acclamation of the cardinal's name. Moreover, the cardinal was not elected by the common inspiration of a multitude of people and clerics; he was nominated or rather "created" by the pope; that is, by St. Peter. Yet with due alterations of details, the

---

[43] On the *Vicarius Dei* title of rulers in general, cf. Jean Rivière, *Le Problème de l'église et de l'état au temps de Philippe le Bel*, Spicilegium Sacrum Lovaniense, VIII (Paris and Louvain, 1926), 435–440, and as a title of the pope, see A. von Harnack, "Christus praesens—Vicarius Christi," *Sitzungsberichte der Berliner Akademie*, 1927, Abh. XXXIV.

[44] See, e.g., *Liber pont.*, II, 361: "Ildebrandum archidiaconum beatus Petrus elegit"; Gregory VII finally was acclaimed: "Domnum Gregorium papam sanctus Petrus elegit." *Ibid.*, II, 296: "'Ter acclamatum est responsumque: 'Paschalem papam sanctus Petrus elegit,' " a place which shows clearly the responsorial character of these laudes. The acclamations to Hadrian IV were probably likewise alternating, cf. *ibid.* II, 389: "' 'Papam Adrianum *a Deo* electum' tam clerici quam laici pariter conclamantes." The form "quem *Deus* elegit" is found also at the elevation of Alexander III (*ibid.*, II, 398); however, if really there was a tendency under Hadrian IV and Alexander III to replace *sanctus Petrus* by *Deus*, this tendency at least did not influence the Orders. Cardinal Deusdedit quotes the acclamation of the *Ordo Romanus IX* without the second line ("In sua sede multis annis sedere" is omitted) so that there results the acclamation customary in his day; cf. Deusdedit, II, c. cxiii, ed. Wolf von Glanvell (1905), 1, 241; see also *Liber cens.*, II, 123, for the *Petrus*-acclamation, and *Ordo Romanus XIV*, in Migne, *PL.*, LXXVIII, col. 1132, for the later period. See above, n. 38, for the *Petrus*-acclamation to Henry V (*Liber pont.*, II, 300), and above, n. 39.

[45] The laudes to cardinals seem to go back to the eleventh century. I find them first mentioned by Leo of Monte Cassino (*MGH. SS.*, VII, 692) when he relates the reception of Frederick of Lorraine, cardinal and abbot of Monte Cassino, later Pope Stephen IX: ". . . ad titulum suum de more cardinalium cum laude perductus est." The forms of these laudes are found in the Orders of Benedict (*Liber cens.*, II, 171, § 5) and Albinus (*ibid.*, II, 91). They seem to have fallen into desuetude by the fourteenth century; cf. *Ordo Romanus XIV*, in Migne, *PL.* LXXVIII, col. 1235, where the cardinal receives simply the acclamation *multos annos* thrice repeated.

laudes to cardinals are nonetheless episcopal acclamations and their form recalls especially the German episcopal acclamations of St. Gall, Freising, and Minden. They cannot be traced earlier than the twelfth century, but may have originated in the eleventh, when the "College of Cardinals" proper was established.[46]

The shouts of *N. papa quem sanctus Petrus elegit* were often to accompany the solemn procession which brought the pope, after his election back to the Lateran Palace. These processional laudes and acclamations are mentioned time and again in the *Liber pontificalis* and elsewhere,[47] and often they refer to the pageantry of the solemn reception of the pope. Procession and solemn reception, that is, observances which originally were an imperial prerogative, were taken over by the Holy See at an early date. However, in the early eighth century it was officially ordered that a pope was to be received with truly imperial honors and the banners of the city of Rome and of the Roman garrison were to be carried before him.[48] The banner procession is not simply an expression of joy. It replaces the triumphal processions of the Caesars and as a privilege apper-

---

[46] See the stimulating study of H. W. Klewitz, "Die Entstehung des Kardinal-kollegiums," *ZfRG.*, kan. Abt. XXV (1936), 115 ff., and "Montecassino in Rome," *QF.*, XXVIII (1937–1938), 36 ff.; in general, Anton Michel, *Papstwahl und Königsrecht oder das Papstwahl-Konkordat von 1059* (Munich, 1936).

[47] See, e.g. *Liber pont.*, I, 368 (Conon, 686 A.D.); I, 371 (Sergius I, 687 A.D.); I, 440 (Stephen II, 752 A.D.); I, 470 f. (Stephen III, 768 A.D.); II, 87 (Sergius II, 844 A.D.); II, 107 (Leo IV, 847 A.D.); II, 140 (Benedict III, 855 A.D.); II, 152 (Nicholas I, 858 A.D.); II, 191 (Stephen V, 885 A.D.). See for John XIII (966 A.D.) Benedict of Mount Soracte, in *MGH. SS.*, III, 719; for Stephen IX (1057 A.D.), see also Leo of Monte Cassino, *MGH. SS.*, VII, 693. *Liber pont.*, II, 282 (Gregory, VII, 1073 A.D.); II, 296 (Paschal II, 1099 A.D.); II, 313 (Gelasius II, 1118 A.D.); II, 327 (Honorius II, 1124 A.D.); see for Victor IV (1159 A.D.) *MGH. Const.*, I, 261, No. 188; for Clement III (1182 A.D.) *Annales Romani*, in *Liber pont.*, II, 349; and for Innocent III, the *Gesta Innocentii*, c. 7, Migne, *PL.*, CCXIV, col. xxi. The text of these laudes is rarely transmitted; see, however, above, n. 44, and *Liber pont.*, II, 191, the acclamation to Stephen V (885 A.D.) which has the following text:

"Domnum Stephanum
presbyterum
Deo dignum
omnes volumus,
omnes querimus
et petimus
nobis preesse pontificem . . ."

[48] *Liber pont.*, I, 390; the emperor orders in honor of Pope Constantine (708–715) that "omnes iudices ita eum honorifice susciperent quasi ipsum presentaliter imperatorem viderent." Here the *imperial* honors are actually mentioned; a reception *cum gloria*, however, was offered at Constantinople to Pope John I (523–526), cf. *Liber pont.*, I, 275; and the processional reception was staged at Rome for Pope Conon in 686; cf. *ibid.*, I, 368: "omnes iudices una cum primatibus exercitus pariter ad eius salutationem venientes in eius laude omnes simul adclamaverunt." Further, in the *Ordo Romanus I*, c. 21, in Migne, *PL.*, LXXVIII, col. 948, which belongs to the eighth century but may be even earlier, the "milites draconarii, id est qui signa portant," are mentioned in the papal procession. For this whole problem, cf. Carl Erdmann, "Kaiserliche und päpstliche Fahnen im hohen Mittelalter," *QF.*, XXV (1933–1934), 15 ff. See also Batiffol, *op. cit.*, pp. 211 f., and 213, n. 2, for the hails *Confessor Christi*, *Confessor Christi* (Migne, *PL.*, XLI, col. 835) as a processional acclamation.

taining to the emperor it is found in the Donation of Constantine, written in the middle of the eighth century, where it is said *expressis verbis* that the emperor had ceded to Pope Sylvester "also the banners and the whole procession of the imperial majesty."[49] Thus, the banner procession and right to display it is one of the many prerogatives enumerated in the Donation which actually were customary with the Holy See long before the forged document was drafted.[50] But it was not before the time of Gregory VII that the display of the banner procession within Rome was proclaimed as an exclusively papal prerogative which not even the emperor could claim.[51]

PAPAL LAUDES IMPERIALIZED

Our knowledge of the papal ceremonial between the ninth and the early twelfth centuries is very scant. The Roman liturgy and Roman liturgical writing, in decline for a long time, but activated by the stimulating influence of Charlemagne, decayed definitely during the "Age of Iron." They only recovered under the new impulses which proceeded from the Reform Papacy in the eleventh century. After the Reform, our earliest evidence for the staging of Roman ecclesiastical performances dates from *ca.* 1140, when the Canon Benedict of St. Peter's wrote his *Liber Politicus* during the pontificate of Innocent II (1130–1143).[52] Benedict's work, momentous in every chapter, is of outstanding importance with regard to our knowledge of Roman acclamations. He records the Franco-Roman laudes to be sung to the emperor at his coronation and on the occasion of Church festivals when by chance the emperor was present in Rome. Benedict records also the laudes to cardinals as well as the quaint and archaic *laudes Cornomanniae*,[53] facetious acclamations of Greek and prob-

---

[49] *Constitutum Constantini*, c. 14, in Mirbt, *Quellen*, 111, lines 25 ff.: ". . . conferentes . . . et conta atque signa, banda etiam et diversa ornamenta imperialia et *omnem processionem imperialis culminis* . . ."

[50] It is generally known that the forger, on the whole, records and mythicizes and, above all, summarizes customs, prerogatives, and privileges such as the Holy See was granted or had adopted long before the eighth century, beginning in the age of Constantine. See, e.g., Klewitz, in *ZfRG.*, kan. Abt., XXX (1941), 108 f., with reference to the papal crown.

[51] In fact, the Roman banner procession was withheld from the emperors since the coronation of Henry V (1111), that is, after the Investiture Strife; cf. Erdmann, *op. cit.*, p. 17, n. 1. A splendid description of the papal procession and reception is offered by Boso, *Vita Alexandri*, in *Liber pont.*, II, 340.

[52] *Liber cens.*, II, 141 ff.; see Duchesne in the Introduction to the *Liber cens.*, I, 105 ff.

[53] On this celebration, cf. Duchesne, *ibid.*, I, 107–113; for the text, see *ibid.*, II, 171 ff.; Cabrol, *DACL.*, VIII, 1910 ff., *s.v.* "Laudes pueriles"; Paul Fabre, "Le Polyptique du chanoine Benoît à la Vallicelliane," *Mélanges d'archéologie et d'histoire*, X (1890), 384 ff.; V. Tommasini, "Sulle laudi greche conservate nel *liber politicus* de Canonico Benedetto," *Mélanges Ernesto Monaci* (Rome, 1901), 377–386; Fedor Schneider, "Ueber Kalendae Januariae und Martiae im Mittelalter," *Archiv für Religionswissenschaft*, XX (1920–1921), 390 ff., and the same author's *Rom und Romgedanke im*

ably pagan origin offered to the Roman bishop on the Saturday after Easter. In addition, Benedict gives a full account of the various species of laudes offered to the pope on different occasions.

In the papal laudes recorded by Benedict, the great change in the pope's general position after the Investiture Strife is reflected very clearly. The pope had changed from a Roman bishop to a Roman monarch, and accordingly we find, still side by side, episcopal and "monarchic" hails to the pope in the same work. There is on record a formulary of the acclamations which the *judices*, the papal Judges Palatine, rendered to the pope. At the celebration of the great festivals, the pope, on his return from the service in St. Peter's, was received by the judges either at the Lateran Palace or else at one of the Roman Station-Basilicas, and after being granted the papal benediction the judges chanted their laudes:[54]

Hanc diem	multos annos!
Tempora bona habeas!	Tempora bona omnes habeamus!

It is evident that these hails represent nothing but episcopal acclamations.

The performance of the judges was preceded by a similar one staged by the cardinals. On horseback, they had accompanied the pope from St. Peter's to the Lateran, or to a Station-Basilica. On their arrival they descended from their horses while the pope still remained on his white mount; they asked and received from the pope the blessings and chanted the following laudes:

Summo et egregio antistiti, beatissimo	
pape Innocentio, vita!	Deus conservet eum.
Salvator mundi	tu illum adiuva.
S. Maria	tu illum adiuva...
Omnes sancti	adiuvate illum.[55]
Kyrieleison....	

This is a *vita*-acclamation which, however, is not preceded by the *Exaudi Christe* of the imperial acclamations; it is followed instead by the cry

---

Mittelalter (Munich, 1926), 29 ff.; see also F. Cabrol, *Les origines liturgiques* (Paris, 1906), Appendix C, pp. 203–210. See, for similar *laudes pueriles*, L. Traube, "Ein altes Schülerlied," *N.Arch.*, xxv (1900), 620 ff.

[54] *Liber cens.*, II, 146. On the "Stations" in Rome, see Hartmann Grisar, S.J., *History of Rome and the Popes in the Middle Ages*, trans. and ed. by Luigi Cappadelta, I (London, 1911), 145 f., § 103. In the *Ordo Romanus IX* (cf. above, n. 42) we find the *patroni regionum* as singers; Deusdedit, II, c. cxiii, ed. Wolf von Glanvell (1905), I, 241, replaces them by the *notarii regionum*; Benedict has *iudices* instead; on their position, see L. Halphen, *Études sur l'administration de Rome au moyen âge*, Bibliothèque de l'école des hautes études, CLXVI (Paris, 1907), 37 ff., 81 ff.; P. E. Schramm, "Studien zu frühmittelalterlichen Aufzeichnungen über Staat und Verfassung," *ZfRG.*, germ. Abt. XLIX (1929), 198 ff.; Bonizo, *Liber de vita christiana*, ed. Perels (1930), 242, n. 1.

[55] *Liber cens.*, II, 146.

Deus conservet, a formula proper to the episcopal acclamations, so that these laudes, too, must be considered "episcopal." In fact, we can distinguish without difficulty the two patterns of epicsopal acclaims, namely, those beginning *Hunc diem* and the others beginning *Te pastorem*, and thus recognize the well-known form of German episcopal acclamations. This is obvious if we join together the laudes chanted by judges and cardinals in the following way:

Judges:	Hanc diem	multos annos!
Cardinals:	Summo et egregio antistiti . . .	Deus conservet eum.
	Salvator mundi	tu illum adiuva.
	S. Maria	tu illum adiuva . . .
	Omnes sancti	adiuvate illum.
Judges:	Tempora bona habeas . . .	

This matches the formularies of St. Gall, Freising, and Minden. Their context has been distributed, in Rome, to two different groups of chanters—judges and cardinals—whereas in Germany we find one undivided litany. The dependency of the German and Roman forms on one another can hardly be denied, though it is difficult to tell who borrowed from whom. However, it is remarkable that these papal acclamations match the German forms only and have very little similarity to the French episcopal laudes, for instance of Autun,[56] at least not so far as their structure is concerned. Moreover, the papal form is recorded in Rome not earlier than the twelfth century, whereas we find the corresponding form in St. Gall already in the first half of the ninth. Although this might be ascribed to the contingencies of manuscript transmission, it is nevertheless very likely that the priority is indeed with the German forms, which may have been passed on to Rome through one of the various channels, known and unknown,[57] in Ottonian times when the Franco-German liturgy exercised its decisive influence on the liturgy of Rome.[58]

However, in the early twelfth century we find the pope still acclaimed in the manner in which the bishops were acclaimed. This, at least, is true with reference to those laudes which were rendered to him in the open and on his return from the divine service. But there is no doubt that these episcopal acclamations to the pope were about to die away. They gradually were replaced by the laudes which were sung

---

[56] For St. Gall, Freising, and Minden, cf. above, notes 11, 12, 36, 37; for Autun, cf. above, n. 21.

[57] *Liber cens.*, I, 350, c. 24; the monastery of Reichenau was required to deliver to Rome "pensionis nomine in sui (sc. abbatis) consecratione codicem Sacramentorum unum, Epistolarum unum, Evangeliorum unum, equos albos ii." Cf. Andrieu, *Ordines*, I, 515 ff. For the adoption of the German liturgy by Rome, see Klauser, "Die liturgischen Austauschbeziehungen," *HJb.*, LIII (1933), 185 ff.

[58] Andrieu, *loc. cit.*, and Klauser, *loc. cit.*

in church and during the Mass. Benedict of St. Peter's is the first author to offer the formulary of papal Mass laudes, and in his Order the two patterns—the episcopal acclamations to the pope and the papal Mass laudes—still overlap, or rather they are kept apart very carefully. We have every reason to assume that sixty years after Benedict the episcopal acclamations were definitely discarded. Albinus and Cencius, as well as the author of *Ordo XIII* who wrote under Pope Gregory X (1271–1276), would, it is true, mention the fact that the pope received the laudes when the great procession reached the Lateran Palace or one of the basilicae, but they no longer record the forms of these acclamations.[59]

The next author to mention the laudes to be sung in the open is Cardinal Jacobus Gaetani Stefaneschi († 1343). He explains in his *Ordo XIV* that the judges, conducted by a cardinal, sing to the pope out of doors "the very same laudes which the Prior of the Cardinal Deacons had chanted during mass before the Epistle and after the Collect."[60] Cardinal Gaetani, therefore, is our first evidence for the fact that the episcopal form of acclamations to the pope has been abolished and replaced by the Mass laudes. His witness is indeed of a very late date and therefore seemingly of little value for the earlier times. Yet, through the medium of the thirteenth-century *Missal of the Papal Chapel* Cardinal Gaetani draws on the *Ordinarium* of Innocent III, composed *ca.* 1200, so that the *Ordo XIV* reflects, to a great extent, the ceremonial observed under this great pope.[61] Consequently, it is probable that the old form of episcopal acclamations to the pope was abolished under Innocent III, who ostentatiously assimilated papal and imperial acclamations with each other, and that ever since his time the acclaims rendered to the pope after the great procession, and in the open, were the same as those chanted during the Mass in church. Perhaps it was even the intention of the pope's biographer to put these two performances into parallel, since he emphasizes that Innocent III at his inauguration received the laudes "in St. Peter's Basilica as well as before the Lateran Palace."[62]

---

[59] See, for Albinus, *Liber cens.*, II, 124; for Cencius, *ibid.*, I, 290, 298 f., and Migne, *PL.*, LXXVIII, col. 1065 (*Ordo Romanus XII*, c. 2): "Tunc iudices et advocati veniunt ei obviam sub gradibus in porticu; ibique prior cardinalis sancti Laurentii foris murum cum iudicibus et advocatis ei faciunt laudes"; cf. *ibid.*, c. 35, 38, and *passim*. For the *Ordo Romanus XIII*, c. 9, and *passim*, see Migne, *PL.*, LXXVIII, col. 1111B.

[60] *Ordo Romanus XIV*, c. 41, Migne, *PL.*, LXXVIII, col. 1138: ". . . prior presbyterorum cardinalium ordinatis iudicibus et scrinariis in filo, faciet idem laudem, sicut diaconus cardinalis fecerat in Missa ante Epistolam post Orationem."

[61] See the brilliant reconstruction of this stemma by Michel Andrieu, "L'Ordinaire de la Chapelle Papale et le Cardinal Jacques Gaétani Stefaneschi," *Eph. Lit.*, XLIX (1935), 230–260.

[62] *Gesta Innocentii*, c. 7, Migne, *PL.*, CCXIV, col. xxi, with reference to the pope's coronation: "Factaque laudes tam in Ecclesia S. Petri quam ante Lateranense Palatium . . ."

However, the abolishment of the episcopal laudes to the pope and their replacement by the Mass laudes may even antedate by several years the accession of Innocent III. This surmise becomes almost certainty if we consider the chanters who sang the laudes outdoors. According to Benedict the following ceremonial was observed:

First came the Cardinal Prior of San Lorenzo with the Deacons and began to intone the laudes; the responses were sung by the cardinals. There followed the *primicerius*, the first of the Roman Judges Palatine, who acted as precentor while the judges responded. Each group, cardinals and judges, chanted different laudes.

This arrangement was also that of Albinus,[63] who wrote about 1189. In the *Ordo XIV* (c. 41), we find a new ceremonial:

The Prior of the Cardinal Priests arranges the judges and notaries in one rank; the prior then had to intone the invocations of the Mass laudes to which the judges and notaries—and not the cardinals—sang the responses.

This is a great change. Instead of two groups of chanters—cardinals and judges—we find one "combined group," namely a cardinal as precentor with judges and notaries as choir. It is evident that this change is closely connected with the equalization of Mass laudes and laudes in the open. The episcopal acclamations, which formerly had served on the second occasion, were easily distributed in two groups; similar to the Autun formulary, there were two sections of hails, one referring to the feast day (*Hanc diem*) and the other to the person acclaimed, bishop or pope. The new formulary of Mass laudes, however, represents an indivisible unit; this chant, accordingly, was sung by a "combined group" of singers of which the cardinals as a corporation were excluded. It is remarkable that this latter arrangement of chanters agrees perfectly with both the *Ordo XIII* ("presbyter cardinalis . . . cum tabellionibus et iudicibus") and the Order of Cencius (*Ordo XII:* "prior cardinalis . . . cum iudicibus et advocatis").[64] Neither Cencius nor the *Ordo XIII* offer the text of these laudes; but there follows by implication that the Mass laudes, intoned by a cardinal as precentor and responded to by the judges, must have replaced the episcopal laudes by 1196–97, the date of the Cencius Order, so that the abolishment of the episcopal acclamations to the pope was carried through just before the accession of Innocent III.

The form of papal laudes that henceforth remained valid and was sung exclusively on every occasion has a simple litanizing text.[65]

---

[63] *Liber cens.*, II, 124.
[64] Above, n. 59.
[65] The form quoted is that of Albinus, *Liber cens.*, II, 145 f., because Benedict does not offer the full list of saints; cf. *ibid.*, pp. 131 ff. Albinus quotes the laudes at the celebration of Easter, Benedict at Christmas and Easter, and Cencius (*ibid.*, I, 290) at Christmas alone, but mentions (*ibid.*, I, 289) that the very same form was sung at the Mass on Easter and on all other laudes days.

Exaudi Christe	Domino nostro Innocentio a Deo decreto summo pontifici et universali pape vita. (ter)
Salvator mundi	tu illum adiuva.
S. Maria	tu illum adiuva.
S. Michael	tu illum adiuva.
S. Gabriel	tu illum adiuva.
S. Raphael	tu illum adiuva.
S. Johannes	tu illum adiuva.
S. Petre	tu illum adiuva.
S. Paule	tu illum adiuva.
S. Andrea	tu illum adiuva.
S. Stephane	tu illum adiuva.
S. Laurenti	tu illum adiuva.
S. Vincenti	tu illum adiuva.
S. Silvestre	tu illum adiuva.
S. Leo	tu illum adiuva.
S. Gregori	tu illum adiuva.
S. Benedicte	tu illum adiuva.
S. Basili	tu illum adiuva.
S. Saba	tu illum adiuva.
S. Agnes	tu illum adiuva.
S. Caecilia	tu illum adiuva.
S. Lucia	tu illum adiuva.

Kyrie eleison. Christe eleison. Kyrie eleison.

In a way, and especially in regard to the long and uninterrupted sequence of saints (it here follows the order of the Litany of the Saints), these laudes are reminiscent of the German episcopal acclamations, and consequently also of those sung to the cardinals and by the cardinals to the pope.[66] Yet, this new form is no longer an episcopal acclamation, for it alludes neither to the pope as *antistes* nor to the pope's episcopal see. Also it does not display the response characteristic of the acclaims to bishops— *Deus conservet*. Instead, we find the *vita*-acclamation in the form of the Franco-Roman imperial laudes with the cry *Exaudi Christe* preceding. Moreover, the pope's title matches verbatim the one found in the Franco-Roman forms and disagrees with those found in the papal-episcopal laudes. Another point should perhaps not be overstressed, but it may be mentioned nevertheless that, within the Mass, this new form was voiced between the first Collect and Epistle, that is the customary place of the imperial laudes, whereas in the *Ordo IX* they have their place after the *Gloria*.[67] The essential thing, however, is that the new formulary differed from all episcopal acclamations. The new hails to the pope were clearly distinguished from those to any other member of the hierarchy. Furthermore, this formulary was to equal, as may here be anticipated, the new form of imperial laudes introduced under Innocent III.

[66] Above, notes 45, 46, 56.
[67] Above, n. 42 and Chap. III, notes 65, 71.

What is the age of the new form which we shall call *laudes papales?* In the *Ordo IX* it is mentioned that the pope was offered laudes to be sung to him after the *Gloria*. Unfortunately, the redactor of the Order has omitted to record their form; he records only the papal-episcopal acclamations rendered by the *patroni regionum*, who in their capacity as chanters were later replaced by the judges or notaries. Of course, it is not impossible that the Mass laudes of the *Ordo IX* were the same as those of the Order of Benedict, but it is not likely. In the first place, the Litany of the Saints can hardly be expected to appear in a Roman Order as early as the eighth century (cf. above, Chap. II, pp. 34 f.); it would represent the earliest evidence thus far known, whereas in fact the Franco-Roman forms show clearly how hesitatingly Rome added the files of saints to the acclamations. Second, if it be accepted that the papal-episcopal laudes with the long series of saints depended on the German model, this consideration would lead us to the late tenth or early eleventh century as the date of the introduction of this particular species in Rome. And on this pattern, in turn, the papal Mass laudes depend. That the German acclamations should have been formed under Roman influence is not altogether impossible. However, it is not probable. The general trend of liturgical influences was from North to South in that period; also, a similar influence of a Roman model is not felt in the episcopal laudes of France or any other country. Third, there is not one formulary of *laudes papales* on record antedating the Order of Benedict, whereas a number of early papal-episcopal laudes (without the series of saints) have been transmitted. Finally, the replacement of the old papal-episcopal acclamations by the Mass laudes of Benedict's Order makes it likely that the form of the latter was "new" and of a more recent date, since usually it is a new invention that supersedes an old tradition. In short, the Mass laudes of the *Ordo IX* probably were a form of early episcopal acclamations without invocations of series of saints.[68] Thus, it is not without reason that our first evidence for the new *laudes papales* remains the Order of Benedict which presents rites and ceremonies in the form in which they had been arranged by the popes of the Church Reform during the latter half of the eleventh century. Indeed, only against the background of the Reform Papacy does the new pattern of *laudes papales* achieve its full relief.

---

[68] Klewitz, "Die Krönung des Papstes," *ZfGR.*, kan. Abt. XXX (1941), 112 ff., indicates that the development of the papal tiara during the eleventh century signifies at the same time an innovation and a harking back to the earlier times (eighth and ninth centuries), when the pope by wearing the so-called *camelaucum* was then clearly distinguished from other bishops. In a similar way, which, however, we cannot ascertain, the *laudes papales* might be considered not only as an innovation but also as a revival of Mass laudes of the time of the *Ordo IX*. But since their form is unknown, it is useless to indulge in further hypotheses.

It will be recalled that within the domain of secular princes the laudes were closely connected with the celebration of crownings or festival crown-wearings. Until the eleventh century a papal coronation did not exist. The pope was consecrated but not crowned for the simple reason that originally there was no crown he could have worn.[69] Whatever the papal headgear may have been like in the earliest centuries, a special headgear of the pope is not mentioned before the time of Pope Constantine I (708–715). Pope Constantine is said to have worn the so-called *camelaucum,* a white silk cap, high and conical, which was an insignia of the Byzantine emperor and other Eastern rulers. It was adopted probably by one of the Greek popes of Rome and worn as a nonliturgical headgear at the papal processions.[70] To wear this cap was a papal privilege even before the Donation of Constantine "legalized" the right of wearing it. In the great forgery it is said that the Emperor Constantine conceded his diadem of gold and gems to Pope Sylvester, who, however, refused to wear the crown over his clerical crown, the tonsure, and who therefore was given the white silk cap which in the forged document is called *frygium* and which is the same as the *regnum* in other documents.[71] This headgear, originally, was worn only at the papal processions and in this connection it is mentioned also in the *Ordo IX.*[72] However, at an unknown date between the ninth and the early eleventh century this headgear, perhaps in a slightly different form, became, under the name of the *mitra Romana,* a liturgical headdress which the pope did not remove during the service of the Mass. Moreover, to don the mitre was no longer a privilege of the pope alone; the cardinals, too, enjoyed this prerogative and eventually the mitre was granted as an insignia of honor also to a few individual bishops. It was Pope Leo IX (1049–1054), who first granted to bishops the privilege of wearing the mitre.[73] By the end of his pontificate there existed, in fact, no headdress the wearing of which was exclusively a papal prerogative.

It was probably Pope Nicholas II (1058–1061), who created an ex-

---

[69] For the following, see the excellent study of Klewitz, *op. cit.,* pp. 97 ff., with which I became acquainted just in time to unburden my apparatus criticus and to straighten out certain lines of development which I had pointed out years ago; cf. Jordan, in *ZfRG.,* kan. Abt. XXVIII (1939), 145, n. 1. Also, my circumstantial argumentation concerning the festival crown-wearings of the pope—a subject not dealt with before— could be condensed to a short paragraph.

[70] *Liber pont.,* I, 390; cf. Klewitz, *op. cit.,* pp. 109 f.

[71] This whole problem, it seems to me, has been solved by Klewitz as far as it could be solved at all. Eichmann, "Der sogenannte Salische Kaiserordo," *ZfRG.,* kan. Abt. XXVII (1938), 22, tries to distinguish between *frygium* and *camelaucum* and polemizes against Braun, *Die liturgische Gewandung* (1907), 495 ff., but he is not consistent and considers the two words as designations of the same cap in his article "Von der Kaisergewandung im Mittelalter," *HJb.,* LVIII (1938), 276.

[72] Migne, *PL.,* LXXVIII, col. 1007: "accedit prior stabuli et imponit ei in capite regnum . . . Et tunc demum ascendit (sc. papa) super equum . . ."

[73] Klewitz, *op. cit.,* p. 113.

clusively papal insignia. The mitre, it is true, remained the liturgical headdress which the pope shared with the bishops; but the *frygium* was reintroduced, as a nonliturgical head ornament. Pope Nicholas II was apparently the first to add to the *frygium* a golden crown.[74] Thus, the famous papal headdress with crown, styled also *tiara*, was created for considerations both hierarchical and political—hierarchical in order to provide the pope with a badge which he did not share with any bishop and which clearly distinguished him among the members of the hierarchy; political in order to emphasize the temporal power of the pope, a *signum imperii* according to Innocent III's definition, and also a prerogative inferred by the Donation of Constantine which the Reform Papacy had set out to materialize to the letter.

It was in the period of the Church Reform and of the establishment of the world-mastering papacy that the papal inauguration changed from the consecration of a bishop to the coronation of the pope-emperor. Ample evidence for this change is available. There is recorded the "coronation" of Pope Paschal II (1099–1118), Pope Calixtus II (1119–1124), and later pontiffs, in the crowned cap.[75] Henceforth the Roman bishops really wore Constantine's "imperial diadem" over the *tiara* which, however, during the service was, and still is, replaced by the customary mitre. The mitre, according to Innocent III, was the insignia of the spiritual power, the crown the insignia of the temporal power, "mitram quoque pro sacerdotio, coronam pro regno."[76] It was the obvious emblem of the pope as *sacerdos et imperator*.

The eleventh century was the high tide of the *coronamenta*, the crown-wearings, and festival coronations, on the part of the secular rulers. The Roman pontiff, being himself a crown-bearer by that time, did not hesitate to follow the model of emperors and kings. In Benedict's *Liber Politicus* we find for the first time a section unknown to any earlier ceremonial which has the rubric: "These are the festivals on which the pope must be crowned."[77] There follows a list of eighteen holidays— Christmas, Easter, Pentecost, Epiphany, Ascension, the pope's anniversary, and twelve other days—which were to be observed as the pope's crown-wearing days. Incidentally, our earliest evidence for a papal crown-wearing on feast days refers to Gregory VII who, on Christmas in 1075, paraded "coronatus et cum omni laude" from S. Maria Maggiore to his

---

[74] See Klewitz' discussion (*op. cit.*, pp. 97 f., 114 ff.) of the famous passage in Benzo of Alba, *Ad Henricum*, VII, c. 2, *MGH. SS.*, XI, 671 f.

[75] *Liber pont.*, II, 297; Klewitz, *op. cit.*, p. 98, n. 7.

[76] Migne, *PL.*, CCXVII, col. 665, cf. col. 481, as well as the interesting remark of Bruno of Segni (Migne, *PL.*, CLXV, col. 1108) quoted by Klewitz, *op. cit.*, p. 106: "Summus autem pontifex propter hoc et regnum portat, . . . quia Constantinus imperator olim b. Silvestro omnia Romani imperii insignia tradidit."

[77] *Liber cens.*, II, 165, § 2, and 90, § 1.

palace.[78] And ever since the end of the eleventh century the chronicles abound in reports that the pope, on these occasions, wore an *ornamentum imperiale* formed like a helmet and surrounded by a gold circle; or the headgear is described in similar terms.[79]

The "imperialization" of the Church is one of the outstanding features of the Reform Papacy. Gregory VII, in his *Dictatus*, goes so far as to declare "that only the pope was entitled to use the imperial insignia";[80] and the author of the so-called *"Dictatus* of Avranches" adds that the wearing of the *regnum* and other imperial array at processions was exclusively a papal prerogative.[81] To this array there belonged above all the *cappa rubea*, the imperial purple, which the pope donned immediately after his election and which constitutionally was even more important than the tiara with crown. The purple, introduced in the age of the Reform, was considered the true symbol of papal dominion.[82] Its reception was effected also by the Donation of Constantine where the *clamis purpurea* is mentioned among the raiments ceded to the pope, a garment styled in the *"Dictatus* of Avranches" a *signum imperii et martyrii*.[83] Similar imperial tendencies are traceable to all sections, political and administrative, of the papal government. It was only then that the pope became the feudal lord of princes and kings;[84] that feudalism was put into full force within the patrimony,[85] and that the offices at court such as chamberlain, cupbearer, marshal, dapifer, and seneschal were added to the papal staff.[86] Then the custom began to style the papal household the *Curia Romana*, a Roman Court in the meaning of both the royal court

[78] *Liber pont.*, II, 282.

[79] To the rich collection of places referring to the papal festival crownings in France, which Klewitz (*op. cit.*, pp. 100 ff., notes 11–14) has collected, there may be added the earliest evidence. It refers to a crown-wearing of Pope Urban II at Limoges, on Christmas in 1095, and it is mentioned by Geoffrey of Vigeois (c. 27), in Bouquet, *RHF.*, XII, 428: "Triumphaliter coronatus ad sedem Apostolicam Episcopalem rediit, ubi reliqua solemnitatis officia peregit." The queer expression "sedes Apostolica Episcopalis" refers to the cathedral of St. Martial in Limoges because its saint was claimed as an apostle. For St. Martial's alleged apostleship, cf. Duchesne, in *Annales du Midi*, IV (1892), 319 ff.; Leclercq, *DACL.*, IX, col. 1109 ff., *s.v.* "Limoges."

[80] Gregory VII, *Registrum*, II, *Ep.* 55a, ed. Caspar, in *MGH. Epist. sel.*, I, 204. The interesting suggestions of Julia Gauss, "Die *Dictatus*-Thesen Gregors VII. als Unionsforderungen," *ZfRG.*, kan. Abt. XXIX (1940), 1–115, who links the famous document with Gregory's Eastern policy, must be seriously taken into consideration.

[81] S. Löwenfeld, "Der *Dictatus Papae* Gregors VII.," *N.Arch.*,XVI (1891),200: "Soli pape licet in processionibus insigne quod vocatur regnum portare cum reliquo paratu imperiali."

[82] Klewitz, *op. cit.*, p. 120.

[83] Löwenfeld, *op. cit.*, p. 200; Klewitz, *op. cit.*, p. 120, n. 77.

[84] Beginning with the infeudation of the South Italian Norman Princes; cf. Jordan, *op. cit.*, pp. 71 ff.; Erdmann, *Kreuzzugsgedanken*, pp 116 ff., 173 ff.; P. Kehr, "Die Belehnungen der süditalienischen Normannenfürsten durch die Päpste (1059–1192)," *Abh. Preuss. Akad.*, Berlin, 1934, Abh. 1, pp. 1–52.

[85] Karl Jordan, "Das Eindringen der Lehensidee in das Rechtsleben der römischen Kurie," *ArchUF.*, XII (1931), 13–110.

[86] Karl Jordan, "Die Entstehung der römischen Kurie," *ZfRG.*, kan. Abt. XXVIII (1939), 139 ff.

(household) and the king's court (law court).[87] There was established in Rome a *capella papalis* with papal chaplains after the model of the much older secular institution of the King's Chapel where royal chaplains attended to the administrative requirements of the realm.[88] In the very same period the pope began to act as a general of both the ideal Christian army and his own papal army and to display, in this capacity, papal banners and standards with which kings and princes were feudally invested and which the pontiff did not hesitate to carry against Christian rulers.[89] By the twelfth century, the Roman Church was conceived of, and styled accordingly, as the true and new *Imperium Romanum*,[90] while the College of Cardinals appeared as *Senatus Romanus*.[91] It was in this period that the pope first was depicted in the *Maiestas*, that is enthroned as a world-ruler like the Lord or the emperor, whereas in former days the pope was depicted in the humble way in which saints were represented.[92]

---

[87] Jordan, *ibid.*, pp. 97 ff. On the office of the papal *cancellarius*, successor of the *bibliothecarius* in the earlier period, see P. Kehr, "Scrinium und Palatium," *Mitteilungen des Österreichischen Instituts für Geschichtsforschung*, Ergänzungsband VI (1910), 70 ff., and the new study by H. W. Klewitz, "Cancellaria. Ein Beitrag zur Geschichte des geistlichen Hofdienstes," *Deutsches Archiv*, I (1937), 45–79.

[88] Jordan, *op. cit.*, pp. 145 f.; Borwin Rusch, *Die Behörden und Hofbeamten der päpstlichen Kurie des 13. Jahrhunderts* (Königsberg, 1936), 77–90.

[89] Erdmann, "Kaiserliche und päpstliche Fahnen im hohen Mittelalter," *QF.*, XXV (1933–1934), 1–48; and the same author's *Kreuzzugsgedanken*, especially Chap. VI ("Vexillum sancti Petri"), and *passim*.

[90] Gervase of Tilbury, *Otia imperialia*, in *MGH. SS.*, XXVII, 378; Fr. von Schulte, "Zur Geschichte der Literatur über das Dekret Gratians," *Sitzungsber. Akad.*, LXIV (Vienna, 1870), 111, 132; J. B. Sägmüller, "Die Idee von der Kirche als Imperium Romanum im kanonischen Recht," *Theologische Quartalschrift*, LXXX (1898), 69 ff.; see also Greven, "Frankreich und der fünfte Kreuzzug," *HJb.*, XLIII (1923), 23 ff., for the papal leadership of the Crusades.

[91] The image is old; cf. Hieronymus, *Ep.* XXXIII, 5, *CSEL.*, LIV, 259, who styles the Roman clergy "Senatus," though in a derogatory sense; see Gmelin, in *Deutsches Archiv.* II (1938), 527, n. 7. See also the *Donation of Constantine*, c. 15, ed. Mirbt, *Quellen*, p. 111, the concession to the Roman clergy to use all the insignia "sicut noster senatus." In the age of the Church Reform these terms are found frequently; see, e.g., Petrus Damiani, *Contra philargyriam*, c. 7, Migne, *PL.*, CXLV, col. 540. Damiani, in his *De picturis principum apostolorum*, c. 1, *ibid.*, col. 589C–D, mentions "Petrus qui senatus apostolici princeps est." This image should not be confounded with the one mentioned before. The transcendental "apostolorum senatus" is found, e.g., in the *Ordo commendationis animae*, in Migne, *PL.*, CLI cols. 925 f.; see also the anthem sung on the Day of the Apostles (". . . dies, in quo summi regis senatores, Apostolorum principes Petrus et Paulus, ad supernam angelorum curiam . . . pervenerunt") for which Gastoué, "Le chant gallican," *RCGr.*, XLII (1938), 12, claims Gallican origin. This, however, does not refer directly to the cardinals as senators, an idea which is still found in Pius X's *Codex Juris Canonici*, c. 230: "S. R. E. Cardinales Senatum Romani Pontificis constituunt." For the problem, see Schramm, *Renovatio*, I, 255, and *passim;* Ingeborg Schnack, *Richard von Cluny*, Historische Studien, 146 (Berlin, 1921), 105, n. 214; for the thirteenth century, see Kantorowicz, *Ergänzungsband*, p. 200.

[92] Cf. G. Ladner, *Theologie und Politik vor dem Investiturstreit*, Veröffentlichungen des Österreichischen Instituts für Geschichtsforschung, I (Brünn, Leipzig, and Prague, 1935), 155 f., and his article "I mosaici e gli affreschi ecclesiastico-politici nell'antico palazzo Lateranense," *Rivista di Archeologia Cristiana*, XII (1935), 265 ff.; a fuller account will be found in Professor Ladner's *Die Papstbildnisse des Altertums und des Mittelalters*, Monumenti di Antichità Cristiana, pubblicati dal Pontificio Isti-

And it was a quite logical development that St. Peter, and eventually the pope himself, was considered and styled the virtual emperor,[93] the *princeps*[94] and *verus imperator*,[95] of the Western world.

There can be no doubt but what the new form of *laudes papales* falls in with this general development. The pope had become a "crowned head," and whenever he presented himself *in corona*, at his coronation and on the days of festival crown-wearings, he was tendered the laudes.[96] All this developed quite logically and was consistent in itself. By means of the new form of unmistakably papal laudes the uniqueness of the pope's office, as compared with the episcopal dignity in general, was emphasized, and at the same time the papal ceremonial was assimilated to that of emperor and king. The idea underlying the introduction of the *laudes papales* thus hardly differed from that of the other innovations: the new form stood out against the episcopal acclamations and at the same time presented itself as an antitype of the acclamations to the emperor.

The world had become pope-centered. No longer was there that self-contained equilibrium of all ranks of human society which the Gallo-Frankish and Franco-Roman laudes had displayed with perfect clarity; no longer were there the numerous intentions for the various powers on earth, interlaced with the invocations of various groups of saints—for the pope the apostles, for the king the Déesis group, for the queen the virgins,

---

tuto di Archeologia Cristiana, Ser. II (Città del Vaticano, 1941), of which apparently no copy has as yet reached America. See also Joseph Wilpert, "Die Kapelle des hl. Nikolaus im Lateranpalast, ein Denkmal des Wormser Konkordats," *Festschrift Georg von Hertling* (Kempten and Munich, 1913), 232 f.

[93] See, e.g., the letter of Gregory VII, *Registrum*, III, 15, ed. Caspar, I, 276, with reference to the Normans: ". . . beato Petro, quem solummodo dominum et imperatorem post Deum habere desiderant." See also Joannes Diaconus, *Liber de Ecclesia Lateranensi*, in Migne, *PL.*, LXXVIII, col. 1385C (a very bad text; cf. Klewitz, "Die Entstehung des Kardinalkollegs," *ZfRG.*, kan. Abt. XXV [1936], 123, n. 1): "Quando papa S. Petri vicarius . . . missam celebrat, ipsi, qui sacerdos est regalis et imperialis episcopus immo patriarcha et apostolicus, predicti vii episcopi debent assistere . . .' Between 1073 and 1081, documents were dated in the Burgundian kingdom "domno nostro papa Gregorio Romanum imperium tenente"; *Cartulaire de l'abbaye de Saint-Bernard de Romans* (Romans, 1898), I, 203 ff., Nos. 186, 188.

[94] Emmy Heller, "Der kuriale Geschäftsgang in den Briefen des Thomas von Capua," *ArchUF.*, XIII (1935), 242, n. 3; cf. 265 f., Nos. 14 and 15; 269 f., Nos. 21 and 22; 283, No. 47; 285, No. 51. The pope had been addressed "Your Majesty" even before, though only occasionally; cf. Bouquet, *RHF.*, VII, 559 (Charles the Bald to Nicholas I), and *ibid.*, X, 436 (Abbo of Fleury to Gregory VII); cf. Hauck, *Kirchengeschichte Deutschlands* (3d and 4th eds., Leipzig, 1906), III, 263, n. 4.

[95] Cf. above, n. 93; Kantorowicz, *Ergänzungsband*, p. 19. The idea of the *papa augustus* can be traced back very far indeed. Not to mention the Donation of Constantine, see, e.g., Walahfrid Strabo, *De exordiis*, c. 32, *MGH. Capit.*, II, 515: "Comparetur ergo papa Romanus augustis et caesaribus." See also Schramm, *Renovatio*, I, 24.

[96] Benedict, c. 19, *Liber cens.*, II, 145 f., and *passim*. Cf. *Liber pont.*, II, 296 f., for the coronation of Paschal II. In this connection the slip of Albinus, *Liber cens.*, II, 91, is interesting, for he heads the Franco-Roman imperial laudes with the wrong rubric: "Incipiunt laudes festis diebus quando domnus *papa* [read: "imperator"] coronatur." See the following note.

the confessors for the bishop, and the martyrs for the army. Had the Holy See sought to continue this tradition, it would have been easy to order the chanting of the old Franco-Roman laudes on the pope's festivals.[97] But the compact balance of the Romanesque Age, which had reflected the harmony of the universe, was about to wane, and with the rise of the Gothic Age the forces of heaven and earth began to focus in one man who, according to Innocent III, "is set between God and man, below God but above man, less than God but more than man, who judges all man but is judged by no one." The harmony of the cosmos was no

---

[97] Were the Franco-Roman laudes ever chanted in Rome except on those occasions when the emperor was present? The indications in favor of this practice are few, and none is convincing.

(1) The rubric of the Franco-Roman forms is always "Incipiunt laudes festis diebus." This can mean either the Church festivals in general (Christmas, Easter, and Pentecost), or festivals of the emperor such as his coronation in Rome, or his crown-wearing in Rome, which took place for the last time in 1133, when Lothar III and Innocent II wore their crowns; cf. Klewitz, "Festkrönungen," *ZfRG.*, kan. Abt. XXVIII (1939), 56, n. 3.

(2) Whatever the practice may have been, Albinus' rubric (*Liber cens.*, II, 91; above, n. 96) does not make sense and must be an error. The Franco-Roman laudes were not sung when the pope was crowned, for Albinus himself records the form of the laudes to be sung at the papal coronation and crown-wearings, namely, the normal *laudes papales*. We therefore must read "quando imperator coronatur."

(3) Benedict, *Liber cens.*, II, 169, makes the following statement:

"Leo III constituit in laude imperatoris dici *Piissimo augusto a Deo coronato, magno et pacifico imperatori vita et victoria* ante sacram confessionem beati Petri Apostoli et plures sanctos invocari ab archidiacono et diaconibus, primicerio et cantoribus et notariis. Haec laus sit in corona eius ad altare sancti Mauritii ubi coronatur imperator a Romano pontifice."

This suggests that Leo III ordered the singing of the laudes to the emperor on "normal occasions" at the *Confessio;* on the emperor's coronation, however, they were to be rendered before the altar of St. Maurice. This evidence, however, is almost without value once we realize that the first sentence is borrowed from the description of Charlemagne's coronation in the *Liber pont.*, II, 7, where it is said that Charlemagne's coronation laudes were sung at the *Confessio* of St. Peter's. We know nothing about an enactment of Leo III according to which this homage was to be perpetuated. In fact, the passage does not really deal with the laudes; it deals with the consecration of the emperor. Schramm, "Die Ordines des Kaiserkrönung," *ArchUF.*, XI (1929), 332 ff., discusses the problem. Quite obviously, Benedict tries to explain the incongruity of the practice of his own time (consecration of the emperor at the altar of St. Maurice) with the authentic description of the first coronation at the *Confessio* (Charlemagne was not anointed in 800). He therefore distinguishes between (a) laudes at the coronation before the altar of St. Maurice, and (b) a fabulous constitution of Leo III about laudes before the *Confessio;* but (b) refers merely to Charlemagne's enhancement, so that Benedict cannot be adduced as a witness for the singing of festival laudes in the Franco-Roman form within Rome—unless the emperor himself was present. But there is an explanation of Benedict's inconsistency. In 1133 Benedict saw with his own eyes Lothar III and Innocent II wearing their crowns on Whitsunday. On this occasion an unction did not take place; hence, the altar of St. Maurice was not the scene of a liturgical act. But a coronation took place—the festival imposure of the crown through the pope—and this act was staged, quite correctly, at the *Confessio;* and consequently the laudes, too, were sung at the *Confessio*, a custom which Benedict traces back to Leo III. After all, Benedict does not say that the laudes were sung to the emperor when the latter was not personally present.

Thus, there is no evidence for the singing of the Franco-Roman laudes on feast days in Rome. It would be most illuminating if the imperial laudes containing an intention for the emperor had actually been discarded as a festal acclamation and replaced by the new monarchical *laudes papales*. But this does not seem to be so.

longer reflected in the concord of various social groups; the whole was represented by the pope alone. Therefore, the exclusion of all other powers from the new *laudes papales* must be considered as a significant feature of the new papal monarchy. The chant contains only one acclaim, the acclaim to the pope; and all ranks of saints are invoked as intercessors for him who would soon be considered the "summus pontifex . . . qui potest dici ecclesia."

IMPERIAL LAUDES PAPALIZED

The task of representing the *Rex et Sacerdos* ideal in this world had been passed on from the emperor to the pope. It is logical that the increase of "imperial" authority on the part of the pontiff should entail a decrease of the clerical or "sacerdotal" elements which formerly were inherent in the office of the Roman emperor. In Carolingian and Ottonian times a sacerdotal kingship after the model of Byzantium seemed to be not wholly impossible. But once the rigid hierarchism of Rome had conquered, the Byzantine solution lost every chance in the West. Rome considered the emperor a papal subordinate. In spite of similar trends in Byzantium, the basileus nevertheless remained the lord and superior of the consecrating patriarch. The model of St. John the Baptist, whose irrational power was as preponderant in the East as was the rational hierarchic power of the "Prince" of Apostles in the West, may have fostered the conception that the *consecratus* could hold a rank higher than the *consecrator:* "A knight baptizes the king, a serf the Lord, St. John the Saviour."[98] This may elucidate the relationship between patriarch and basileus. In the West, however, the proportion was inverse. At an early date, in the age of Nicholas I and John VIII, Rome began to lay stress on the word of the Apostle: "The less is blessed of the better" (Heb. 7:7).

---

[98] See the antiphon:
> "Baptizat miles regem, servus dominum, Johannes Salvatorem. Aqua Jordanis stupuit, columba protestatur, paterna vox audita est: Hic est filius meus."

This antiphon is older in the West than Hermann Usener, *Kleine Schriften,* IV (1913), 429 ff., seems to assume. It is found in the Worcester Cathedral Cod. F. 160, fol. 58; it appears at an even earlier date in the Breviary, and it has been arranged as a hymn, cf. *Analecta Hymnica,* XXXIV, 208, No. 255 ("Miles regem baptizavit . . ."). Its origin is oriental; cf. F. C. Conybeare, *Rituale Armenorum* (Oxford, 1905), 173, § 40, and pp. 421 and 426, § 28. In *De caerim.,* I, 3, p. 41, similar phrases are used as an acclamation to the emperor. They belong to the oriental ritual of the Blessing of the Waters on the eve of Epiphany, a ceremony with which the West became acquainted in the eleventh century when it appears first in a manuscript from Salzburg (not Viviers); cf. De Puniet, in *DACL.,* II, 704, and for the manuscript (Paris, Bibl. Nat. Lat. MS 820) Leroquais, *Pontificaux;* see also A. Franz, *Die kirchlichen Benediktionen,* I, 193 ff., § 10. The ritual was rarely incorporated in the Western liturgy and remained an Eastern curiosity ("Benedictio aquarum theophaniarum secundum ordinem orientalium ecclesiarum"); only in Southern Italy did it belong to the official rite of some churches. For the origin of the feast, see Dom Anselm Strittmatter, "Christmas and Epiphany: Origins and Antecedents," *Thought,* XVII (1942), 617 ff., where the modern literature on the subject will be found.

And in the age of Innocent III no man would have thought of arguing about the truth of the pope's sentence: "Kings are anointed by priests, not priests by kings. Lower thus is he who is anointed, than he who anoints, and more dignified the anointer than the anointed."[99] The age of sacramental kingship began to pass away, and the emperor's sacerdotal character, so far as it went, was never to be restored again within the Church after the blows which the idea of an imperial Church government had suffered during the Investiture Strife and its aftermath.

The abrogation of the priestly essence resident in the emperor's office presents itself as a long process at the end of which we find the name of Innocent III. The imperial coronation ceased to be a part of the High Mass as was true of the papal coronation; it took place before Mass began. The coronation garments of the emperor were no longer considered "liturgical" robes with which he was dressed at the service; the emperor donned his coronation robe in his chamber before he entered the cathedral. He was not consecrated before the *Confessio sancti Petri*, now reserved to the pope alone, but before the altar of the militant St. Maurice in the side aisle of St. Peter's. Moreover, the emperor's head was no longer anointed, but only his shoulders and arm; and the unction was accomplished not with chrism, but with unconsecrated catechumen oil.[100] It would be strange had these encroachments not affected also the manner of acclaiming the emperor.

As late as the twelfth century, Roman public opinion seems to have considered it an imperial privilege to be offered the laudes. This is expressed plainly in the so-called Cornomannic laudes, a gay and almost carnivalesque mockery of the pope staged on the Saturday after Easter. The Roman crowds, on this day, would march behind a fool's priest, who was mounted on an ass and disguised as a kind of Silenus. The people would sing quaint Greek songs and would shout on their arrival at the papal palace: "Open the doors to us! We come to see Pope Innocent! We want to salute him, salute and honor him, and sing to him laudes such as those sung to the Caesars."[101] The crowd, when singing this archaic song, was not quite wrong. The papal laudes, in fact, derived from those offered to the emperors in bygone days. But by the time of the twelfth century

---

[99] Innocent III, *Registrum de negotio imperii*, *Ep.* 18, Migne, *PL.*, CCXVI, col. 1012. See Eichmann, "Königs- und Bischofsweihe," *Sitzungsber. Bayr. Akad.* (Munich, 1928), Abh. 6, pp. 69 f., who quotes some additional evidence for the Western conception; see, however, G. Tellenbach, *Church, State and Christian Society at the Time of the Investiture Contest* (Oxford, 1939), 57, n. 2, and 65.

[100] Eichmann, *op. cit.*, pp. 59 ff.; Schramm, *op. cit.*, p. 353, n. 4.

[101] *Liber cens.*, II, 172. Duchesne, *ibid.*, Introd., 1, p. 111, n. 1, explains that the imperial laudes were considered in Rome in the twelfth century as an imitation of the papal laudes; but this is not suggested by the poem which, at any rate, is much older than the twelfth century. Cf. *Graphia Libellus*, c. 19; Schramm, *Renovatio*, II, p. 101. See above, n. 53.

the current had certainly changed its course, for now the text of the papal formularies began to affect the imperial acclamation.

A first attempt to alter the text of the Franco-Roman laudes is registered in the Order of Cencius Savelli, later Pope Honorius III. (Cf. below, Appendix IV.) In the formulary transmitted in his Order the interlacement of acclamations and invocations of the saints is abolished. Four hails—to the pope, the emperor, the empress, and the army—open the song; then follows as in the *laudes papales* an uninterrupted series of saint invocations, thereafter the *Christus vincit* with a small number of laudatory invocations and the doxology in an abbreviated form. It is a simplified pattern of Franco-Roman laudes and discloses the tendency to assimilate the imperial acclamations to the new form of papal laudes.

Cencius Savelli's solution was a half measure which Innocent III apparently did not accept. He carried through a radical change of forms. In 1209, at the coronation of Otto IV, which in general was more secular than the preceding consecrations of emperors, the new form of imperial laudes was heard probably for the first time. It has the following text:[102]

Exaudi Christe	Domino nostro invictissimo Romanorum imperatori et semper augusto salus et victoria! (ter)
Salvator mundi	tu illum adiuva.
S. Maria	tu illum adiuva.
S. Michael	tu illum adiuva.
S. Gabriel	tu illum adiuva.
S. Raphael	tu illum adiuva.
S. Johannes Bapt.	tu illum adiuva.
S. Petre	tu illum adiuva.
S. Paule	tu illum adiuva.
S. Andrea	tu illum adiuva.
S. Marce	tu illum adiuva.
S. Stephane	tu illum adiuva.
S. Laurenti	tu illum adiuva.
S. Vincenti	tu illum adiuva.
S. Alexandre...	tu illum adiuva.

Kyrie eleison. Christe eleison. Kyrie eleison.

The poverty of the form, as compared with that of the ancient Franco-Roman laudes, is striking. There is no *Christus vincit, Christus regnat, Christus imperat* left in this mutilated chant. There are no laudatory invocations of Christ, no doxological praises, nor is there an acclamation to any other person or to the army. It is the emperor alone who is hailed. He is "monarch," is "individual," and not part of the structure of the universe and of the universal human society. As far as this singleness is concerned, the emperor is presented as a true antitype of the pope, and

---

[102] See for the so-called *Order of the Third Period*, Eichmann, "Die Ordines der Kaiserkrönung," *ZfRG.*, kan. Abt. II (1912), 1–43; Schramm, *op. cit.*, pp. 337 ff.

the similarity of papal and imperial forms makes us think of the doctrine of the Two Powers established by Providence to govern harmoniously this world. But a closer inspection of the document proves that, rather than the unity of two equal powers, it is the notorious metaphor of Sun and Moon which is illustrated by the new form. In the ancient Franco-Roman laudes, and even in those of the Cencius Order, we still find the two offices carefully balanced. There was an acclamation to the pope:

> Domino nostro a Deo decreto summo pontifici et universali pape vita

and one to the emperor:

> Domino nostro a Deo coronato magno et pacifico imperatori vita et victoria.

This parallelism of titles reflects, as it were, the equilibrium of the double choirs of Romanesque cathedrals, a unison of powers and a general balance which we find definitely disturbed after the victory of the hierarchy. In Pope Innocent's formulary the emperor is no longer styled *a Deo coronatus;* he is deprived of his immediate relationship with God. He is no longer the *rex pacificus* and is thus deprived of his eschatological background and essence as well. He is *invictissimus Romanorum imperator,* it is true; but even this attribute is empty and void of a spiritual dimension, for in conquering and being unconquered he fulfills a task dictated to him and imposed on him by the Holy See. He is, as Innocent III would have it, merely the "fighting arm of the Church" and for doing this duty he is anointed on shoulder and arm.[103] His office is de-spiritualized.

All this follows clearly from the new formulary of laudes. It shows the assimilation of the two offices to each other and, at the same time, displays by this similarity the supremacy of the *papa imperialis* over the *imperator papalis.*[104]

It is not only the impoverishment of the liturgical emperor worship that strikes us, but also the fact that this worship itself seems to have lost its basis in life. The image of Christ the Emperor and King began to fade away in the West and so did that of Christ the Commander

---

[103] Innocent III, *Reg.,* VII, *Ep.* 3, Migne, *PL.,* CCXV, cols. 282 f. The emperor became a *miles beati Petri* from whose altar the sword was taken up at his coronation; cf. Eichmann, *op. cit.,* p. 32; F. Kern, *Gottesgnadentum und Widerstandsrecht* (Leipzig, 1915), 115 f., n. 207.

[104] Most interesting, in this connection, is the acclamation to Henry V in Rome (1111 A.D.), perhaps a first effort to assimilate imperial with papal acclamations; cf. *Liber pont.,* II, 300: ". . . eandem laudem ei, ut alii ferebant, referentes atque dicentes 'Henricum regem sanctus Petrus elegit!' " This sounds like a joke; but it obviously meant that the emperor was considered no longer *a Deo coronatus*—like a cardinal, he was "created" by the pope, i.e., by St. Peter. As the emperor was not "vicarius Petri," the acclamation cannot be interpreted otherwise than as a token of the imperial dependency on the pope. This hail, therefore, should not be confounded with similar phrases used, e.g., in a papal letter to Pepin ("Beatus Petrus qui vos in reges unxit"); cf. *Codex Carolinus,* in *MGH. Epist.,* III, 501, No. 10.

when the word "Crusade" degenerated to a means of imposing taxes and waging European wars. The imperial image of Christ had dominated from the Constantinian Age until the end of the Romanesque Age. Then the Gothic and Renaissance ages established a new image of Christ, more human and intimate, which in essence was by no means imperial or royal. That king or emperor should represent on earth, as it were, the living Christ no longer made sense, since the claim was deprived of its inner truth. It is true that the imposing glory of the Church in this world made it reach to the heavens during the Later Middle Ages and that the mystic ingredients within the service were increased in that period. But the living mystery of the descent to earth of the Celestial Jerusalem and the true mystery character of the liturgy, whose "realism" had linked the mediaeval Church—even the Church in the West—to the mystery cults of the Hellenistic-Roman past, all began to wane in the Gothic and Renaissance ages.[105] Thus, the triumphant phrases of *Christus vincit, Christus regnat, Christus imperat* lost their substance and became unreal, too. They fell into oblivion or else were used as magic words, but life had gone from the realistic conception of an interrelationship between the Emperor Christ in heaven and his antitype on earth. As a consequence the whole performance of singing the ancient laudes to the ruler was to be discarded. A liturgical ruler-worship had become unessential.[106]

The chant, though with a different emphasis, has been revived in our day. The revival is closely connected with the ecclesiastical revival of the image of *Christus Rex*. But before completing the circle and inspecting the development of the laudes in modern times, it seems appropriate to give an account of the diffusion of these acclamations in the countries which did not directly belong in the Frankish orbit.

[105] See the excellent discussion by Anton L. Mayer, "Renaissance, Humanismus und Liturgie," *JLW*., XIV (1938), 123–171, esp. pp. 166 ff., and also his earlier article "Liturgie und Gotik," *JLW*., VI (1930), 68 ff.

[106] It was not abolished completely; even the Protestant Churches preserved a certain ruler worship; cf. Hans Liermann, "Untersuchungen zum Sakralrecht des protestantischen Herrschers," *ZfRG*., kan. Abt. XXX (1941), 311–383.

CHAPTER V

DALMATIAN AND VENETIAN LAUDES

Acclamations to the Ruler in Dalmatia

THE LITURGICAL history of the Balkan kingdoms belongs, on the whole, to the Græco-Slav orbit of culture; but the Dalmatian littoral forms an exception. Eastern and Western rites overlapped in this ancient Byzantine province which for centuries was the sport of rival Adriatic powers. The Dalmatian laudes betray their kinship with Byzantium, it is true. But at least they present themselves in Frankish or Roman attire. Therefore, and because they belong to the Western Church, they shall not be neglected here, especially since their study proves to be worth our while. The varied destinies to which the Dalmatian maritime towns were doomed during the Middle Ages are very distinctly reflected in the formularies of the politico-liturgical acclamations; and the scattered references to Dalmatian laudes, though not very numerous, indicate with a surprising clarity the legal and constitutive momentum of the acclamations in these regions. The Dalmation species of laudes has hitherto attracted very little, if any, attention among historians, so that a collection of even fragmentary material may prove to be useful.[1]

As late as the eleventh century, the Dalmatian littoral belonged to the Byzantine *thema* Dalmatia. Under Greek domination it was naturally the Eastern emperor who would be remembered in the laudes on feast days. We possess reliable evidence of this practice. John the Deacon reports in his chronicle[2] that in 997 the Emperor Basil II had agreed, with certain reservations, to the petition of some Dalmatian towns and allowed them to accept the protectorate of the Republic of Venice. Accordingly, on Ascension Day in 1000, the Doge Pietro Orseolo sailed forth with a fleet to take over the new province in the name of St. Mark; and a later widespread tradition would have it that it was this event which later was commemorated annually, with glittering pomp, as the doge's "Marriage to the Adriatic Sea."[3] Pietro Orseolo spent Whitsuntide in Ossero, where

---

[1] Joannes Lucius, *De Regno Dalmatiae et Croatiae* (Vienna, 1785), II, c. vi, pp. 72–74, is still fundamental; cf. Bona, *Rerum liturgicarum libri duo* (Paris, 1672), II, c. v, 8, p. 359. A musicological study has been published by A. Zaninović, "Un Christus vincit en Dalmatie au XIIᵉ siècle," *RCGr.*, XXX (1926), 130–133. For the laudes in the Venetian possessions see the study of Cardinal Silvio Giuseppe Mercati, "Laudo cantato dal clero greco di Candia per il pontifice Urbano VIII e l'arcevescovo Luca Stella," *Bessarione*, XXXVIII, (Rome, 1922), 9–21.

[2] *MGH. SS.*, VII, 32; ed. G. Monticolo, in *Fonti per la storia d'Italia* (Rome, 1890), I, 157 f.

[3] Cf. Ferdinand von Šišić, *Geschichte der Kroaten*, I (Zagreb, 1917), 195. Usually it is Venice's naval victory in 1177, over Barbarossa's son Otto, which is claimed as the event commemorated; cf. W. Lenel, *Die Entstehung der Vorherrschaft Venedigs an der Adria* (Strasbourg, 1897), 12 ff.

he received the acclamations of the clergy and people and had the laudes chanted to him. This was not meant to be a single welcoming ceremony. The bishops of Traù, Veglia, and Arbe pledged themselves to glorify henceforth on all festivals on which the solemnity of laudes was due the name of the doge immediately after that of the Byzantine emperor.[4] That is to say that they recognized the Venetian overlordship after that of Byzantium.

The pledge of the bishops agrees with the general Church policy in these regions. Ever since the Synods of Spalato (925 and 928) the Dalmatian maritime towns, though politically dependent on Byzantium, belonged in ecclesiastical matters to the administrative orbit of Rome.[5] As far as her ecclesiastical status was concerned, Dalmatia, therefore, was already severed from Byzantium. The recognition of the doge's power as secondary only to that of the Byzantine emperor prepared the way for a severance in secular politics as well. Hence, papal and dogal politics worked in the same direction, and the eager pledge of the Dalmatian bishops to acclaim the name of the doge in the laudes illustrates these conditions.

In fact, the name of the Eastern Roman emperor soon disappeared from the liturgical acclamations of Dalmatia. The coastal cities, it is true, until the end of the eleventh century continued to consider themselves, whenever it fitted into their political program, as being under Byzantine rule; in 1091 and 1095 their documents were still dated according to the years of the Greek emperor's reign.[6] Meanwhile, however, the Croatian kings had successfully contested both the Greek and Venetian domination of the coastal regions. Byzantium had yielded to the pressure of the Croats who were protected by Gregory VII as feudatories of the Holy See; and the move against the Croatians by the Signoria, whose doge had proudly adopted the title of "Duke of Dalmatia and Croatia" in 1090 after the extinction of the old Croatian dynasty,[7] proved likewise unsuccessful in the end. This failure of both St. Mark and Byzantium is reflected in the laudes of Zara of that time. For we find in the Zara formulary no acclamation either to the emperor or the doge, but instead one

[4] Johannes Diaconus, *MGH. SS.*, VII, 32: ". . . sacrum diem pentecosten solemniter celebrantes, predicto principi laudis modulamina decantaverunt . . . Insuper episcopi eisdem sacris confirmaverunt, quo feriatis diebus, quibus laudis pompam in aecclesia depromere solebant, istius principis nomen post imperatorum laudis preconiis glorificarent." Cf. Dandolo's *Chronicon Venetum*, in Muratori, *Scriptores*, XII, 228, who follows John the Deacon; see also Šišič, *loc. cit.;* Lenel, *loc. cit.;* Lucius, *op. cit.,* p. 119.
[5] The acts are conveniently published by Rački, *Documenta Historiae Chroaticae,* in *Monumenta Historica Slavorum Meridionalium,* VII (1877), 187 ff., No. 149; cf. Šišič, *op. cit.,* pp. 129 ff.
[6] Rački, *op. cit.,* p. 154, No. 128 (1091 A.D.); 159, No. 131 (1095 A.D.); Lenel, *op. cit.,* pp. 15 ff.
[7] Lenel, *op. cit.,* p. 15.

addressed to the new ruler who was then striving toward the Adriatic, King Koloman of Hungary (1095–1114).[8]

With King Koloman there begins the Hungarian sway over the littoral, which lasted, though by no means unopposed, for many centuries. In the laudes of Zara, he is hailed along with his son Stephen,[9] the bishop of Zara, and the Hungarian magnate Cledinus, who governed the city as a count.[10] Needless to say, the pope, Paschal II, was acclaimed first as in all Western formularies. As the first *acclamatus*, however, he replaced, audibly and visibly, the Byzantine emperor in these regions.[11]

It is probably not merely by chance that the oldest Hungarian form of laudes known to us originated in Zara. This place was the Dalmatian coronation city. At Zara King Koloman celebrated in 1097 his marriage with the daughter of Roger I of Sicily, and here, in 1102, he allowed himself to be crowned king of Dalmatia.[12] It is possible and even likely that the laudes formulary was used also as a crowning acclamation, although in the first place it must be considered a form of "festival" laudes. We know already through the events at Ossero in 1000 that it was the Dalmatian custom to voice that chant at Church festivals. Moreover, this practice is attested for Christmas and Easter celebrations by a rubric in the Zara formulary.[13] These festal days are mentioned again in a decree of 1192 which the papal legate, Gregory of Saints Apostles, issued for the Church of Traù.[14] It may be assumed that Traù, at that time, included in

---

[8] Berlin, Staatsb. MS Theol. Lat. Quart. 278, fol. 1ᵛ, an Evangelary of the Collegiate Church of S. Simeone in Zara, contains on the first and last leaves the laudes and a few documents in a twelfth-century hand other than the one that wrote the text of the codex. The formulary is printed by F. Bianchi, *Zara Christiana* (Zara, 1877), I, 538 f.; Brunelli, *Storia di Zara*, I (1815), 275 f.; T. Smičiklas, *Codex diplomaticus Regni Croatiae, Dalmatiae, et Slavoniae* (Zagreb, 1904), ll, 392.

[9] He was born in 1101 and ruled, after his father, from 1114 to 1131. He had the royal title probably as heir to the throne, but may have been made as well king of Dalmatia during the lifetime of his father.

[10] His name occurs frequently in Dalmatian documents; in 1102, Cledinus is witness to the coronation of King Koloman at Zara (Smičiklas, *op. cit.*, ll, 9 f., No. 6); in 1105, he is witness to a document at Zara (*ibid.*, p. 15, No. 10); in 1116–1117 he signed a document as "princeps et banus" (*ibid.*, p. 393, No. 2). See also for the year 1111, *ibid.*, pp. 22, No. 19; 24, No. 21. This magnate can thus be traced from 1102 to 1117; since Pope Paschal II ruled from 1099–1118 and Bishop Gregory of Zara from 1101–1111, the formulary must fall in the period 1102 to 1111.

[11] Lucius, *op. cit.*, p. 74.

[12] Cf. Smičiklas, *op. cit.*, II, 9, No. 6, and *ibid.*, p. 147, the charter for Santa Maria di Zara: "Ego Colomannus . . . postquam coronatus fui Belgradi supra mare in urbe regia." Dalmatian coronations of the Hungarian kings are frequently mentioned; cf., e.g., Rački, *op. cit.*, pp. 19, No. 16; 50, No. 49; 53, No. 52, with reference to Traù in the years 1108 and 1142; see also concerning Spalato in 1207, the charters published by Smičiklas, *op. cit.*, lll, 69, No. 61; 71, No. 63: "cum autem ad vos coronandus aut vobiscum regni negotia tractaturus venero." This formula must not always refer to an actual coronation; it is a routine formula "in adventu regis" in order to secure certain services of the cities whenever the king comes to Dalmatia.

[13] The rubric is "Laus que in pascha et natali die post Evangelium dicitur"; cf. above, n. 8.

[14] See Giovanni Lucio, *Memorie istoriche di Tragurio* (Venice, 1674), 477, the letter of Archibishop Peter of Spalato says with reference to Traù ". . . super duobus

this chant an intention for the Hungarian king. This at least is proved by a document of 1200, in which it is mentioned that King Bela III, while visiting Traù, was tendered the laudes by the clergy and people of the city.[15]

Thus, in spite of the changes from Byzantine to Venetian, and then to Hungarian rule, there was no break in the liturgical tradition. Hungary appeared as the legal successor of Byzantium, though not Hungary alone. From the days of Gregory VII the Holy See had aimed at the feudal overlordship of Dalmatia, and occasionally the popes were successful in their claims. It is sometimes difficult to tell whether laudes sung in the Adriatic provinces referred to the Roman pontiff in his quality as pope or as feudal overlord. However, in 1199, the Serbian Prince Vucan, who styled himself king of Dioclea (today Podgoritza, Albania) and who in his struggle for the Serbian throne was supported by the Holy See and by Hungary, then the papal champion in the Balkans, wrote to Innocent III and assured him that in his little kingdom he had ordered *laudum praeconia* to be sung in celebration of the pope's accession to the Holy See.[16]

In this connection a Greek acclamation to Innocent III may be mentioned. After the crusaders under Venetian leadership had conquered Constantinople in 1204, the liturgical commemoration of the pope met with considerable resistance within the Greek Church. In Constantinople this issue was settled in a not quite perspicuous way. Enrico Dandolo, so we are told, did not force upon the Greek Church the inclusion of the name of the pope in the diptychs of the Mass; but the Greeks were supposed to chant the laudes to the pope in the manner which was used customarily for the *euphemia* of the basileus.[17]

This seems a political rather than an ecclesiastical measure, especially if we consider the constitutional importance attributed to the laudes by

perperis (hyperperis) laudum, uno in Pascha, alio in Natali Domini persolvendo;" cf. Smičiklas, *op. cit.*, II, 254, No. 328.

[15] Smičiklas, *op. cit.*, II, 361, No. 333; J. Kukuljevič de Saccis, *Regesta documentorum regni Croatiae, Dalmatiae et Slavoniae saeculi XIII* (Zagreb, 1896), 3, No. 9. Zara had expelled the Venetian officers in 1181.

[16] Smičiklas, *op. cit.*, II, 333, No. 310; A. Theiner, *Vetera Monumenta Slavorum Meridionalium*, I (Rome, 1863), 6, No. 10; Innocent III, *Reg.*, II, *Ep.* 176, in Migne, *PL.*, CCXIV, col. 726. For Dioclea and its ecclesiastical status, see Moriz Faber, "Das Recht des Erzbischofs von Antivari auf den Titel Primas von Serbien," *Wissenschaftliche Mitteilungen aus Bosnien und der Herzegowina herausgegeben vom Bosnisch-Herzegowinischen Landesmuseum in Sarajevo*, XI (Vienna, 1909), 345 ff.; and Duchesne in the Introduction to the *Liber censum*, 1, 49 ff. For Vucan and his relations with the Holy See, cf., Dragutin Franič, "Die Lage auf der Balkanhalbinsel zu Beginn des 13. Jahrhunderts," *Wissenschaftliche Mitteilungen aus Bosnien* . . . V (1897), 313 f., 320 f.; Maria Luise Buria, "Die Krönung des Stephan Prvovenčani und die Beziehungen Serbiens zum römischen Stuhl," *Archiv für Kulturgeschichte*, XXIII (1933), 148 f. See also L. Karaman, in *Byzantion*, IV (1927–1928), 321–336.

[17] Johannes Baptista Cotelerius, *Ecclesiae Graecae Monumenta* (Paris, 1686), III, 519; see above all the important article by Silvio Giuseppe Mercati, *op. cit.*, p. 11: Ἰννοκεντίου δεσπότου πάπα τῆς πρεσβυτέρας Ῥώμης πολλὰ τὰ ἔτη.

the Venetians. The political significance of the acclamations is revealed very obviously in the conflicts arising between Venice and Hungary over the domination of Dalmatia. One bone of contention was Zara. It is well known how brutally this city had been sacked by the Venetians and the crusaders in 1202. Two years later Venice bullied the citizens of Zara into promising that twice a year, at Christmas and Easter, they would voice the laudes to the doge, the patriarch of Grado, and to the city count whom the Signoria claimed the right to appoint.[18] Yet, a few months later, King Andrew II of Hungary very energetically claimed this prerogative as his due in the neighboring city of Nona. He took Nona under his protection and confirmed the communal privileges, but in exchange he demanded the solemn assertion that "in accordance with the old usages of his faithful subjects in the littoral" the clergy and people of Nona would render homage to the king and his successors by singing the laudes and acclaiming the king's name on the customary feast days.[19]

The strong emphasis laid on the rendering of the liturgical acclamations indicates how important an act this ceremony was considered to be by both Venice and Hungary. It was a token of submission and public recognition of the respective overlord and at the same time a pledge binding the Church as well as the people. We have every reason to believe that in this case Byzantine conceptions of sovereignty exercised a decisive influence on both Venice and Hungary. The original and primarily political nature of the laudes, which was never dismissed in Byzantium, was distinctly brought into prominence in Dalmatia at a time when the genuine and intrinsic value of liturgical acclamations was about to be obscured in the Western realms. It was due to the survival of Byzantine tradition that southeastern Europe remained conscious of the true meaning of these ecclesiastical hails until modern times. (Cf. below, p. 182.)

The Form of the Hungarian Laudes in Dalmatia

The form of the Dalmatino-Hungarian acclamations was preserved for many centuries with some insignificant changes. At our disposal are the formularies of Zara of the early twelfth century and of Ossero of the fourteenth,[20] not to mention a vast number of late mediaeval and even mod-

---

[18] Smičiklas, *op. cit.*, III, 45, No. 42: "Clerus autem bis in anno in nativitate domini et in pascha resurrectionis laudes cantabunt in maiori ecclesia solempniter domino Duci et domino patriarche atque archiepiscopo suo et comiti omni anno, propter quod benedictionem recipient consuetam. Eligent Jadratini semper comitem de Venetiis . . ."

[19] Smičiklas, *op. cit.*, III, 51, No. 46: "Laudes regio nostro nomini, sicuti est consuetudo fidelium nostrorum de Marittimis, pro honorificientia regia consuetis diebus solemnibus per suum clerum et populum deprecabuntur." Cf. F. Bianchi, *Zara Christiana*, II, 527, cf. I, 536 f., on the acclamations in general.

[20] Vatican, Borg. MS 339, fol. 59ᵛ, a supplementary leaf of a twelfth-century manuscript, the fragment of an Evangelary from Ossero; cf. A. Ebner, *Quellen und For-*

ern laudes of the littoral under Venetian and Austrian domination. (Cf. below, p. 182.)

The oldest text, that of Zara, *ca.* 1102,[21] is as follows:

Exaudi Christe! (ter)
Christus vincit, Christus regnat, Christus imperat! (ter)
Paschali summo pontifici et universali pape sàlus et vita perpetua (ter)
Colomanno Ungarie, Dalmatie et Croatie almifico regi vita et victoria (ter)
Stephano clarissimo regi nostro vita et victoria.
Gregorio venerabili Jadere presuli salus et vita.
Cledin inclyto nostro comiti vita et victoria.
Cunctis inclytis vita!

The form of Ossero refers to King Louis the Great of Hungary and falls in the years 1378–1382.[22] It is written in a very bad Latin and has the following text:

Exaudi Christe! (ter)
Domino pape Gregorio sumo pontifice et universali pape salus, honor et vita perpetual
Cunctis incliti vita!
Domino Lodouico regis Ungarie salus, honor et vita victoria.
Cunctis incliti vita!
Domino Michaeli episcopo Absarense et tocius insule salus, honor et vita perpetua.
Domino Saraceno[a] comite Absarense et tocius insule[b] salus, honor et vita victoria.
Cunctis incliti vita!

[a] name cancelled with a thin stroke and "in Paradisio" interlined.
[b] "una cum iudicibus suis" in margin.

These two formularies disclose very clearly the peculiarities of the Dalmatian laudes. Their structure reminds us immediately of the Byzantine acclamations voiced at synods and on other occasions: a number of hails but no effort to arrange them in a formal or litanylike way. There are no invocations of saints. The laudations with the responding *Christus vincit* are lacking; so are the doxologies, and also the shouts of *feliciter* with the *tempora bona* wishes. Nor is the army acclaimed.[23] The Dalmatian laudes have the *Exaudi Christe* in common with the Western litany; it is the

*schungen zur Geschichte und Kunstgeschichte des Missale Romanum im Mittelalter.
Iter Italicum* (Freiburg, 1896), 153, n. 2, who dates the document incorrectly; he has it refer to Gregory X and King Ladislaus. Bishop Michael of Ossero ruled from 1364 to 1390, cf. Daniele Farlato, *Illyrum Sacrum* (Venice, 1775), V, 198 f., so that the pope must be Gregory XI (1378–1389) and the king, whose name is mentioned, is Louis the Great (1342–1382).
[21] Cf. above, notes 8 and 12.
[22] Cf. above, n. 20; the offenses against grammar and orthography are not corrected.
[23] There is, however, an acclamation to the count which is not found in Western laudes, although the count is frequently found in other prayers, e.g., in the *Praeconium Paschale;* cf. Ladner, "The 'Portraits' of Emperors in Southern Italian *Exultet* Rolls," *Speculum,* XVII (1942), 187, 192, and the *Exultet* of the Barberini Lat. MS 592, leaf 5, and the Madrid, Bibl. Nac. Lat. MS 289 (153), fol. 115ᵛ; cf. E. Kantorowicz, "A Norman Finale of the Exultet and the Rite of Sarum," *Harvard Theological Review,* XXXIV (1941), plate facing p. 129; see also Biehl, *op. cit.,* p. 91. The duke of Normandy is mentioned in the laudes of Rouen; but he was, after all, a "sovereign"; cf. below, Chap. VI, p. 167.

opening cry, remindful of the original Roman or Franco-Roman, forms. The title of the pope, however, agrees with the Gallo-Frankish forms rather than with the Franco-Roman, whereas the *Christus vincit*, which we find in the Zara form intercalated between the *Exaudi* and the acclamations proper, may be borrowed from any Western model. The three beats of the *Christus vincit* have disappeared from the text of Ossero, but even in that of Zara they are almost unessential, since they do not influence the mood of the whole song as in the West. A peculiarity of the Dalmatian laudes is the hail *Cunctis inclytis vita*. It concludes the Zara form and is repeated after each acclaim in the Ossero formulary; it can be found nowhere in the West and is therefore, almost certainly, of Byzantine origin. Moreover, the musical accompaniment of the Zara laudes deviates from all Western patterns.[24]

The Hungarian laudes of Dalmatia follow, on the whole, the Byzantine model; but they are amalgamated with elements deriving from Gallo-Frankish or Franco-Roman acclamations, so that it is justifiable to style them "Franco-Byzantine" laudes.

The Laudes in the Venetian Colonies

Dalmatian usages cannot be dealt with adequately without taking into account the Republic of Venice, which had been colonizing the coastal regions ever since the year 1000. Unfortunately, we know next to nothing about the singing of laudes in the liturgy of Venice proper. It is true. a few notes, not very specific, suggest that the doge on some occasions, for example at his investiture, would be greeted with acclamations.[25] But no text of laudes seems to have been preserved from San Marco. This is not surprising because the laudes belonged to the episcopal mass and the *ecclesia ducalis S. Marci* was not ruled by a bishop but by a dogal chaplain, the *Primicerius*. The cathedral church of Venice was San Pietro di Castello, on the little island of San Pietro to the east of the Arsenal. But

---

[24] Cf. Zaninovič, *loc. cit.* See below, p. 204, n. 52.

[25] The ceremonial observed at the investiture of the doge does not seem to have been studied in recent years; see, however, Flaminius Cornelius, *Ecclesiae Venetae Antiqua Monumenta* (Venice, 1749), X, 90, who mentions that, in 1071, the people of Venice welcomed the new doge and "unanimiter acclamavit et ipsum cum hymnis et laudibus in S. Marci ecclesiam nondum completam duxit, qui investitionem cum vexillo suscepit." The source is not mentioned, but the author may refer to the later constitutions; cf. *ibid.*, X, 237: "Ipse vero dux dare debet capellanis pro suo introitu libras denariorum venetorum viginti quinque ad grossos, et si capellani iverint ad Ducissam, priusquam veniat in palatium et laudes ei cantaverint, tunc Ducissa pro renumeratione libras denariorum xxv eis persolvere debet." The mention of the doge's name in the Canon of the Mass was introduced, at a comparatively late date, by the Synod of Grado, in 1296; cf. Mansi, *op. cit.*, XXIV, 1166, § 5: "Quia in toto patriarchatu nostro Regem vel Principem non habemus. . . . nisi inclytum Ducem nostrum Venetiarum, statuimus ut in loco Canonis misse in secreta, ubi dicitur *Una cum papa nostro et Episcopo nostro* . . . immediate iungantur *et Duce nostro*, expresso nomine, et *pro bono statu Venetiarum* . . . que ibidem sequuntur."

this see was eclipsed by that of the patriarchs of Grado who practically transferred their residence from the island of Grado to Venice in the twelfth century. Yet no formulary of Grado seems to have come to light. But since the chanting of laudes is attested in the patriarchate of Aquileia, the duplicate of Grado (the formulary preserved falls in the years 1145–1153),[26] and since we know that the people of Zara were compelled, after 1204, to offer acclamations to the patriarch of Grado also, we may assume that Grado was familiar with this practice.

However, the Signoria always brought into prominence the legal and constitutional importance of the laudes within her colonial empire. It was ever one of the fundamentals of Venetian domination to insist upon the recognition of Venice's sovereignty by imposing the laudes on the conquered people, almost on the very day she established her rule in a colony. This practice is proved clearly by a document of September, 1211, when the Venetians brought Crete under their sway. Immediately after the occupation of the island, the Doge Pietro Ziani stipulated that the laudes be sung to him and his successors in all the Cretan cathedrals four times a year: namely, at Christmas and Easter, on the day of St. Titus—apostle to the Cretans and their patron—and on that of St. Mark. The celebration of St. Mark's day is most remarkable, for at that time there was no church in Crete dedicated to the patron of the Signoria.[27] The demands of the doge, which were obeyed in October of the same year,[28] were repeated by the Signoria in 1222.[29] All this agrees perfectly with the practice observed at Ossero, in 1000, and at Zara, in 1204; and incidentally it was a Venetian, Enrico Dandolo, who immediately after the conquest of Constantinople ordered the singing of laudes in honor of Pope Innocent III.

It was thus clearly an essential part of the Venetian technique of colonization and belonged to the whole system of Venice's domination to make St. Mark's sovereignty promptly evident also in the liturgy of the subject people. Just as the colonizing cities of ancient Greece had transplanted the cults of their gods to the new foundations, so Venice did in imposing the cult of St. Mark, the mother city's tutelary "deity," upon her daughters. Hence we find in Crete the acclaim:[30]

> Illustrissimo et serenissimo Domino nostro, Domino N.,
> Dei gratia Duci Venetiarum, salus, honor, vita, triumphus.
> S. Marce   tu nos adiuva.

This political practice prevailed throughout the Later Middle Ages. The

---

[26] B. M. de Rubeis, *Monumenta Ecclesiae Aquilejensis* (1740), 588 f.
[27] Mercati, *op. cit.*, p. 12; Flaminius Cornelius, *Creta Sacra* (Venice, 1755), II, 3, 229.
[28] Cornelius, *op. cit.*, II, 235.
[29] *Ibid.*, II, 258.
[30] Cf. above, n. 27.

Signoria was anxious to keep this token of her domination from falling into oblivion or from suffering any encroachment. A decree of the Senate expressly ordered that in Dalmatia the singers of the laudes be paid with public funds so that this ancient custom should not cease to be observed.[31] Therefore, countless Venetian colonial formularies of laudes have survived from the Later Middle Ages as well as from modern times. We have formularies from Traù, Zara, Spalato of the fifteenth and sixteenth centuries,[32] and others of the same period from Crete;[33] forms of later centuries are preserved from Lesbos, Chios, and Athens;[34] and since the observance outlasted the days of Venice's glory, there are modern formularies of the Hapsburg period transmitted. (Cf. below, p. 182.)

Not all these laudes follow the same pattern. In Dalmatia, where Venice was the successor of the crown of Hungary, we find the following form:

Exaudi Christe!

Christus vincit, Christus regnat, Christus imperat.

Sanctissimo et beatissimo patri et domino nostro clementissimo domino NN. divina providentia sacrosanctae Romanae et universalis Ecclesiae summo pontifici laus, honor et decus et celestis triumphus.

Christus vincit, Christus regnat, Christus imperat.

Serenissimo ac excellentissimo principi et domino nostro gratiosissimo Domino, Domino NN., Dei gratia inclyto duci Venetorum laus, honor, gloria et perpetuus triumphus.

Christus vincit, Christus regnat, Christus imperat.

Illustrissimo et reverendissimo Domino, Domino NN., Dei et apostolica gratia episcopo Traguriensi laus, honor, vita et gaudium sempiternum. . . .

Christus vincit, Christus regnat, Christus imperat.

Exaudi Christe.   Exaudi Christe.[35]

This form agrees with the early laudes of Zara under Hungarian domination; only the titles of the *acclamati* have grown baroque and the phrase *Cunctis inclytis vita* is replaced by the *Christus vincit* which is repeated after each hail.

---

[31] Lucius, *De regno Dalmatiae*, 73; ". . . ex Veneti senatu decreto pro antiqui moris continuatione solvit aerarium publicum capituli Tragurii quotannis libras xv. . . ."

[32] Lucius, *op. cit.*, p. 73. The laudes are not dated, but the titles of the authorities acclaimed suggest fifteenth or even sixteenth century; the forms tally almost verbatim with the laudes mentioned by Gerola, "Una descrizione di Candia del principio del seicento," *Atti dell'accademia degli Agiati in Rovereto*, Ser. III, Vol. XIV (Rovereto, 1908), 270 f., 278–281; cf. Mercati, *op. cit.*, pp. 13 f. In the description of Crete published by Gerola the military and political character of the laudes ceremonial is shown very clearly.

[33] Mercati, *op. cit.*, pp. 20 f., cf. 12 ff.

[34] *Ibid.*, pp. 15 f.; see also H. J. W. Tillyard, "The Acclamations of Emperors in Byzantine Ritual," *The Annual of the British School at Athens*, XVIII (1911–1912).

[35] In this formulary, which is published by Lucius, *loc. cit.*, there follow intentions for the count or captain of the city, the chamberlain and the heads of the corporations, for the canons and the clergy, the judges, counsellors, and the nobility, and for the citizens and people of Traù, Zara, and Spalato, respectively.

On the other hand, the laudes which Venice introduced in the archipelago, that is, in cathedrals which had not been previously under Hungarian domination, display a close relationship with the Western and Frankish types. They open with the *Christus vincit,* followed by the acclamation, and contain invocations of saints with the response *tu nos adiuva.*[36] Their general composition is not so exuberant as that of the Gallo-Frankish formularies; yet these Venetian colonial laudes derive clearly from the Frankish pattern, and, therefore, it may be assumed that it was via Venice that Frankish elements also pervaded the laudes to the Hungarian kings when they ruled in Dalmatia.

---

[36] Cornelius, *op. cit.,* II, 31 ff.; Mercati, *op. cit.,* pp. 12 f.

CHAPTER VI

THE LAUDES IN THE NORMAN REALMS

SICILY

THE CHURCH IN SOUTHERN ITALY, though organized and built up under the auspices of Rome as the Norman conquest proceeded, abounds in liturgical peculiarities. Until the sixteenth century, the archbishop of Benevento wore a tiara as his headgear;[1] Cosenza and other cathedrals celebrated the blessing of the waters according to Byzantine style on the eve of Epiphany;[2] the *Exultet* was written on scrolls and decorated with images;[3] the *Praeconium Paschale* displayed the most varied forms;[4] elements of the Ambrosian rite survived in the local liturgy of Benevento and other Lombard principalities;[5] petty princes were anointed and kings wore the mitre. In this symphony elements of the "Gallican" rite or of the French ritual style could not be lacking.

Indeed, the connection of Southern Italy with France, especially with Normandy, and further with Norman England was never broken. Ever since the Norman conquest, there existed a continual coming and going between Norman South and Norman North.[6] French remained the language of the Sicilian court until the end of the Norman dynasty.[7] As early as the eleventh century, chroniclers styled William the Conqueror master not only of England but also of Apulia and Sicily; and Rouen, whose coins were current in Southern Italy as late as the twelfth century, could bask in the splendor of two regal scions, the duke-king of Normandy and the king of Sicily.[8] A number of bishoprics and many more prebends of the South were occupied by Normans from England and

---

[1] Eugène Müntz, "La tiare pontificale du VIIIᵉ au XVIᵉ siècle," *Mémoires de l'académie des inscriptions et belles-lettres*, XXXVI:1 (1897), 238; cf. H. W. Klewitz, "Die Krönung des Papstes," *ZfRG.*, kan. Abt. XXX (1941), 110, n. 47.

[2] Adolph Franz, *Die kirchlichen Benediktionen im Mittelalter*, I (1909), 194.

[3] Myrtilla Avery, *The Exultet Rolls of South Italy* (1936), offers perfect reproductions; cf. Ladner, in *Speculum*, XVII (1942), 181 ff.

[4] Kantorowicz, in *Harvard Theological Review*, XXXIV (1941), 129 ff.

[5] Dom René-Jean Hesbert, "Les dimanches de carême dans les manuscrits Romano-Bénéventains," *Eph. Lit.*, XLVIII (1934), 198 ff.

[6] The intensity of these interchanges has been brought to light, above all, by C. H. Haskins; see his *Norman Institutions* (Cambridge, 1918), *passim; Studies in Mediaeval Science* (Cambridge, 1924), 185 ff., and the study "England and Sicily in the Twelfth Century," *English Historical Review*, XXVI (1911), 433 ff. See also Lynn Townsend White, *Latin Monasticism in Norman Sicily* (Cambridge, 1938), and Evelyn Jamison, "The Sicilian Norman Kingdom in the Mind of Anglo-Norman Contemporaries," *Proceedings of the British Academy* (1938), 237–285.

[7] Guill. Apul., *Gesta Roberti Wiscardi*, I, 167 f., *MGH. SS.*, IX, 244.

[8] Alexander of Telese, *Gesta Rogerii*, III, c. 8, IV, c. 1, in Del Re, *Cronisti e scrittori sincroni della dominazione normanna nel regno di Puglia e Sicilia* (Naples, 1845), I, 133, 146. See the poem on Rouen by an unknown author, published by Ch. Richard, "Notice sur l'ancienne bibliothèque des échevins de la ville de Ro_en," *Précis analytique des travaux de l'academie royale ... de Rouen* (1845), 163, of which Haskins, *Nor-*

Normandy. Even the see of Palermo was held, at times, by Anglo-Normans and so were those of Messina and Girgenti. We do not know enough about the lower clergy, but Northerners can be found among the canons of Palermo's cathedral,[9] and the powerful influence of Anglo-Norman monasticism penetrated the southern kingdom in successive waves.[10]

The liturgy of the Church of Southern Italy, therefore, could not avoid being strongly affected by these currents. We learn that the monks of Saint-Evroul, who came to settle in the South, strictly observed the customs of Normandy and continued to sing the chants which they were wont to sing at home in the mother convent.[11] Among the countless Sicilian manuscripts of the National Library in Madrid there is a Gradual closely related to one of Rouen which, however, displays some significant variants demonstrating the way in which the liturgy of Normandy was adapted to Southern usage.[12] A Troper in Madrid, in spite of its Rouenese features, comes from the Sicily of King Roger II.[13] There may be added also the so-called *Missale Gallicum* of Palermo which falls in the twelfth century and indicates how strongly the Gallo-French rite had worked upon the liturgy of the Church of Southern Italy.[14] These strong ties between South and North are again noticeable in a formulary of laudes in a late manuscript preserved in the Cathedral Archives of Palermo.[15]

---

man Institutions, p. 144, n. 72, has printed the first part referring to the Norman duke-king; the second section refers to Sicily:

"Ex te progenitus, Normanno sanguine clarus,
Regnat Rogerus victor, sapiens opulentus.
Te Rogere potens, tu maxima gloria regum;
Subditur Ytalia et Siculus, tibi subditur Afer;
Grecia te timet et Syria et te Persa veretur;
Ethiopes albi[!] Germania nigra [!] requirunt
Te dominante sibi, te protectore tueri.
Vera fides et larga manus tibi septa dedere;
Te dignum imperio solum diiudicat orbis."

[9] Haskins, *Studies in Mediaeval Science*, p. 187, and in *Eng. Hist. Rev.*, XXVI (1911), 436 f.

[10] White, *op. cit.*, pp. 47 ff.

[11] Ordericus Vitalis, *Ecclesiastica historia*, ed. A. Le Prevost (Paris, 1838–1855), II, 89 ff. One of the monks, Robert Gamaliel, who joined Robert Guiscard, in 1060, together with Abbot Robert of Grantmesnil, was a famous cantor; cf. Handschin and David, in *RCGr.*, XL (1936), 17.

[12] L. Delisle, "Un livre de choeur normano-sicilien conservé en Espagne," *Journal des Savants* (1908), 42–49; cf. Kantorowicz, *op. cit.*; p. 131, n. 8. The manuscript is Madrid Bibl. Nac. Lat. 132.

[13] Madrid, Bibl Nac. Lat. MS 289 (153); cf. Karl Young,"Some texts of Liturgical Plays," *Publications of the Modern Language Association of America*, XXIV (1909), 325 ff.; Kantorowicz, *op. cit.*, p. 129.

[14] Palermo Cathedral MS 544; cf. Johannis de Johanne, *De divinis Siculorum officiis tractatus* (Palermo, 1736); La Mantia, "*Ordines iudiciorum Dei*" *nel missale Gallicano del XII secolo* (Palermo-Turin, 1892).

[15] Palermo Cathedral MS 601, fols. 107–110. The fifteenth-century manuscript (see Pls. XIII and XIV) has the title *Cantus diversi ad usum S. Panormitanae Eccle-*

Christus vincit, Christus regnat, Christus imperat.

R/ Exaudi Christe.

Domino nostro regi Friderico, magnifico
et triumphatori ac invictissimo, vita
perpetua!   Exaudi Christe.

Salvator mundi	tu illum adiuva
Redemptor mundi	tu illum adiuva
S. Trinitas	tu illum adiuva
S. Maria	tu illum adiuva
S. Michael	tu illum adiuva
S. Gabriel	tu illum adiuva
S. Raphael	tu illum adiuva
S. Johanne Baptista	tu illum adiuva

Regi nostro Friderico glorioso et trium-
phatori pax sempiterna!   Exaudi Christe.

S. Petre	tu illum adiuva
S. Paule	tu illum adiuva
S. Stephane	tu illum adiuva
S. Laurenti	tu illum adiuva

Pacifico rectori et piissimo gubernatori
regi nostro Friderico lux indeficiens et
pax eterna!   Exaudi Christe.

S. Sylvestre	tu illum adiuva
S. Maria Magdalena	tu illum adiuva
S. Christina	tu illum adiuva
S. Agatha	tu illum adiuva

Christus vincit, Christus regnat, Christus imperat.

R/ Exaudi Christe.

Ipsi soli honor et gloria, virtus et victoria per infinita secula
seculorum.   Amen.

This chant is composed unmistakably after the model of the Gallo-Frankish laudes. But the model has been followed rather vaguely; composition and structure—and it may be added the intonation, too—differ widely from all the forms which have so far been discussed. That the laudatory section is lacking and that the doxology falls short are minor deficiencies. More interesting is the fact that the *Exaudi Christe* follows after the acclamation instead of preceding it. This, as we shall see, is the style of Rouen (cf. below, p. 167), so that the whole problem of dependency and origin is brought to a close almost before being broached. The most striking feature, which is without precedent or parallel, is the

---

siae; it contains several liturgical pieces from Norman times. For a description of the manuscript I am indebted to the kindness of Monsignore Enrico Parricone, of Palermo, who provided me also with the photographs of the laudes. The formulary has been published repeatedly; cf. J. de Johanne, *op. cit.,* 116 f.; Giovanni Maria Amato, *De principe templo Panormitano* (Palermo, 1728), 425; Huillard-Bréholles, *Historia diplomatica Friderici Secundi,* I, 9, n. 1.

threefold acclamation to the king as *dominus*, as *rex*, and as *rector et gubernator*, and the absence of an acclamation to the pope, to any member of the hierarchy, or to any other person at all. We feel the spirit of Norman statesmanship. There is no haggling over a suppressed or granted a *Deo coronatus* or over other symbols of spiritual or secular supremacy. Here the state has engulfed the Church.

That the formulary is Norman should not be doubted. It is true, the name of the sovereign acclaimed, Frederick, is in itself not an evidence for the date. The Palermo manuscript is late (fifteenth century) so that the name might refer to one of the Aragonese kings of this name. Yet the absence of Spanish saints suggests that the form can hardly refer to one of the Spaniards.[16] Also, the saints' names make it likely that this copy is to be placed in a Norman setting, that is, in the twelfth century. In general, the sequence of saints agrees with that of the Litany of the Saints which by that time had become uniform in the West. The invocation of the Holy Trinity is unique because it is not preceded by the customary invocations of the individual members of the Trinity.[17] This, however, may have no meaning or may be due to local conditions. Indicative of the date are perhaps two female saints, Mary Magdalen and Christina. Mary Magdalen, whose veneration was very popular in France,

---

[16] I was not in a position to ascertain whether or not laudes were sung in Spain. Aragon and Navarra are not likely to have observed this rite at the coronations, cf. Schramm, "Die Krönung im katalanisch-aragonesischen Königreich," *Homenatge a Antoni Rubió i Lluch* (Barcelona, 1936), III, 577–598. In Castile the general conditions were more favorable because the kings claimed the imperial title and adopted the rite of imperial coronations; cf. in general Peter Rassow, "Die Urkunden Kaiser Alfons' VII. von Spanien," *ArchUF.*, X (1928), 327 ff.; A. Schunter, *Der weströmische Kaisergedanke ausserhalb des einstigen Karolingerreiches* (Munich, diss., 1926); Herman Hüffer, "Die Leonesischen Hegemoniebestrebungen und der Kaisertitel," *Spanische Forschungen der Görres-Gesellschaft*, Erste Reihe, III (1931), 337–384. A Coronation Order for the "Imperator Hispaniae" existed in the thirteenth-century Toledo, Cathedral MS 39–12, fols. 146–173ᵛ, according to Ludwig Fischer, "Sahagun und Toledo," *Spanische Forschungen*, Erste Reihe, III (1931), 301 ff. Unfortunately the Order has not been published and may be destroyed or lost by now. Hüffer, *op. cit.*, pp. 374 f., quotes the acclamation "Vivat Adefonsus imperator!" The Order, according to Fischer, followed that of the imperial coronation in Rome with some appropriate changes, e.g., "Confessio Beatae Mariae" instead of "Confessio S. Petri"; also the Spanish emperor-king becomes a knight of St. Mary and not one of St. Peter. However, since the laudes belonged to the Roman coronations, we might expect to find them in Castile, too.

For the *Christus vincit* on Spanish coins, cf. below, p. 228, n. 32. A theological work, the *Planeta*, written about 1218 for Diego de Campos, chancellor of Ferdinand III, begins with the words:

"In nomine Ihesu Christi incipit planeta. Liber primus Christus vincit, Christus regnat, Christus imperat."

The three clauses, written in huge letters and with inks of various colors, fill half a page of the Madrid, Bibl. Nac. Lat. MS 10108; cf. Z. G. Villada, *Paleografía Española* (Madrid, 1923), I, 286, and Pl. LI; cf. Peterson, *Untersuchungen*, p. 315.

[17] See, e.g., the Litany in Migne, *PL.*, CXXXVIII, col. 889. The English laudes of 1068 (Maskell, *Monum. Lit.*, II, 85) begin with the invocations of God the Father, the Son, and Holy Ghost; these may have been simply replaced in Sicily by that of the Trinity. Cf. Haseloff, *Eine thüringisch-sächsische Malerschule*, Pl. XXXI, 67.

had no early connections with Sicily. But she became important to the Norman royal family in the late twelfth century, for King William II, in 1184, began to construct in the cathedral of Palermo a chapel dedicated to her and destined to be the last resting place of the Norman queens and princes.[18] St. Christina became a Sicilian saint after 1160, for in this year her bones were translated from Tyre to Palermo. King William I dedicated a chapel to her which William II completed in 1185, some ten years after the archbishop of Palermo, Walter Offamil, had founded a little church in her honor.[19] At any rate, the saint names suggest the twelfth century as the date of the formulary, and this consideration, together with the Rouenese style of the text, may justify the attribution of the Palermo laudes to Frederick II, the Hohenstaufen emperor.[20] They fall in his early period when he was merely king of Sicily and not yet king, or emperor, of the Romans. But whether they really represent the laudes which were sung at his coronation, as is generally assumed, is a different matter.[21]

Our knowledge of Sicilian politico-liturgical customs is fragmentary. Apart from the Palermo formulary, no other texts of laudes have yet come to light. The surmise of a South Italian scholar that the chant was spread beyond Palermo cannot be proved[22] unless he had in mind acclamations or laudes to bishops, which of course were well known and politically important;[23] we learn that even the abbot of Monte Cassino was rendered

---

[18] Antonio Mongitore, *Bullae, privilegia et instrumenta Panormitanae ecclesiae* (Palermo, 1734), 53, publishes a document, issued by Archbishop Walter Offamil in March, 1187, wherein the archbishop mentions "capella regia S. Marie Magdalene . . . in qua pretiosa corpora illustrissimorum ducum et reginarum recolende memorie quiescebant"; cf. Amato, *op. cit.*, pp. 50 ff. The cult of the saint was introduced also in Rome at a comparatively late date; cf. P. Ketter, *Die Magdalenenfrage* (Trier, 1929), 45.

[19] The date of the translation is not quite certain, cf. Luigi Boglino, *Palermo e Santa Cristina* (Palermo, 1881), 64; however, it took place under William I (1154–1166) and Archbishop Hugh of Palermo (1144–1166). For Christina in the laudes, cf. Boglino, *op. cit.*, p. 74; and *ibid.*, pp. 86 ff., 97 ff., for the construction of the two shrines; see also Amato, *op. cit.*, pp. 257 f.; Octavus Cajetanus, *Vitae Sanctorum Siculorum* (Palermo, 1657), II, 145 ff., and n. 58. See also Eiríkr Magnusson, "A Fragment of the Old Danish Version of St. Christina," *Transactions of the Cambridge Philological Society*, V (1902), part 3. In the sixteenth century St. Christina was relied on for the healing of lues, cf. Johannes Laurentius Anania, *De natura daemonum* (Venice, 1589), 152.

[20] Only De Johanne, *op. cit.*, pp. 116 ff., seems to attribute the laudes to the Aragonese. See, however, Huillard-Bréholles, *loc. cit.*; E. Winkelmann, *Jahrbücher Philipps von Schwaben und Ottos IV. von Braunschweig* (Leipzig, 1873), I, 119 f. A later marginal note in the manuscript simply indicates: "per il Re Friderico."

[21] Unfortunately the political liturgy of South Italy in Norman times has hardly been studied. Investigations on the subject have to proceed from local liturgical manuscripts, not to mention those preserved in Madrid. I consulted the liturgical manuscripts in Naples and of some cathedrals near Naples—all that could be done during a short visit in the south. The following notes, therefore, do not pretend to offer more than a tentative approach to the problem.

[22] De Johanne, *op. cit.*, pp. 116 f.

[23] For Sicilian episcopal laudes, cf. *MGH. Const.*, II, 544, No. 413, and above, chap. IV, n. 27, p. 120.

laudes at his accession.[24] Concerning the Norman rulers, however, our sources are silent, and only a few scattered notes disclose the curious ecclesiastical position which the Norman princes obtained from early times.

Amatus of Monte Cassino relates in his *History of the Normans* that Richard of Aversa, after he had conquered Capua and was elevated to a princely rank, visited the Abbey in 1058. He was received by the monks in solemn procession, *comme roy*. The church was decorated as on Easter, the lamps were lit, and the cloisters resounded with chants and laudes in honor of the prince.[25] The description shows that Richard was granted the liturgical reception which belonged by right only to princes who were anointed. This regulation, it is true, is of a later date.[26] But even if it had existed in the eleventh century, we may wonder whether the prince of Capua had not been fully entitled to claim, in his own right, the liturgical reception with the canopy carried over him, with incense smoking, lamps burning, and laudes chanted, such as he was offered at Monte Cassino. For the Norman princes in Southern Italy enjoyed the privilege of anointment otherwise restricted to kings, and indeed to few kings only.[27]

There can be no doubt that the princes of Capua and Salerno were anointed, and perhaps those of Benevento, too.[28] It is reported of Richard

[24] Leo Ostiensis, *MGH. SS.*, VII, 704 (but see below, n. 29); abbatial acclamations are not rare; see, e.g., the intention for Abbot Bovo of Corvey in the ninth-century laudes of Corvey; Lehmann, "Corveyer Studien," pp. 71 f. For modern laudes to the abbot of Maria Laach, cf. Urbanus Bomm, in *Liturgisches Leben*, I (1934), 337 ff.

[25] Amato di Montecassino, *Storia de' Normanni*, IV, c. 13, ed. Vincenzo de Bartholomeis, in *Fonti per la storia d'Italia* (1935), 191:

> "Il fu rechut e procession comme roy. Et fu aornée l'eglise coment lo jor de Paque; et furent aluméez les lampes; et lacort resone del cant et de la laude del Prince."

I am indebted to Dr. Carl Erdmann, in Berlin, for drawing my attention to this passage. See also Leo Ost., *MGH. SS.*, VII, 708: ". . . venit ad hoc monasterium, recipitur honorifice nimis cum processione solemni: erat enim admodum glorie appetens."

[26] Potthast, *Regesta Pontificum*, n. 6584; cf. above, p. 72, n. 27. The liturgical procession was granted, however, also to the duke of Aquitaine; see the *Ordo ad benedicendum ducem Aquitaniae*, in Bouquet, *RHF.*, XII, 453. Its date, according to Schramm, *English Coronation*, pp. 48 f., is about 1200. The *Pontificale Romanum* contains (probably since Durandus) an *Ordo ad recipiendum processionaliter principem magnae potentiae*.

[27] By then, only the German emperors and kings, the kings of France, England, and Jerusalem (after 1100) enjoyed the privilege of anointments. Aragon received the unction in 1204, Navarra in 1257, Scotland in 1329; Castile may have received this privilege immediately before the thirteenth century; cf. Marc Bloch, *Les rois thaumaturges*, pp. 194 f., 460 f., where an interesting passage is cited from the Hostiensis (*Summa aurea*, I, c. 15): "si quis de novo ungi velit, consuetudo obtinuit, quod a papa petatur sicut fecit rex Aragonum et quotidie instat rex Scotie." Portugal never achieved the unction; cf. Schramm, "Die Krönung in Deutschland," p. 184, and his paper mentioned above (n. 17), pp. 3 f., 7 f., for the unctions in Aragon and Navarra, and below, p. 181, n. 5, for Bohemia.

[28] This fact, which hitherto had escaped notice, has been brought to light by Paul Kehr in his latest studies, cf. *Regesta Pontificum Romanorum. Italia pontificia*, VIII: *Campania et Apulia* (Berlin, 1936), 36, No. 135, and "Die Belehnungen der süditalienischen Normannenfürsten durch die Päpste," *Abh. Preuss. Akad.*, Berlin, 1934, Abh. 1, pp. 37 ff.; see also his note in *QF.*, XXV (1933–1934), 311 ff.

of Capua that, in 1058, he was received by the people of Capua and was "consecrated" their prince.[29] He was followed by another Richard, whose "consecration" in 1098 is reported.[30] Then, in 1120, the chronicler Falco of Benevento relates that the Capuans made Richard III, son of Robert of Capua, their prince who was "consecrated" in the presence of many South Italian bishops by the archbishop of Capua on Ascension Day of that year.[31] Finally, and according to the same source, Robert II was inaugurated in a particularly solemn way, in January, 1128, in the presence of Pope Honorius II and the South Italian high clergy who filled the cathedral of Capua to assist at Robert's "anointment." The anointment was performed by the archbishop of Capua "in agreement with the privileges enjoyed by his predecessors in the Capuan See."[32] That is to say that the right to consecrate and anoint the ruler, which in many countries had given rise to disputes, belonged to the Capuan hierarch in accordance with traditions which were obviously much older than the Norman domination.

This at least may be gathered from the conditions in Salerno. In that old Lombard principality it was not the metropolitan who acted as *coronator* of the princes, but the bishop of Capaccio. We learn that Bishop Alfanus of Capaccio anointed, in 1127, Roger II as prince of Salerno and that he carried this action through in the presence of his metropolitan, the archbishop of Salerno.[33] This prerogative of a bishop must go back to the tenth century when Capaccio (ancient Paestum) was the capital of the Lombard principality of Salerno and still harbored the body of St. Matthew before this relic was transferred to Salerno. The evangelist became, of course, the patron saint of the Norman princes of Salerno; his image was displayed on their coins which, on the obverse, showed the princes in thoroughly "royal" attire with scepter and orb in their hands

---

[29] Leo Ost., *MGH. SS.* VII, 707: "recipiunt hominem, sacrant in principem." The value of this source has been greatly reduced by the researches and discoveries of H. W. Klewitz, "Petrus Diaconus und die Montecassineser Klosterchronik des Leo von Ostia," *ArchUF.*, XIV (1936), 414–453. In our case, however, it makes almost no difference whether Leo or Peter is the author of the respective passages, the less so since the essence of his notes is supported by other authors, at least so far as the consecrations of princes are concerned.

[30] Petrus Diaconus, *MGH. SS.*, VII, 764: "Capuani (Riccardum) sibi in principem consecrarent."

[31] Falco of Benevento, in Del Re, *Cronisti*, I, 180: "et eo constituto Capuanus archiepiscopus convocatis episcopis aliisque viris prudentibus . . . die ascensionis Domini . . . principem illum consecravit."

[32] *Ibid.*, pp. 195 f.: "Pontifex Honorius archiepiscopos et abbates accersiri precepit, quatenus ad principis unctionem convenirent, qui euntes die statuto exultatione ingenti ad Capuanam ecclesiam convenere. Archiepiscopus itaque Capuanus iuxta predecessorum suorum privilegium presente tanto ac tali pontifice Honorio . . . predictum Robertum in principatus honorem inunxit et confirmavit."

[33] Romuald of Salerno, *MGH. SS.*, XIX, 418: "Qui in eadem civitate ab Alfano Caputaquensi episcopo est unctus in principem. Dehinc Regium veniens ibidem in ducem Apuliae est promotus." On the right of Capaccio-Paestum of supplying the *coronator*, see the arguments of Paul Kehr, in *QF.*, XXV, 312.

and a crown with pendants on their heads.³⁴ However, the right of anointing had apparently not been passed on to Salerno, but remained a privilege of Capaccio which this see may have enjoyed in Lombard times.

We do not know³⁵ whether the dukes of Apulia were anointed, nor is there any certainty about a consecration of the princes of Benevento. According to an obscure account, Arichis, the first prince of Benevento, had been anointed and crowned after Charlemagne had conquered the Lombard kingdom in the north.³⁶ But there is no indication that this became a Beneventan tradition, although in other duchies the anointment of Norman princes seems to have taken place in continuation of a Lombard tradition.

What had been the custom of Norman petty princes could not be withheld from the Norman kings. The privilege of being anointed was expressly granted to Roger II by the Holy See.³⁷ This, however, does not define the unusual position of the Norman kings within the Church. From the times of Count Roger I, the grand counts and kings of Apulia and Sicily possessed the powers of papal legates. Probably as a consequence of the legatine office we find that the attire of the Norman kings was closely related to that of a bishop, apparently even more so than that of other Western rulers. The king wore the mitre, the dalmatic, and the sandals as well as other insignia of the episcopal office.³⁸ It is necessary to realize these peculiarities, which amazed Anglo-Norman visitors to

³⁴ Arthur Engel, *Recherches sur la numismatique ... des Normands* (1882), Pl. VI, 1–7, 10; Pl. II, 1, 2, 4, 6. The somewhat odd cap with pendants (Pl. VI, 5–6) obviously represents a simplified crown, cf. Pl. VI, 4.

³⁵ See, however, above, n. 33: "in ducem Apuliae est promotus." Reggio, Calabria seems to have been the place of the consecration. Whether this implied an anointment is doubtful.

³⁶ Erchempert, *MGH. SS.*, III, 243; Leo Ost., *MGH. SS.*, VII, 586: "Ab episcopis (Arichis) ungi se fecit et coronam sibi imposuit." The report is unreliable in itself but may reflect conditions of the Lombard period.

³⁷ Falco of Benevento, in Del Re, *Cronisti*, 1, 201 f. For the other sources of Roger's coronation, see Erich Caspar, *Roger II. und die Gründung der normannisch-sicilischen Monarchie* (1904), 508, Reg. n. 69a, and for the bull of Pope Anacletus II (September 27, 1130), *ibid.*, pp. 506 f., Reg. n. 65.

³⁸ E. Caspar, "Die Legatengewalt der normannisch-sizilischen Herrscher im 12. Jahrhundert," *QF.*, VII (1904), 189–219. The papal privilege concerning the legatine power of the Norman count is dated July 5, 1098; but Roger I had styled himself legate months before; cf. Klewitz, "Studien über die Wiederherstellung der römischen Kirche in Süditalien durch das Reformpapsttum," *QF.*, XXV (1933–1934), 138 f. The papal concession to Roger II of wearing episcopal insignia—ring and staff, dalmatic, mitre and sandals—is transmitted in an indirect way only; see the letter of the Romans to Conrad III, Ph. Jaffé, *Bibliotheca rerum Germanicarum*, I (1864), 334, and Caspar, *Roger II*, p. 402, n. 3, as well as the remarks of White, *op. cit.*, p. 127, n. 4, concerning some iconographical errors. For the iconography, see Sigfrid H. Steinberg, "I ritratti dei re normanni di Sicilia," *La Bibliofilia*, XXXIX (1937), 29–57. A survey of the episcopal raiments of the Sicilian king is offered by Eichmann, "Kaisergewandung," *HJb.*, LVIII (1938), 294 f.; but his interpretation of *virga et baculus* as two names for the same thing, namely, for the crozier, is hardly correct, for neither expression signifies, not at least in this connection, the staff of the bishop. The meaning of *virga* is the "rod," and of *baculus* either the short staff (scepter) or the

Sicily,[39] in order to appreciate the strange laudes of Palermo which do not contain intentions for either the pope or the clergy but show the unique scheme of hailing the king alone. Apparently the Normans tried to stress the ruler's absolute and independent mastery of the Sicilian Church such as it resulted from the legatine power. The laudes indeed suggest that the king, within his realm, considered himself almost his own pope, or that he was anxious to avoid any possible encroachments on his privileges which an acclamation of the Roman pontiff might entail. Hence, the Norman ruler really appears as the *pacificus rector* of the Sicilian State Church and as the kingdom's *sanctissimus dominus*, a title after the Byzantine pattern which had already been applied to the grand counts.[40] At any rate, it may be held that it is the idea of royal absolutism in its then harshest form which we find reflected in the laudes of Palermo.

Nothing certain is known about the time when the laudes were brought into use in Sicily. It is likely, however, that not only the kings but also the Norman princes were offered the laudes at their consecration. The *Christus vincit, Christus regnat, Christus imperat* as a legend on princely coins[41] and also the influence of Rouen, where the duke of Normandy received a special acclamation in the laudes (cf. below, p. 167), seems to support this surmise. On the other hand, the custom of singing festival laudes on the feast days of the Church must be taken into account. Here again we have to confess our lack of knowledge. However, King Roger II, in a charter of 1148, granted to the abbot of San Giovanni degli Eremiti in Palermo the privilege to act, on all solemn occasions, as the king's *precipuus cappellanus*, to celebrate Mass in the royal chapel on feast days and to take precedence of all other prelates of the kingdom.[42] These arrangements suggest that the custom of royal crown-wearings on feast

---

long thin staff of kings; cf. Schramm, "Frankreich," *ZfRG.*, kan. Abt. XXVI (1937), 209 f. The mitre was a headgear of the German emperor long before the time of Roger II; Nicholas II had granted it, in 1059, to Duke Spitignew of Bohemia.

A later prerogative of the Sicilian king was his active participation in the divine service if the pope was present. In this case the king had to read the Epistle; should the emperor be present, too, the latter was to read the Gospel; cf. *Ordo Romanus XIV*, c. 47, Migne, *PL.*, LXXVIII, col. 1182, which is a later insertion borrowed from the *Caeremoniale* of the cardinal-archbishop of Rouen. The ceremonial became complicated if at this papal service the king of France should join the emperor and the king of Sicily, for then France would read the first and Sicily the second part of the Epistle; cf. Martène, *De antiquis ecclesiae ritibus*, II, c. ix (1736), II, 593; Schramm, *ibid.*, p. 246, n. 2; Biehl, *op. cit.*, p. 101. Another privilege, granted to Charles II of Anjou, was the anointment "sicut inunguntur reges Francie"; cf. L. H. Labande, "Le cérémonial Romain de Jacques Cajétain," *BÉCh.*, LIV (1893), 72.

[39] Cf. E. Jamison (above, n. 6), p. 268, for the interest taken by Englishmen in the legatine power of Roger II and on the exaggerations of Radulphus Niger, *MGH. SS.*, XXVII, 335; cf. Caspar, *Roger II*, p. 402, n. 3.

[40] Klewitz, in *QF.*, XXV, 145 (cf. above, n. 38).

[41] Cf. above, p. 10 (Chap. I, notes 31–33).

[42] Caspar, *Roger II*, p. 570, reg. 216; White, *op. cit.*, pp. 127 f.

days was introduced also into the Norman kingdom, which makes it likely that the laudes were voiced on these occasions.

The formulary of Palermo has generally been regarded as the coronation laudes of Frederick II. However, since his coronation took place on Whitsunday (May 17, 1198), we cannot tell whether the laudes referred to the crowning or to the feast day of the Church. Frederick's father, Henry VI, was likewise crowned on a feast day (Christmas, 1194),[43] and so were Roger II (Christmas, 1130) and William I (Easter, 1154). Only King William II was crowned on an ordinary weekday (May 17, 1166), and this is true also for his second coronation which took place together with the first coronation of his English-born queen (February 13, 1177). By chance, the only Siculo-Norman Coronation Order to be preserved and identified seems to refer to William II's second coronation, and in this Order we actually find the rubric "post epistolam cantetur laus regis."[44] Hence, the singing of laudes belonged indeed to the Sicilian coronation rite. This will become all the more obvious when we consider the Anglo-Norman customs.

NORMANDY

As in many other provinces of France, the laudes were commonly chanted in Normandy. In addition to several formularies of the Later Middle Ages and of modern times,[45] there have survived two older texts from the Church of Rouen, one of the eleventh century,[46] the other of the twelfth.[47] Furthermore, a Gradual of the end of the twelfth century or the early thirteenth, though it contains no text of this litany, yet indicates in a rubric that the laudes were chanted on feast days.[48] The text of the eleventh-century form follows.

---

[43] Otto of St. Blasien, c. 40, *MGH. SS. rer. Germ.*, ed. Hofmeister (1912), 63, "cunctis laudes affatim acclamantibus," refers to Henry's reception, not to the coronation ceremonial.

[44] The Order has been published from a Beneventan manuscript of the twelfth century by Schwalm, in *NArch.*, XXIII (1898), 17 ff.; the editor, however, mistook "laus regis" for the *Incipit* of a hymn or a prayer. The Order can hardly refer to any other South Italian coronation than that of William II and Joan of England; cf. Schramm, *English Coronation*, p. 60, n. 2, who also points out some remarkable similarities between the South Italian Order and the rite observed at the second coronation of Richard I.

[45] Rouen, Bibl. Mun. MS 256 (A 284), fols. 134ᵛ–136, a sixteenth-century Antiphonary from Rouen, of which a facsimile is found in *Le graduel de l'église cathédrale de Rouen au XIIIᵉ siècle*, publiée par V. H. Loriquet, Dom Pothier et Abbé Colette (Rouen, 1907), I, Pls. iv-vii. For the eighteenth-century laudes from Rouen, cf. Le Brun Desmorettes, *Voyages liturgiques*, pp. 323 ff. See also below, Chap. VII, p. 183, and Bukofzer, below, pp. 199 ff., on the various laudes of Rouen.

[46] Rouen MS 489 (A 254), fol. 71, on an additional leaf among the works of Boethius; a facsimile and transcription is found in *Graduel de Rouen*, I, 69, and Pl. i. The saints hint at Fécamp.

[47] Rouen MS 537 (A 438), fol. 90; cf. *ibid.*, I, 69.

[48] Paris, Bibl. Nat. Lat. MS 904, fol. 108ᵛ: "Si archiepiscopus presens fuerit, cantetur ante epistolam *Christus vincit* ad vesperas." The complete manuscript has been published by Pothier, *Graduel de Rouen;* see, for the rubric, I, 69. The same rubric is found in the Bibl. Nat. Lat. MS 905, which seems to be a copy of MS 904.

Christus vincit, Christus regnat, Chris-
tus imperat.
Exaudi Christe.
Illo summo pontifici et universali pape
vita!
S. Petre
S. Paule
S. Johannes
Christus vincit, Christus regnat, Chris-
tus imperat.
Exaudi Christe.
Illo Francorum regi in Christi pace vita
et victoria!
S. Michael
S. Gabriel
S. Raffael
Christus vincit, Christus regnat, Chris-
tus imperat.
Exaudi Christe.
Guillelmo, Normannorum duci, salus et
pax continua!
S. Maurici
S. Sebastiane
S. Adriane
Christus vincit, Christus regnat, Chris-
tus imperat.
Exaudi Christe.
Omnibus pontificali honore sublimatis
salutaris vitae gloria!
S. Ambrosi
S. Martine
S. Benedicte
Christus vincit, Christus regnat, Christus
imperat.
Exaudi Christe
Omnibus christiane legis principibus
et judicibus salus eterna!
S. Georgi
S. Tiburci
S. Frodmunde
Christus vincit, Christus regnat, Chris-
tus imperat.
Exaudi Christe
Rex regum et dominus dominorum
Gloria et spes nostra
Misericordia et auxilium nostrum
Fortitudo et victoria nostra
Arma nostra invictissima
Lux, via et vita nostra

R/ Christus vincit, Christus regnat,
Christus imperat.
Exaudi Christe.

Exaudi Christe.
tu illum adiuva.
tu illum adiuva.
tu illum adiuva.
Christus vincit, Christus regnat,
Christus imperat.
Exaudi Christe.

Exaudi Christe.
tu illum adiuva.
tu illum adiuva.
tu illum adiuva.
Christus vincit, Christus regnat,
Christus imperat.
Exaudi Christe.

Exaudi Christe.
tu illum adiuva.
tu illum adiuva.
tu illum adiuva.
Christus vincit, Christus regnat,
Christus imperat.
Exaudi Christe.

Exaudi Christe.
tu illos adiuva.
tu illos adiuva.
tu illos adiuva.
Christus vincit, Christus regnat,
Christus imperat.
Exaudi Christe.

Exaudi Christe.
tu illos adiuva.
tu illos adiuva.
tu illos adiuva.
Christus vincit, Christus regnat,
Christus imperat.
Exaudi Christe.
Christus vincit.
Christus vincit.
Christus vincit.
Christus vincit.
Christus vincit.
Christus vincit.

Ipsi soli regnum et imperium per immortalia saecula saeculorum. Amen.	Christus vincit.
Ipsi soli laus et gloria per omnia saecula saeculorum. Amen.	Christus vincit.
Christe audi nos	Christe audi nos.
Kyrrieleyson	Kyrrieleyson
Christe eleyson	Christe eleyson
Kyrrieleyson	Kyrrieleyson.
Feliciter (ter)	Feliciter (ter)
Tempora bona maneant (ter)	Redempti sanguine Christi
Feliciter (ter)	Feliciter (ter)
Regnum Christi veniat (ter)	Deo gratias. Amen.

This is, on the whole, a Gallo-Frankish formulary; but it deviates from the model in several details. Most startling is the extravagant use made of the *Christus vincit.* Not only does it open the chant, but it opens also every single acclamation, and as a response it is found not only in the laudatory section but also in the doxology. The laudations, incidentally, fall short. They seem to be brought into line with the acclamatory section, as it were, an acclamation to Christ the "Rex regum et dominus dominorum" who receives six hails replacing the three saint invocations connected with the terrestrial powers. His acclamation ends in the doxology which likewise is adapted to the rhythm of the whole song. The composition is very artful and symmetrical, much more so than even the Gallo-Frankish forms, not to mention the Franco-Roman in which acclaims and laudations seem to break asunder.[49] If we take into account the slow but steady crescendo of the whole song, which ends in the cry "Regnum Christi veniat," we may maintain that of all laudes forms hitherto inspected that of Rouen is by far the most balanced and artful specimen.

These early Norman forms are of great interest also for political reasons because they contain a special acclamation for the duke of Normandy. In the form adduced, we find a hail for Duke William, and in that of the twelfth century there is an intention for "N., Normannorum duci invictissimo." Elsewhere an individual acclamation to a duke is unusual, if not unknown.[50] The one of Rouen, therefore, must be looked upon as a

---

[49] Cf. above, Chap. III, p. 110. The triadic composition of the song is noteworthy. There are always three saints invoked after each acclamation; including the acclamation of the laudatory section, the song has six sections; and the laudatory section contains six acclaims. Schramm, "Ordines-Studien III: Die Krönung in England," *ArchUF.*, XV (1938), § 10, p. 317 f., makes a similar observation with reference to the English Coronation Order of William I's times, published by John Wickham Legg, *Three Coronation Orders*, H. Bradshaw Society, XIX (London, 1900), 54 ff. See also above, Chap. II, p. 19, n. 15, and below, Appendix I, p. 194.

[50] Exactly what is the meaning of "N. ductori pacifico" in the Bamberg laudes to Henry II (Migne, *PL.*, CXL, col. 54; *AA. SS.*, July III, 699) is not evident. The acclaim to the city count in Dalmatia refers to an official and representative of the king. See Chap. V, n. 23.

token of the curious sovereignlike position which the duke of Normandy enjoyed in his duchy. This does not imply that the French king was expropriated. Hails to the pope and the king of France precede the acclamation to the duke which naturally was omitted in later centuries after Normandy had fallen to the crown of France. Still, the duke is not simply one among the many feudal princes who are acclaimed in the fifth section of our formulary. He represents a class of his own, remindful perhaps of the *proles regalis* which in other formularies is often found in this place.[51]

So much for the texts which permit us to trace the Norman laudes back to the eleventh century.[52] There is yet another, nonliturgical, evidence for the laudes. We find in the Chartulary of Rouen Cathedral a letter of William Giffard, bishop of Winchester and one time chaplain of William I and chancellor of William Rufus.[53] In this letter, written between 1101 and 1103, the bishop attests that under the two Williams no chancellor nor chaplain had been entitled to give orders to the choir of Rouen Cathedral or ever had ordered anything concerning the singing of the *Christus vincit*.[54] Exactly what the bishop alludes to is no longer obvious to us. Apparently there had arisen malpractices when chaotic conditions were rife in Normandy, and the chancellor or chaplain seems to have ordered the singing of laudes on his own responsibility or on behalf of the ruler, an action to which the chapter of Rouen objected. The whole issue is obscure, since laudes would be voiced by the clergy on those occasions and days when laudes were due. Apparently, however, either the duke himself or his officials had interfered by ordering the chant on other occasions. The question thus seems to have been whether it was the business of the court or of the archbishop to order the singing of laudes. A ray of light falls on the strife if we take English customs into consideration. In England, indeed, the king, and not the bishop, paid the *presbyterium* to the chanters of laudes, and Henry III ordered the singing of the solemn acclamations whenever he saw fit to do so. Perhaps we may

---

[51] Cf. Schramm, in *ArchUF.*, XV (1938), § 8, p. 316, and *idem, English Coronation*, p. 31. A parallel is found in the Franco-Roman laudes in the Munich Cod. Lat. 14510 (cf. above, p. 106), containing a special acclamation to Louis the German in addition to that to Louis the Pious. The laudes in the Montpellier MS 409 have acclamations for the young kings as *proles regalis*, whereas in the Munich manuscript King Louis the German is sovereign himself.

[52] The eleventh-century form referring to "Duke William" must not necessarily antedate the Conquest because the twelfth-century form, too, contains an acclamation for the "Duke" only, not for the English king.

[53] Rouen MS 1193, fol. 49; *Inventaire-Sommaire des archives départementales. Seine-Inférieure, Archives ecclésiastiques*, sér. G, III (Paris, 1881), 123, No. 3623:
   "Notum sit . . . quod . . . nullus cancellarius vel capellanus habuit potestatem in ecclesia Rothomagi aliquid in Choro disponendi vel cantandi *Xristus vincit* vel aliquid aliud faciendi."
Cf. L. Valin, *Le duc de Normandie et sa cour* (Paris, 1910), 258, No. III; J. H. Round, *Calendar of Documents preserved in France* (London, 1899), I, 1, No. 4; Haskins, *Norman Institutions*, p. 82, n. 59.

[54] *Christus vincit* is the customary name for the laudes, especially in England.

assume that also in Normandy the prince considered the ordering of laudes his business, a fact (if it is one) which would emphasize the legal or political import attributed to the laudes in Normandy—a kingly prerogative like the right to parade under a canopy or to use the *Dei gratia* formula which is found in ducal charters.[55]

An effort has been made to connect the laudes of the eleventh century with the Council of Lillebonne.[56] This may be right or wrong, but it is beside the point because the council opened on Whitsunday, in 1080, when laudes were due in any event. Another surmise is that they were chanted at the duke's inauguration, so to speak, as ducal coronation laudes.[57] Here a *non liquet* must be the answer. The acclamations are not mentioned either in the Order of the ducal consecration (a twelfth-century extract from an English Order),[58] or in the two detailed descriptions of the ceremonial observed at Rouen under Richard I and John.[59] Nonetheless it is not improbable that laudes were sung at the duke's consecration, not only because girding the duke with the sword of Normandy was considered an equivalent to the rite of crowning, or because Rouen considered itself ranking as high as Rome,[60] but because English

[55] The *Dei gratia* formula of the Norman dukes makes its appearance almost with the laudes. The dukes, prior to 1066, avoided the formula with great care and replaced it by *nutu Dei*; cf. Haskins, *Norman Institutions*, pp. 258, 261, and *passim*. Only after the conquest did the duke, even though he might not have been king of England— e.g. Robert Curthose—style himself "Dei gratia dux et princeps Normanorum"; Haskins, *op. cit.*, pp. 288 f., 73. The practice of the South Italian Normans was different, for they did not refrain from using the form "gratia Dei dux Apulie," etc; cf. H. W. Klewitz, in *QF.*, XXV (1933–1934), 143. Even South Italian barons would use the formula "Dei gratia Domini regis Baronus et Consanguineus," cf. White, *Latin Monasticism in Norman Sicily*, p. 267, No. XXVII. Accordingly, the Sicilian officials and captains of Frederick II used the *Dei gratia* formula very freely; cf Kantorowicz, *Ergänzungsband*, p. 198. The theory of the lawyers in Italy would have it that no secular prince was entitled to use the formula "nisi sit imperator vel rex vel alter [!] qui sui capitis recepit unctionem"; cf. Selden, *Titles of Honour* (London, 1672), 90 ff., who refers to Pietro dei Boattieri, *Rosula novella*, c. 111 (this seems to be the *Rosellula novella* of the Milan, Ambros. MS B. 132 Sup., representing an extract from the *Rosa novella*; cf. Fedor Schneider, in *QF.*, XVIII [1926], 196); see also Fritz Kern, *Gottesgnadentum und Widerstandsrecht* (Leipzig. 1914), 307, and the literature quoted by him.

[56] *Graduel de Rouen*, I, 67, quotes for evidence Loth, *La cathédrale de Rouen. Son histoire, sa description*, p. 557, which was not accessible to me. Cf. below, p. 176, n. 89. The combination is sheer guesswork.

[57] Valin, *op. cit.*, p. 44.

[58] H. A. Wilson, *The Benedictional of Archbishop Robert*, Bradshaw Society, XXIV (London, 1903), 157 f.; Marc Bloch, *op. cit.*, pp. 496 f., and 194, n. 1; Schramm, *English Coronation*, pp. 46 ff.; P. L. Ward, in *Speculum*, XIV (1939), 176, n. 4.

[59] These coronations are described by Benedict of Peterborough, *Gesta Henrici regis* (ed. Stubbs, Rolls Series, 49), II, 73; Radulph de Diceto (ed. Stubbs, Rolls Series, 68), II, 66 f.; Roger of Wendover (ed. Coxe, Rolls Series, 51), III, 138 f.; Matthew of Paris, *Chronica maiora* (ed. Luard, Rolls Series, 57), II, 454. Cf. Haskins, *op. cit.*, on the oaths delivered by the dukes.

[60] See Guillaume le Maréchal, ed. Paul Meyer (Paris, 1891), 344, line 9555: "a Roëm fu dus ceint d'espée"; Valin. *op. cit.*, p. 45. For the claims of Rouen to be Romelike, see the poem quoted above, p. 158, n. 8:
"Imperialis honorificentia te super ornat;
Tu Rome similis tam nomine quam probitate,
ROTHOMA, si mediam removes, et ROMA vocaris."

customs may have retroacted on Normandy. And in England, from the days of the Conquest until the fourteenth century, the laudes always were connected with the coronation rite, a fact which has not always been sufficiently emphasized.[61]

ENGLAND

Texts of English laudes are not too rare. At the present time four formularies are known. The oldest is a text found in a Pontifical of the eleventh century. It contains acclamations to Pope Alexander II, William the Conqueror, Queen Matilda, and Archbishop Ealdred of York, and it has been accredited to the coronation of Matilda, which was performed by Archbishop Ealdred at Winchester in 1068.[62] This attribution may be correct, although the episcopal acclamations appended to this form suggest a pattern of festival rather than of coronation laudes.[63] Another formulary is found in a twelfth-century Pontifical of Canterbury (or Ely?); it has its place within the Coronation Order of a king and queen so that it might refer to the sacring of Henry II and Eleanor of Poitou in 1154.[64] A third form is known from a thirteenth-century Antiphonary of

---

Like the pope, the archbishop of Rouen claims that he can be judged by no one; see the Anonymous of York, in *MGH.*, *Libelli de lite*, III, 656 ff., especially 658, lines 4 ff., and H. Böhmer, *Kirche und Staat in England und in der Normandie* (Leipzig, 1899), 179, No. IV, 186, and 437 ff., No. II.

[61] Schramm, *English Coronation*, p. 31, still says that all traces of laudes disappeared in England in the course of the twelfth century, but corrects himself in *ArchUF.*, XV (1938), 324 f.

[62] Brit. Mus. Cotton. MS Vitellius E. XII, fols. 159ᵛ–160; the form has been published by Maskell, *Monumenta Ritualia*, II, 85 f., after it was first edited by W. G. Henderson, *Liber pontificalis Chr. Bainbridge archiep. Eboracensis*, Surtees Society, LXI (Durham, 1875), 279 ff., and Introd., xxvi ff. The scope for dating the document is very limited. Matilda was crowned by Archbishop Ealdred of York in 1068 (May 11) at Winchester, and the archbishop died in 1069 (September 11) so that the form must fall in these sixteen months.

The English forms are closely related to those of Rouen. They are likewise impregnated with the *Christus vincit* triad which is repeated before every acclamation. The latter, however, is not followed, but preceded, by the *Exaudi Christe*. The triadic scheme (cf. above, n. 49) is observed most rigidly in all the English forms, since even the laudatory section displays three times three acclamations with the responses of *Christus vincit* or *regnat* or *imperat* in alternation, a custom which first is noticed in the twelfth-century form. The laudations are incorrectly arranged in the prints.

[63] This consideration does not exclude the probability that these laudes were sung also at Matilda's coronation, but it includes the possibility that they were sung, e.g., at the Easter crown-wearing at Winchester in 1069 as well. The form of the episcopal laudes, or rather the deprecatory prayer for the bishop, is as follows:

"Benedicat vos divina majestas Domini.

Benedicat vos spiritus sanctus qui in specie columbe in Jordane fluvio super Christum requievit.

Ille vos benedicat qui de coelo dignatus est descendere in terram et de suo sancto sanguine nos redemit.

Benedicat Dominus *sacerdotium vestrum* et introitum vestrum."

[64] Cambridge, Trinity College Lat. MS 249, fols. 108ᵛ; the form has been published by Henderson, *op. cit.*, p. 283; H. A. Wilson, *The Pontifical of Magdalen College*, Bradshaw Society, XXXIX (London, 1910), 252 f. The saints Dunstan and Elphegus are from Canterbury, but provenance from Ely is assumed by M. R. James, *Catalogue of Western Manuscripts in Trinity College. Cambridge* (1900), I, 348. The attribution to

Worcester Cathedral.[65] It is a form of laudes to be used at the service on feast days, and this is true also of the copy found in the Gradual of Worcester which differs from that in the Antiphonary only in that the name of St. Edward is added to the saints invoked for the king.[66]

These are the four texts. To these there may be added a copy of poetical laudes of the eleventh century which is appended to the formulary of 1068.[67] Moreover, if we confine ourselves to liturgical sources, there are some rubrics concerning the laudes. In the first place, there is the Missal of Westminster, written about 1383–84 for Nicholas Lytlington, abbot of Westminster, which shows in the coronation ceremonial the marginal note: "ante epistolam cantetur solempniter *Christus vincit.*"[68] This entry repeats to the letter a marginal note found in the Coronation Office of Edward II of 1308.[69] Thus, according to liturgical sources, laudes are known in connection with the coronations of the twelfth century (1154?), of Edward II (1308), of Richard II (1377), and probably with that of Queen Matilda (1068).

This, however, is not all the evidence available of coronation laudes in England. Geoffrey of Monmouth in his History of the Kings of Britain reports a story, entirely mythical, about the designation of Constantine

---

Henry II and Eleanor is tentative and remains doubtful, for Eleanor may never have been crowned in England; cf. Schramm, *English Coronation*, p. 57; see also P. L. Ward, "The Coronation Ceremony in Mediaeval England," *Speculum*, XIV (1939), 176.

[65] Worcester Cathedral Cod. F. 160, fol. 201; the form has been published by W. H. Frere, *The Winchester Troper*, Bradshaw Society, VIII (London, 1894), 130 f., and pp. xx, n. 2, xxvi; a facsimile is found in *Paléographie musicale*, XII (1922), fol. 201, and a transcription, which is not quite correct so far as the laudations are concerned, on p. 74 f. Cf. below, Appendix I, p. 194, the analysis of these laudes by M. F. Bukofzer; see also below, pp. 217 ff.

[66] This Gradual is a part of the Worcester MS F. 160; cf. *Paléographie musicale*, XII, 74, n. 6.

[67] Cf. above, n. 62, for the prints. The intentions for king and queen are as follows:
"Moribus ornatum Salomonis fonte repletum
Poscimus Anglorum nostrum salvet *basileum*,
    Qui super astra.
Poscimus et nostram salvet Christus *basileam*,
Nobilem atque piam gestantem dogmatis ydram,
    Gloria victori."
For the British *basileus* title, see F. Hardegen, *Imperialpolitik Heinrichs II. von England* (Heidelberg, 1905), App.; E. A. Freeman, *History of the Norman Conquest* (1870–1879), I, 620 ff.; Stengel, in *Deutsches Archiv*, III (1939), 3 ff.

[68] John Wickham Legg, *Missale ad usum ecclesiae Westmonasteriensis*, Bradshaw Society, V (London, 1897), III, 1523, referring to col. 714, and II, 714, n. 3. On the date of the manuscript (*Westminster Abbey, Missale Westmonasteriense*), see J. A. Robinson and M. R. James, *The Manuscripts of Westminster Abbey* (Cambridge, 1909).

[69] Brit. Mus. Harleian MS 2901, fol. 35; this Coronation Order of Edward II, in which the laudes rubric precedes the "leccio epistole beati Petri Apostoli," has been brought to light by H. G. Richardson, "Early Coronation Records," *Bulletin of the Institute of Historical Research*, XVI (London, 1938), 11; cf. Schramm, in *ArchUF.*, XVI (1939), 284, who maintains that in spite of the entries in the two missals (the Westminster and the Harleian) the laudes were not sung at the coronations of Edward II or Richard II, but omits giving reasons for his assertion.

of Brittany as English king by "Archbishop" Guethelinus of London
who acclaimed the king-to-be in the following way:[70]

> Christus vincit, Christus regnat, Christus imperat.
> Ecce rex Britannie deserte.   Adsit modo Christus.
> Ecce defensio nostra.   Ecce spes nostra et gaudium.

This is a mutilated and botched form of Gallo-Frankish laudes, of which
the opening triad, the acclamation to the king, and the fragments of
laudations are still distinguishable. Of course, this fictitious acclamation
is not relevant to the legendary past to which Geoffrey pretends to refer;
but it is a testimony for Geoffrey's own time, for he attributed to the
bishop nothing but the acclamations of the twelfth century such as were
then customary in England.[71]

Geoffrey of Monmouth wrote during the reign of Stephen of Blois
(*ca.* 1140), and by coincidence another contemporary relates that at a
festival crowning of Stephen strife arose between the monks and the
secular clergy when they were singing the *Christus vincit*.[72] We are not
told what the subject of the strife may have been. Presumably, however,
monks and clerics were quarreling over the question of who was to voice
the litany, since this was more than a point of honor. We know from the
liturgical documents of other countries that the cantors of the *Christus
vincit* received for their chanting a small sum of money, two sous in
Rheims, twelve *nummi bone monete* in Laon, ten sous in Rouen, two
hyperpers in Traù, three soldi in Rome, and similar sums in other cathedrals.[73] In England the *presbyterium* or reward for chanting the laudes to
the king amounted to twenty-five shillings. This gratuity was paid in the
Continental cathedrals by the bishop to whom the laudes were offered.[74]

[70] Geoffrey of Monmouth, *Historia regum Britanniae*, VI, c. 4, ed. Edmond Faral, *La légende Arthurienne. Études et documents*, Bibliothèque de l'école des hautes études, CCLVII (Paris, 1929), III, 169.

[71] For other contemporaneous reflections in Geoffrey, see J. S. P. Tatlock, "Certain Contemporaneous Matters in Geoffrey of Monmouth," *Speculum*, VI (1931), 206 ff.; Schramm, in *ArchUF.*, XV (1938), 328 f., § 17. Professor Tatlock, to whom I feel greatly indebted for several valuable suggestions, kindly called my attention to the magical application of the *Christus vincit* formula in Osborn's *Vita S. Dunstani*, c. 19 (ed. W. Stubbs, Rolls Series, 63), 145; cf. Helinand of Froidmont, *Chronicon*, XLVII, ad a. 1073, Migne, *PL.*, CCXII, col. 960A.

[72] Gervase of Canterbury (ed. W. Stubbs, Rolls Series, 73), I, 527: "Facta est autem altercatio inter monachos et clericos, dum utrique *Christus vincit* cantarent"; the place is quoted by Schramm, *English Coronation*, p. 31, p. 31, n. 5, and *ArchUF.*, XV, 324, § 12a.

[73] Prost, *Quatre pièces*, pp 170 f.; Léon Gautier, *Histoire de la poésie liturgique au moyen âge* (Paris, 1896), I, 82 f.; for Traù, cf. above, Chap. V, n. 14; for Rheims, see above, Chap. IV, n. 31; for Rouen, see the accounts of the archiepiscopal treasurer wherein assignments for the cantors of the *Christus vincit* are found in the years 1402 and 1403; cf. *Inventaire-Sommaire des archives départementales. Seine-Inférieure* (above, n. 53), Sér. G, I (1866), 6 f., Nos. G. 18–19.

[74] Cf. above, chap. IV, n. 31.

In England, it was the king who gave the money. This implies that the laudes were voiced only in the king's presence as an honor intended for him and not for the bishop. In fact, the *laudes regiae* in England never became episcopal acclamations "for the Pall," as in France, and consequently they vanished when the idea of liturgical kingship disappeared with Richard II. At any rate, in England, more than on the Continent at that time, the laudes had the character of a state ceremony.

To the historian the English practice has a great advantage. Since every expense of the king is almost bound to appear somewhere in the carefully kept rolls of the English Exchequer, we may expect to find entries in the royal accounts referring to the laudes. Indeed, the *Liberate Rolls* in particular, but other accounts as well, offer considerable material which in connection with the laudes has so far not been utilized. The earliest entry known to me is found in the Pipe Roll of Henry II, an assignment dated June 5, 1188, in which it is said that the clerics "qui cantaverunt *Christus vincit* die Pentecoste ante regem" were to receive twenty-five shillings.[75] More numerous are the assignments of King John. December 28, 1201, John ordered the payment of twenty-five shillings for the singing of the *Christus vincit* on Christmas,[76] and the same amount was assigned, on April 24, 1204, to the cantors who were to sing the Easter laudes on the following day, April 25.[77] We know also of John's donation to the cantors on Easter in 1205.[78] More interesting, however, than these entries referring to festival laudes is the one in the roll of 1200, dated October 10, in which it is said:[79]

Liberate de thesauro nostro xxv solidos Eustacio capellano et Ambrosio, clericis nostris, qui cantaverunt *Xristus vincit* ad secundam coronationem nostram et ad unctionem et coronationem Jsabelle regine uxoris nostre.

In this example the character of the chant as "Coronation laudes" is actually on record. Moreover, we should note that this coronation of King John along with the consecration of his queen was not celebrated on a Church festival but on an ordinary Sunday, October 8, 1200. Thus laudes were voiced in Westminster only because of the coronation. Fortunately this is not the sole evidence of its kind. The same observation can be made concerning both John's predecessor and his successor. A

[75] *Pipe Roll 34, Henry II, 1188,* p. 19, to which Mr. Austin Lane Poole, in Oxford, kindly directed my attention.
[76] *Rotuli de Liberate ac de Misis et Praestitis regnante Johanne,* ed. T. Duffus Hardy (London, 1844), 25.
[77] *Ibid.,* p. 93.
[78] *Rotuli litterarum clausarum, King John,* ed. T. Duffus Hardy (London, 1833), I, 26.
[79] *Rotuli de Liberate,* p. 1; see also T. Duffus Hardy in the Introduction to his edition of *Rotuli litterarum patentium in Turri Londinensi asservati* (London, 1835), p. xxv.

chronicler's relation testifies that on Richard's second coronation at Winchester, April 17, 1194, three cantors sang the *Christus vincit* after the first Collect.[80] On the other hand, on February 10, 1237, Henry III lavishly assigned one hundred shillings to Walter of Lench, the favorite cleric of the royal chapel, for his and his assistants' part in singing the laudes at the king's festival crown-wearing and the inaugural coronation of Queen Eleanor at Westminster on January 20, 1236.[81] This coronation likewise took place on an ordinary Sunday; therefore it may be taken for granted that in England the laudes belonged to the crowning rite as well as to the service on the great feast days.

This latter custom is proved not only by the formularies of Worcester mentioned before, but also by a great number of entries in the rolls. It is surprising to find how rapidly the occasions on which the *Christus vincit* was chanted began to be multiplied by the time of Henry III. This is a most startling fact. Admittedly, the laudes days were also increased on the Continent in the twelfth and thirteenth centuries, above all in Rome where the pope was crowned and tendered the laudes on eighteen occasions, and also in France where the chant, by that time, was definitely connected with the hierarchical representation.[82] Yet, the increase of laudes days under Henry III was quite extraordinary and abnormal. In the first years of his reign, it is true, it can be ascertained from his orders of payment—although the *Liberate Rolls* are not completely preserved—that in 1227,[83] 1228,[84] 1229,[85] and 1230[86] the laudes were chanted regularly thrice a year, namely, on the three great Church festivals. This was quite normal and agreed with the general usage. The increased voicing of laudes seems to begin in 1233. Although the *Liberate Roll* of this year breaks off as early as October, the laudes had nevertheless been chanted ten times in the preceding months. In addition to the three festivals, the *Christus vincit* had been ordered sung on the days of St. Mary's Purification, Ascension, Trinity, Midsummer, St. Mary's Ascension, St. Mary's Birthday, and on the Translation of Edward the Confessor.[87] Even this great number of laudes increased in the ensuing years, or else the days

---

[80] Gervase of Canterbury, ed. Stubbs, I, 526: "Post primam orationem collecta dicta est pro rege. Deinde *Christus vincit* a tribus personis"; the place is quoted by Schramm, *English Coronation*, p. 31, n. 5, and *ArchUF.*, XV, 326, n. 1.

[81] *Liberate Rolls, Henry III*, 1226–1240, I, 255.

[82] The days of pall-wearings in England are listed by Maskell, *Monum. Rit.*, II, 320. See also *Graduel de Rouen*, I, 65 f., where eight laudes days are mentioned; for the pope, see Albinus in *Liber cens.*, II, 90.

[83] *Liberate Rolls*, I, 14 (Jan. 18); I, 27 (April 18); I, 39 (June 20).

[84] *Ibid.*, I, 69, 79, 87 (Feb. 22, April 28, June 23).

[85] *Ibid.*, I, 115, 128, 139 (Jan. 20, May 5, July 19).

[86] *Ibid.*, I, 164, 177 (Feb. 3, April 19). The *Liberate Rolls* are lacking for the years 1231 and 1232.

[87] *Ibid.*, I, 197, 208, 218, 221, 231, 234, (Feb. 4, April 16, June 7, 28, Sept. 16, Oct. 13). The Rolls are lacking for the period October 1233–October 1236.

were changed. In 1237, the chant was sung also on Epiphany;[88] in 1238, on All Saints;[89] in 1239, on Circumcision (January 1), on the Day of St. Botulph (June 17)—in order to celebrate the birth of a prince, later King Edward I (June 16)—on the Queen's purification (July 31), on St. Edmund's Day (November 20), on St. Edward's Day (January 5), and all this in addition to the greater part of the festivals mentioned for the year 1233. In other words, between Epiphany in 1239 and Epiphany in 1240 the laudes were sung to Henry III no less than sixteen times.[90] In 1240, the laudes occur likewise on the Day of St. Leger (October 2) because of another "puerperium reginae,"[91] and in 1241 the ceremony was staged at least twelve times.[92]

This accumulation of laudes days and the obviously quite deliberate royal orders to perform this litany throws, perhaps, some light on Normandy and the otherwise enigmatic letter of the bishop of Winchester. On the other hand, this cumulation of *Christus vincit* performances is certainly less remarkable as an indication of the development of English liturgical observance than it is of the king's condition of mind. To be sure, it is possible that Henry III tried to compete with the pope and the *dies coronae* observed in Rome. But this is not likely. Rather, we should assume that from the increase of laudes days we can read off as from a fever-curve the progress of this king's religious zeal. In another connection, it has been observed by historians that the king's extravagant mania for collecting relics began about 1234, and that, in some inner relationship with this passion, the building and completing of Westminster Abbey began to occupy his mind to an ever-increasing extent.[93] "The less he was clever in his actions within this present world," says a contemporary writer,[94] in an oft-quoted passage, "the more he indulged in dis-

---

[88] *Ibid.*, 1, 255 (Feb. 10), where 100 shillings are assigned for the coronation (above n. 81) and another 75 shillings for Christmas, Epiphany, and St. Mary's Purification.

[89] *Ibid.*, 1, 311 (Jan. 29), where 100 shillings are assigned for Easter and Whitsun in 1237 and for Epiphany in 1238; the amount, however, indicates a fourth singing of the laudes, probably on Christmas in 1237.
Ibid. 1, 364 (Feb. 4), an assignment of 10 pounds for eight performances of the laudes, namely, on Midsummer, St. Mary's Ascension, Translation of St. Edward, All Saints, Christmas in 1238, and Circumcision, Epiphany, Purification in 1239.

[90] For 1239, see the last three days mentioned in n. 89; and further *ibid.*, I, 406 (Aug. 8), an assignment of 8 pounds 15 shillings for seven laudes, and *ibid.*, I, 441 (Jan. 15), 10 pounds for eight laudes, of which five refer to 1239 and three to 1240.

[91] For 1240, see above, note 90. Within six days, from Circumcision to Epiphany, the laudes were sung thrice. See further *Liberate Rolls*, I, 496 (Oct. 5), for the *puerperium* of the queen.

[92] *Liberate Rolls*, II, 32 (Feb. 21), an assignment of 15 pounds for twelve laudes, beginning Epiphany 1240. In the following years the Rolls no longer refer to the *Christus vincit*, but the custom did not disappear, for a single assignment (Feb. 24, 1245), shows that the litany was sung on the day of the queen's purification; *ibid.*, II, 292.

[93] E. F. Jacob, "The Reign of Henry III. Some Suggestions," *Transactions of the Royal Historical Society*, 4th ser., X (1927), 34 f.

[94] Rishanger, *Chronica* (ed. Riley, Rolls Series, 28), pp. 74 f.

playing his humility before God. On some days, he heard the mass three times and, as he longed to hear even more masses, he had them celebrated privately to him and constantly attended them. And when the priest elevated the body of the Lord, he grasped at the priest's hand and kissed it." This report is obviously true to the very letter, for so unbiased a man as the famous Bolognese lawyer Francesco d'Accursio, the son of an even greater father, mentions, in an address to Pope Nicholas III, King Henry's devotion "in missis diurnis quam plurimis audiendis."[95] It is also well known that St. Louis disapproved of Henry III's excessive piety, and according to a story which is, if not true, at least significant, the French king suggested to King Henry the hearing of sermons rather than of innumerable Masses. But Henry is said to have answered he would prefer to see a friend than to hear even good news about him, and for this reason he preferred to witness the sacrifice of the Mass.[96] In this very same period Henry III began to indulge in the veneration of Edward the Confessor, a cult to which posterity owes, after all, Westminster Abbey. In 1237, the Day of the Confessor was added to the festival calendar of the universal Church at the king's urgent request, and the chroniclers report how King Henry, on St. Edward's Day, went in procession, barefooted and in surplice and cope, offering to his patron a crystal containing the blood of the Lord, and how his staring eyes were fixed on the crystal which he bore in his hands.[97] Henry III sought religious excitement, and the symptoms mentioned may explain his desire to have the laudes sung to him as frequently as possible and to borrow from this victory song the self-confidence which in many respects he lacked.

Interesting as this is, it does not tell us how the laudes became a part of the English coronation ritual. They were not mentioned either in the French or the German Orders of Coronation. In Rome, it is true, the chant was sung regularly at the imperial sacring, and it once happened that an English king, Canute the Great, witnessed this celebration (1027) which deeply impressed him. Hence the possibility that England may have borrowed the laudes in the coronation rite from Rome cannot be

---

[95] Cf. G. L. Haskins and E. H. Kantorowicz, "A Diplomatic Mission of Francis Accursius and His Oration before Pope Nicholas III," *English Historical Review*, LVIII (1943), p. 443, n. 1.

[96] Rishanger, *Chronica*, ed. Riley, p. 75.

[97] Matthew of Paris, *Chronica Maiora*, ed. Luard, VI, 138–144, cf. IV, 643. In this connection, the lines of John of Garland, containing a very positive, but almost unknown judgment, may be adduced; cf. his *Exempla honestae vitae* (ca. 1258 A.D.), ed. Edwin Habel in *Romanische Forschungen*, XXIX (1911), 151:

"Rex dilecte Deo, regum largissime, sanctum
Qui colis Edwardum, quem veneraris amas . . .
Istud Londoniis rex sanctam videt ad aram
Corpus, adorat, cum sacer ille Dei."

ruled out completely. However, this solution is farfetched and hardly convincing, less so since the English forms are not Roman, but unmistakably Gallo-Frankish or even Rouenese. The laudes were unknown in the Anglo-Saxon Church, at least they are never mentioned. They must have been brought to England, along with many other innovations, by the Normans.[98] In agreement with the ritual observances in Normandy, the laudes were sung also in Norman England at the festivals. But how was it that the festival laudes of Normandy became the coronation laudes of England? The first Norman coronations in England seem to have been decisive. The Conqueror himself was crowned on Christmas in 1066. Queen Matilda was crowned at Winchester on Pentecost, May 11, 1068. Thus the first two Norman coronations in England coincided with Norman laudes days. The succeeding coronations did not coincide with Church festivals, but Geoffrey of Monmouth's testimony, as well as the Coronation Order of the twelfth century, provide satisfactory evidence that by that time the laudes had become an integral part of the coronation ceremony. The conclusion can be drawn easily. In keeping with the ritual of Normandy, laudes were chanted at Church festivals in England. The first two Norman coronations in England took place on laudes days; and the ceremonial of the first two coronations determined the rite for the future, even though coronations might take place on a weekday or ordinary Sunday. The possible influence of the Roman model should not be disregarded. The existence, however, of English coronation laudes can be explained satisfactorily without this model.

We may now draw from England a conclusion for the other Norman realms. The *Ordo* of the ducal consecration in Rouen was but a cutting taken from an ancient English coronation ritual. It was introduced in the late twelfth century when under Richard I and John the inauguration of the Norman duke became almost the equivalent of a ducal coronation. It therefore seems likely that English observance began to retroact on Normandy and that owing to English influence the ancient festival laudes of Normandy were chanted, in the late twelfth century, also at the consecration of the duke of Normandy. Furthermore, it becomes comprehensible that laudes are found in the coronation rite of Palermo, too. The South had borrowed this observance from England. In the form of festi-

[98] For the violence in introducing the Norman way of chanting to England, see the story about Thurston of Glastonbury, who summoned soldiers against the Anglo-Saxon monks because they refused to abandon their customary chant in favor of the way of singing as represented by William of Dijon; that is to say that in conquered England it was liturgy which became the mouthpiece of the political opposition; cf. H. Böhmer, *Kirche und Staat in England*, pp. 120 f.; E. Sackur, *Die Cluniacenser*, II (1894), 353 ff.; for William of Dijon, cf. J. Handschin and D. L. David, "Un point d' histoire grégorienne. Guillaume de Fécamp," *RCGr.*, XXXIX and XL (1935–1936), especially XL, 13 ff.

val laudes, this liturgical acclamation traveled from Normandy to England, and was returned by England in the form of coronation laudes to the two Norman realms, Normandy and Sicily. That the three Norman states had not only many features in common, but even formed, in many ways, a unity in culture, administration, and learning has been indicated by many modern studies. This holds true for liturgy as well. The liturgical unity of the three Norman states becomes more and more visible,[99] although in detail many items still remain to be clarified.

[99] See the studies quoted above, n. 6, p. 157; also Schramm, *English Coronation*, p. 60, n. 2, and E. Kantorowicz, "A Norman Finale of the Exultet and the Rite of Sarum," *Harvard Theological Review*, XXXIV (1941), 129–143.

CHAPTER VII

THE LAUDES IN MODERN TIMES

IN SPITE OF its serious background, the latest development of the laudes seems somewhat like a caricature of a former life. Ancient forms and rites might be restored; but the rhythm of life that had vouched for the inner truth of ceremonies in bygone days cannot be conjured up again. Nevertheless, caricatures of life are instructive, all the more so since the latest renewal of the laudes completes the circle and brings us back to the origins. When the mediaeval conception of Christ the Emperor and King faded away, along with the corresponding conception of the emperor or king as the vicar and the likeness of Christ, the chant of the *laudes regiae* was doomed to disappear from the liturgico-political realm. The laudes reappeared when in Europe the modern dictators established a new ruler or "leader" cult and when the Church rejoined the cult by instituting the feast of "Christ the King."

Very little is known about the moment at which, in the various countries, the solemn acclamations of the liturgy passed into desuetude. In England, the fourteenth century is apparently the time when this observance expired, and it must be considered at least a symbolical coincidence that the *Christus vincit* is mentioned, for the last time, in a marginal note to the Coronation Order of Richard II with whom a period of kingship came to an end (see, however, Pl. VIII).

In Sicily, the laudes seem to have disappeared with the Normano-Suabian dynasty. They are no longer contained in the Angevin and Aragonese rites of coronation or mentioned otherwise.

The practice in Germany remains obscure. The festival laudes must have dropped out of use by the early twelfth century. There seems to be not a single German formulary transmitted from the Hohenstaufen period. Most likely this break of tradition has something to do with the Investiture Strife the reactions of which upon the liturgy deserve a special study.[1] The laudes survived only in connection with the Roman coronation of the German emperor. They still were sung in the fifteenth century at the coronation of Frederick III in Rome and in the sixteenth at that of Charles V, in 1530,[2] when, in Bologna, the polite Medici pope apologized to the no less polite emperor for asking him to kiss the pontiff's foot.[3]

---

[1] The only form preserved of the Hohenstaufen period seems to be the one from Aquileia; cf. above, p. 115.

[2] Augustinus Patricius Piccolomineus, *Sacrae cerimoniae Romanae Ecclesiae*, in Chr. G. Hoffmann, *Nova scriptorum et monumentorum collectio* (Leipzig, 1733), II, 350 f.; the form agrees with that quoted above, p. 144; cf. Biehl, *op. cit.*, 111, n. 4.

[3] "Osculatis autem pedibus dixit papa: Veniam det mihi Celsitudo Tua, invitus passus sum osculari pedes meos, sed lex ceremoniarum ita cogit." Luther, *Werke*

It would be interesting to know whether the house of Hapsburg continued the observance. An acclamation referring to Ferdinand I together with Charles V is preserved, but, since it was offered by the Council of Trent, the form of these laudes is that of conciliar acclamations, which differs widely from that of the ancient Gallo-Frankish or Franco-Roman laudes.[4] It is not impossible that within the Hapsburg monarchy the kingdom of Bohemia may have known the *laudes regiae*.[5] No form, however, has been transmitted and the only formulary of "Bohemian laudes" in print is but a joke of the historian Bernard Pez, an invective hurled against his scholar foe, the Jesuit Father Hansiz.[6] But the genuine laudes

---

(Weimar edition, 1934), Briefwechsel, V, 275; the interesting place is quoted by Hans Liermann, "Untersuchungen zum Sakralrecht des protestantischen Herrschers," *ZfRG.*, kan. Abt. XXX (1941), 318, n. 18.

[4] Mansi, *op. cit.*, XXXIII, 196, § viii (December 4, 1563). The laudes were chanted by the cardinal of Lorraine while the whole assembly made the response. The style is quite baroque; the intentions for the emperors have the following text.:

> *Cardinal:* Caroli quinti imperatoris et serenissimorum regum, qui hoc universale concilium promoverunt et protexerunt, memoria in benedictione sit.
> *Patres:* Amen, Amen.
> *Cardinal:* Serenissimo imperatori Ferdinando semper augusto orthodoxo et pacifico, et omnibus regibus, rebus publicis et principibus nostris multi anni.
> *Patres:* Pium et christianum imperatorem, Domine, conserva. Imperator coelestis terrenos reges, rectae fidei conservatores, custodi ..."

See also the acclamations of the Council of Florence, in 1573; Mansi, *op. cit.*, XXXV, 804 f., § lxiii.

[5] Cosmas of Prag, *Chronica Boemorum*, II, c. 38, *MGH. SS. rer. Germ.*, ed. Bretholz (1923), 141, 1086 A.D.:

> "Trevirensis archiepiscopus ... unxit in regem Wratizlaum et imposuit diadema super caput tam ipsius quam eius coniugis Zuatane cyclade regia amicte, clericis et universis satrapibus ter acclamantibus: 'Wratislao regi quam Boemico tam Polonico, magnifico et pacifico, a Deo coronato, vita, salus et victoria!' "

Manitius, in *Mitteilungen des Österreichischen Instituts für Geschichtsforschung*, VIII (1887), 482, suggests that Cosmas simply borrowed the acclamation to Charlemagne voiced at the latter's coronation in 800; see, however, Loserth, in *Archiv für Kunde österreichischer Geschichtsquellen*, LIV (1876), 11 ff. For the right to crown the duke of Bohemia on Church festivals, cf. *MGH. Const.*, I, 236, No. 170, and the *Continuatio Cosmae* by the Monk of Saaz, in *Fontes rerum Bohemicarum*, I (Prague, 1879), 249, quoted by Klewitz, "Die Festkrönungen der deutschen Könige," *ZfRG.*, kan. Abt. XXVIII (1939), 71.

[6] Bernard Pez, *Ad ... P. Marcum Hanzizum ... Epistola* (Vienna, 1731), 48 f., criticizes severely the chronological and editorial blunders of Hansiz's edition of the *Vita S. Ruperti* and invents *ad hoc* the following laudes.:

"Ruperto, magno Noricorum Apostolo   vita et victoria!
Germaniae Benedicto   vita et victoria!

Christus vincit, Christus regnat, Christus imperat!

Ruperto Juvavensi, Caranthano, Tauriscico, Carno,
Vinidico, Langobardico, Slavico, Pannonico, Hunico,
Bajuvarico, Boico,   vita sempiterna!

Theodoni primo duci Bojorum circa annum DCXII a
S. Ruperto ex Pannonia et Hunnia (*in marg.: Hunia seu Hunnia hodie Austria!*) invitato, feliciter baptizato
et a deo coronato principi   vita et victoria!

survived in another part of the monarchy—in Dalmatia. Here this observance outlasted the Venetian rule and when, in 1875, Emperor Francis Joseph visited Zara, the capital of the Austrian Province of the Littoral, he was received by a chant of the imperial part of the ancient Dalmatian laudes which, after all, had come down from Byzantine times.[7] Correspondingly, in the cathedral of Zara Pope Pius IX was offered the papal part of the laudes when he celebrated his priestly jubilee, in 1869, and on his pontifical jubilee in 1871.[8] The old usage of singing festival laudes to the ruler on Christmas and Easter was observed in Zara until the most recent times. On Easter in 1918, Charles, the last Hapsburg emperor, was the last to receive the liturgical acclamation, shortly before the breakdown of Central Europe wrenched and shattered all the traditions by which the Austrian crown had been linked, almost visibly, with that of the Eastern Roman Emperors.[9]

In Italy, where the laudes had never been very popular outside of Rome,[10] the observance had passed out of existence probably long before.[11] Even at the papal court, whose traditions, like those of the English crown, have never been affected by the contingencies of history to the same extent as those of other courts, the acclamations on Church festivals seem to have fallen into disuse by the fifteenth century.[12] Only the conciliar acclamations survived, and so did, perhaps without a break, the custom of singing the laudes at the papal coronation. If ever this tradition had been abandoned, at least it was resumed again; for at the enthronement of Pope Pius X, in 1903, a little pamphlet was printed containing text and music of the coronation laudes. The text tallies with the form first transmitted by Benedict of St. Peter's in the twelfth century.[13]

Pez, to whose letter Dr. N. Fickermann, in Berlin, kindly called my attention, was not the first to invent malicious laudes, for they had been composed against the Byzantine emperor by Liutprand of Cremona; cf. his *Legatio*, c. 10, *MGH. SS. rer. Germ.*, ed. Dümmler (1877), 181; and *ibid.*, pp. 86, 111, 172, 190, and *passim* his reports about Byzantine acclamations.

[7] F. Bianchi, *Zara Christiana* (Zara, 1877), I, 536 f.

[8] *Ibid.*, I, 536; for the survival of the laudes within the Venetian Empire, cf. Lucius, *op. cit.*, p. 74; De Santi, *op. cit.*, p. 593, n. 1; Mercati, in *Bessarione*, XXXVIII (1922), 10 ff.; above, p. 151.

[9] Cf. *RCGr.*, XXX (1926), 130 ff.

[10] Laudes from Italy are very few, namely (1) the forms of Verona, (2) the laudes of Chieti, both of the ninth century, (3) those of Ivrea of the eleventh century, and (4) of Aquileia of the twelfth century. After the thirteenth century, however, the Durandus laudes beginning with *Christus vincit* may have been received also in Italy; cf. above, p. 113, n. 4.

[11] See the Roman Pontifical of about 1485 according to which laudes were sung merely "in quibusdam ecclesiis"; *DACL.*, VIII, 1907 f., *s.v.* "Laudes Gallicanae," and above, p. 118, n. 23.

[12] The later mediaeval *Ordines Romani* quote the laudes only on the occasion of a papal or imperial coronation.

[13] *Laudes in die coronationis . . . Pii PP. X.* (August 9, 1903), published in Rome, by Forzan & Cie., a photostat of which Professor G. B. Ladner of Toronto, was kind enough to send me.

At this time, however, a more general revival of the laudes and the *Christus vincit* triad as well as the *Christus vincit* ideology becomes palpable. It is interesting to watch History setting, as it were, her traps. The revival began, in the most unpolitical way, on the part of learned musicologists. In 1887, Dom Mocquereau had founded at Solesmes the *Paléographie musicale* as an organ for the reform of the Gregorian chant, and in the course of this movement, which was championed by the Benedictines with the truly scholarly battle cry "Back to the sources," the almost forgotten chant of the laudes was resurrected from oblivion. It seems as if the laudes were reintroduced in Rome at the coronation of Pius X, to whose heart the reform of Gregorian chant was so very dear.[14] However, in France the tradition of the *Christus vincit* had never faded away entirely; here it could be revived. In some French cathedrals such as Rheims, Orléans, Lyons, or Vienne this litany in the form of episcopal laudes had been chanted as late as the eighteenth century, most probably until the outbreak of the French Revolution.[15] In Rouen, the usage survived even this great break of historical continuity; the laudes have been sung here as an "Acclamation to the Pall" until the present war.[16] In many respects the liturgy of Rouen was momentous for the musical reformers, and it seems as though the stimulation emanated from the music of the laudes rather than from the text, as may be gathered from the work of Dom Gastoué.[17]

Eventually, however, the reform of Gregorian music merged with other ecclesiastical activities, above all with the "Liturgical Movement." The latter's far-flung aims are not easily described; but it is not exaggeration to maintain that the truly vital forces within the Roman Church have been gathered in this movement. It does not intend to purge only the liturgy of its baroque accretions and deformations and to revive the old, but it endeavors also to revive an unbroken and unreflected approach to liturgy in general and thereby affects, to an extent that cannot yet be gauged, the attitude toward religious life of millions of people.[18] Important though this movement may be for its own values, it is important to the historian for the fact that it discloses and reflects a general European development of mind which is not confined to the Roman Church.

However this may be, the reform of Gregorian music and the Liturgical Movement joined to compose, for modern use, new formularies of laudes

[14] See, e.g., Gastoué, *op. cit.*, pp. 236 ff.

[15] *DACL.*, VIII, col. 1901, n. 20; for Vienne, see also David, in *RCGr.*, XXVI (1922), 7.

[16] See *Notes and Queries*, CLVIII (1930), 118; *JLW.*, IX (1929), 178, n. 84; Jocelyn Perkins, *The Cathedrals of Normandy* (London, 1935), 43.

[17] Gastoué, *op. cit.*, pp. 168 ff.

[18] The *Jahrbuch für Liturgiewissenschaft*, published since 1921 in Maria Laach and edited by O. Casel, A. Baumstark, and A. L. Mayer, is perhaps the most prominent medium of communication of this movement.

so that a modernized *Christus vincit* made its appearance. These reorganized acclamations have been chanted on various festal occasions and finally have been incorporated in official and semiofficial editions of the Gregorian chant published before and after the First World War.[19] However, it was only in the 'twenties of our century that the *laudes regiae*, revived by learned musicologists and liturgiologists, began to reappear also on the political stage of postwar Europe, and, by the irony of which History is so fond, this chant made its reappearance along with what was believed the new lodestar of political life: totalitarianism and dictatorship.

The impact of the new ideas was felt in Rome earlier and more intensely than elsewhere. The two eventual partners of the Vatican Treaties moved almost at the same time to Rome from Milan: in February of 1922, Achille Ratti was crowned Pope Pius XI, and in October, 1922, Benito Mussolini achieved the political leadership of the kingdom of Italy. Frictions between the Vatican and the Palazzo Chigi, between the papal and the Fascist sees, arose almost inevitably in the early days of the new order. Fascist challenges were answered, without closing the door completely, by the papal counterchallenges when Pius XI, at the end of the Holy Year of 1925, instituted the new feast of "Christ the King." The new feast was an outcome of the Liturgical Movement; but it was also a political act. The totalitarian aims of Italian Fascism were capped by the no less totalitarian, if transcendental, ideal of the Universal Empire of *Christus Rex*. The papal encyclical refers, in very distinct terms, "to the plague of anticlericalism, its errors and impious activities," which had come into being "as the Empire of Christ over all nations was rejected" and "the right, which the Church has from Christ himself, to teach mankind, to make laws, and to govern people in all that pertains to their eternal salvation was denied."[20] A new Mass, in accordance with ecclesiastical convention, was established for the new "Feast of the Kingship of Christ," and it became customary to include the chant of the laudes, in the form in which it had been revived by the promoters of Gregorian music, in the divine service of this particular feast day as well as others. How quickly the ancient text and its melody again became popular can be learned from the last papal election—that of Pius XII in March, 1939—when the throng crowding the square in front of St. Peter's saluted the new pontiff, as he gave

[19] Cf. Beat Reiser, O.S.B., *Laudes festivae. Lectionarium et cantatarium pro diversitate temporum et festorum* (Vatican, 1932), 223 ff.; L. Camattari, S.J., *Cantemus Domino. Manuale di canti sacri* (Rome, 1924), 316, No. 567; Gastoué, *op. cit.*, p. 200. Cf. below, pp. 213 f.

[20] Cf. Lord Clonmore, *Pope Pius XI and World Peace* (New York, 1938), 96 f.; Joseph Husslein, S.J., *Christ the King* (New York, The American Press, 1926) 14 ff.

his benediction from the balcony, by bursting spontaneously into the old, and yet new, chant of *Christus vincit, Christus regnat, Christus imperat*.[21] Any revival of the past, however, is two-edged and cuts both ways. When Pepin revived the ideal of *rex et sacerdos* together with the biblical anointment of kings, he could not possibly have foreseen that this innovation would be counteracted immediately by the Donation of Constantine and thus help to promote the hierarchical antitype of *sacerdos et imperator*. Nor could the leaders of Fascist authoritarianism have foreseen that they would provoke an even stronger answer on the part of the Vatican, or Pope Pius XI, that the rallying cry of *Christus Rex* would have surprising political repercussions. It became a catchword of Franco's Spain. It became the battle cry of the young Mexicans of the Catholic Association, styled the "Soldados de Cristo Rey," who defied the anticlerical government decrees and who, when executed, fell with the cry on their lips "Viva Cristo Rey ... Viva el Papa!"[22] In Belgium, the "Rexist" party, in close connection with the leaders of the Catholic Youth, shifted rapidly to National-Socialist ideologies. And in Italy, once Palazzo Venezia and Vatican were reconciled, the laudes became an integral part of Fascist devotion.

Political acclamations have been resuscitated systematically in the authoritarian countries. They are indispensable to the emotionalism of a Fascist regime.[23] Moreover, the Italian program of a *Renovatio Imperii*

[21] See the *New York Times*, Friday, March 3, 1939, p. 3: "Suddenly and apparently spontaneously the whole crowd was singing. The noble notes of the hymn with the chorus *Christus vincit, Christus regnat, Christus imperat* rolled up to the sky with an intensity and volume of sound that moved even skeptical observers. With this hymn the crowd wished the Pope peace, a long life and glory." The text is found in *The St. Gregory Hymnal and Catholic Choir Book*, compiled, edited, and arranged by Nicola A. Montani (Philadelphia, 1940), 578, No. 310, where it is said that the chant is "rendered on Solemn Functions, at the Reception of Archbishops or Bishops, or any other festival occasion."

[22] Professor Max Radin kindly called my attention to the fact that the Bancroft Library of the University of California, Berkeley, has a number of most interesting pamphlets referring to these events; see also Francis McCullagh, *Red Mexico* (New York, 1928), 215 ff.; Lord Clonmore, *op. cit.*, pp. 283 f. Cf. below, n. 23.

[23] E. K. Rand, *The Building of Eternal Rome* (Cambridge, Mass., 1943), 230, likewise stresses, in an amusing footnote (n. 65), the inner relations between dictatorships and acclamations. He considers the *vita*-acclamations as less appropriate in formal democracies because a shout such as "O President, live forever!" might be resented by the party out of power. Professor Rand, too, has observed that in Italy the cry "Viva Cristo Rè!" was opposed to "Viva il Duce!" He felt disappointed, however, at the Nazi acclamations containing series of moral maxims such as *Stärke! Tapferkeit! Ewigkeit!* This can only be a slip of the great scholar. The *Historia Augusta* contains many acclamations such as *Virtus tua! Fortitudo tua! Aeternitas tua!* (see above, pp. 13 f.), which reappear in the laudatory section of the laudes as *Virtus nostra! Fortitudo nostra!* with reference to Christ, whereas the Nazi acclamations are strangely egocentric: *Ein Volk erkennt sich selbst!* ran an acclamation in 1933. The acclamation of March, 1938, following the occupation of Austria, was *Ein Reich, Ein Volk, Ein Führer!* the stemma of which leads via Barbarossa (*unus Deus, unus papa, unus imperator;* cf. Rahewin, *Gesta Friderici*, IV, c. 66) to the εἶς Θεός acclamations so brilliantly discussed by Peterson, *Untersuchungen*, pp. 254 f. See above, Chap. II, n. 31, for the rhythm.

Romanorum suggested, all by itself, a revival of acclamations by which the Imperator was recognized recurrently during his reign. It is true that the way of acclaiming the ancient Caesars has not literally been renewed, nor has a modern *Exaudi Dux* replaced the ancient related hails. But a step in this direction was taken by the Fascist Ministry of Education which published a national hymnbook containing a modern formulary of *laudes regiae*. Full scope to meditations was given to the listener—and if he happened to be a historian, to meditations on the dangers implicit in his profession of excavator of the past—when he heard the Italian Balillas sing:[24]

> Christus vincit, Christus regnat, Christus imperat!
> Pio summo pontifici et universali patri pax, vita et salus perpetua!
> Regi nostro Victorio Dei gratia feliciter regnanti pax, vita et salus perpetua!
> Duci Benito Mussolini italicae gentis gloriae, *pax*, vita et salus perpetua! ...
>
> TEMPORA BONA VENIANT!

---

[24] Achille Scinelli, *Canzoniere nazionale. Canti corali religiosi e patriottici* (Roma, Provveditorato Generale dello Stato, 1929), 66, Nos. 27, 28. The formulary displays the Franco-Byzantine type of Dalmatian laudes. Its date is obvious because the king is not yet styled "Imperator Aethiopiae, Rex Albaniae." The acclamation to Benito Mussolini is one of the few examples of laudes to officials; its text agrees with the acclaim for the city-count of Zara or Ossero (above, p. 152) rather than with that for William the Conqueror (above, p. 166, n. 46).

APPENDICES

APPENDIX I

THE MUSIC OF THE LAUDES

BY

MANFRED F. BUKOFZER

CONTENTS

THE MUSIC OF THE LAUDES

BY

MANFRED F. BUKOFZER

INTRODUCTION

THE ACCLAMATIONS or laudes belong musically to the liturgical recitative which forms an integral part of plainsong. In Gregorian chant three melodic styles must be distinguished: the syllabic, the neumatic, and the melismatic. Peter Wagner has shown that these styles were not arbitrarily selected, but correspond to certain liturgical functions.[1] The syllabic style is characterized by its close connection with the text, and by simple recitation with one note to each syllable. Since the text of these recitations is usually taken from the psalms, the group as a whole is called psalmody.[2] The syllabic style has its proper place in the liturgy as the antiphonal psalmody of the Office.

The neumatic style differs from the syllabic in that it employs more than one note to one syllable, but usually not more than two or three. Such groups of tones could be represented graphically by a single neum, hence the name. The melodic pattern of the neumatic style does not differ basically from that of the syllabic style. Both follow the formula of the psalm-tones which, if set in the neumatic style, appear to be embellished or melodically more flexible. The liturgical place of the neumatic style is the antiphonal psalmody of the Mass.

The melismatic style, finally, stands apart from the other two styles because it is soloist's music, not choral music. The melodies are highly florid, and one syllable of the text may carry a great number of notes. The melisma or (p)neuma could be represented only by a whole group of neumes. This solo style is reserved in the liturgy for the nocturnal responses of the Office and the responsorial chants of the Mass.

In the present study I am only concerned with the syllabic and the neumatic styles. The music of the laudes appears in the manuscripts most frequently in neumatic form. From this observation the liturgical place of the laudes can be inferred: they belong to the psalmody of the Mass. We shall see later that the laudes were not sung antiphonally, as one would expect. The position of the laudes in the liturgy must be regarded in many respects as exceptional. Although the proper place in the service was not rigidly regulated, usually they were sung after the *Gloria*

---

[1] Peter Wagner, *Einführung in die gregorianischen Melodien, III, Gregorianische Formenlehre*, 1921, 15 ff.

[2] For the psalmody in general, see the summary in Gustave Reese, *Music in the Middle Ages* (New York, 1940), 172 ff.

in excelsis between the first Collect and the Epistle. However, a rubric of the Durandus formulary[3] directs that the laudes be sung before the *Gloria in excelsis.* This lack of uniformity is also reflected in the fact that the laudes had no assigned place in the Mass book. Not only do they occur on flyleaves or empty spaces selected at random, but they also appear in tropers[4] or other not strictly liturgical books. Although the laudes are not tropes themselves,[5] the occurrence in early tropers seems to indicate that they stood outside of the liturgy and were originally denizens of the Mass.[6] Lack of uniformity can also be observed in the extant melodic versions, which range from a syllabic to a highly neumatic style.

For the strictly syllabic psalms, prayers, and lessons it was not necessary to notate the complete music because the recitation was regulated by the psalm-tones or the stereotyped formulas of the *toni lectionis.* In general the laudes differ from the psalmody in that they are always given a fully notated melody aside from the fact that their text is not taken from the psalms. The laudes are similar in this respect to the recitations of special prayers which were sung only on certain days of the liturgical year or on special occasions. Both these special prayers and the laudes are generally supplied with the fully notated music. The most important of these pieces are the *Te Deum,* the *Exultet* with the *Praeconium Paschale,* and the Lamentations of Jeremiah.[7] All of them have melodies of their own, although they all have long syllabic sections which follow a *tonus currens* more or less closely. But the neumatic sections of these chants make the complete notation necessary.

The music of the laudes has been discussed previously by Pothier,[8] Gastoué,[9] David,[10] Delasilve,[11] D. P. S.,[12] Zaninovitch,[13] and De Santi.[14]

[3] No. 12 of the list of sources given below. For other variations, see above, pp. 112 ff.

[4] Léon Gautier, *Histoire de la poésie liturgique au moyen âge. Les tropes,* 1886, p. 82. Cf. above, p. 19.

[5] Gautier (*op. cit.,* p. 150) incorporated the laudes in his list of tropes although he felt "une très vive hésitation" to do so. He hastens to point out that the acclamations are not "tropes proprement dits." According to Gautier's own definition, the laudes cannot be classified as tropes. Their litany structure, moreover, clearly indicates that they have nothing to do with tropic interpolation.

[6] For a historical confirmation of this point, see above, pp. 89 f. Also Peter Wagner (*op. cit.,* p. 260, n. 2) stresses the extra-liturgical origin of the laudes.

[7] See Peter Wagner, *op. cit.,* p. 224 ff.

[8] *Le graduel de l'église cathédrale de Rouen,* ed. Loriquet, Pothier, and Colette (Rouen, 1907), 200 ff.

[9] Amédée Gastoué, *La musique de l'église* (2d ed.; Lyons, 1916), 168 ff. "Le chant gallican," *RCGr.,* 41 (1937), 101, 131, 167; 42 (1938), 5, 57, 107, 146, 171; 43 (1939), 7, 44; also *Revue St. Chrodegang de Metz* (1937), No. 6, 110. This last study was inaccessible.

[10] Dom Lucien David, in *RCGr.,* 26 (1922), 1.

[11] Joseph Delasilve, "Une acclamation liturgique," *RCGr.,* 12 (1906), 197.

[12] Dom P. S. "Un Christus vincit du XVIᵉ siècle," *RCGr.,* 26 (1922), 84.

[13] Antoine Zaninovitch, *RCGr.,* 30 (1926), 130.

[14] Review of "Le 'Laudes' nel'Incoronazione del Sommo Pontefice," by C. Respighi in *Rassegna Gregoriana,* 2 (1903), 455.

Several versions of the music of the laudes have been published in the studies of Delasilve and Pothier. Gastoué, the only scholar who has investigated the melody of the laudes from a comparative standpoint, gives a general but incomplete survey of the musical sources in *La musique de l'église* (p. 195). He also was instrumental in bringing about a revival of the laudes in the present-day liturgy. The article by Pothier is concerned primarily with showing an alleged scheme of the development the nature of which is rather hypothetical (see below, p. 199). The other articles add new material and record variants of the melody. On the basis of the above material and some other sources, not previously discussed from a musical point of view, the following study will endeavor to survey the musical aspects of the laudes and to elucidate their musical origins.

SOURCES

The available musical sources are listed in chronological order.[15]

1. Laudes of Autun: Diptych (Ivory plate) containing on the back laudes *ca.* 900. Facsimile Richard Delbrück, *Die Konsulardiptychen. Studien zur spätantiken Kunstgeschichte*, Berlin, 1929, II, Pl. 27; see Pls. VII and XII. Notated with clef- and staffless neumes.

2. Laudes of Limoges: Paris, Bibl. Nat. Lat. MS 1240, fol. 65, *ca.* 935. Facsimile excerpt in *Analecta Hymnica*, vol. 7, second facsimile at the back of the book. Staff- and clefless neumes, however in diastematic Aquitanian notation (point-neumes).[16]

3. Limoges: Paris, Bibl. Nat. Lat. MS 1118, fol. 39^v, *ca.* 990. Music excerpt in A. Gastoué, *La musique de l'église* (1911), 181. Clefless diastematic notation (Aquitanian point-neumes).

4. Autun: Paris, Arsenal MS 1169, *ca.* 1000. Music excerpt in Gastoué, *op. cit.*, 197. Same kind of notation as in no. 3 ?

5. Fécamp: Rouen, Bibl. Munic. MS 489, fol. 71. Eleventh century. Facsimile *Le graduel de l'église cathédral de Rouen*, 1907, Pl. 1. Clef- and staffless neumes.

6. Zara: Berlin, Staatsbibl. MS Theol. Lat. quart. 278. 1107–1109. Published by Zaninovitch in *RCGr.*, 30 (1926), 130. Clef- and staffless neumes. The reliability of the transcription is questionable.

7. Narbonne: Paris, Bibl. Nat. Lat. MS 778, late twelfth century. Music excerpt in D. Lucien David's article in *RCGr.*, 26 (1922), 6. Probably notated on a staff with clef.

8. Ritual of Soissons: Paris, Bibl. Nat. Lat. MS 8898, fols. 30^v–32, late twelfth century. Pl. XI; see below, p. 215. The publication of Abbé Poquet (see above, p. 116, n. 15), *Rituale seu mandatum insignis ecclesiae Suessionis tempore episcopi Nivelonis exaratum* (Soissons, 1856) was not available. This manuscript, like all the following ones, is notated in the regular plainsong notation and offers no problems.

---

[15] Owing to political circumstances several manuscripts were inaccessible and the writer had to rely reluctantly on copies and excerpts from books and articles. The ensuing discussion is, therefore, offered with some reservation.

[16] For a survey of the notation and special literature, see Reese, *op. cit.*, p. 138.

9. Beauvais: Brit. Mus. Egerton MS 2615, fols. 42–43. *ca.* 1230. Facsimile excerpt (fol. 43) in H. C. Greene, "The Song of the Ass," *Speculum*, 6 (1931), 540–541.[17]

10. Antiphonary of Worcester Cathedral Lib. MS F. 160, thirteenth century. Facsimile in *Paléographie musicale*, XII (1922), 201–202.

11. Paris: Brussels, Bibl. Roy. MS 1799, fols. 62–63ᵛ, end of the thirteenth century. Manuscript copy of the musical beginning.

12. Durandus laudes: Rome, Vatican Lat. MS 4743, fols. 20–20ᵛ, fourteenth century. Pls. IX and X. Music almost the same as the version published in *RCGr.*, 26 (1922) 84 ("Un Christus vincit du XVIᵉ siècle").

13. Palermo, Cathedral Lib. MS 601, fols. 107ᵛ–109, *ca.* 1400. Pls. XIII and XIV; see below, pp. 220 f.

14. Troyes, Bibl. du Grand Séminaire, no signature, fifteenth century. Published by Delasilve, "Une acclamation liturgique notée," in *RCGr.*, 12 (1906), 197.

15. Rouen, Bibl. Munic. MS 256, fifteenth century. Published in *Graduel de Rouen*, Vol. I, Facsimile, Pls. IV–VIII, and p. 202.

16. Rouen, version of the seventeenth or eighteenth century. Published in *Graduel de Rouen*, I, 202.

17. Modern laudes for the coronation of Pope Pius X, 1903. Printed Rome, Forzan & Cie., 1903.

18. Modern laudes, two versions as printed in *Chants divers pour les saluts du très saint sacrement* (3d ed.; Tournai, Desclée, 1924) pp. 251, 252.

Of these laudes the music of the Soissons version (no. 8), the elaborate Worcester version (no. 10), and the interesting variant of Palermo (no. 13) appear in full at the end of this study. Only relevant sections of the others will be given in transcription.

FORM

The general outlines of the laudes resemble the litanies with their series of invocations of the saints. The historical relations between the Litany of the Saints and the laudes have been discussed extensively (pp. 34 ff.). The artistic similarities between the two forms strike the eye immediately: both have a tripartite main body flanked by an introductory and a closing section. Both employ the contrast of a group of soloists and the responding chorus. Both make use of the *seriatim* principle.

The introductory section of the Litany consists of the *Kyrie eleison*, *Christe exaudi nos*, and the invocations concluded each time with *miserere nobis*. The first main part is formed by the series of saints to which the response *ora pro nobis* is sung. This first part is the longest. The middle part is characterized by the *libera nos* response. The third part contains the series beginning consistently with *ut* and ending with the *audi nos* response. The closing section starts with the *Agnus dei* and is rounded off by the return to the *Christe audi nos* of the introduction.

---

[17] Friedrich Ludwig drew attention to this version of the laudes in his *Repertorium organorum* (Halle, 1910), I, 230.

Thus, the Litany of the Saints is a well-organized artistic whole. Its all-pervading spirit is that of submission and contrition. In contrast to the spirit of humility the character of the laudes can be described as almost aggressive. The militant exuberance leaves no place for submission, and even the series of saints which the two litanies have in common is followed here not by *ora pro nobis*, but by *Tu illum adiuva* which, in the general setting, acquires almost the strength of a command.[18]

The general mood is set by the triumphant tricolon *Christus vincit, Christus regnat, Christus imperat* which forms the introduction and recurs as a refrain throughout the whole. It is thrice repeated. Threefold division, as established by the beginning, is carried through much more systematically in the laudes than in the litany. The first main part contains the acclamations. The subdivisions of the first part vary in number according to the number of persons acclaimed. There are usually four or five subdivisions for the pope, the ruler, his consort, the bishop and clergy, and, as a rule, the army. Each is begun by the bold *Exaudi Christe* and continued by the recitation in which the acclaimed are directly addressed by name. Each acclamation is followed in turn by a series of saints. The series is frequently opened by the call to either the *Salvator*[19] or the *Redemptor Mundi*. Then follow the individual saints. It is interesting to note that the number of saints is frequently, but not always, restricted to three. In the most highly organized laudes, however, the number was three, in keeping with the general triadic scheme, as in Autun (no. 1), Fécamp (no. 5), Soissons (no. 8), and Worcester (no. 10).

The *laudes Christi* form the central part of the chant. The response to the short laudatory exclamations constantly repeats the refrain *Christus vincit*.

The third and last part consists of the doxology *Ipsi soli . . . secula seculorum, amen*, again sung three times in slightly different wordings, each repeated by the chorus. With the doxology which might be rounded off, as in England, by another repetition of the *Christus vincit* formula the laudes proper are concluded.

The closing part might consist of several appendices. One of them is typical of the episcopal laudes. This addition begins with the words *Te pastorem* or *Hunc diem*. It is significant to observe that the refrain formula is here no longer taken from the *Christus vincit* but now changes to *Deus*

---

[18] This is true almost literally. In the Byzantine army, where Latin was the language of command at least until the eighth century, the imperative *adiuta* was shouted at a charge of the troops. When the attacking army had approached the enemy at arrow's shot, the commanding officer would give the command *parati!*, whereupon one soldier had to shout *adiuta* while the army responded with *Deus* and then charged. Cf. Ernst Stein, *Studien zur Geschichte des byzantinischen Reiches* (Stuttgart, 1919), 132. [E.H.K.]

[19] Cf. above, p. 45, n. 114.

conservet.[20] The second closing section is the so-called polychronion *multos annos, tempora bona.*[21] It does not always appear in the formularies. A third manner of closing consists of a threefold *Kyrie* and *Christe audi nos* as sung in the litany. The laudes do not necessarily contain all three concluding appendices. Some manuscripts, such as Bibl. Nat. Lat. MS 13159 and Fécamp (no. 5), record all three sections, while others, such as Worcester (no. 10), Palermo (no. 13), and Rouen (no. 15), omit them altogether.

The version of the Sarum use from Worcester (no. 10), the most consistent and artistic variant of the laudes, deserves special attention. The outlines of the form are precisely the same as given above. However, the triadic scheme is pushed to its extreme by a judicious insertion of the *Christus vincit, Christus regnat, Christus imperat* formula from beginning to end.

While ordinarily the extolling *Christus vincit* tricolon is heard only once for the introduction, it appears here at the beginning of every subsection of the first part before *Exaudi.* The Worcester laudes have altogether five subsections, each with a series of three saints.[22] The central part, the *laudes Christi,* is also strictly organized in a threefold division. For the usual *Christus vincit* responses a progressive refrain is substituted which uses in turn the verbs *vincit, regnat,* and *imperat.* Thus textual and musical variety is achieved. The procedure is repeated, as is to be expected, three times, so that three times three *laudes Christi* result. The triadic structure of the central part is a unique feature of the English specimens,[23] because its organization usually follows the archaic *seriatim* principle, without any prescribed length.

The third doxological part likewise displays the usual ternary structure. In Worcester, however, each sentence of the doxology is answered by the full tricolon *Christus vincit, Christus regnat, Christus imperat,* which concludes the whole acclamation exactly as it was begun. There is no appendix or closing section which would have destroyed the balance of the form.[24]

Since the style of the music might be either syllabic or neumatic, the

[20] The laudes of Worcester judiciously use the phrase *Deus conservet* at two places only. The acclamations for the king, the queen, and the army end with *salus et vita* or *salus et victoria,* whereas the two acclamations for the archbishop and the bishop end with *Deus conservet.* The wording clearly indicates that a relic of the episcopal laudes has survived in the *laudes regiae* of the Sarum use. Cf. above, pp. 113 ff., 123.

[21] Cf. above, p. 20.

[22] The last series of saints seemingly forms an exception to the rule because four names appear in the manuscript. This fact, however, is due to a mistake of the scribe. The name of St. Dunstan which belongs to the second series is erroneously repeated in the last series and must be deleted.

[23] Cf. above, p. 19, n. 15.

[24] The failure to recognize the form of the laudes seems to be the reason for the faulty transcription by Dom Mocquerau in the *Paléographie musicale,* XII, 74–75.

textual organization determines the musical. The threefold *Christus vincit* formula which governs the text and its ternary form governs likewise the music of the laudes. There are basically only two musical ideas that make up the threefold formula:

The second musical idea follows directly with:

The music for *Christus vincit* and *Christus regnat* is identical, the *Christus imperat* employs the significant cadence to the lower fourth descending from the *tonus currens, tenor,* or *tuba.* This cadential figure is of the greatest importance for the music of the laudes. The identical cadence is used for the invocations of the *Salvator* or *Redemptor Mundi* which often introduce the series of saints. It is similarly sung to the name of each saint and musically repeated in the chorus's response *Tu illum adiuva.* Thus, this cadence is the most frequently repeated musical figure of the laudes. It appears both with the same and with changed words in alternation.

In contrast to the manifold use made of the music to *Christus vincit-imperat,* the music of the *Exaudi Christe* stands quite by itself and does not appear with any other text. In all versions the music here reaches the highest point of the entire melody as is appropriate for this invocation. The music of the acclamation proper which names the pope and the ruler is always composed in strict psalmodic style on the *tonus currens.* Only strongly accented words receive an accent by means of a higher note as *a déo coronato* or *víta et victoria.* The recitative is concluded again by the same music as is heard with *Christus imperat.* This recurrent cadence has been indicated in the transcriptions by square brackets.

The music of the central part, the *laudes Christi,* is ordinarily derived from the *Christus vincit* formula which consists only of the *tonus currens* with its lower and higher inflection. Sometimes, however, the *laudes Christi* end with the music of the *imperat* cadence, as in Soissons (no. 8) and in Fécamp (no. 5). The alternation of the *imperat* and the *vincit* cadence makes this form musically more attractive. The *laudes Christi* receive, moreover, more emphasis.

The doxology is composed on the *tenor*, but ordinarily with more freedom than at the other places where the *tonus currens* is used. The leading up to the *tenor* from the second below is noteworthy. This peculiarity makes the impression of a rudimentary *initium* which is otherwise not found in the *laudes*. I shall come back to the question of the *initium* in the discussion of the different *tenores* of the laudes.

The possible appendages either follow the same formulas as previously employed in the main body of the laudes or have music of their own. The refrain of the episcopal laudes *Deus conservet* usually follows the melodic pattern of the *imperat* formula which is the same music as the *Tu illum adiuva* of the acclamatory response. This is also true of the Durandus laudes, although they differ essentially in other respects. The music of the *Kyrie* appendix forms a striking contrast to the musical style of the laudes. It is the only melismatic section of the music, and is thus easily recognizable as something that does not really belong to the laudes proper. The melody used has nothing to do with the formulas of the laudes. Melodic analysis will bring out the appendix character of the *Kyrie* much more than the mere consideration of the text alone.[25] The phrase *Christe audi nos* makes it at once clear that the *Kyrie* section must be a part of the litany and not of the *Kyrie* of the Ordinary. This statement will be confirmed by melodic comparisons. For the discussion of the formal side it may suffice to point out the fact that the *Kyrie* section is an appendix. It must be regarded as a survival of the times in which the laudes had not yet broken out of the framework of the litany.[26] The high degree of unity which can be observed throughout the music of the laudes corresponds exactly to the textual structure of the form.

[25] See the discussion of the *Kyrie* below, p. 208.

[26] The *Kyrie eleison* in connection with the laudes is found in all Carolingian and German formularies except the laudes of Chieti (see above, p. 105, n. 130) and of those in the Munich Cod. Lat. 14322 (see above, p. 99, n. 118). In France it is found, for instance, in Beauvais, Arles, Nevers, and Rheims; but it is missing in Autun, Limoges, Narbonne, Chartres, Paris, as well as in the form of Ivrea. Furthermore, the *Kyrie* is missing in the Sicilian, Norman, and English laudes, in those of Dalmatia and of Aquileia, and in all the Franco-Roman forms (except those transmitted by Benedict of St. Peter's), including the formulary of *Cencius II*. However, the papal laudes and the papalized imperial forms do have the *Kyrie*. The material offered here is fragmentary, since the writer of this study was heedless of the problem before the musical investigation had been carried through by Professor Bukofzer. It would be premature to draw any conclusions; the surmise, however, may be advanced that the *Kyrie*, although musically a stranger in the laudes proper, goes back to the early union of laudes and Litany of the Saints in Carolingian times and thus survived above all in the empire. When transferred to other countries (Sicily, Normandy, England, Dalmatia) as well as to Rome, the laudes lost the *Kyrie* which in fact has nothing to do with these acclamations. Its reappearance in the papal (and papalized imperial) laudes may be due to the fact that these forms were made similar to the Litany of the Saints; see also the episcopal laudes of Minden (p. 123, n. 36), as well as above, p. 88, notes 73, 74, and below, p. 208. [E.H.K.]

PERFORMANCE

All sources of the laudes that give us any indications of the performance at all, agree in assigning the singing to two responsorial groups. The chanting of the laudes is performed in responsorial style, namely solo recitation with chorus response. The classification of the laudes as responsorial is not quite unequivocal. In strictly responsorial music only one soloist sings the solo sections and the whole chorus answers him. In the laudes there are almost without exception at least two solo singers.[27] In this respect the laudes again resemble the litany, which is likewise performed by two soloists in constant alternation with the chorus. The practice of having a small group of soloists in opposition to the chorus leans toward the antiphonal practice of singing in two alternating half-choruses. Nevertheless, the singing of the litany and the laudes is responsorial in principle. The rubrics of the laudes manuscripts, however, sometimes specify a much greater number of singers for the solo group than two. The Durandus formulary[28] prescribes the precentor, four good adult singers plus four boys for the solo group; that means altogether nine singers. The effect of this particular performance would be practically antiphonal singing.

We observe here the straddling of border lines which makes the exact liturgical classification of the laudes so difficult. The same ambiguity is reflected in the melodic style which might be either syllabic or neumatic.

The Narbonne version[29] assigns the singing of the soloists' sections to four older men of the chorus and requires for the response not the whole chorus but only four boys. In this rather exceptional case we have an almost completely soloistic performance. Usually the boys enhance the timbre of the solo group. In the performance of Narbonne the timbre of the men's voices is set off by the bright color of the boys' group. This dramatic juxtaposition of tone color is also known from the singing of sequences which came up during the ninth century.[30]

The response of the chorus *Christus vincit* or *Tu illum* might have been originally a response of the whole congregation. As early as the first quarter of the ninth century, however, it was the business of the specially trained chorus of clerics. The congregation was only a passive onlooker

---

[27] The rubrics are discussed above, pp. 121 f. The laudes of Paris, late twelfth century, Bibl. Nat. Lat. MS 9505, fol. 82, have the following rubric: "Sequitur Triumphus qui nunquam nisi celebrante Episcopo cantatur. De duobus vel tribus subdiaconis sericis indutis cantatur, pueris post eos respondentibus." See, however, above, p. 133, for the cardinal prior of San Lorenzo as soloist.

[28] See above, no. 12 (Durandus).

[29] See above, no. 7 (Narbonne).

[30] Also the *laudes hymnidicae* (see above, pp. 73 f.) are sequences. For the performance, see Peter Wagner, *Einführung in die gregorianischen Melodien* (3d ed.; 1911), I, 263; III, 483.

and listener.[31] The only action recorded in the manuscripts is given in some rubrics which prescribe that the whole congregation shall rise.[32] Standing during the performance of the laudes thus contrasts with the performance of the litany for which prostration is required, quite in keeping with the general spirit of the litany.[33] No further action for the singing of the laudes is indicated in the sources. The episcopal laudes, coming after the completion of the *laudes regiae*, prescribe that the two soloists advance toward the throne of the archbishop in order to receive the presbyterium, walking slowly enough to arrive at the foot of the throne as the music ends.[34] Here the altar of the church becomes almost a stage. This dramatization of the liturgical action has its parallel in the liturgical plays for Christmas, New Year, and Easter which became so numerous in the tenth and the following centuries.[35] It is not by coincidence that acclamations are preserved in tropers such as St. Gall MS 381, and British Museum Egerton MS 2615 which also contain liturgical plays. The latter manuscript contains the highly dramatized Office of Beauvais for New Year, a day on which the laudes were sung in this cathedral.

We learn from the Durandus formulary one important fact about the manner of singing the laudes. It not only insists that the soloists must be good singers, but adds that they intone *alta voce*. The performance of the laudes with clamorous voices is quite in keeping with the triumphant character of the whole prayer. It might be expected that the solo recitation had to be rather loud, judging from the fact that not necessarily professional singers, but knights and even the cellarer might take the lead in the laudes.[36] Such chanters would sing the soloists' part, if not beautifully, at least forcefully.

Here again the performance of the laudes stands in striking contrast to that of the litany. The recitation for the litany is carried out *sotto voce* in humble softness, the voice being muffled by prostration or the bowed heads of the singers. In the performance of plainsong in general the proper

---

[31] Cf. the Cologne and Verona manuscripts, above, p. 86. On the participation of the congregation in the singing of the chant see Wagner, *op. cit.*, I, 73, Besseler, *Musik des Mittelalters und der Renaissance* (1931–1935), 80, and Ursprung, *Katholische Kirchenmusik*, (1931–1933), 57, and 99.

[32] The laudes of Ponthion (876) expressly refer to the standing up of the congregation (see above, p. 70). Also the rubric of the Soissons laudes (no. 8) specifies before the acclamation of the pontiff: *hic surgant omnes si pontifex presens fuerit.* See above, p. 79, n. 45, for the Council of Tribur (895), and *Avellana*, No. CIII, § 30, *CSEL.*, XXXV, 487, for a Roman council (495).

[33] The prostration is discussed above, pp. 90 f.

[34] See above, pp. 121 f.

[35] Coussemaker, *Drames liturgiques du moyen âge*, 1860; E. K. Chambers, *The Mediaeval Stage*, 1903, II; Karl Young, *The Drama of the Medieval Church*, 1933; Otto Ursprung, *op. cit.*, p. 76; cf. La Piana, above, p. 49, n. 125.

[36] See above, p. 31, n. 61.

intensity of the voice for the different prayers was required. Thus the *Musica Enchiriades* of the ninth century says: "nam affectus rerum quae canitur, oportet ut imitetur cantionis affectus, ut in tranquillis rebus tranquillae sunt neumae, laetisonae in iucundis, moerentes in tristibus."[37] A tract on music ascribed to Odo of Cluny (d. 942) and also to Berno of Reichenau (d. 1048) remarks similarly: "in tractu vero et gradalibus plane et protense humiliataque voce incedere videtur."[38]

MELODIC COMPARISON

Style.—Although the melodic versions of the laudes show a common origin in principle they may vary in regard to the melodic style. Some of the versions are extremely syllabic, others highly neumatic. In the discussion of Dom Pothier[39] three versions are compared. The first one, allegedly the version of the eleventh century, is obviously taken from the article by Delasilve,[40] who published the fifteenth-century laudes of Troyes. Pothier contends that syllabic style characterizes the oldest form of the laudes and substitutes the version of the fifteenth century for the really archaic version of the eleventh century. While it is true that neumatic style generally appears in later forms of the chant, the scheme of development as traced by Pothier cannot be accepted without qualifications. Although the early clefless neumes cannot be transcribed with any degree of certainty so far as the pitches are concerned, they do permit us to recognize clearly the melodic style of the music. Several versions of the tenth and eleventh centuries are preserved of which only the Autun formulary (no. 1) is strictly syllabic. The Fécamp version of the eleventh century has a neumatic group on the second syllable of *Christus*. Apparently, syllabic and neumatic forms existed side by side. The preponderance of the slightly neumatic versions of the *Christus vincit* over the strictly syllabic forms makes the moderately neumatic style the most important.

In table 1 (p. 200), the three most syllabic versions are compared (nos. 1, 2, and 14). Since the music of the *Christus vincit* formula and the following *Exaudi Christe* supply the basis of the whole chant, only these sections are offered. It should be kept in mind that the first two give definite information only about the numbers of the notes. The Limoges version (no. 2) is diastematically notated, but it is not clear whether the cadence on *adiuva* falls to the fourth or the fifth.

The syllabic versions show the character of the *Christus vincit-imperat*

---

[37] Gerbert, *Scriptores ecclesiastici de musica*, 1784 (Facs. ed.; 1931), I, 172. The treatise is not by Hucbald.
[38] Gerbert, *op. cit.*, I, 276.
[39] *Graduel de Rouen*, p. 202.
[40] *RCGr.*, XII (1906), 197.

formula in its bare outlines, (1) recitation on one tone with its lower inflection (whole tone), and (2) at the end the cadence of a fourth. The call *Exaudi Christe* is always composed neumatically, even in the other-

TABLE 1

wise syllabic versions. The neume is indicated in the transcriptions by means of a slur.

In table 2 the moderately neumatic versions are compiled (nos. 4, 5, 7, 8, 9, and 11). The group of two either ascending or descending notes might appear in these versions either to the first or second syllable of *Christus* (nos. 4, 8, 9, and 11) or on the first syllable of *vincit* (nos. 5 and 7). In the Fécamp version (no. 5) the neumatic group appears twice on *vincit* and the third time on *Christus*. It should be noted that each

TABLE 2

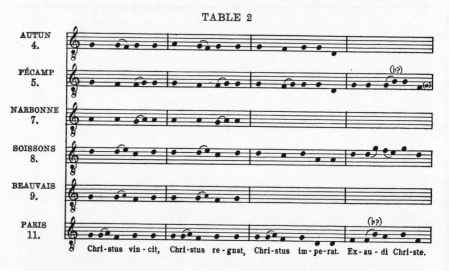

section of the *Christus vincit, Christus regnat, Christus imperat* formula contains only a single neume, quite in contrast to the highly neumatic versions.

The three highly neumatic versions are nos. 10, 13, and 15. They approach melismatic style. Each single syllable is supplied with a group of two and even three notes.[41]

The three versions are practically the same melodies except for the final cadence to the fifth in the Palermo version which will be discussed later. It is significant that all melodies preserve the fundamental struc-

TABLE 3

Chri - stus vin - cit, Chri-stus re - gnat, Chri-stus im - pe - rat. Ex-au - di Chri - ste.

ture of the formula in spite of melodic elaboration. The greatest variety is shown in the melody of *Exaudi Christe*. Comparing the versions from tables 1, 2, and 3 we observe that in all versions the syllable -*au*- has a group of two or three notes which is always ascending. The upward skip varies between a third or a fourth, and the descending cadence might similarly fall to the fourth or to the third, the former being the favored cadence. The insistence on the fourth tallies with the cadential fourth in the *Christus imperat* formula, so that we have here two structural fourths of the following pattern:

The structure cannot be explained as a system of tetrachords that survived possibly from ancient Greek music.[42] However, it should be noted that the primitive interval structure of a fourth is consistently adhered to, and the only variation is achieved by means of transposition. The structural fourth is simply transposed a third higher for the music of *Exaudi Christe*. This kind of transposition within a melody must be regarded as an archaic feature of melodic organization. The upper fourth is reached either from the *tonus currens* directly by going up a third and falling to the fourth at the end (nos. 13 and 14), or it is approached from the tone below the *tonus currens* by skipping up and falling by a fourth (nos. 10, 11, and 15).[43]

---

[41] The notes in small print indicate liquescent notes in the original notation (the so-called *plica* of polyphonic music). For the liquescent signs in plainsong notation, see Peter Wagner, "Der Gregorianische Gesang," *Handbuch der Musikgeschichte*, ed. Guido Adler, 1930, I, 94.

[42] See Wagner, *op. cit.*, III, 27.

[43] No. 10 forms an exception in that it falls to the third, not to the fourth.

The Tuba or Tenor.—The term *tonus currens*, which is taken from the tone of recitation in the psalmody, is not used here to imply that the laudes are regulated by one of the psalm-tones. Peter Wagner has pointed out that liturgical recitations like the *Exultet* and the *Te Deum* do not fit any psalm-tone and that they originated at a time antedating the concern with the church modes.[44] This statement applies also to the laudes. In our particular case it can be said definitely that the laudes must come from a practice which was not yet touched by the psalm-tones. One of the most important factors in the music of the laudes is the absence of the *initium*. The *initium* of the psalm-tone always leads up to the tenor from the note of the *finalis*. The *tonus currens* of the laudes begins in the good sources always without *initium*. Only the hybrid sources like the late Rouen form (no. 15), which is also textually a hybrid, begin the recitative section with a real *initium*.

The recitative sections of the laudes (the acclamation proper and the doxology) are similar to two important prayers of the Canon of the Mass: the preface *Vere dignum* and the *Pater noster*. The oldest (Mozarabic) form of the *Pater noster* and also the old prayer *Libera nos* of the Ambrosian service recite their texts on the tenor *a* without an *initium*.[45] The music of the syllabic section of the laudes is therefore practically the same. It should be kept in mind, however, that in the laudes the line *Ipsi soli* usually starts with the note below the tenor. This beginning might be considered an incipient form of *initium*, but the lower inflection of the tenor is touched upon in the recitation several times without ever developing into a full-fledged *initium*. The absence of the *initium* furnishes an important clue to the origin of the laudes music which will be discussed in a later paragraph.

Besides the *initium* the absolute pitch of the tenor is of significance. The *tonus currens* of the extant laudes is either *g* or *a*. The earliest sources unfortunately, do not give us any help in determining the pitch. Nevertheless the archaic Troyes version (no. 14) stands on *g* in the manuscript not on *a* as the printed edition indicates. The transposition was made by Delasilve in order to conform with the unreliable, and undeservedly too popular, Rouen version (no. 15). The versions of Beauvais (no. 9) and of Paris (no. 11), both excellent French sources of the thirteenth century, also give *g*. A fourth manuscript, Soissons (no. 8), shows a remarkable

[44] Wagner, *op. cit.*, III, 27.
[45] *Ibid.*, III, 58, and 68.

deviation from the rule. The *Christus vincit, regnat, imperat* formula is always recited on *d*. This might be simply a transposition of the tenor from *a* to its lower fifth (or upper fourth). However, the *Exaudi Christe* rises from *d* to its upper fourth and the following acclamations recite on the tenor *g*. Consequently, the Soissons version belongs to the group of laudes in which the tenor stands, at least in part, on *g*. Double tenors such as the one used in the Soissons version are not uncommon in the psalmody. The music of the preface, the *Pater noster*, and the litany is sometimes built on a double *tonus currens*.[46] But in the laudes the Soissons version is the only one known to employ a double tenor.

Since four good sources stand on *g*, among them the archaic one of Troyes, the clefless manuscripts have been transcribed likewise on *g*. They might, of course, equally well be put on any other degree, and no claim is made that the transcriptions offered are final as regards the pitch. It might very well be that the intervals of the *Exaudi Christe* should be transcribed to agree with the Soissons version, with or without a double tenor. The other versions of the laudes recite on *a* (nos. 7, 10, 13, and 15). It has been claimed that the tone of recitation on *g* was characteristic of the Ambrosian psalmody.[47] Yet, while tenors on *g* are not rare, recitations on *a* are at least equally frequent in the Ambrosian and also Mozarabic chants. It might be pointed out that a certain archaism is connected with *g* as the tenor of a psalmody. Apparently, *g* was the original *tuba* of both the fourth psalm-tone and the litany which had to give way later on to *a* and *c* respectively.[48]

The importance of the tenor pitch should not be exaggerated. It is relevant only for the different forms of what has been styled the subtonal and subsemitonal recitations.[49] The difference lies in the higher and lower inflection of the tenor. If *g* is the tenor, the higher and lower neighbor are both whole tones, the inflection thus being either subtonal or supertonal. If *f* is the tenor, its higher neighbor would be *g*, a whole tone, its lower *e*, a half tone, the inflection thus being supertonal and subsemitonal respectively. Wagner has shown that the line of development runs consistently from the original tonal to the younger semitonal inflection.[50] It is not surprising to find that the music of the laudes confirms his observation. All laudes recite subtonally except the version of the Durandus manuscript (no. 12) which shows the tenor on *f* with subsemitonal inflection. The thirteenth century was particularly fond of the modern subsemitonal recitation. In the thirteenth century it was incorporated in the Dominican

---

[46] *Ibid.*, III, 63, 71, 263.
[47] Delasilve, *loc. cit.*, p. 202.
[48] Wagner, *op. cit.*, III, 110, 27.
[49] *Ibid.*, III, 26.
[50] *Ibid.*, III, 524.

reform of the chant,[51] and it seems likely that version no. 12 dates from this time. The laudes of Zara (no. 6) of the early twelfth century cannot be considered in this connection because the printed transcription seems to chose the tenor *c* arbitrarily. If correctly transcribed, this tenor would also recite with the subsemitone.[52]

However, the great majority of the laudes recite subtonally. The versions with the tenor on *a* do not differ from those on *g* in this respect. While the supertonal inflection of the tenor on *g* is beyond question, upper inflection of the tenor *a* might be either *b flat* or *b natural*. Only the late sources like no. 16 actually prescribe a *b flat*. The tritonal effect achieved by the omission of the flat speaks again for a certain archaism in the music of the laudes. The tritone is one of the characteristic intervals of the Ambrosian chant. Also in the tenors on *g* most of the sources do not indicate a *b flat*. Only in the Troyes version of the fifteenth century is it prescribed. Troyes might be archaic in respect to the syllabic style of the melody, but modern in respect to the harmonic interpretation. The absence of the *b flat* in the versions on *g* creates a marked tritone skip on *Exaudi Christe* and by no means can it be proved that we have to supply a flat as a matter of course. In contrast to the slight tritonal effect[53] which results from the supertonal inflection of the tenor *a*, the tritone in the *g* version appears in the structural interval and, therefore, might well be intentional.

It has been noted before that the recitation sections follow the tenor closely, but that the tonic accent of important words usually receives careful consideration. In this respect the tenor of the free recitatives like the laudes and the *Exultet* shows a marked independence of the stereotyped cadential inflections (like *flexa* and *mediatio*) as used in the strict psalm-tones. In the recitation of the psalm-tones the tonic accent is sometimes deliberately disregarded, particularly at the final cadence. Here the musical formula governs the declamation: "omnis enim tonorum depositio in finalibus mediis vel ultimis *non est secundum accentum verbi,* sed secundum musicalem melodiam toni facienda."[54] Different stages of flexible declamation can be discerned in the laudes. The early version from Autun (no. 1) clearly considers the tonic accent of important words. The

---

[51] *Ibid.,* III, 41.

[52] The version of Zara is so irregular that, for the present, it cannot be taken into consideration until the transcription has been verified. The modern polyphonic version of the laudes in Zara, given in Zaninovitch's article (p. 133), are of some interest. The author fails to point out that the melody lies in the lower voice, the tenor. It preserves, at least in rudimentary form, the melodic formula, but in the modern subsemitonal inflection. The clef of the tenor is incorrectly printed as baritone clef. It must be the regular bass clef.

[53] Also Pothier (*Graduel de Rouen,* p. 201) points out that the *b* in the Rouen version is simply an escape note without harmonic importance.

[54] *Instituta patrum de modo psallendi* (tenth century) in Gerbert, *op. cit.,* I, 6 b.

word "important" should be stressed because the accent is not brought out for every word, but usually only for the significant ones. Thus the Autun version (no. 1) deviates from the rigid tenor as follows:

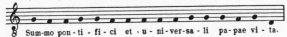

Sum-mo pon - ti - fi - ci et · u - ni - ver-sa - li pa-pae vi - ta.

The version of Troyes (no. 14) is the only one which recites on the tenor without any inflection. Comparison with the oldest laudes preserved shows that this part of the Troyes version cannot be archaic. Apparently the rigid recitation of the psalm-tone has influenced the recitation of the Troyes laudes, but only the recitation section, not the rest of the melody.[55]

A point of considerable interest comes to light if the recitative sections of Beauvais (no. 9) and Rouen (no. 15) are compared with the one from Worcester (no. 10). Whenever the tonic accents of the words are expressed in the music by a higher note, the departure from the tenor is usually not greater than a whole or a half step. In many northern sources, however, the accent is more emphatically stressed by raising the step to a skip of a third. Peter Wagner was the first to draw attention to the difference between northern and southern dialect in Gregorian chant.[56] Wagner associated the "Germanic" dialect primarily with German sources although it is found also in English manuscripts.[57] In the following table the versions quoted above are superimposed. It shows that in the Worcester version the step of the "Romanic" dialect is consistently raised to a skip, and, in addition, the skip of a third on *im*mortalia appears as a fourth.

TABLE 4

BEAUVAIS 9.

WORCESTER 10.

NB. NB. NB. NB. NB.

Ip - si so - li im-pe - ri - um glo-ri - a - que po - tes - tas per im-mor-ta - li - a se - cu - la.

ROUEN 15.

---

[55] The statement of Delasilve (*loc. cit.*, 202) that the Rouen version "n'est que la mélodie troyenne enrichie" is not quite correct and must be qualified so far as the recitative section is concerned. The recitation in Troyes appears to be a reduction of the originally more flexible recitation in the old laudes compositions. It follows that Pothier's tacit assumption that the Troyes version represents the most archaic stage of the melody must be questioned. Pothier presents the Troyes version on the table (*Graduel de Rouen*, p. 202) as "la forme syllabique du premier âge, c'est-à-dire des Xe et XIe siècles" without qualification and without notifying the reader that the melody is transposed from the original tuba *g* to *a*.

[56] "Germanisches und Romanisches im mittelalterlichen Chorgesang," *Bericht über den 1. musikwissenschaftlichen Kongress der Deutschen Musikgesellschaft*, Leipzig, 1926.

[57] Wagner's sweeping statement that the English were on the side of the "Romanic" dialect (*op. cit.*, p. 22) must be rejected. The Worcester version of the laudes proves

A similar expansion of the basic intervals can be observed in the music of the laudatory paıt of the Worcester laudes. In no other version is the music to *Rex regum, Rex noster*, and so on, so exuberant as here.

The Melodic Formula.—After having considered the tenor of the laudes we turn to the *Christus vincit, Christus regnat, Christus imperat* formula. No similar formulas can be found in the otherwise similar chants of the *Te Deum* and the *Exultet*. Both use an *initium* foreign to the laudes. The connoisseur of the psalm-tones might at once think of the fourth tone which resembles the *Christus vincit-imperat* music. But it has been pointed out above that the laudes originated before the time in which the psalm-tones began to be systematized.[58] In the *Commemoratio brevis de tonis et psalmis modulandis*[59] the fourth tone is supplied with an *initium* like all the other psalm-tones. A recitation using this archaic form with *initium* can be found in the oldest music of the *Gloria in excelsis*.[60] The music of the laudes comes from another stratum of the chant. The only musical parallels can be found outside of the Roman sphere in the Mozarabic, Ambrosian, and Gallican forms of the chant. They recite like the laudes without *initium*, within the structural interval of the fourth. The frame interval of the fourth can also be found in the *tonus ferialis* of the Ambrosian lessons which consists of nothing but a recitation on the tenor and a cadence on the lower fourth.[61]

The *Christus vincit-imperat* formula recites in its first half with the lower (and naturally always subtonal) inflection, and falls in its second half to the fourth. This skip downward might be filled in by steps, as in the neumatic versions, or stand by itself. In table 5 the oldest formulas of the Mozarabic *Pater noster*,[62] the Ambrosian salutation[63] of the Mass,

that the English followed, at least in this case, the "Germanic" dialect. The narrow term "Germanic" should be replaced by the broader term "Northern."

[58] The earliest treatise dealing with psalmody was written by Aurelian of Réomé in the ninth century; see Gerbert, *op. cit.*, I, 42 ff., and also Wagner, *op. cit.*, III, 83.

[59] Probably of the ninth century by an anonymous author, not Hucbald; see Gerbert, *op. cit.*, I, 213.

[60] *Graduale Romanum*, No. XV, in festis simplicibus.

[61] *Antiphonale missarum juxta ritum Sanctae Ecclesiae Mediolanensis* (Rome, 1935), 623. This is possibly the most archaic formula of recitation in the whole chant. It is also found in primitive music.

[62] Quoted by Wagner, *op. cit.*, III, 58. Wagner does not refer to the source from which his quotation is taken. However, in his article "Der mozarabische Kirchengesang und seine Ueberlieferung," *Spanische Forschungen der Görresgesellschaft*, 1. Reihe, I (1928), 137, Wagner describes a *Pater noster* formula from the *Missale Mixtum* (1500) which seems to be identical with the one quoted. If so, a difficulty arises. The *Pater noster* of the *Missale Mixtum* was published in facsimile by Germán Prado in his study "Mozarabic Melodics," *Speculum*, III, (1928), 228. This version recites on *d*, not on *a* as does the Wagner version. There are some additional divergencies. Prado points out that *Pater noster* as sung in the liturgy of today differs from the version of the *Missale Mixtum*. Wagner either quotes the present-day melody

the *tonus evangelii,* and the response of the Ambrosian litany[64] are compared with the syllabic and melismatic forms of the laudes formula.

The main point in comparing the music is not the correspondence of the few notes which is clear enough, but the fact that all the compared sections represent repeated formulas. Gastoué has drawn attention to the correspondence of the music to *Exaudi Christe* with the music of the Gallican *preces.*[65] Thus, the two main formulas of the laudes do not belong to the Gregorian chant proper, namely the Roman chant, but to the non-Roman periphery of the chant of which the Mozarabic, Ambrosian, and Gallican forms are the main constituents.

TABLE 5

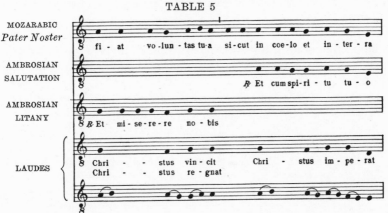

It is not by coincidence that the modern Roman papal laudes (no. 17) do not adhere to the formula of the old laudes. The papal laudes are styled after the music of the litany. The only difference lies in the tenor. The litany recites in the modern fashion on *c* subsemitonally while the laudes recite subtonally on *a.* But the music of *Tu illum adiuva* is otherwise identical with the response of the litany *ora pro nobis.* In this case the laudes have been completely "Romanized."

A glance at the version of Palermo[66] (no. 13) shows that the cadence to

---

which is of ancient origin or transcribes the version of the *Missale Mixtum* incorrectly.

[63] See *Antiphonale . . . Mediolanensis* (1935), 616 and 624. This melody differs from the one quoted by Zaninovitch (*loc. cit.,* 132) whose quotation seems to be based on the version given in Giulio Bas, *Manuale di canto ambrosiano* (1929), 4.

[64] *Antiphonale . . . Mediolanensis* (1935), 635.

[65] Gastoué, "Le chant gallican," *RCGr.,* XLIII (1939), 45.

[66] The music of the Palermo MS is notated with an exceptional *F*-clef. Usually the two vertical strokes of the *F* surround the *F*-line of the staff. In our case the lower stroke of the *F*-clef is sitting directly on the line. The clef indicates here an *F*-space, not an *F*-line. The above reading of the clef is confirmed by the occasional use of the *C*-clef. It should be noted that the laudes of Palermo appear in a manuscript that contains tropes and sequences. They are preceded by a trope to *Ave Maria* and followed by the old St. Martial sequence *Alma chorus Domini,* which is notable for its being composed in hexameters. This is another instance of the laudes appearing in the surroundings of tropers (see above, notes 4 and 5).

the lower fifth stands apart from all other known versions. If the version of Limoges (no. 2), discussed above (p. 199), should be transcribed as suggested in parentheses in table 1, there would be one important old parallel. The solution as given in parentheses seems, however, unlikely. All the more striking, then, is the unique cadence of the Palermo version. Other exceptional features are the abundance of liquescent notes, comparable only with the Worcester version, and the attempts at mensural notation of the music. Certain notes which accompany short syllables are written not as *longae* but as rhombic *breves* in order to indicate in the manner of a *cantus fractus* the shortness of the note values. The words follow all the same-pattern of long, two or three shorts, long:

$$\underline{}\ \breve{}\breve{}\underline{}\ \underline{}\ \underline{}\ \underline{}\breve{}\breve{}\underline{}\ \underline{}\breve{}\breve{}\underline{}\ \underline{}\breve{}\breve{}\breve{}\underline{}$$
Domino nostro, invictissimo, piissimo, indeficiens

At least a hint of mensural notation can also be observed in the Worcester version, but the notation is more equivocal than in the Palermo manuscript.

The Kyrie Appendix.—As stated before, the *Kyrie* does not always form an integral part of the laudes. The melodic style is always neumatic

TABLE 6

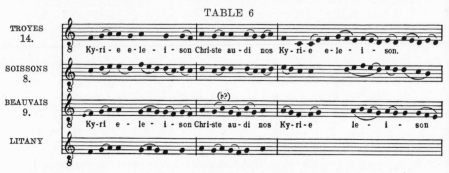

TROYES 14.

SOISSONS 8.

BEAUVAIS 9.

LITANY

Ky-ri - e e-le - i - son Chri-ste au - di nos Ky - ri- e   e - le - i - son.

or melismatic, thus forming a distinct contrast to the remainder of the laudes. The phrase *audi nos* is taken from the litany and suggests that the music might correspond to it also. This suggestion proves to be correct. The melodies of the *Kyrie* vary not only in the different laudes, but also in the different versions of the litany.[67] Nevertheless a close correspondence of some *Kyries* of the laudes with one of the litany can be easily observed. The first *Kyrie* of no. 14 tallies with nos. 9 and 8 (the latter standing a fifth higher). The Beauvais version (no. 9), in turn, is almost the same as the *Kyrie* of the litany preserved in a North Italian Carthusian manuscript of the twelfth century[68] (see above, table 6).

It should be noted that the tritone makes itself strongly felt at the

---

[67] Wagner, *op. cit.*, III, 260.
[68] *Ibid.*, III, 261 and II, 309.

Christe audi nos of the Beauvais version (no. 9). The two French sources nos. 8 and 9 are identical also in the last and usually most elaborate *Kyrie* which reads differently in version no. 14. The two French manuscripts thus show a certain relationship emphasized by the fact that both laudes recite on the archaic tenor *g*.

The contrast between the melodic style of the laudes proper and the *Kyrie* does not stand alone. A similar break can be observed if the tonal relations of the *Kyrie* to the preceding section are analyzed. None of the *Kyrie* fits tonally the formula of the laudes. They have different finals and different beginnings. The *Kyrie* examples quoted belong to laudes which recite on *g*. The melodies of the *Kyries*, however, do not adhere to the structural fourth *g–d*. Only the last *Kyrie* of no. 14 ends on *d* (the final of the laudes), yet reaching down to *c* at the beginning. The *Kyries* clearly set themselves off as an alien element in the laudes, both in regard to their melismatic melodic style and their tonal organization. Thus, the analysis of the music confirms the view expressed at the beginning (p. 196) that the *Kyrie* does not belong formally to the laudes.

Historical Conclusions

Having analyzed the music of the laudes we are now able to summarize the results in regard to the possible origin of the laudes. The most outstanding point is the correspondence of the laudes to the music of certain non-Roman formulas as found in the Mozarabic, Ambrosian, and Gallican rites. The interrelations between the Ambrosian and Mozarabic liturgy have been investigated by Bishop[69] and Wagner,[70] mainly on the basis of literary and liturgical sources. Rojo[71] and Prado tried to show musical correspondences, but their melodic comparisons do not rest on a solid foundation because our present knowledge of the melodies is still too restricted. The actual close kinship between the Ambrosian, Mozarabic, and Gallican chants can be more easily shown by pointing at the parallelism of the liturgies in general. Table 7[72] (p. 210) gives the terms used in the different rites for the chants of the Proper of the Mass. We see at once the singularity of the Roman terminology and the similarity between the three others. While these chants are all identical in their liturgical functions, their names vary in the different rites.

---

[69] W. C. Bishop, *The Mozarabic and Ambrosian Rites*, 1924.

[70] Peter Wagner, "Der mozarabische Kirchengesang . . . ,"*Spanische Forschungen der Görresgesellschaft*, 1. Reihe, I (1928), 102, and "Untersuchungen zu den Gesangstexten und zur responsorialen Psalmodie der altspanischen Liturgie," *ibid.*, II (1930), 67.

[71] Casiano Rojo and Germán Prado, *El Canto Mozárabe, Estudio histórico-critico de su antiguedad y estado actual* (Barcelona, 1929).

[72] After Wagner, "Der mozarabische Kirchengesang . . . ," *Spanische Forschungen*, 1. Reihe, I (1928), 129–130.

Gastoué has summarized the little that is known about the Gallican chant.[73] That it was related to the Mozarabic and Ambrosian more closely than to the Roman is certain, although many questions still remain to be answered.[74]

The music of the laudes has been called non-Roman for lack of a better term. What is meant is that the music does not conform with the Roman unification of plainsong which, beginning in the ninth century, eventually stamped out the regional dialects and brought about the unified version known as Gregorian chant. It might be pertinent to add that the term "Gregorian Chant," significantly enough, was first used in the ninth cen-

TABLE 7

ROMAN	AMBROSIAN	MOZARABIC	GALLICAN
Introitus	Ingressa	Praelegendum	Praelegendum
Graduale	Psalmellus	Psallendum	Responsorium
Alleluia cum Versu	Versus in Alleluia	Laudes	Laudes
Tractus	Cantus	Cantus	
Offertorium	Offertorium	Sonus (Sacrificium)	Sonus
	Confractorium	Confractorium	Confractorium
Communio	Transitorium	Accedentes	Trecanum

tury,[75] at a time when the tendency toward strict centralization became more and more obvious. The laudes cannot have originated in Rome because in that case the music would almost certainly be regulated by a psalmtone. The correspondence to the regional Ambrosian, Mozarabic, and Gallican dialects is so close that the evidence points definitely to a birthplace outside of Rome. The fact that the chant faithfully preserved its old or archaic features warrants the conclusion that Rome received the music from abroad without being able to destroy its idiomatic qualities: the archaic recitation on *g*, the subtonal recitation, the lack of an *initium*, the flexibility of tenor, and the recitation within the structural fourth.

---

[73] Gastoué, "Le chant gallican" *loc. cit.*, and also his *Histoire du chant liturgique à Paris* (Paris, 1904), I. See also J. B. Thibaut, *L'ancienne liturgie gallicane, son origine en Provence sous Cassien et St. Césaire d'Arles*, 1928.

[74] A chant that the Mozarabic and the Gallican rites have in common is the *preces* (see Rojo and Prado, *op. cit.*, p. 74, and Reese, *op. cit.*, p. 112 for a musical example). In the text of the *preces* the phrase *Exaudi Christe*, which is rare in the Roman liturgy, occurs several times in the *versus*:
        "Ad te clamantes *Exaudi Christe* . . . and
        Exaudi Christe rugitum nostrum . . .
See also Higini Anglès *El Còdex Musical De Las Huelgas* (1931), I, 12 ff., and *La Musica a Catalunya fins a Segle XIII* (1935), 36 ff. and 239 ff. Cf. Prado, in *Speculum*, III (1928), 235.

[75] Wagner, *Einführung*, I, 196, n. 2.

The music of the *Kyrie* permits us to draw some conclusions about the relations between the litany and the laudes. The presence of the *Kyrie* appendix represents a survival of the litany of which the laudes formed originally a part.[76] The musical contrast between the laudes and the *Kyrie* reflects the much greater contrast between the triumphant spirit of the laudes and the submissive spirit of the litany. While the laudes were certainly styled formally after the litany, their spirit and music were incompatible with their formal model. This fact comes out very clearly in the diametrically opposed manner of performance of the two prayers. A new, independent prayer was then created in the Visigothic or Gallican sphere, and it proved its inner strength by the resistance it offered to a potential Romanization when it was eventually sung in Rome. Some of the laudes never dropped the *Kyrie*, retaining it as a relic of the litany, whereas others, notably the most exuberant and highly neumatic versions, abandoned it and thus finally achieved independence and artistic unity.

THE INFLUENCE OF THE LAUDES ON OTHER MUSICAL FORMS

The text of the laudes eventually exercised an influence on several other forms. The influence on the finale of the *Praeconium paschale: Exultet jam angelica turba* has been discussed above.[77] A musical correspondence of the laudes to the *Exultet* finale cannot be observed. There are two other instances in which the laudes served as a model for other forms. The first refers to an antiphon belonging to the Feast of the Trinity. It is found in the Sarum Antiphonary[78] and has the short text:

> Spes nostra
> Salus nostra
> Honor noster
> O beata Trinitas!

The short exclamatory statements have the same textual structure as the laudatory part of the laudes and, moreover, the same phrases occur in both laudes and antiphon in the same order (see Appendix IV, p. 242). It should be emphasized that this Trinity antiphon does not exist in the Roman liturgy but apparently only in the Sarum rite. A polyphonic setting of *Spes nostra* is known to exist in the form of a three-voiced composition which uses the plainsong melody as *cantus firmus*. The piece was written by an anonymous English composer[79] of the early fifteenth cen-

---

[76] See the discussion on p. 196.
[77] See above, pp. 23 f. The music of the *Exultet* can be found in Wagner, *op. cit.*, III, 228.
[78] Worcester F. 160, *Paléographie musicale*, XII, 158.
[79] Bologna, Liceo Musicale, Cod. 37, no. 183. The composer is designated as *"de anglia."*

tury. Again, the nationality of the composer points to the English origin of the antiphon. If the text of the antiphon was really fashioned after the text of the laudes, it would be an additional argument in favor of their non-Roman origin.

How popular the text of the laudes must have been in the thirteenth century can be inferred from a curious and very clear quotation of the *Christus vincit-imperat* formula in a motet of the Notre Dame school.[80] The manuscript is of Franco-Spanish origin and dates from *ca.* 1250.[81] The two-voiced motet is based on the tenor *Domino quoniam* which borrows a section of the chant for its tenor in the typical fashion of a motet. The plainsong section on which the motet is constructed stems from the Easter gradual *Haec dies*,[82] one of the most solemn graduals of the entire liturgy. The *versus* of the gradual has the following text: *Confitemini Domino quoniam bonus, quoniam in saeculum misericordia eius.* The second and third word of the *versus* make up the whole text of the tenor and the music for these words corresponds with the plainsong note by note. The text of the duplum or upper voice comments upon the liturgical text of the gradual in the manner of a trope.[83] The new text clearly marks itself as an interpolation by taking up the first word of the liturgical text *Domino* and ending in assonance with the word *quoniam*.

> Dominus glorie
> resurgens hodie
> morte mortem domuit,
> aditum restituit
> vite iam perdite
> cuncti plaudite.
> *Christus victor*[84] superat, liberat,
> quos culpa ligaverat,
> triumphans *regnat, imperat.*

As is traditional in the early stage of motet development, the text is closely related to the original liturgical function of the gradual on which the composition is based. It furnishes a commentary on the resurrection of Christ. In our particular case the commentary is notable for the fact that it refers back to the liturgical phase which immediately preceded the singing of the gradual. The gradual is sung directly after the reading of

---

[80] Published by H. Husmann, "Die Motetten der Madrider Handschrift und deren geschichtliche Stellung," *Archiv für Musikforschung*, 2 (1937), 182.

[81] The manuscript, formerly in Toledo, bears the signature Madrid, Bibl. Nac. MS 20486 (*olim* Hh 167). A thorough description of the contents can be found in Ludwig, *Repertorium*, 125.

[82] *Graduale Romanum*, Dominica Resurrectionis.

[83] See Manfred F. Bukofzer, "Speculative Thinking in Mediaeval Music," *Speculum*, XVII (1942), 175, where special literature is quoted.

[84] The substitution of the noun *victor* for the verb *vincit* in this paraphrase serves to emphasize the idea of the victorious and triumphant Christ.

the Epistle, which in turn is preceded by the laudes. Examples of motet texts which quote preceding or following phases of the same liturgy do not occur very frequently. They show the tendency to emphasize the unity of outstanding Masses like the one for Easter. The quotation of the most important formula of the laudes is interwoven in the motet, the words *regnat, imperat* being placed in a strategic position: at the end. The quotation appears here as a commentary within a commentary which is a typical procedure of mediaeval elaboration. It should be observed that the word *triumphans* clearly indicates the full appreciation of the thirteenth century for the triumphant character of the laudes. In this connection it becomes doubly significant that in Paris, and only in Paris, the laudes were called by the special term *Triumphus*.[85]

Finally a word about polyphonic settings of the laudes. Only two settings are known to exist: one for two voices of Zara (see note 52), certainly not composed before *ca.* 1500; another preserved in a North Italian manuscript of the first half of the fifteenth century.[86] Its composer, Hugo de Lantins, was a well-known Flemish musician active in Italy around 1420. Lantins' *Christus vincit* is composed for three voices with a leading upper voice and two supporting (instrumental) parts. It is the earliest polyphonic setting of the laudes thus far known. Which one of the formularies was used as text cannot be decided so long as the manuscript is inaccessible. It is not improbable that the Durandus formulary, which was at that time popular in Italy, forms the basis of the composition. Lantins' melody bears no resemblance to any of the monophonic laudes. Although only the first three measures are at present available, it can be safely concluded that no traditional melody of the laudes is borrowed. The composition is written freely without *cantus firmus* in the Italian song-style of the early fifteenth century.

The Modern Versions of the Laudes

There are at least two modern versions of the laudes, both printed in *Chant Divers*.[87] The first, the "short acclamations," is a modern chant composition by A. Kunc which unfortunately enjoys official sanction. In an eclectic manner the music of the tricolon is composed around the common chord. The composer has rearranged the words to the following:

Christus vincit, Christus regnat,
Christus, Christus imperat.

---

[85] Cf. above, p. 3, see also, p. 196, n. 26.

[86] Bologna, Bibl. Univ. MS 2216, fols. 30ᵛ–31. A thematic catalogue of this manuscript is offered in Johannes Wolf, *Geschichte der Mensural-Notation* (1904), I, 203, from which the first three measures of the *Christus vincit* (no. 47) can be transcribed. Only the first two words of the text are given in the catalogue.

[87] Edited by F. Tourte and M. Kaltnecker (3d ed.; Tournai, Desclee & Cie. 1924), pp. 251, 252.

Through this small but telling change the austere strength of the three invocations has been sacrificed for a shallow symmetry of meter which the composer apparently held to be more "pleasing." The arrangement of Kunc's melody in four-part harmony by Nicola A. Montani[88] inflates the composition in a pseudo-Verdi style which is beyond criticism.

The second modern version, the long acclamations, fortunately adopt the old melody, yet in a version that does not exactly agree with any of the previously recorded ones. It appears to be modeled after the Troyes and Rouen melodies as published in the *Graduel de Rouen*.

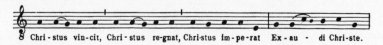

Chri - stus vin - cit, Chri - stus re-gnat, Chri-stus im - pe -rat   Ex - au - di Chri-ste.

The text seems to be a hybrid of the formulary of *Cencius II* (see below, Appendix IV) and the Gallo-Frankish forms. It is formally inferior.

The melody of the Rouen version (no. 16) has also been arranged in four-part harmony by Montani[89] with the same unfortunate textual addition as in the modern version quoted above. This arrangement neatly destroys the most characteristic and strongest feature of the melody, namely, its cadence to the lower fourth. Montani forces the melody to end on *f* in order to conform with modern key feeling. Incompetence in the matter of "harmonizing" the Gregorian chant could not be demonstrated by a more drastic example.

---

[88] *The St. Gregory Hymnal*, comp. by Nicola A. Montani (rev. ed.; Philadelphia, The St. Gregory Guild, Inc., 1940), No. 310.

[89] Montani, *op. cit.*, No. 248. To the harmonization a footnote is added stating that the melody dates from the year 1080 and was sung at the Council of Lillebonne for William the Conqueror, a claim that is without foundation (see above, p. 170, n. 56). Montani, in fact, made use of the Rouen version of the eighteenth century (no. 16)! Had he dated the melody at 1800 rather than 1080 he would have been closer to the truth.

LAUDES OF SOISSONS (no. 8)

Laudes of Soissons (no. 8)—*continued*

LAUDES OF WORCESTER (no. 10)

I

Chri-stus vin-cit, Chri-stus re-gnat, Chri-stus im-pe-rat. Ex-au-di Chri-ste!

Sum-mo pon-ti-fi-ci et u-ni-ver-sa-li pa-pe vi - ta

Sal-va-tor　mun - di　　Tu il-lum ad-iu-va.
Sanc-te　Pe - tre　　Tu il-lum ad-iu-va.
Sanc-te　Cle - mens　Tu il-lum ad-iu-va.
Sanc-te　Six - te　　Tu il-lum ad-iu-va.

Chri-stus vin-cit, Chri-stus re-gnat, Chri-stus im-pe-rat. Ex-au-di Chri-ste!

[Re-gi An-ge-lo-rum] a de-o co-ro-na-to sa-lus et vic-to-ri-a

Re-demp-tor mun - di　　Tu il-lum ad-iu-va.
Sanc-te Ae[d]-mun - de　Tu il-lum ad-iu-.va.
Sancte Er-min-gil - de　Tu il-lum ad-iu-va.
Sanc-te Os-wal - de　　Tu il-lum ad-iu-va.

Chri-stus vin-cit, Chri-stus re-gnat, Chri-stus im-pe-rat. Ex-au-di Chri-ste!

[Re-gi-ne An-glo-rum] sa-lus et vi-ta

Re-demp-tor mun - di　　Tu il-lum ad-iu-va.
Sanc-ta Ma-ri - a　　Tu il-lum ad-iu-va.
Sanc-ta Fe-li - ci-tas Tu il-lum ad-iu-va.
Sancta Ae-thel-dri - da Tu il-lum ad-iu-va.

Chri-stus vin-cit, Chri-stus re-gnat, Chri-stus im-pe-rat. Ex-au-di Chri-ste!

Ar-chi-e-pis-co-pum et om-nem cle-rum si-bi com-mis-sum de-us con-ser-vet.

LAUDES OF WORCESTER (no. 10)—*continued*

Sal - va - tor mun - di   Tu il - lum ad - iu - va
Sanc - te Eal - phe - ge   Tu il - lum ad - iu - va
Sanc - te Tho - ma   Tu il - lum ad - iu - va
Sanc - te Dun - sta - ne   Tu il - lum ad - iu - va

Chri - stus vin - cit, Chri - stus re - gnat, Chri - stus im - pe - rat. Ex - au - di Chri - ste

E - pis - co - pum et om - nem cle - rum si - bi com - mis - sum de - us con - ser - vet.

Sal - va - tor mun - di   Tu il - lum ad - iu - va
Sanc - te Os - wal - de   Tu il - lum ad - iu - va
Sanc - te Ul - sta - ne   Tu il - lum ad - iu - va
Sanc - te Eg - wi - ne   Tu il - lum ad - iu - va

Chri - stus vin - cit, Chri - stus re - gnat, Chri - stus im - pe - rat. Ex - au - di Chri - ste

Om - ni - bus prin ci - pi - bus et cunc - to ex - er - ci - tu - i an - glo - rum sa - lus et vic - to - ri - a

Sal - va - tor mun - di   Tu il - los ad - iu - va
Sanc - te Mau - ri - ci   Tu il - los ad - iu - va
Sanc - te Gre - go - ri   Tu il - los ad - iu - va
Sancte Se - bas - tia - ne   Tu il - los ad - iu - va

Chri - stus vin - cit, Chri - stus re - gnat, Chri - stus im - pe - rat. Ex - au - di Chri - ste

II

Rex re - gum Chri - stus vin - cit

Rex no - ster Chri - stus re - gnat

Glo - ri - a no - stra Chri - stus im - pe - rat

Au - xi - li - um no - strum Chri - stus vin - cit

LAUDES OF WORCESTER (no. 10)—*concluded*

For - ti - tu - do   no - stra Christus re - gnat

Li - be - ra - ti - o   et re-demp-ti - o   no - stra Christus im - pe - rat.

Vic - to - ri - a   no-stra in - vic - tis - si - ma Christus vin - cit

Mu-rus no-ster in - ex - pu - gna - bi -lis Christus re - gnat

De - fen-si - o   et ex-ul - ta - ti - o   no - stra   Christus im - pe - rat.

III

Ip-si so-li im-pe-ri-um, glo-ri-a et po - te-stas per im-mor-ta-li-a se-cu-la se-cu-lo-rum a-men.

Chri - stus vin - cit, Chri - stus re - gnat, Chri - stus im - pe - rat

Ip-si so-li laus et iu-bi-la-ti-o et be-ne-dic-ti-o per in-fi-ni-ta se-cu-la se-cu-lo-rum a-men.

Chri - stus vin - cit, Chri - stus re - gnat, Chri - stus im - pe - rat

Ip-si so-li ho-nor et cla-ri-tas et sa-pi-.en-ti-a per in-fi-ni-ta se-cu-la se-cu-lo-rum a-men.

Chri - stus vin - cit, Chri - stus re - gnat, Chri - stus im - pe - rat

LAUDES OF PALERMO (no. 13)

Laudes of Palermo (no. 13)—*concluded*

Pa - ci - fi - co rec -to - ri et pi - is-si - mo gu- ber -na - to - ri

re - gi no - stro Fri - de - ri - co lux in - de - fi - ci - ens

et pax e - ter - na. Ex - au - di Chri - ste.

Sanc - te Sil - ves - ter Tu il - lum. ad - iu - va
Sancta Maria Magda - le - na Tu il - lum ad - iu - va
Sanc - ta Chri - sti - na Tu il - lum ad - iu - va

Sanc - ta A - ga-tha Tu il - lum ad - iu - va.

Part II *omitted in ms.*

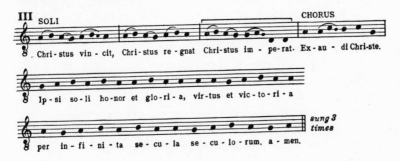

III Chri - stus vin - cit, Chri - stus re - gnat Chri - stus im - pe - rat. Ex - au - di Chri-ste.

Ip - si so - li ho -nor et glo -ri - a, vir-tus et vic - to - ri - a

per in - fi - ni - ta se - cu - la se - cu - lo - rum. a - men. *sung 3 times*

APPENDIX II

The custom of copying, even of imitating, the coinage of foreign sovereigns or foreign states must not be confounded with counterfeiting; nor is that custom confined to the Later Middle Ages or any other single period in history. In our time, we are quite used to seeing smaller nations adhere to one of the leading currencies, and we gladly recall the amenities of the former Latin Monetary Convention, lasting until 1918, by which the currencies of Italy, Belgium, Switzerland, Austria, Serbia, Rumania, and Greece were standardized on the basis of the French franc.[1] France, after the First World War, ceased to represent "European Standard" in monetary affairs, but it should not be forgotten that her coinage, once before, had become emblematical of the currency of a great number of dynasts. The problem of the diffusion of the *Christus vincit* legend on coins is of great interest, because the adoption of this French device, especially by German petty princes on the western marches of the empire, illustrates very clearly the interrelationship of monetary, cultural, and political spheres of influence.[2]

European gold coinage as an international instrument of trade begins, as is well known, in Florence in the thirteenth century. The florin, displaying the image of John the Baptist and the Florentine lily, enjoyed a high esteem because of the reliability of its monetary value; its weight, fineness, standard, and general appearance were soon imitated by princes and lords having the right of coinage.[3] However, not only the florin, but also the French gold denier, first minted by St. Louis in 1266, became a

---

[1] The Austrian gold coins of ten and twenty crowns have been considered copies or imitations of the French pieces of ten and twenty francs. The Austrian coins were designed to drive out the French currency especially from the principalities of the Danube; cf. C. Ernst, "Die neuen österreichischen Goldmünzen," *Num. Z.*, II (1870), 567.

[2] The following notes are supposed to contribute a few items to this problem only so far as it is connected with the French policy of expansion after 1300. The material is incomplete; the observations here presented are based upon notes taken sporadically and casually; and even these notes could not always be evaluated owing both to the war and to the fact that standard numismatic works and periodicals, not to mention local numismatic studies, were not accessible to me. Nevertheless the material offered seems ample enough to indicate the problem at least; also, it might be a help to further investigations on the subject.

[3] Cf. H. Dannenberg, "Die Goldgulden vom Florentiner Gepräge," *Num. Z.*, XII (1880), 146–185, and *ibid.*, XVII (1885), 130 ff.; for the Netherlands, see R. Serrure, "Le florin d'or de Florence et ses imitations," *Bull. Num.*, V (1898); A. de Witte, "Les relations monétaires entre l'Italie et les provinces belges au moyen âge et à l'époque moderne, *Atti del congresso internazionale di scienze storiche, Roma, 1–9 Aprile 1903* (Rome, 1904), VI, 207 ff. There were "fore-runners" of the Florentine gold coinage, e.g., the *Augustales* of Frederick II which even enjoyed an international market quotation during the thirteenth century; cf. Schaube, "Ein italienischer Kursbericht von der Messe von Troyes aus dem 13. Jahrhundert," *Zeitschrift für Sozial- und Wirtschaftsgeschichte*, V (1897), 252, 296 ff.; cf. Kantorowicz, "Zu den Augustalen Friedrichs II," in *Kaiser Friedrich der Zweite. Ergänzungsband* (1931), 255–263.

European standard coin which, despite royal manipulations in later times, was to be repeatedly copied or imitated. To follow the model of the royal coins was quite legitimate within the French royal house. Charles of France, brother of Louis XI, for instance, was certainly entitled to apply the *Christus vincit* legend to his gold coins.[4] So was Charles VIII of France, when he transferred this motto to the kingdom of Naples, which he thought he had conquered.[5] Not quite so legitimate is the so-called Anglo-Gallic coinage. The Black Prince seems to have been the first to utilize this motto for the Aquitanian coinage,[6] unless it was Edward III himself who started minting that money under his name and in his quality as king of France.[7] Henry V and Henry VI were, so to speak, legitimate kings of France so that nobody could deny them the right to strike French *moutons*, *angelots*, and *Francs à cheval* with the traditional French motto under their own names.[8] However, they did not transfer this custom to England, although, in that very period, the *Christus vincit* triad actually made its appearance also in the British Isles, namely, in Scotland. Robert III (1390–1406) and James II (1437–1460) applied that legend to their gold "lions" and "demi-lions,"[9] and as this was effected under French influence, we find here an example of copying the French model without the political justification of which the English kings could avail themselves.

The taking over of the French model has a more serious bearing on the Continent, where the German princes on the western marches of the empire were the first to adopt the French custom. The idea, of course, of these petty princes was to gain for their currencies the same authority, esteem, and "international" value as that which was enjoyed by the coins of their financially more powerful neighbor, France. Provided the weight, fineness of gold, and general standard of the French model coin was not altered in the princely mints, there was little to object to in the adoption of even the model's device, although these imitations were sometimes so similar to the original that the copy might easily have

[4] Cf. Henri Stein, "Charles de France, frère de Louis XI," *Mémoires et documents publ. par la société de l'école des chartes*, X (1921), 487 f., 490 f.

[5] Cf. Luigi dell'Erba in *Archivio storico per le provincie Napoletane*, N. S., XIX (1933), 61.

[6] Herbert A. Grueber, *Handbook of the Coins of Great Britain and Ireland in the British Museum* (London, 1899), 53, No. 286.

[7] *Ibid.*, p. 50, Nos. 269–271, and Pl. IX; see also E. Caron, *Monnaies féodales francaises* (Paris, 1882), 162, No. 238. As vicar general of the empire, Edward III is said to have minted *Christus vincit* coins in Brabant; cf. V. Tourneur, "Le prétendu monnayage d'Édouard III en Brabant," *Transactions of the International Numismatic Congress in London, June–July, 1936* (London, 1938), 334 ff., Pl. XXI.

[8] Grueber, *op. cit.*, p. 60, No. 323 (Henry V), and pp. 64 f., Nos. 343 f. (Henry VI); see also Blanchet et Dieudonne, *Manuel de numismatique française*, II (1916), 285, fig. 135, and *passim*.

[9] Grueber, *op. cit.*, p. 170, Nos. 38–40, and Pl. XLII; p. 173, No. 50. Cf. Edward Burns, *The Coinage of Scotland* (Edinburgh, 1887), I, 343 ff.; III, Pls. xxv–xxviii, xxxi.

passed for the original French denier. Still, these were not forgeries. The difference between imitating coins and counterfeiting them is very considerable. But it is in the nature of things that the relatively small step from imitating to counterfeiting the original, for example, by lowering the monetary value, was taken not too rarely.[10]

It is not the intention to deal here with the economic and commercial significance of copying the French coinage, but to emphasize the general cultural or even political momentousness of this practice. Not only does the practice of the German princes disclose the more or less desperate monetary conditions in the empire during the Later Middle Ages,[11] but it also clearly outlines the sphere of political and cultural influence of the French crown on the German frontier. France, after the breakdown of the empire during the Interregnum, was on her march toward the Rhine, and the German princes were compelled to succumb, or succumbed quite voluntarily, to the French ambitions. The trend toward establishing a mediaeval Rheinbund is well known, for its beginnings have been described masterfully;[12] and the expansion of the French monetary device bears additional evidence of the effects of France's general cultural propaganda in the fourteenth century.

Among the German princes with strong French sympathies the house of Luxembourg ranks highest. In 1294, Count Henry of Luxembourg, later Emperor Henry VII, entered upon a treaty of eternal feudal allegiance with Philip the Fair.[13] Henry's son, King John of Bohemia, must

---

[10] Among other famous forgers who deserve our attention is Jolantha of Flanders, countess of Bar, who "sub signo regis Francie falsam monetam fabricari et cudi fecit" and who, during the course of her long lawsuit, was excommunicated for her forgeries; *Brussels, Arch. génér. du Royaume. Trésor de Flandre*, 2344 (May 7, 1367). The family of Bar, as well as the counts of Flanders, adopted the images and the legends of the French coinage (see below, notes 25, 31) so that Jolantha also may have fabricated *Christus vincit* coins. Another forger of French coins with the *Christus vincit* legend was William de Beauregard, abbot of Saint-Oyen-de-Joux in Franche Comté (1348–1380), who had a long trial and was excommunicated by the archbishop of Besançon; cf. E. Caron, *op. cit.*, pp. 318 f., No. 551. See also P. Bordeaux in *Revue numismatique*, VIᵉ sér., Vol. V (1901), 76: "*. . . NCIT · XPS · R.*" Frederick II at the Diet of Mainz in 1235, treated alike the copying and counterfeiting of coins; *MGH. Const.*, II, 244, No. 196, 11: "*. . . qui sibi monetam sive formam aliene impressionis usurpant.*"

[11] The efforts to introduce an empire coin after the model of the Byzantine Empire remained without success in both Italy and Germany; for Italy, see H. Bresslau, "I denari imperiali di Federico I," *Atti del congresso internazionale di scienze storiche, Roma, 1–9 Avrile, 1903*, Vol. VI, Sezione numismatica (Rome, 1904), 31–36; and for Henry VII who, in 1312, tried to impose gold *augustarii* as an imperial currency in Italy, see *MGH. Const.*, IV, 718 ff., No. 727; 640, No. 669. In Germany these efforts were even more hopeless, and local monetary unions, e.g., that of the four Rhenish Electors in 1386, were hardly a remedy. See the interesting letter of Charles IV to the bishop of Cambrai (July 25, 1349), published by Serrure in *Révue de la numismatique française*, IIIᵉ sér., Vol. XI (1893), 407 ff.; Eduard Ziehen, *Mittelrhein und Reich im Zeitalter der Reichsreform, 1356–1504* (Frankfort, 1934), was not accessible to me.

[12] Fritz Kern, *Die Anfänge der französischen Ausdehnungspolitik bis zum Jahre 1308* (Tübingen, 1910); for the earlier period, see also W. Kienast, *Die deutschen Fürsten im Dienste der Westmächte*, Vols. I and II:1 (Utrecht, 1924–1931).

[13] F. Kern, *Acta Imperii Angliae et Franciae ab anno 1267 ad annum 1313* (Tübingen, 1911), 64 ff., Nos. 90–91, and *idem, Ausdehnungspolitik*, pp. 168, 328 ff.

be considered almost a French prince in his sympathies and predilections. He fought with the French army at Crécy, in 1346, and was killed in this battle. John's son, the later Emperor Charles IV, was brought up in an atmosphere of French learning and culture and, like many another young German nobleman, spent some years of his youth in Paris.[14] Therefore, it is hardly surprising to find that the Luxembourgs were among the first to adopt the French model of coinage with the legend *Christus vincit, Christus regnat, Christus imperat*. Henry VII does not seem to have gone that far; but the *écus* and *moutons d'or* coined by John of Bohemia (1309–1346) copied the French pattern, and Charles IV in his capacity as a German peer and count of Luxembourg, though not as an emperor, followed the French monetary model until the year 1353.[15] Further, the branch of the Luxembourg family which ruled in Brabant, where this house succeeded that of Louvain, likewise followed this practice. Duke John of Brabant of the house of Louvain was a sympathizer of the French kings and became a French partisan in 1304; his successor, John III (1312–1355), was the first duke of Brabant to coin *moutons* and *francs à cheval* in the French manner and with the *Christus vincit* device. In this he was followed by his Luxembourg successors. Joan and Wenceslaus (1353–1383), and then Joan alone (1383–1406), had *Christus vincit* coins minted for Brabant, and this tradition remained unbroken in the duchy under the dukes of the house of Burgundy, namely under John IV (1416–1427) and Philip of Saint-Pol (1427–1430).[16]

Another famous dynasty on the German marches, the Jülich, began to sympathize with France after 1307.[17] We find members of this widely diffused house, whose seigneuries were scattered on the lower Rhine as well as in modern Belgium and Holland, applying the *Christus vincit* device to their coins in most of their possessions during the fourteenth century. It is true, the coins of the Jülich had often no connection whatever with the French monetary system unless they represented simply base coins of French money. Nevertheless, many of the Jülich adopted the French legend, as is indicated by the following list:[18] Dietrich of Heinsberg, count of Looz (1336–1361); Geoffrey III of Dalenbrok, lord

---

[14] For John, see E. Ficken, *Johann von Böhmen, eine Studie zum romantischen Rittertum des 14. Jahrhunderts* (Göttingen, diss., 1932), and for Charles IV in Paris, A. Gottlob, *Karls IV. private und politische Beziehungen zu Frankreich* (Innsbruck, 1883).

[15] Specimens of these coins are found, e.g., in the Cabinet des Médailles in Brussels.

[16] Brussels, Cabinet des Médailles; Alphons Witte, *Histoire monétaire des comtes de Louvain, ducs de Brabant et marquis du saint Empire Romain* (Brussels, 1894), I, *passim*.

[17] Kern, *Ausdehnungspolitik*, pp. 301, 305.

[18] J. Menadier, "Die Münzen der Jülicher Dynastengeschlechter," *ZfN.*, XXX, (1913), 433 f., No. 10, 445, Nos. 40–45, 456 f., No. 69, 467, No. 10, 468, No. 13, 491 ff., Nos. 3–6. Alfred Noss, *Die Münzen von Jülich, Mörs und Alpen* (Munich, 1927), was not accessible to me.

of Heinsberg, count of Looz and Chiny (1361–1395); John II, lord of Mörs (1364–1372); William II, duke of Jülich (1357–1361); Walram, lord of Borne and Sittard (1356–1378); Reynard I, lord of Schönau (1347–1369); Reynard II, lord of Schonvorst (1369–1396). An interesting specimen was issued by Duke William of Jülich who minted (1372–1375), at the mint of Junkheit near Aachen, a *groschen* for the city of Aachen with the legends

> Reverse: XC : VINCIT : XC : REGNAT
> Obverse: + KAROLUS MAGNUS IMPERAT.

Thus, St. Charlemagne here replaces the name and function of Christ the Emperor.[19]

Of the Jülich princes enumerated, only Dietrich of Heinsberg really adopted the model of the *moutons d'or* of King John the Good of France (1350–1364). The other members of this house seem to have followed the pattern of coinage of the archbishop of Cologne.[20] This brings the practice of the princes of the Church in western Germany to the fore. In Cologne, Archbishop William of Gennep (1349–1362) began with coining *Christus vincit* money; in this he was followed by his two successors in the archiepiscopal see, Adalbert, count von der Mark (1363–1364) and Engelbert III, count von der Mark (1364–1369). In Trier, it was Boemund of Saarbrücken (1354–1362) and Kuno von Falkenstein (1362–1388) who chose to adopt the French pattern for their archiepiscopal coins;[21] and here again political sympathies and monetary usages are found largely coinciding.[22] Furthermore, we find the bishops of Cambrai and Liège issuing coins of French pattern. Cambrai, though politically dependent on the Reich, belonged to the ecclesiastical province of Rheims and its bishops had become vassals of the French crown in relatively early days.[23] Liège had its first pro-French bishop in the person of Theobald of Bar who became a *homo ligius* to Philip the Fair

---

[19] J. Menadier, "Die Aachener Münzen," *ZfN.*, XXX (1913), 354 f., Nos. 92–95; cf. *ibid.*, XXXI (1914), 251.

[20] Menadier, *ZfN.*, XXX (1913), 434, 445, 467, 491.

[21] For Cologne, see A. Noss, *Die Münzen und Medaillen von Cöln: Erzbischöfe von Cöln, 1306–1547* (Cologne, 1913), *passim*; P. Joseph, "Die Münzstempel und Punzen in dem historischen Museum der Stadt Köln," *Num. Z.*, XX (1888), 110. For Trier, see A. Noss, *Die Münzen von Trier, 1307–1556* (Bonn, 1916); A. Engel and R. Serrure, *Traité de numismatique du moyen âge* (Paris, 1894), III, 1216; Menadier, *ZfN.*, XXX (1913), 491. I was not in a position to consult again the books of Noss and to verify the exact quotations.

[22] Trier had a long tradition of pro-French feeling on the part of the archbishops; see, e.g., for Baldwin of Luxembourg, who was also educated in France, Kern, *Ausdehnungspolitik*, p. 260; Edmund Stengel, *Baldewin von Luxemburg, ein grenz-deutscher Staatsmann des 14. Jahrhunderts* (Weimar, 1937).

[23] Kern *Ausdehnungspolitik*, pp. 179, 247 f.; Lotte Hüttebräuker, "Cambrai, Deutschland und Frankreich," *ZfRG.*, germ. Abt., LIX (1939), 88–135; P. Charles Robert, *Numismatique de Cambrai* (Paris, 1864).

in 1304. However, it was not before the time of Bishop John of Arckel (1364–1378) that Liège minted *Christus vincit* coins which likewise were issued by its Bishop John of Bavaria (1390–1417), a member of the house of Wittelsbach.[24]

The relations of the family of Bar with the kings of France went through many ups and downs. Jolantha of Bar (cf. above, n. 10) was entangled in a lawsuit for counterfeiting French money. Other counts of Bar adopted the French model in a less suspect way.[25] Reynald of Bar, bishop of Metz (1302–1319), a brother of the pro-French Bishop Theobald of Liège, did not make use of the *Christus vincit* motto, as this fashion, on the whole, became popular shortly after his time; but he at least began to apply to his coins the French language which is found on the episcopal money of Toul as early as the thirteenth century, under Bishop Gilles de Sorcy (1253–1271), and somewhat later on that of Verdun under Bishop Henry of Apremont (1312–1350), whereas the municipal coins, for example of Metz, displayed at the same time the symbols of the German currency.[26] Thus, the coinage of these bishoprics on the frontier reflects the national as well as the social antagonism within these towns.

Of the house of Wittelsbach, the bishop of Liège, John of Bavaria, has been mentioned. Other members of his house, governing the Bavarian possessions in the Low Countries, likewise began to imitate the French motto. The county of Hainaut had been dependent on the French suzerainty ever since the days of Philip the Fair.[27] Hainaut, at that time, was under the dynasty of Avesnes, which was succeeded by the Wittelsbach. The *Christus vincit* device is found on the coins of the three Wittelsbach counts of Hainaut, William III (1356–1358), Albert of Bavaria (1358–1404), and William IV (1404–1417), a custom thereafter continued by the Burgundian count of Hainaut, John IV (1418–1427).[28] Furthermore, in Holland, under William V of Bavaria (1356–1357), a similar coin was issued.[29] The *Christus vincit* type of money finally became so popular in the Low Countries that even the German emperor of the house of Wittelsbach, Louis IV, had to take the local custom into account and thus coined, between 1338 and 1346, in the mint of Antwerp and perhaps

---

[24] Specimens in Brussels, Cabinet des Médailles.

[25] F. Friedensburg, *Münzkunde und Geldgeschichte der Einzelstaaten des Mittelalters und der neuern Zeit* (Berlin and Munich, 1926), 53 ff., mentions also Vaudémont and Lorraine among those lords who followed the French model; Count Edward of Bar was likewise educated in Paris, cf., Kern, *Ausdehnungspolitik*, p. 290.

[26] Friedensburg, *loc. cit.*

[27] Kern, *Ausdehnungspolitik*, pp. 250 ff.

[28] Renier Chalon, *Recherches sur les monnaies des comtes de Hainaut* (Brussels, 1848), 77, No. 94, and *passim*.

[29] Brussels, Cabinet des Médailles.

even in that of Frankfort, an *écu d'or*[30] which displayed the legend
XPC : VINCIT : XPC : REGNAT : XPC : IMPERAT. The popularity of the French monetary pattern is further reflected in the county of
Flanders, where Louis van Maele (1346–1384), the last ruler of the house
of Dampierre, coined his *écus, francs à cheval,* and other deniers in accordance with the French models. Here again the succeeding dynasty, in the
person of the Burgundian Philip the Bold (1384–1406), continued this
usage for a while until the anti-French attitude of the Burgundians
brought a change also concerning the monetary policy. But even so, the
Burgundian Chamber of Accounts was conscious of the fact that the new
Flemish *ridders* were nothing but French deniers.[31]

There were, to be sure, many other princes who considered it advisable
to follow the general fashion and copy the French *Christus vincit* legend.
The lords of Élincourt, who were Luxembourgs, the lords of Réthel, Rum-
men, Utrecht, Duke Gerard of Berg, and Wallerand III, count of Ligny,
also a Luxembourg, all followed the same practice.[32]

---

[30] W. Schwinkowski, "Die ersten sächsischen Goldgulden und die Goldprägungen
im Mittelalter," *ZfN.,* XXVII (1910), 321; cf. Luschin von Ebengreuth, *Num. Z,*
XXVIII (1896), 321; Arthur Suhle, "Der Groschenfund von Schoo bei Essen," *ZfN.,*
XLI (1931), 68.

[31] See, e.g., *Brussels, Arch. génér. du Royaume.* Chambre des Comptes, MSS 579
and 580, containing monetary tables. In the introduction (MS 579, fol. 5–5ᵛ; MS 580,
fol. 1 with a Flemish translation on fol. 2) the author traces the monetary system of
the fifteenth century to St. Louis. The text of the interesting paragraph is as follows:
"Notandum est quod circa annum domini MCCL tempore Sancti Ludovici
francorum regis celebrata certa conventio fuit super facto monetarum in
civitate parisiensi, in qua comparuerunt deputati multorum principum, tam
citramontanorum quam ultramontanorum, et ibi sequendo vestigia pre-
cedentium et futurum providere volentes concluserunt, . . . [there follow the
regulations about weight, etc.]. Idem Rex Ludovicus fecit cudi unum de-
narium auri vocatum Regale . . . Anglici vero predictum fundamentum
tenentes cuderunt dimidium nobile pro duplo, Italici et Ultramontani
ducatos, Almani Alti florenum Ungarie. Postmodum vero Rex francorum
scutum vetus, dux Burgundie Philippus equitem dictum *Rider,* qui omnes
denarii sunt similes auro valore et pondere Regali predicto."
Specimens of the coins of Flanders are found in Brussels, Cabinet des Médailles.

[32] Cf. Freiherr von Schrötter, *Lexikon der Münzkunde* (1930), 402, *s.v.* "mouton
d'or." For Gerard of Berg, see Menadier, *ZfN.,* XXX (1913), 491, No. 3; for Wallerand
of Ligny (1371–1415), cf. E. Caron, *op. cit.,* p. 394, No. 665. Ligny, in the Barrois,
belonged to the empire. It is interesting to observe similar conditions prevailing also
in the south, in the ancient kingdom of Arles (Burgundy), where as late as 1365
Emperor Charles IV was crowned king. *Christus vincit* coins were minted by William
de la Garde, bishop of Arles (1359–1375), and by Raymond IV of Orange (1340–1393);
cf. Caron, *op. cit.,* pp. 239, No. 405, and 245, No. 420. The influence on France's
southwestern borderland, Spain, does not seem to have been so effective as in the
eastern provinces. However, two kings of Castile and Leon, Henry III (1390–1406)
and Henry IV (1454–1475), issued xps vincit coins not only in gold but also in silver
and (a singular feature to which Miss Lucie E. N. Dobbie kindly called my attention)
in copper; cf. Aloïss Heiss, *Descripción general de las monedas hispano-cristianas desde
la invasión des los Arabes* (Madrid, 1865), I, 79–82, Nos. 1–4, 10–14, 17, 25 (p. 85, n. 1
has the legend iesus vincit, iesus regnat, iesus imperat), and pp. 101, 103, 106,
Nos. 4, 20, 51; see also *Memorial Numismatico Español* (1873), III. Gold reali with
the *Christus vincit* were minted during the thirteenth century by the early Aragonese
kings of Trinacria, that is, by Peter of Aragon and Costanza of Hohenstaufen (1282–

Although the list offered here of princes using the French device on coins is casual and certainly not complete, the instances cited are enough to make it evident how the money design, and frequently also the monetary system, of the Low Countries as well as of western Germany gradually fell prey to the French standard of currency and, at the same time, to the French "device." This monetary penetration of the German marches by France began, roughly, in the second decade of the fourteenth century, that is to say that it followed closely on the epoch of Philip the Fair. This name, in turn, stands for the first phase of France's endeavors to carry, both aggressively and peacefully, the cultural and political sphere of her influence toward the Rhine. In 1308, after the German king Albrecht of Hapsburg had been killed by the Swiss, a number of German princes signed a convention for the election of a new ruler. The instrument was drafted neither in Latin nor in German, but in French. In this convention the western German princes promised to support one another against anyone whomsoever "except our Lords, the Kings of Germany and France."[33] These princes, all of whom enjoyed French pensions, were the duke of Lorraine and Brabant, the count of Hainaut and Holland, Henry of Luxembourg, John of Flanders, Guy of Flanders, the count of Jülich, and the count of Looz and Chiny. This is practically the same group of petty sovereigns which introduced, some ten years later, the French currency or the French legend on coins into their own duchies and counties.

Thus, the "numismatic" invasion of the western marches of the Reich evidently was the corollary of the political conditions which resulted from the weakness and impotence of the empire. The simple fact that so many German princes (among them two emperors, Louis of Bavaria and

---

1285), James of Aragon (1285–1296), and Frederick II of Aragon (1296–1337); but the tradition was Sicilian rather than French. Cf. V. Capobianchi, in *Archivio della società romana*, XIX (1896), 369 f.; Mariano Amirante, "Il *reale* di Giacomo d'Aragona," *Circolo numismatico napoletano, Studi e ricerche*, 1926, pp. 31 f.; Rodolfo Spahr, "Il *reale* di Federico II d'Aragona," *Bollettino del circolo numismatico napoletano*, 1927, pp. 37 f. It was legitimate for Turin to strike *Christus vincit* coins in the period 1538–1542 because Turin then was under the domination of Francis I of France; cf. Maggiora-Vergano, "Alcune nuove monete dei Principi Sabaudi e del Piemonte," *Bollettino della società piemontese di archeologia e belle arti*, XV (1931), 139 f.; cf. *ibid.*, IX (1925), 64. A Venetian coin with the legend CHRISTUS IMPER has nothing to do with the triad; it means "Christus imperator" and replaced the former money of the Signoria which displayed the name of the emperor (ENRICUS IMPER.); cf. *Num. Z.*, II (1870), 224 f. Papal coins with the *Christus vincit, Christus regnat, Christus imperat* are numerous in later centuries; see, for instance, for Sixtus V and Pius VI the notes of Barbier de Montault, *Œuvres complets*, III (1893), 392, 405. The earliest specimen is a papal florin of Gregory XI (1370–1378) minted at Avignon; the reverse shows the pope enthroned and in a *mándorla* like the Christ of the Roman florins; cf. Camillo Serafini, *Le monete e le bolle plumbee pontifice del Medagliere Vaticano* (Milan, 1910), I, 79, n. 74, and Pl. XII, 18.

[33] *MGH Const.*, IV, 200 ff., Nos. 237–238; Guy of Flanders appears in the second document only.

Charles IV, in their qualities of German seigneurs on the western marches) were easily won over by France as well as by her clear-cut monetary system indicates that these regions in matters of civilization and of cultural influences had virtually slipped away from the Reich and had exchanged its dubious protection for that of France. The blending, and even the melting down of French and German capabilities finally found its most felicitous expression, during the fifteenth century, in the very peculiar culture of the Burgundian States astride the Franco-German frontier. However, the magnetism of French culture as well as its emissions and propaganda had been effective long before the fourteenth century so that the adoption of the French model of coins by so many German princes is but one additional item illustrating the bonds by which these German lords were connected with France. On the other hand, the monetary alienation from the Reich was not restricted to princes; it is found also in the cities. It is worth while to mention that Frederick III, the long-ruling (1440–1493) Hapsburg emperor, after having granted the people of Cologne the right to mint their own money, was obviously disappointed in the symbols which the citizens designed for their new coin, and he asked them to put the eagle of the empire on their money. But the people of Cologne refused and called the emperor's attention to the fact "wie die gulden mit dem adelaer am Ryne nye gankafftlich geweist synt"; that is to say, on the Rhine the florins with the eagle had never been current. Cologne, therefore put an orb on its florins, whilst it applied to its *groschen* the legend of *Christus vincit, Christus regnat, Christus imperat.*[34]

[34] For the privilege, cf. J. Chmel, *Regesta chronologico-Diplomatica Friderici III Rom. Imp.* (Vienna, 1840), No. 6828; A. Noss, *Die Münzen der Städte Köln und Neuss 1474–1794* (Cologne, 1926), No. 1; A. Suhle, "Zum Münzrecht der Städte Köln, Werl und Marsberg," *ZfN.*, XXXIX (1929), 188 f. The reply of the people of Cologne has been published by A. Suhle, "Der Groschenfund von Schoo bei Essen," *ZfN.*, XLI (1931), 188, from a Memorial in the Archives of Cologne (Kölner Briefbuch, 31, fol. 146ᵛ; December 19, 1476).

APPENDIX III

THE NORMAN FINALE OF THE EXULTET

IT IS well known that until late in the eleventh century an archaic form of the *Exultet*[1] was used in several South Italian cathedrals, the so-called *Vetus Itala*, which differed considerably from the text of the *Missale Romanum*.[2] Another South Italian peculiarity remained unnoticed, a Norman version of the doxology of the *praeconium paschale* differing from both the *Vetus Itala* and the *Missale Romanum*. In the Roman Missal we find the customary doxology:

Per eumdem dominum nostrum Jhesum Christum filium tuum qui tecum vivit et regnat in unitate spiritus sancti Deus per omnia secula seculorum.

The *Vetus Itala* shows the variant:

Qui vivis cum patre et spiritu sancto et regnas unus Deus in s.s.

Quite different from either of these is the third version:

Qui semper *vivis, regnas, imperas* necnon et gloriaris solus Deus solus altissimus, Jhesu Christe, cum sancto spiritu in gloria Dei patris.

This form cannot be traced farther back than the twelfth century, and since it seems to occur exclusively in the three Norman states—Sicily, Normandy, and England—its name should be the "Norman finale."

Our earliest evidence of this form is from Norman Southern Italy, where it is found in the following manuscripts:

1. Madrid, Bibl. Nac. Lat. MS 289 (153), fol. 115ᵛ. Cf. above, p. 158, n. 13; for a facsimile see *Harvard Theological Review*, XXXIV (1941), facing p. 129.

2. Madrid, Bibl. Nac. Lat. MS, 132, fol. 99ᵛ. Cf. above, p. 158, n. 12; to a facsimile, found in Dom Grégoire Mᵉ Suñol, *Introduction à la paléographie musicale grégorienne* (Paris, Tournai, and Rome, 1935), p. 247, pl. 58, Professor Manfred Bukofzer kindly called my attention.

3. Palermo, Cathedral, MS 544; cf. above, p. 158, n. 14.

4. Troia, Cathedral, "Exultet" Roll, twelfth century; cf. Myrtilla Avery, *The Exultet Rolls of South Italy* (Princeton, 1936), Pl. CLXXXV.

5. Naples, Bibl. Naz. MS VI.G. 34, fol. 82. This is a *Processionale* from Troia, about the middle of the twelfth century, containing a reference to "gloriosissimo rege nostro ill." For the place of origin see fol. 136: "Horum festa plebs troiana colat et apulia." The manuscript is mentioned in *Analecta Hymnica*, XLVII, p. 25, No. 105.

6. New York, Morgan Library MS 379, fol. 111, twelfth-century missal of uncertain origin.[3]

---

[1] A more detailed discussion of the problem will be found in my article "A Norman Finale of the Exultet and the Rite of Sarum," *Harvard Theological Review*, XXXIV (1941), 129–143. To the literature there mentioned (n. 1), should be added the important article of Gerhard Burian Ladner, "The 'Portraits' of Emperors in Southern Italian *Exultet* Rolls and the Liturgical Commemoration of the Emperor," *Speculum*, XVII (1942), 181–200.

[2] H. M. Bannister, "The *Vetus Itala* text of the Exultet," *Journal of Theological Studies*, XI (1910), 43–54.

[3] The manuscript, which I feel I must study anew before venturing to offer a a definite opinion, contains in the *Praeconium* (fol. 111) a commemoration for the

These are Sicilian manuscripts; they are all from the twelfth century. In Normandy the same finale is found in two manuscripts, both of the early thirteenth century:

7. Paris, Bibl. Nat. Lat. MS 904, fol. 96ᵛ; cf. above, p. 166, n. 48.
8. Paris, Bibl. Nat. Lat. MS 905, fol. 96, a copy of No. 7.

It is found also in the *Missale secundum usum insignis Ecclesiae Rothomagensis*, printed on parchment by Mag. Martin Morin (Rouen, 1499), which I consulted in the British Museum. In England, this finale is found

---

emperor ("gloriosissimo imperatore nostro ill."), and, as natural, a second commemoration in the Orations on Good Friday (fol. 105), where an interlinear addition, "romano imperio" is superscribed over the "xristia" of "pro xristianissimo imperatore." Ladner, in the article mentioned above, has made it definitely clear that the mention of the emperor in these prayers, especially in the *Orationes solemnes*, is not prejudicial to the origin of a manuscript. "Emperor" in these prayers is a metapolitical idea, not a political power or a "national" designation. It is a commemoration, says Bishop, *Liturgica Historica*, p. 297, "which we may read, but do not say." A curious illustration of this can be adduced from the New York Public Library MS 20, fol. 98ᵛ, a Missal of Bristol of 1410–1420, where we find the commemoration for the pope erased from the *Orationes solemnes* (obviously a manipulation of the sixteenth century), whereas that for the emperor is not touched: the latter was not said in any event, whereas the former was. Hence, the Morgan Library MS, so far as the emperor commemoration is concerned, could easily be of South Italian origin or at least a copy of a South Italian manuscript, made perhaps in Spoleto, as has been suggested, because (fol. 120) three Spoletan saints (Gregorius, Pontianus, and Ysaac) are mentioned. A later Spoletan manuscript (Naples, Bibl. Naz. MS VI.G. 3), mentioning SS. Eleutherius, Pontianus, and Anastasius, is of no avail, since it follows Roman usage and it may reasonably be doubted whether Spoleto ever followed a rite other than Roman. The copyist of the manuscript, if he was really a Spoletan, was at any rate startled by the unusual *Praeconium*, for in the lemma following after this prayer (fol. 120) he writes: "Benedictione cerei finita *secundum teutonicum ordinem* ascendat lector ad legendam lectionem."

It has been suggested by a previous student of the manuscript that "teutonicus ordo" may hint at the Teutonic Knights whose master is indeed mentioned in the *Praeconium* of the thirteenth-century Vatican, Barb. Lat. MS 699 (XIV, 72), fol. 104, of which G. B. Ladner, then in Rome, kindly made a copy for me in 1937; for the Barberini MS, see Ebner, *Quellen und Forschungen zur Geschichte und Kunstgeschichte des Missale Romanum im Mittelalter* (1896), 152. But this suggestion is beside the point because the Teutonic Order did not exist when the Morgan MS was written. "Teutonicus ordo" is opposed to "Ordo Romanus" in the sense of Gregory VII's famous decision:

"Romani autem diverso modo agere ceperunt, maxime ab eo tempore, quo Teutonicis concessum est regimen huius [sc. Lateranensis] ecclesie. Nos autem et ordinem Romanum investigantes et antiquum morem nostre ecclesie statuimus fieri sicut superius prenotavimus antiquos patres imitantes."

G. Morin, in *Rev. bénéd.*, XVIII (1801), 179, and in his *Études, textes découvertes*, I (Maredsous and Paris, 1913), 460; Ludwig Fischer, *Berardi cardinalis et Lateranensis Ecclesiae prioris 'Ordo Officiorum Ecclesiae Lateranensis,'* Historische Forschungen und Quellen, 2–3 (Munich and Freising, 1916), 77. That the antagonism between the two rites, Teutonic and Roman, also affected the finale, is shown by Bernold of Constance, *Micrologus*, c. 6, Migne, *PL.*, CLI, col. 981, who complains of the intolerance of the *moderni* because even in Rome the ancient form of the finale "iam non sine scandalo locum habere possit." In this case, however, it was the position of the word *Deus* in the doxology that was disputed. Thus, the scribe of the Morgan MS, when noticing the deviation from the Roman usage in the Praeconium, seems to have taken it for granted that this deviation was Teutonic, whereas in fact it was the Norman finale that may have puzzled him.

in practically all the manuscripts containing the ritual of Salisbury, which was introduced during the thirteenth century, but it does not seem to appear in an earlier text.[4]

The finale "Qui vivis, regnas, imperas" is evidently influenced by the three clauses of the laudes. This is not surprising if we consider the wide diffusion and the almost proverbial or magic application of the formula in that period. Also we should take into account that the *praeconium paschale*, just as the laudes, was one of the most important manifestations of liturgical ruler worship and that it was sung on Saturday night of Holy Week only a few hours before the laudes were voiced at the High Mass on Easter Sunday. This seems to explain the fact that the finale of the prayer for the ruler was accommodated to the great chant to the ruler.

For the birthplace of this finale, we must exclude England from the outset because the "Rite of Sarum" was introduced in England during the thirteenth century and it depended apparently on the ritual of Rouen. Thus the problem concerning the origin of the Norman doxology is reduced to the question: Normandy or Sicily? It is true, the usual liturgical migration was from north to south and it may be an unfortunate accident of manuscript transmission[5] that our earliest evidence in Normandy does not antedate the thirteenth century whereas Sicilian manuscripts show the Norman finale in the early twelfth. However, a reverse influence from Sicily to Normandy cannot be ruled out as a possibility. It is likely that the *Christus vincit* legend made its first appearance on South Italian coins before it wandered to France (see above, Chap. I); furthermore, the form of the *Exultet* was subjected to irregularities in Southern Italy during that period when it changed from the *Vetus Itala* to the Roman usage; and finally the priority of Sicily is suggested by the manuscripts. Hence, we may assume that the Norman finale of the *Exultet* originated in Southern Italy.

---

[4] Cf. J. Wickham Legg, *The Sarum Missal Edited from Three Early Manuscripts* (Oxford, 1918), 119. I first found the Norman finale in the Antiphonary of Worcester Cathedral (Cod. F. 160, fol. 221; cf. above, p. 172, n. 65), and inspected also the New York, Morgan Library MS 107, fol. 129, and the Oxford, Bodleian Libr. MS lit. 408 (Addit. MS B 20), fol. 67ᵛ (the latter through Mr. D. von Bothmer).

[5] Brit. Mus. Addit. MS 10028, so far as known the only twelfth-century service book of Rouen, unfortunately does not contain the *Exultet;* cf. Bishop, *Lit. Hist.*, 298. That the three later Missals of Rouen (Bibl. Munic. MSS 276, 277, 278) contain the Norman finale may be taken for granted; our earliest evidence, however, remains the Paris Bibl. Nat. Lat. MS 904.

APPENDIX IV

The Nations in the Laudes and the Order Cencius II

IN A STIMULATING study on the "Roman and Christian Ideas of Empire in Early Liturgy," Professor Gerd Tellenbach has outlined very clearly the development of national designations in early mediaeval prayers.[1] He indicates that the original prayer for the *Imperium Romanum* said on various occasions during the ecclesiastical year was frequently changed, in the Frankish service books of the eighth century, into one for the *Imperium Francorum*. During the ninth century, however, the Frankish liturgists quite obviously preferred the conception of *Imperium Christianum* which predominates in the manuscripts. Of course, we cannot expect to find uniformity or a clear-cut change from one designation to the other. Manuscripts were used for many centuries. The old designations would survive and be carried along, and it would rarely happen that these designations were altered in the manuscripts by erasure or superscription.[2] The three designations, therefore, overlapped: *Imperium Romanum*, *Imperium Francorum*, and *Imperium Christianum* appear at the same time. The name of *Imperium Romanum* had the longest tradition, and it might be expected that its name would be found over and over again in the Frankish mass books after Charlemagne's coronation in 800 and the revival of the imperial dignity in the West. This, however, is not the case. In some regions, above all in Italy, a revival of the expression *Imperium Romanum* may be registered, it is true; but on the whole the "Rome enthusiasm" of the Frankish Church is surprisingly modest.

Tellenbach deals with the laudes only in a lengthy footnote (p. 27, n. 3). It seemed to him that in connection with the acclamation to the army the expressions *Francorum, Romanorum, Christianorum, Alamannorum,* or *Teutonicorum* were used so chaotically that he deemed it wiser not to establish a "principle" without a detailed study of the litanies and their history in general. It is beyond the scope of this present note to investigate the evolution of the national designations in the litanies in general. It might be useful, however, to treat the problem with regard to at least one litany, the laudes. This is feasible indeed; for, once the laudes have been classified in a reasonable way, the various national designations appear much less chaotic than might be assumed at first glance.

The ancient Gallo-Frankish laudes contain, with two significant excep-

---

[1] Tellenbach, "Römischer und christlicher Reichsgedanke in der Liturgie des frühen Mittelalters," *Sitzungsber. Heidelberg,* 1934, Abh. 1, especially pp. 24 ff. See also E. H. Kantorowicz, "The Problem of Mediaeval World Unity," *The Quest for Political Unity in World History,* ed. Stanley Pargellis (=Vol. III, The Annual Report of the American Historical Association for the Year 1942; Washington, 1944), pp. 35 ff.

[2] See, however, Tellenbach, *op. cit.,* p. 53, No. 2, the variants, and also pp. 58, No. 10; 59, No. 13.

tions, the acclamation to the *exercitus Francorum*. This custom lasts until the late ninth century. One exception to this rule is found in a formulary of St. Gall (858–867). It refers to Pope Nicholas I, King Louis the German, and Queen Emma. The army here is styled *exercitus Francorum et Alamannorum*.[3] The reason for the addition of *Alamanni* may be sought in the parochial pride of the monastery which Louis the German seems to have visited at the end of 859 after his deplorable campaign against his brother Charles the Bald. The more plausible ground, however, is that a prayer for the *exercitus Francorum* without restriction would have included also the army of Louis' West Frankish brother and enemy. Hence, the term *Alamannorum* serves to distinguish the Eastern Frankish army from the "French" army of Charles the Bald. This does not imply necessarily a "national" tendency, not at least in a sentimental way. It is a distinction which reflects the haziness of the term "Frankish" in the times of the fratricidal wars, a limitation rather than an amplification of the hails to the army.

The second exception to the rule does not refer to "separatism" but has almost the opposite meaning. The expression *exercitus Christianorum* appears, for the first and only time in the forms of the Carolingian era, in the laudes of Chieti to the Emperor Louis II and the Empress Angilberga. The date is presumably 865–866. Tellenbach (p. 36 ff.) has rightly emphasized that the conception of a "Christian imperialism" as reflected in the phrase *Imperium Christianum* was closely connected with the war against infidels or "bad Christians." Every army fighting the Moslems would consider itself as championing the whole Christian world or the universal idea of a politically nonexistent *Imperium Christianum*. This is true with reference to the laudes of Chieti. During the winter 865–866, Louis II camped near Chieti with an army which he had levied by extremely severe measures for the war against the Moslems in Southern Italy.[4] Hence, this acclamation to the army presents itself as an early evidence confirming the thesis that the terms *Imperium Christianum* and *exercitus Christianus*, notwithstanding their significance in the absolute, were applied in the relative in order to stress the contrast against the infidels.

Exercitus Christianus, with or without an implicit antithesis against the infidels, remained the standard phrase within the realms which emerged from the collapse of the Carolingian monarchy. The German laudes in the times of the Ottonian and Salian emperors do not contain a term other than *exercitus Christianus* to designate the army. In the

---

[3] Prost, *Quatre pièces*, pp. 175 f.
[4] Vatican, Reg. MS 1997 fol. 160ᵛ; for the date, see Gaudenzi in *Bullettino dell'Istituto Storico Italiano*, XXXVII (1916), 376; for the events L. M. Hartmann, *Geschichte Italiens im Mittelalter*, III:1 (Gotha, 1908), 265 ff. The items referring to German, English, Norman, and French forms can be found easily through the General Index at the end of this book.

Franco-Burgundian laudes, and in those of the former Frankish depend-
encies, Aquitania and Septimania (see below, Appendix V), only a
Christian army is mentioned. This is true also for the hails to the army
in France from the times of Hugh Capet to Philip Augustus (see, however, the Laudes of Soissons). Only one French province forms an exception to this rule—Normandy.

The first change toward a "nationalism" in the acclamation to the
army originated not within the old Carolingian Empire but in England.
From early times the English prayers are remarkable for stressing the
"national" rather than the "universal" character. In the laudes sung
to William I and Queen Matilda in 1068, it is still the *exercitus Christianus* which is hailed, though only along with *omnibus principibus
Anglorum*. In the formulary of the twelfth century, however, we find
acclamations not only to the *rex* and *regina Anglorum* (thus replacing the
rex pacificus of the earlier forms), but also to the *exercitus Anglorum*. The
same is true with reference to the forms of Worcester in the thirteenth
century. This English "nationalism" in the laudes seems to have its
source, or rather one of its sources, in conditions in Normandy. William I
was acclaimed *Normannorum dux* in his duchy. Consequently, the dukes'
feudal overlord, the king of France, who was usually acclaimed *Serenissi-
mus a Deo coronatus magnus et pacificus rex*, was almost compelled to
receive likewise a national designation. He was suddenly acclaimed in
Rouen as "King of the French," *Francorum rex*. Moreover, in order to
avoid difficulties the acclamation to the army was entirely omitted—in
Normandy of all countries! Indeed, it might have been difficult to tell
whether Rouen was to pray for the French or for the Norman army. In
France proper national designations for the king do not occur earlier than
the thirteenth century, and it is illuminating to find that apparently
Rheims made the start in "nationalizing" its laudes. The "religion of
Rheims" in the time of St. Louis could not be expected to be anything
but "national," and thus we find in the Rheims laudes of 1257 the acclamations to the *excellentissimo regi Francorum a Deo coronato et pacifico*
and to his French army. It may be noted that, whereas the English title
then was simply *Rex Anglorum a Deo coronatus*, the French maintained
the eschatological note of mediaeval rulership and combined with the
national designation the image of the liturgical *rex pacificus*.

Within this general development the Franco-Roman laudes (as opposed to the Gallo-Frankish) have an exceptional place. Never was the
phrase *exercitus Christianus* adopted by Rome. The Holy See, after all,
was universal not because its holder was a Christian bishop but because
he was the Roman bishop, the successor of the Prince of Apostles. The
Church, too, the *Sancta Romana Ecclesia*, was universal by virtue of

Rome. The Church was Roman and so was, from a Roman point of view, the imperial army. The physical soldiers representing the emperor's army might be Franks or Teutons—these designations were exchangeable in the Roman forms—but metaphysically the imperial army was always and above all else considered an *exercitus Romanorum*. The laudes of Ratisbon of 824–827, in which the word *Romanorum* has been omitted so that there figures merely an *exercitus Francorum*, is not really an exception to this rule. This form is a Franco-Roman specimen adapted to the use of King Louis the German; it is a provincialized form in which the Emperor Louis the Pious is commemorated, it is true, but the army acclaimed is that of the Eastern Frankish king and not that of the emperor, and for this reason *Romanorum* is ruled out. For this one exception, however, the Franco-Roman laudes would always display the name of the Romans, and this designation would always precede that of every other nation, for instance: *exercitus Romanorum et Francorum*.

We do not know when the epithet *Francorum* was exchanged for *Teutonicorum* because no formulary of Franco-Roman laudes falling in the period between the ninth and the early twelfth century (Benedict of St. Peter's) seems to be extant. In the twelfth-century laudes transmitted by Benedict we find an acclamation to the *exercitus Romanorum et Teutonicorum*. It is true that the laudes in the Vatican Lat. MS 7114, and in the Codex Gemundensis contain the odd reading *exercitus Francorum, Romanorum et Teutonicorum*. They have been claimed as representing the "form of transition" from the Frankish to the German Empire and they have been dated accordingly as laudes of the ninth or tenth century.[5]

This suggestion, however, is not likely to be correct. To begin with, the only manuscript extant which contains the three nations and at the same time is datable, the Vatican Codex, is late thirteenth, or even fourteenth century. Second, the sequence (1) *Francorum*, (2) *Romanorum*, and (3) *Teutonicorum* is by no means convincing and looks like patchwork. For during the epoch in which *Teutonicorum* could have been used, the word *Francorum* would have indicated already the "French" and not the Frankish army. Moreover, the designation *Romanorum* always took

[5] Eichmann, "Die Ordines der Kaiserkrönung," *ZfRG.*, kan. Abt. II (1912), 10 f., follows the arguments of J. Schwarzer, "Die Ordines der Kaiserkrönung," *Forschungen zur Deutschen Geschichte*, XXII (1882), 201 ff. The expression "exercitus Teutonicorum" in the time of Arnulph of Carinthia (887–899), with whom Eichmann, Schwarzer, and Biehl (p. 110) try to connect this formulary, sounds anachronistic. In the laudes which actually refer to Arnulph the army is acclaimed "exercitus Francorum," cf. Lehmann, "Corveyer Studien," p. 71 f. The word for "German" during the ninth century is more often *Theodiscus* than *Teutonicus*, cf. Vigener, *Bezeichnungen für Land und Volk der Deutschen* (1901), 25, 33, whose collection, however, is not complete and somewhat superannuated. *Regnum Teutonicorum* is found as early as 919–920, cf. Bresslau, "Die ältere Salzburger Annalistik," *Abh. Preuss. Akad.* (Berlin, 1923), Abh. 2, p. 58 f. In papal records the word *Teutonicus* does not seem to appear before 965, cf. Vigener, *op. cit.*, p. 41.

the first place, and to find it framed between the French and the Teutons must arouse our suspicion. What Schramm has said about the Order of the Coronation to which these laudes are attached,[6] namely, that this Order showed amplifications added at a time when the Order itself was no longer used, holds good also for the acclamations to the army. The very reasonable and appropriate formula of Benedict of St. Peter's (*exercitus Romanorum et Teutonicorum*) was the authoritative model, but it was turned into nonsense by the preceding *Francorum* which the late redactor borrowed perhaps from some earlier acclamations and placed before the correct hail. On the other hand, it is almost impossible that a formula reading *Francorum et Romanorum* should have been augmented and "modernized" by an additional *Teutonicorum* for the very simple reason that such a formula did not exist. *Romanorum* always took precedence of *Francorum*, and a "modernization" in Ottonian times, if really *Francorum* was to be preserved and a new designation to be added, would have probably created the form *Romanorum, Francorum et Teutonicorum* and not the one actually found in the late manuscripts.

In addition to these arguments there is yet another detail to make us wonder whether these garbled laudes can belong to an early period. For there is the remarkable fact that these acclamations are incorporated in the Orders of the Coronation. Although the laudes were sung at the imperial coronation in Rome, as well as at some royal coronations, this song after its separation from the Litany was always recorded separately and not within the *Ordines* proper. In the Vienna MS 1817, fol. 183ᵛ, we find it is true, a formulary of Gallo-Frankish laudes referring to Pope Sylvester II and King Henry II appended to a Coronation Order of the German king. But these laudes are appended to and not arranged within the Order (cf. Andrieu, *Ordines*, I, 397; Migne, *PL.*, CXXXVIII, col. 1119). The custom of inserting the laudes in the Coronation Orders at their proper place within the divine service, namely between the first Collect and the Epistle, does not seem to occur earlier than the twelfth century. Benedict of St. Peter's is the first to incorporate a formulary of *laudes papales* in his Order. Chronologically there follows the English Order of the twelfth century where the laudes follow after the *Sta et retine*. In the Sicilian Order of the twelfth century the laudes at least are mentioned *post epistolam*. The laudes to the emperor are inserted in an Order of the imperial coronation for the first time by Cencius Savelli in the last decade of the twelfth century. We find them, at their correct place, also in the imperial Order of 1209 which remained in force until the sixteenth century. In short, Coronation Orders containing the laudes within the liturgical action are almost mushrooming in the twelfth century,

---

[6] Schramm, "Ordines," *ArchUF.*, XI (1929), 355, n. 2.

whereas earlier evidence is lacking. It is, therefore, not likely that the Vatican Lat. MS 7114 and the Codex Gemundensis should have anticipated by three hundred years a practice which was connected with the general liturgical development after the Age of Gregory VII. The later compilers obviously acted under the influence of authorities of the twelfth century or of their own time, and the laudes as well as other elaborations must be considered later *additamenta* inserted at a time when the superannuated *Ordo* had fallen into desuetude for many centuries. At any rate the odd acclamation to a "Frankish, Roman and Teuton Army" betrays the efforts of a compiler to bring his work up to date.

The argument concerning the nonincorporation of the laudes in the *Ordines* at a date earlier than the twelfth or late eleventh century should be taken into consideration also with reference to the so-called *Cencius II*, the second of two Orders of the Imperial Coronation transmitted by Cencius Savelli, papal chamberlain and later Pope Honorius III. I would have declined to deal with the controversial date of this Order, which oscillates between the times of Otto I and Henry VI, had not recently Dr. Biehl (see below), influenced by Professor E. Eichmann, made the laudes in *Cencius II* one of the main arguments for proving that this Order falls in the tenth century. Professor Eichmann's thesis—and following him that of Biehl—is that the Cencius laudes (merely the question of the laudes will be treated here) display a form similar to the early Frankish formularies rather than to the "shorter form which became customary in the twelfth century," a statement implying among other things that the "early Frankish" (that is Franco-Roman) formularies flourished only in Carolingian and Ottonian times.[7] Translated into our terminology, this means that the imperial laudes in *Cencius II* show more similarity with the Franco-Roman imperial forms than with the papal laudes introduced in the late eleventh or early twelfth century. Thus the similarity of imperial laudes with imperial laudes, or the dissimilarity of imperial laudes to papal laudes, prompts Eichmann to date the Cencius Order as far back as possible. He dates it "tenth century."

Professor Eichmann's statement confounds so many facts that it would need a long dissertation to disentangle the threads. However, there are a few points which it seems worth while to stress in order to clarify the problem.

---

[7] For the last phase of the controversy, see Eichmann, "Das Officium *Stratoris et Strepae*," *Historische Zeitschrift*, CXLII (1930), especially pp. 29 f., 30, n. 1, and the replication of Robert Holtzmann, "Zum Strator-und Marschalldienst," *ibid.*, CXLV (1931). For the older literature about the date of *Cencius II*, see Schramm, *op. cit.*, pp. 289 f. The place quoted is found in Eichmann's article, *ZfRG.*, kan. Abt. II (1912), 10 f.; L. Biehl, *Das liturgische Gebet*, pp. 110 f.

1. One reason for the confusion is that Professor Eichmann does not distinguish clearly enough between papal and imperial laudes in the twelfth century. His statement is a truism so far as it implies that the *imperial* acclamations of Cencius have more resemblance to the *imperial* acclamations of the distant past than to the papal acclamations of the twelfth century. Actually, however, even this truth, which seems obvious and yet means nothing as to the date, is only half correct, as I will prove.

2. The statement implies that the *papal* formulary transmitted by Benedict and Albinus was the "customary form" of all Roman laudes in the twelfth century. This is a generalization which is completely without basis and must be rejected. The imperial laudes were indeed "papalized" but, to our knowledge, not before 1209 and not before the relatively new form of papal laudes had become dominant within the papal ceremonial; this last took place shortly before the accession of Innocent III (cf. above, pp. 132 f.). Professor Eichmann's error results apparently from the misleading and ill-founded distinctions between "Gallican" and "Roman" laudes (see above, pp. 101 f.) which prompted the surmise that the form of papal laudes as transmitted by Benedict was the form of Roman laudes (papal and imperial) without limitation or distinction. That is to say, it is assumed that there was only one species used in Rome, whereas in fact both Benedict and Albinus show that the Franco-Roman forms were used for the emperor and the papal forms for the pope.

3. Benedict and Albinus have handed down two formularies of laudes used in Rome during the twelfth century, one papal (including several variations, namely, papal-episcopal and papal-monarchic laudes) and one imperial, the latter being a normal Franco-Roman formulary modernized by the acclaim to the army as *exercitus Romanorum et Teutonicorum*. Hence, Benedict and Albinus distinguish clearly between (a) chants to the pope and (b) the chant to the emperor along with other authorities. This juxtaposition and simultaneity of the two forms is known to Professor Eichmann as well as it is to anyone familiar with the matter. However, the coexistence of the two forms would not have fitted the cause defended by Professor Eichmann since *Cencius II* can be dated back to Ottonian or Salian times only if the Cencius laudes precede (in time) the papal form of the twelfth century and follow (in time) the Franco-Roman forms of the Carolingian era. Thus, according to Eichmann, the Cencius laudes must fall between the Franco-Roman form (which he considers out of date by, probably, the tenth century) and the papal form of the twelfth century. Therefore, the evidence produced by Benedict and Albinus had to be either ignored or invalidated.

4. Professor Eichmann chooses the second expedient and declares that the imperial laudes in Benedict and Albinus (despite their containing an acclamation for the "Army of the Romans and Teutons"!) represent an "old Carolingian form of the time of Pope Hadrian II (867–872)."[8] It was not easy to figure out where Professor Eichmann had discovered a Franco-Roman formulary referring to Pope Hadrian II and Emperor Louis II. Biehl, however, whose discussion of the Cencius laudes is rich in misinterpretations and distorted judgments,[9] quotes on page 157 what he calls a "Franco-German Formulary" of the time of Louis II, dated 870, which presents itself as an offprint of the Albinus text (*Liber censuum*, II, 91). Albinus, of course, mentions neither Hadrian nor Louis. He simply uses, as Benedict does, the sign · *H* · so that we read "Domno · *H* · pape . . . Domno · *H* · imperatori . . ." This · *H* · as usual

---

[8] Eichmann, *Hist. Zeitschrift*, CXLII, 30, n. 1.

[9] What Biehl, *op. cit.*, pp. 110 f., and 111, n. 3, produces is, to say the least, confused and inconsistent. The place of the singing of the laudes has nothing to do with the place within the Mass of the crowning ceremony which, in *Cencius II*, was not consummated "between Epistle and Gospel," but preceded the Mass.

stands for *N = nomen*. Professor Eichmann, however, seems to consider these signs as abbreviations of names, or rather as initials, and supplements *H*[adrianus] and *H*[ludovicus]. Through this emendation Professor Eichmann indeed rids himself of the inconvenient evidence of Benedict and Albinus for the survival of the imperial laudes in the Franco-Roman form until the twelfth century. For it is clear that the formularies of Benedict and Albinus lost their relevance for the twelfth century, if they really copied verbatim and in an antiquarian manner a superannuated Carolingian formulary. Their evidence, in this case, might well be considered negligible by Professor Eichmann.

5. Unfortunately, Professor Eichmann failed to take into account the consequences of his "emendation." If Benedict's and Albinus's formularies were in fact literal copies of "Hadrian laudes," this would imply that Pope Hadrian II and Emperor Louis II were given the pleasure of hearing the chanters sing in 870: "Exercitui Romanorum et Theutonicorum [!] vita et victoria." This, I believe, closes the discussion.[10]

So long as another twelfth-century pattern of Roman imperial laudes has not been detected, we are entitled to hold that the forms transmitted by Benedict and Albinus were those used in their own times. There is no ground for the theory that the Franco-Roman form, revised by the exchange of *Teutonicorum* for *Francorum*, should not have survived until the end of the twelfth century. By that time (in 1191 or 1197), indeed, Albinus's friend, the chamberlain Cencius Savelli, made a new redaction of the imperial Coronation Order and also rearranged the laudes on this occasion. This is their form:[11]

Exaudi Christe!	Domino nostro C[elestino?] a Deo decreto summo Pontifici et universali Pape vita!
Exaudi Christe!	Domino nostro a Deo coronato magno et pacifico Imperatori vita et victoria!
Exaudi Christe!	Domine nostre N. eius coniugi excellentissime Imperatrici vita!
Exaudi Christe!	Exercitui Romano et Theutonico vita et victoria!
Salvator mundi	tu illos adiuva
Sancte Michael	tu illos adiuva
Sancte Gabriel	tu illos adiuva
Sancte Raphael	tu illos adiuva
Sancte Petre	tu illos adiuva
Sancte Paule	tu illos adiuva
Sancte Johannes	tu illos adiuva
Sancte Gregori	tu illos adiuva
Sancte Maurici	tu illos adiuva
Sancte Mercuri	tu illos adiuva

Christus vincit, Christus regnat, Christus imperat.

R/ Christus vincit, Christus regnat, Christus imperat.

---

[10] Cf. above, n. 5. What Louis II, the "Italian" and son of Lothar, would be doing with a German army—even if we assume that the expression *Teutonicus* might have been used at so early a date—is anything but clear.

[11] It is found in *Liber censuum*, I, 5*; cf. Schramm, *op. cit.*, p. 384.

Spes nostra	Christus vincit
Salus nostra	Christus vincit
Victoria nostra	Christus vincit
Honor noster	Christus vincit
Murus noster inexpugnabilis	Christus vincit
Laus nostra	Christus vincit
Triumphus noster	Christus vincit

Ipsi laus, honor et imperium per immortalia secula seculorum.   Amen.

It is quite obvious, and it has always been noticed, that the Cencius laudes represent a form of transition from the old Franco-Roman formularies to the papalized emperor laudes of 1209. In *Cencius II* there are no invocations of saints interrupting the sequence of acclamations. The saints form a continuous sequence just as in the *laudes papales* of the early twelfth century and the papalized imperial laudes of the early thirteenth. The emperor still is styled "a Deo coronatus" which he is not in the later formulary. The acclaim to the army is remarkable, for we find that the national designation is given in the form of adjectives rather than in that of nouns: *Romano et Theutonico* has replaced *Romanorum et Theutonicorum* of the Benedict and Albinus forms. We take this as another indication of the date. This adjective form did not fall in with the earlier tradition because it was incompatible with the Frankish acclamation to the army: *exercitui Franco* did not exist because it would have been a cacophony. Actually, the adjective form cannot have been developed without the intermediary stage of the Benedict and Albinus texts in combination with which the evolution also becomes clear "acoustically":

1. *Carolingian:* Exercitui Romanorum et Francorum vita et victoria!
2. *Benedict:*   Exercitui Romanorum et Theutonicorum vita et victoria!
3. *Cencius II:* Exercitui Romano et Theutonico vita et victoria!

The evolution 1, 3, 2 is not only unlikely, but it also disagrees with the chronology of the manuscript transmission.

However, the fact is decisive that the Cencius laudes show for the first time the tendency to "papalize" the imperial laudes. Therefore, they cannot possibly antedate the *laudes papales* as such; and these *laudes papales* make their appearance not earlier than the twelfth century. It may be safely maintained that the Cencius laudes are "exactly as old as they are" and that their date falls in the time when they were written by Cencius, namely in the last decade of the twelfth century.

APPENDIX V

The Franco-Burgundian Laudes

THE LAUDES of Ivrea[1] sung to Emperor Henry IV and his antipope Clement (III) display certain peculiarities which have been mentioned in their proper places. The most striking feature is the acclamation to the pope as *prime sedis episcopus*. It discloses Henry's political program according to which the pope was to be merely the first among the imperial bishops. Thus the laudes of Ivrea certainly do not reveal a tendency to curtail imperial prerogatives. All the more remarkable is the fact that the saints invoked for the emperor are not those that follow customarily in the German royal and imperial laudes after the acclamation to the ruler, namely the Déesis group (Mary, the Archangels, and John the Baptist) which has disappeared completely. In their place we find other saints, important yet of minor rank, namely Maurice, Denis, and Victor. Ivrea apparently followed a tradition different from that of Germany. In this, however, the laudes of Ivrea display a similarity to those of Arles and Besançon which tally verbatim with each other.[2] These two forms have Maurice, Sigismund (the Burgundian king), and Victor as royal patrons, and the Déesis group likewise has disappeared. Ivrea has thus Maurice and Victor in common with Arles and Besançon. It is, perhaps, permissible to treat these three formularies as a whole and to style them "Franco-Burgundian" laudes. That is to say that these laudes, or a type similar to them, probably were used for the kings of Burgundy whose realms emerged after the collapse of the Carolingian Empire.

This hypothesis is countenanced by the formularies of yet another Burgundian cathedral, Autun, of which two specimens are known, one of the early tenth century and the other of the period 996–1024.[3] The saints invoked for the king are not Burgundian but French (Denis, Médard, Martin, Corneille). However, the Déesis group has been omitted as in the forms of Ivrea, Arles, and Besançon, and St. George figures as an army saint in all these forms. All this holds true also for the laudes of Narbonne, the capital of Septimania,[4] so that the question thrusts itself upon us

---

[1] Cf. above, pp. 25, 100, 116.

[2] The laudes of Besançon are found in the eleventh-century Vatican Borg. Lat. MS 359, fols. 135–136; those of Arles are extant only in the edition of Du Cange, V, 46; cf. Migne, *PL.*, CXXXVIII, 889. The relationships between the two forms have been stressed by Erdmann, *Kreuzzugsgedanke*, p. 257, n. 31.

[3] For the laudes of Autun, see Kantorowicz, "Ivories and Litanies," pp. 57 f.

[4] Paris, Bibl. Nat. Lat. MS 778, fols. 217ᵛ–218ᵛ, an Antiphonary of Narbonne, belonging to the twelfth century. By means of marginal notes of a later hand, the formulary has been made suitable for the period 1272 to 1276, for the names of Pope Gregory X (1271–1276), Bishop Peter of Montbrun (1272–1286), and King Philip III (1270–1285) have been added. The form, as yet unpublished, has the following lemma:

> "In die sancto Pasche inter collectam et epistolam ante Dominum Archi-episcopum hec letania decantetur (*in margine:* Tres persone si adsunt vel

whether the ancient Carolingian Déesis group of saints invoked for the ruler was not first discarded in the Carolingian successor states whereas it survived in France and in Germany as a royal and imperial prerogative.

tres antiquiores incipiunt et dicunt ter [*Christus vincit*...] R/ pueri respondent ter. Postea dicunt illi tres *Exaudi Christe*. R/ pueri dicunt *Domino summo* . . . Postea dicunt maiores *Salvator mundi* et pueri respondent *Tu illum adiuva* et sic deinceps).''

The saints of the pope are Salvator mundi, Peter, Paul, and Laurence; of the bishop: Mary, Justus, and Pastor; of the king: Salvator mundi, Andrew, and Denis; of the army: John, Vincent, and George.

PLATES

XPC Vincit XPC Regnat XPC Imperat: *a*, St. Louis, *Ecu d'or*;
b, Philip the Bold, *Reine d'or*; *c*, Philip the Fair, *Masse d'or*; *d*,
Philip the Fair, *Chaise d'or*; *e*, Iron Shield of Don Juan of Austria

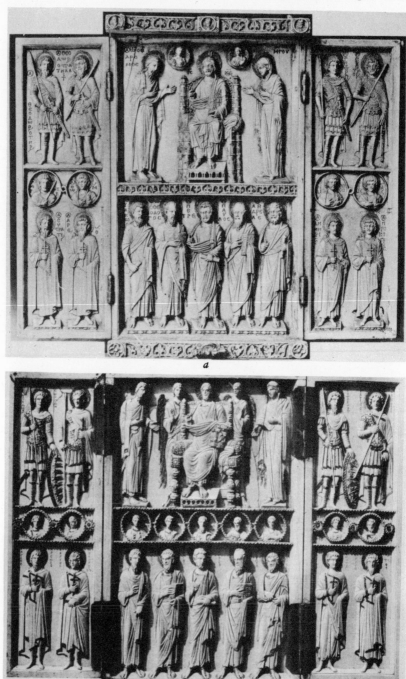

Ivory Triptychs: Déesis. *a*, Louvre, Harbaville Triptych; *b*, Vatican, Museo Christiano

cū epis ꝫ ꝑesbr̄īs hīnande psīar
tīs. Ceterīs in choro breuiter psal
lentibus letaniā que sequitur.

Ryneley son.
Xpistre eleyso.
Kyrieleyson.
Xpe audi nos.

Pater de cælis
deus miserere nob.
Fili redēptor
mūdi ds. ꝯ. n.
Spr sce deus. ꝯ.

Kyrie Eleison: The King's Prostration

a

b

a, Rex et Sacerdos; b, Liturgical Reception

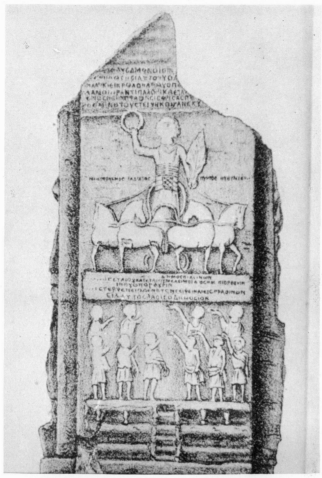

a

b   *c*

a, Charioteer Acclaimed in the Circus; *b*, *Allocutio* and *Acclamatio*;
c, Triumphal entry of Constantius II

Laudes Regiae of Autun

Vivat Rex!
Title page of the Cranmer Bible

Durandus Laudes: Rubric

Durandus Laudes: Text

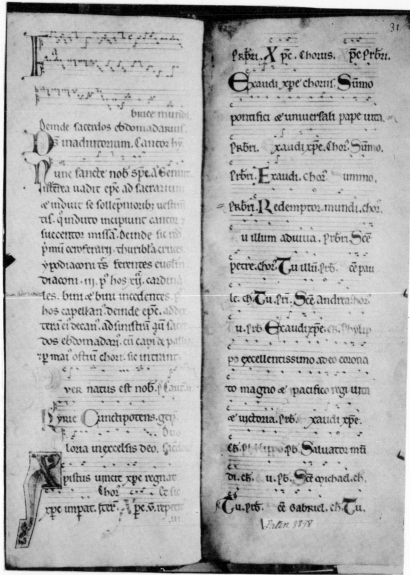

Laudes Regiae of Soissons

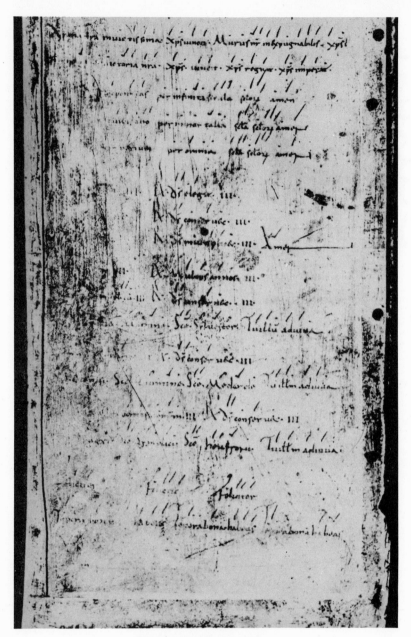

Episcopal Laudes of Autun

Laudes Regiae of Palermo (fol. 107ᵛ)

Laudes Regiae of Palermo (fol. 108ʳ)

Litany. *a*, Déesis group; *b*, Apostles

INDICES

INDEX OF MANUSCRIPTS

(The material within square brackets refers to the General Index.)

GENERAL INDEX

(AB. = Archbishop; B. = Bishop; Ct. = Count; D. = Duke; E. = Emperor;
Ess. = Empress; K. = King; Q. = Queen.)

Aachen, 3, 52, 59, 63, 99, 226; "Lateran," 63; *sedes Davidica*, 63

Abbo of Fleury, 6 n. 17, 140 n. 94

Abbot. *See* Acclamations

Abraham, B. of Freising, 99 n. 120, 115 n. 12

Acclamations:

  Proffered to: emperor (Roman, Byzantine), 8, 13 ff., 16 ff., 20, 24 ff., 27 n. 44, 65–76, 87 n. 71, 96, 119 n. 25, 143; pope, 82 n. 56, 125–142, 160; cardinals, 127 f.; bishops, 17 n. 6, 29 n. 48, 64, 74 n. 31, 87 f., 112–121 (to ordainer), 122, 123 ff., 134, 161; abbots and monks, 45 n. 114, 106, 124, 161 f., 162 n. 24; duke, 168 f. (*see also* Princes); officials, 32, 119 n. 25 (*see also* Judges); crown, 93 f., pall, 93 f., 101, 174, 183; images, 17 n. 7, 72 n. 25, 85 n. 62, 102 f.

  Form: angelic, 87 n. 71; conciliar, nn. 7 and 10, 57 n. 148, 68 ff., 71, 76, 77 n. 38, 83, 152, 181 (*see also* Councils); constitutive (legal), 65, 76 ff., 82 ff., 103, 110 f., 119 f., 147, 150 ff.; electoral (inaugural), 31, 76 ff., 119 (*see also* Coronation); festival, 85 ff. (*see also* Coronamenta); Hebrew, 27 n. 44; litanylike (concluding litany), 40 ff., 48 n. 123, 58 f., 69 n. 15, '10; memorial, 99 n. 120, 125 n. 40, 181 n. 4; poetical, 50 n. 129, 58 n. 153, 70 n. 15, 73 ff. (*see also* Laudes, Hymnidicae: receptions); soteriological, 18 n. 14, 74 f., 76 n. 34

  Formulae: *a Deo coronatus* (*see* Ruler); *a Deo decretus* (*see* Papal); *Augustus*, 66, 74 n. 30, 77 n. 38, 93 n. 92, 103; *Basileus, Basilea* (Western), 77 n. 38, 172 n. 67; *Christus Rex*, 185; *confessor Christi*, 128 n. 48; *Dignus* (ἄξιος), 119 nn. 24 f., 125; *Exaudi Caesar*, 17, 66; *Fiat*, 79, 119 n. 25; *Imperator*, 96, 103, 160 n. 16, 186; *Murus* (τεῖχος), 29 n. 50; *Parati—adiuta Deus*, 193 n. 18; *Rex et sacerdos*, 47, 70, Pl. V, *a* (*see also* Priest-kingship); *Rex pacificus*, 74, 107 n. 137, 145, 159, 236; *Te Deum*, 79, 94 n. 96; *tu vincas*, 26 n. 39, 28 n. 47; *vita*, 16 f., 18, 39, 42, 44, 59, 65, 102, 111, 123, 126, 130, 134, 185 n. 23; *Vivat rex*, 59, 79, Pl. VIII. *See also* Laudes; Litany; Liturgical formulae

Acre, 5 n. 14

Adalbert, Ct. von der Mark, AB. of Cologne, 226

Adana, 11

Adoptianism, 47

Adoption, 96

Adventus. See Reception

Aethelberht, K. of Kent, 61 n. 164

Agaune, abbey of, 33 n. 72

Agilulph, K. of Lombards, 50 n. 129

Aix-en-Provence, 100 n. 123, 112 n. 2, 118 n. 23, 121 n. 30; litany of, 40 n. 104, 41 n. 104, 41 n. 105. *See also* Laudes

Alain of Lille, 6

Albert of Bavaria, Ct. of Hainaut, 227

Albinus. *See Ordo*

Albrecht of Hapsburg, K., 229

Alcuin, 47, 60, 62, 70 n. 17 f.

Alexander, Byzant. E., 69

Alexandria, 52, 125 n. 40

Alfanus, B. of Capaccio, 163

Oda (?), German Q., 99 n. 120

Odo of Cluny, 199

Ogerius, B. of Ivrea, 100 n. 122

Oil rituals, 55 n. 142, 90 f. *See also* Anointment

Old Testament, 56 ff., 62 ff., 93 n. 93. *See also* David

Olive branches, 72, 75

Orationes Paschales (Solemnes, in Vigilia Paschae, Oratio Fidelium), 39 n. 100, 40, 232 n. 3

Ordinale. *See* Service books

Ordinations (royal, episcopal), 55 n. 142, 57 n. 148. 79 ff., 90 ff., 92, 115, 117, 119 n. 25, 122 (papal), 126

Ordo, Ordines:

Collections, 33 ff., 45, 54, 104 ff., 109

Ordo: Ad regem ducendum (recipiendum), 72 n. 27, 162 n. 26; *Baptismi*, 55 n. 142; *Commendationis animae*, 35 n. 81, 71, 139 n. 91; *De sacris ordinibus*, 92 n. 87; of St. Amand, 35 n. 83, 108 n. 145; of Farfa, 72 n. 27, 75 n. 33, 76 n. 34; of St. Riquier, 36, 41, 89

Ordines Romani, 89 n. 79, 102 f., 182 n. 12, 232 n. 3; *Romanus I*, 128 n. 48; *Romanus VIII*, 91 n. 84; *Romanus IX*, 107, 126 n. 42, 127 n. 44, 130 n. 54, 134 ff.; *Romanus XI*, Benedict of St. Peter's, 107 n. 139, 111 n. 152, 127 n. 45, 129 f., 132 ff., 135, 137, 140 n. 96, 141 n. 97, 182, 196 n. 26, 237 f., 240 ff.; Albinus, 107, 127 n. 45, 132 f., 140 n. 96, 141 n. 97, 175 n. 82, 240 ff.; Cencius (*Romanus XII*), 132 f.; *Romanus XIII*, 132 f.; *Romanus XIV*, 127 n. 44, 132 f., 164 n. 38

Orders of the Coronation: 19 n. 15, 23 n. 27, 36 n. 89, 39 n. 100, 42 n. 107, 55, 79, 81, 96 f. *passim;* Imperial: Apamea, 122 n. 32; *Cencius I*, 107 n. 141; *Cencius II*, 75 n. 33, 107 n. 141, 111, 144 ff., 196 n. 26, 214, 234, 238 ff., 241 (text); *Gemundensis*, 107 n. 141, 238; Third period (after 1209), 144 n. 102, 238 ff.: England, 80, 87, 171 f., 178, 238, *passim (see also* Cambridge Trinity MS 249); France, 83, 177; Germany, 81 nn. 51 ff., 83, 90 n. 83, 91, 92 n. 87, 177; Normandy, 170; Sicily, 87 n. 70, 166 n. 44, 178, 238; Spain, 160 n. 16

Oriflamme, 3

Orléans, 73 n. 28; Carolingian laudes, 32 n. 71, 86, 87 n. 71, 89 n. 79, 100 n. 123, 123 n. 34; later laudes, 88 n. 76, (text) 123, 183. *See also* Councils

Ossero, laudes of, 147, 149, 151, 152 (text), 153 f.

Ostia, 22

Ostrogoths, 32

Otto (I, II, or III), 99 n. 120

Otto I, E., 25 n. 32, 73 n. 28, 77 n. 38, 92 n. 89, 95, 239

Otto III, E., 77 n. 38

Otto IV, E., 144

Otto, son of Barbarossa, 147 n. 3

Paderborn, 15 n. 4

Paestum. *See* Capaccio

Palermo, 158, (text) 159, 161, 165 f., 192, 194, 201, 207 f., (musical transcription) 220–221. *See also* Laudes; Hugh; Walter, AB.

Pall, 93, 94 n. 96, 101, 120, 175 n. 82

Palm leaves, 72, 75

Papal: coins, 229 n. 32; coronation, 136 ff.; feudalism, 138, 148, 150, 164 f.; insignia, 126, 136 ff., 139 ff.; monarchy, 119 f., 129 f., 131 f., 138 ff., 141 ff.; titles: *a Deo*